Dorset, Hampshire and the Isle of Wight

written and researched by

Matthew Hancock and Amanda Tomlin

Contents

Coast colour section
following p.112

Cool counties colour
section following p.208

◀◀ Kitesurfing at Poole Harbour ◀ Corfe Castle

Introduction to

Dorset, Hampshire and the Isle of Wight

Dorset, Hampshire and the Isle of Wight encompass some of the UK's most dramatic coastline and attractive countryside, much of it within a two-hour drive of London. These three counties have long formed an extended playground for city dwellers: the lure of the New Forest, with its roaming ponies, the long sandy beaches of Bournemouth and the Isle of Wight, and the dramatic coastal paths combine to make this prime territory for day-trippers and weekend-breakers. Yet those in the know return again and again, aware that these stunning regions merit further exploration.

Much of the verdant well-to-do county of Hampshire is commutable from the capital, and provides a comfortable lifestyle for many, much as it did when Jane Austen lived here. Its biggest draw is the **New Forest** and the **sailing** resorts of the Solent. It's also home to two of England's greatest ports: **Southampton**, today with a burgeoning nightlife and great shopping, and the traditional powerhouse of the navy, **Portsmouth**, with its iconic Spinnaker Tower and historic dockyards.

Separated geographically from Hampshire some seven thousand years ago, the **Isle of Wight** – the smallest county in England, at least when the tide is in – lies only a few miles offshore, but has an altogether different

atmosphere. Much of the island has retained a feel of the 1950s, with no motorways, little development, few large-scale buildings and a distinctly laid-back lifestyle. It has long been popular for its small seaside resorts and bracing seaside walks, not to mention its unusual geology, most evident in the rock stacks of the **Needles**, the countless fossils found on its coastline and the striped cliffs of **Alum Bay**. It also hosts some of the country's best **festivals** – including the famous Cowes sailing week, the Isle of Wight music festival, which pulls in the biggest names in rock and pop, and the more independent Bestival.

Literary connections

Some of England's greatest literary figures are associated with the area.
Dorchester p.95. Many of today's buildings are clearly recognizable in Hardy's novels, especially *The Mayor of Casterbridge*.
Clavell Tower Kimmeridge Bay, p.88. P.D. James's *The Black Tower* is a murder mystery based around this remote cliff-top folly, now available for holiday lets.
The Cobb Lyme Regis, p.136. John Fowles' *The French Lieutenant's Woman* is set in Lyme Regis – the film version's most famous scene with Meryl Streep takes place on The Cobb. Lyme Regis also plays a key part in Jane Austen's *Persuasion*.
Chesil Beach p.124. Ian McEwan's award-winning *On Chesil Beach* uses the Dorset landmark as the setting for the novel's fateful romantic excursion.
Tennyson Down Isle of Wight, p.280. The great Victorian (1809–92) took inspiration from walking these cliff-top downs, which now bear his name and a memorial to the poet.

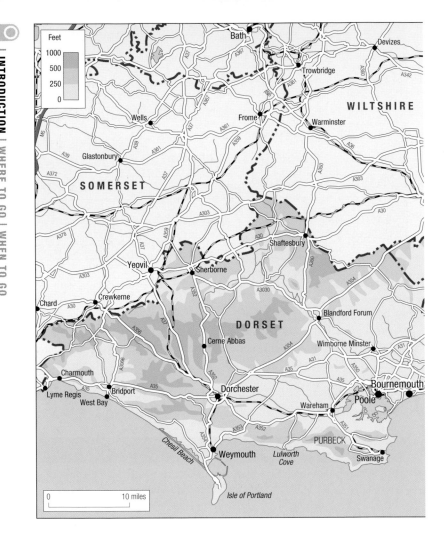

The west of the island overlooks **Dorset**, that much further from the capital and correspondingly more rural and unspoilt. Most visitors flock to its coastline, which boasts some of the best beaches in the UK – from the extensive sands of **Bournemouth** to the extraordinary **Chesil Beach** off Portland Bill. It also embraces the **Jurassic Coast**, England's only natural World Heritage site, whose varied coastline exposes an extraordinary geological mixture of rock stacks, arches and coves. Inland, you'll find the historic towns of **Sherborne** and **Shaftesbury** as well as quintessentially pretty English villages surrounded by rolling downs, heathlands and deep river valleys. This is superb terrain

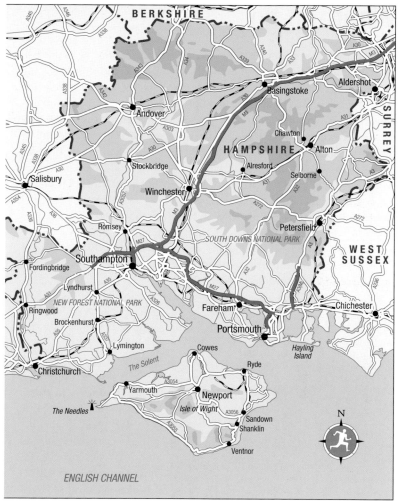

© Crown copyright

for nature lovers, cyclists and walkers, free from the crowds, even when the coasts are heaving.

The region's strategic position between the capital and the coast has made it the home for countless famous people throughout the ages, from the legendary King Arthur (whose supposed Round Table is displayed in Winchester) to Sir Walter Raleigh in Sherborne and the Duke of Wellington, who lived in Hampshire's Stratfield Saye. You can also visit the former residences of Charles Dickens in Portsmouth; Jane Austen, who spent much of her life in Hampshire; T.E. Lawrence, who lived in Dorset; and Thomas Hardy, who is forever associated with his beloved "Wessex".

Where to go

I f you want a beach holiday, there are plenty of options here: the **Isle of Wight** has a variety of beaches – from pebble and shingle to fine sand – and wherever you go on the island, you're never far from the sea. For all the facilities of a large resort, look no further than **Bournemouth** or **Weymouth**, both with fantastic, sandy town beaches. Smaller in scale, **Swanage**, **West Bay** and **Lyme Regis** exude plenty of traditional, bucket-and-spade appeal, while the beaches around **Shell Bay** are hard to beat, backed by miles of sand dunes and heathland. For quieter swimming spots, there's the wonderful pebble beach at **Durdle Door**, the bay at **Chapman's Pool** (accessible only by boat or on foot) and the sand-and-shingle beaches of **Highcliffe** and **Hengistbury Head**, backed by sandstone cliffs. The coasts are also rich in wildlife, with a seahorse reserve in **Studland**, puffins nesting on the cliffs at **Durlston**, Britain's largest colony of mute swans at **Abbotsbury**, and the rare red squirrel thriving on the Isle of Wight and **Brownsea Island**.

▲ Paddling on the Isle of Wight

History fans will find much to explore, too: this area was historic Wessex, where England's first kings – including, perhaps, King Arthur – made their home. Formerly England's capital, **Winchester** offers a fascinating insight into the country's past, while mighty castles include **Corfe Castle**, **Sherborne** and **Carisbrooke** on the Isle of Wight. There's also **Maiden Castle** near Dorchester, a superb example of an Iron Age defensive settlement, while **Cerne Abbas**'s chalk giant dates back at least to Roman times. Maritime history is richly evident in **Southampton** and **Portsmouth**, home to the *Mary Rose* and Nelson's HMS *Victory*.

The best pubs

From beachside inns to thatched rural gastropubs, the region boasts highly alluring drinking-holes. Here are our favourites.

▲ The Square and Compass

Bonchurch Inn Bonchurch (Isle of Wight), p.276. Ancient, highly atmospheric inn that serves great Italian food.

The Mayfly near Stockbridge (Hampshire), p.208. Delicious food, fine beers and an idyllic garden next to the clear-flowing River Test.

The Royal Oak Fritham (New Forest), p.172. Tasty local produce, roaring log fires, a lovely garden and fine walks nearby.

The Royal Oak Bank (New Forest), p.177. Quaint old pub in the heart of the New Forest.

The Ship in Distress Christchurch (Dorset), p.191. A lively bar with a good restaurant serving local fish.

The Square and Compass Worth Matravers (Dorset), p.86. Simply the best pub in Dorset, straight out of a Hardy novel.

Wykeham Arms Winchester (Hampshire), p.208. Wonderful old coaching inn with a warren of rooms, excellent food, and in a great location in the backstreets of Winchester.

Contemporary seafarers are spoilt for choice, too, with major sailing centres at **Lymington**, **Cowes**, **Poole Harbour** and **Portland**, site of the 2012 Olympic sailing events. Other watersports, such as windsurfing, kayaking and kitesurfing are doable all along the coast, while Bournemouth is home to Europe's first artificial **surf reef**. For the less sporty, there are some fantastic museums and family attractions, including the **National Motor Museum** at Beaulieu, **Bovington Tank Museum**, and the fairground rides at **Blackgang Chine** on the Isle of Wight.

For many people, however, it is the rural beauty and timeless quality of the countryside, in particular its two national parks – the New Forest and the South Downs – that make these regions so special. Hikers should look no further than the **South West Coast Path**, Britain's longest footpath, which starts at Poole and follows the Dorset coast to Lyme Regis. And there are fantastic walks inland, including superb river rambles along the **Itchen**, upriver from **Buckler's Hard**, north along the **Test**, and throughout the **New Forest** and the Isle of Wight, both crisscrossed with cycleways and footpaths.

▲ Carisbrooke Castle

When to go

The entire region has a relatively **mild climate**, with a south-facing, sheltered coastline and few extremes of weather. The **summer** is the obvious time to head for the coastal resorts, though you'll be hard pushed to find space to lay your towel on a hot day during the school summer holidays. This is peak time on the roads and for accommodation prices too: other busy times are Easter, Christmas, New Year and the school half-terms, and it is also sensible to avoid travelling on Friday evenings, when people flock down for the weekend. The very best times to visit are May and June, when the countryside is at its most lush, the evenings long and the weather often superb. **Spring** is perfect for exploring the New Forest, when its woodlands and heaths are peppered with ponies and their foals, while **autumn** sees an explosion of spectacular colours, with pigs roaming wild in search of acorns.

Winter, too, has its attractions: it's hard to beat holing up in a country pub in front of a log fire after a long walk on a crisp, sunny winter's day. The flipside is that when it rains, many of the region's best footpaths become virtually unpassable or treacherously slippery. Some of the seaside resorts and more remote attractions and accommodation options may also close in low season. This, however, gives a certain desolate appeal to some of the coastal towns such as Lyme Regis and Swanage, with the additional advantage of quieter roads and easier parking.

18

things not to miss

It's not possible to see everything Dorset, Hampshire and the Isle of Wight have to offer on a short trip. What follows is a selective taste of the city's highlights: quaint pubs, majestic castles, fun activities and intriguing architecture – all arranged in colour-coded categories to help you find the very best things to see and experience. All entries have a page reference to take you straight into the Guide, where you can find out more.

01 Walk the South West Coast Path Page **83** • You can tackle the entire Dorset stretch of Britain's longest footpath, or simply walk some easy sections in a day.

02 **Durdle Door** Page **89** • Swim under this iconic arch from the adjacent pebble beach.

04 **HMS Victory** Page **242** • Explore Nelson's flagship to get an insight into the harsh realities of naval life during the Battle of Trafalgar.

05 **Abbotsbury cygnet hatching** Page **128** • Visit the swannery in May or June, and you'll be surrounded by fluffy cygnets.

03 **Winchester Cathedral** Page **204** • Check out this historic treasure-trove, sheltering everything from the ancient tombs of King Knut and William Rufus to contemporary sculpture by Anthony Gormley.

06 Fossil hunting Page **139** • Head along the Jurassic Coast beaches around Lyme Regis and Charmouth to find the best fossils.

07 New Forest ponies Page **167** • Watch the ponies fearlessly wandering down village streets – but guard your picnic.

08 Old Harry Rocks Page **83** • Walk out along this spectacular stretch of coastal rock stacks high above the Dorset coast.

09 **Corfe Castle** Page **75** • This dramatic hill-top ruin has far-reaching views, overlooking the Swanage steam train puffing along in the valley below.

10 **Brownsea Island** Page **66** • Take a picnic to this delightful car-free island, where red squirrels, ducks and chickens roam wild.

11 **The Hive Beach Café** Page **133** • Enjoy local, freshly caught seafood and fish at this lovely beachside café.

12 **Walk to Tyneham village** Page **88** • Lovely walks and countryside surround this abandoned village, which looks much as it would have done in the 1940s.

13 **Cerne Abbas Giant** Page 107 • This vast priapic figure stands incongruously on a hillside, amid bucolic countryside and thatched villages.

14 **Surfing in Boscombe** Page 56 • Catch the waves at the UK's only man-made surf reef.

15 **The Spinnaker Tower** Page 241 • Take in the great views from this iconic structure, or test your courage by lying on the glass floor and looking down.

16 **Bournemouth beach** Page 51 • Chill out on South England's ultimate resort beach – a fabulous seven-mile stretch of sand, with excellent seaside facilities.

17 **The Needles** Page **280** • These dramatic chalk stacks off the Isle of Wight can be seen from the picturesque eastern side of the island.

18 **Isle of Wight Festival** Page **262** • One of the country's major festivals has featured all the top names in rock and pop, including David Bowie, The Rolling Stones, Iggy Pop and the Sex Pistols.

Basics

Basics

Getting there

The vast majority of people approach the region covered in this Guide by car along the M3 and M27 motorways, or by train – there are direct lines from London's Waterloo station as well as from Bristol, Birmingham and stations in the north. There are also regular National Express coaches from London's Victoria station and most other major cities. Ferry links run to Weymouth, Poole and Portsmouth from France, Spain and the Channel Islands. In addition, the region has two international airports, at Bournemouth and Southampton, with flights from many European countries. Indeed, most of Hampshire and East Dorset is only one to two hours' travelling time from London, though add a good hour to reach the far corners of western Dorset due to the slow rail and road links. Any visit to the Isle of Wight, of course, involves a ferry trip, though this often adds to the charm of the journey.

By car

It's a quick and easy drive along the **M3** and **M27** from London to Southampton (around 90min) or along the **A3** to Portsmouth. Coming from the north, there are good connections using the A34/M3/M27 corridor. Just beyond Southampton, the motorways end – Dorset and the Isle of Wight have no motorways at all – and it's another thirty minutes or so along the **A31** and **A388** to Bournemouth and Poole. Heading further west, however, things slow down beyond Ringwood when the A31 becomes one lane each way and bottlenecks form around Wimborne throughout the summer from lunchtime on a Friday (heading south) and mid-afternoon on a Sunday (heading north). The **A35** from Poole to Lyme Regis is better, having sporadic sections of dual carriageway, though traffic jams often build up around Dorchester, and on the **A354** into Weymouth – though a relief road is being built here in preparation for the Olympics.

By train

Most **trains** into the region are run by South West Trains from London Waterloo (Ⓦwww.southwesttrains.co.uk). In addition, CrossCountry (Ⓦwww.crosscountrytrains .co.uk) runs long-distance trains from the Midlands and the North, while First Great Western (Ⓦwww.firstgreatwestern.co.uk) runs services from Bristol to Southampton and Portsmouth, and Southern Railway

(Ⓦwww.southernrailway.com) serves the south coast between Portsmouth and Brighton.

The Waterloo to Weymouth line serves all the major towns in East Dorset and Hampshire, including Basingstoke (45min), Winchester (1hr), Southampton (1hr 20min), Brockenhurst for the New Forest (1hr 30min), Bournemouth (2hr), Poole (2hr 10min), Dorchester (2hr 45min) and Weymouth (3hr), with trains running approximately every thirty minutes to an hour. Trains to Portsmouth run on a separate line via Guildford every thirty minutes. The far north and west of Dorset is served by trains via Salisbury every two hours to Sherborne (1hr 50min), Gillingham (2hr) for Shaftesbury, and Axminster (2hr 45min) for Lyme Regis and Bridport. For details of fares and specific routes, see Ⓦwww.nationalrail.co.uk.

There are no specific rail passes that cover Dorset and Hampshire, but if you plan to visit the region several times by train, it may be worth getting a **Network Railcard** which gives you a third off the price for up to four adults travelling together and sixty percent off for up to four children: the pass costs £25 for a year and can only be used on off-peak trains (see Ⓦwww.railcard.co.uk/network for details).

By coach

Regular National Express **coaches** (Ⓦwww .nationalexpress.com) from London Victoria serve the main towns in the area, including

Winchester, Portsmouth, Southampton, Ringwood, Bournemouth, Dorchester and Weymouth. There are also less regular services from Gatwick and Heathrow airports and other regional towns in the UK. **Fares** tend to be lower than on the train, especially if you can book in advance and be flexible about when you travel. In addition, iconic US bus company Greyhound runs two routes in the UK, from London Victoria direct to Southampton and Portsmouth. Coaches are comfortable with free wi-fi and newspapers; the journey time is under two hours, and fares start at £1 (Wwww.greyhounduk.com).

By ferry

There are three major **ports**, Portsmouth, Poole and Weymouth, each with **ferries from France** and the first **from Spain**. A fourth port, Southampton – the largest of them all – has no cross-Channel ferries, only boats to the Isle of Wight and huge ocean liner cruise ships.

Portsmouth can be reached from several ports in France: **from Caen**, Brittany Ferries

has 3–4 services daily, varying from 3 hour 45 minutes on the fast catamaran, to 8 hour on the overnight boat: **from St Malo** it has one daily service (9hr), returning overnight; and **from Cherbourg** it runs one daily fast catamaran (3hr), while Condor Ferries has one sailing a week from Cherbourg (5hr). **From Le Havre**, LD Lines has two ships a day (5hr 30min and overnight 8hr). **From Bilbao** in Spain, P&O runs 2–3 ferries a week (36hr), while Brittany Ferries sails twice a week **from Santander** in Spain (24hr).

Poole is served by 2–3 daily services **from Cherbourg** on Brittany Ferries (fast cat 2hr 15min; ferry 4hr 30min or 6hr 30min overnight), and two ferries daily (summer only) **from St Malo** via the Channel Islands (4hr 35min).

Weymouth is served daily by a Condor Ferries fast cat **from St Malo** (5hr 15min) via the Channel Islands.

Fares vary enormously according to the season, the day, the time of day and the route, though LD Lines generally offer the lowest rates.

Four steps to a better kind of travel

At Rough Guides we are passionately committed to travel. We feel strongly that only through travelling do we truly come to understand the world we live in and the people we share it with – plus tourism has brought a great deal of **benefit** to developing economies around the world over the last few decades. But the extraordinary growth in tourism has also damaged some places irreparably, and of course **climate change** is exacerbated by most forms of transport, especially flying. This means that now more than ever it's important to **travel thoughtfully** and **responsibly**, with respect for the cultures you're visiting – not only to derive the most benefit from your trip but also to preserve the best bits of the planet for everyone to enjoy. At Rough Guides we feel there are four main areas in which you can make a difference:

- Consider what you're contributing to the **local economy**, and how much the services you use do the same, whether it's through employing local workers and guides or sourcing locally grown produce and local services.
- Consider the **environment** on holiday as well as at home. Water is scarce in many developing destinations, and the biodiversity of local flora and fauna can be adversely affected by tourism. Try to patronize businesses that take account of this.
- Travel with a purpose, not just to tick off experiences. Consider **spending longer** in a place, and getting to know it and its people.
- Make your trips "**climate neutral**" via a reputable carbon offset scheme. All Rough Guide flights are offset, and every year we donate money to a variety of charities devoted to combating the effects of climate change.

Ferry contacts

Brittany Ferrries ☎0871 244 0744, ⓦwww
.brittany-ferries.co.uk
Condor Ferries ☎01202 207216, ⓦwww
.condorferries.co.uk
LD Lines ☎0844 576 8836, ⓦwww.ldlines.com
P&O Ferries ☎08716 645645, ⓦwww.poferries
.com

By plane

Both Bournemouth and Southampton
airports have regular scheduled flights
throughout the year from many towns and
cities in Western Europe. Ryanair is the main
budget airline to serve **Bournemouth
airport**, with flights from France, Spain,
Portugal, Italy, Scotland and Ireland. Other
airlines that fly to Bournemouth are
Thomsonfly, and Easyjet (winter only) from
Geneva and Grenoble.

Flybe is the main budget airline serving
Southampton airport, with flights from
France, Spain, Germany, Switzerland and
Austria, as well as from several regional
cities in England, Scotland and Ireland.
Eastern Airways has flights to Southampton
from UK regional cities such as Liverpool,
Aberdeen, Leeds and Newcastle.

Airline contacts

Eastern Airways ⓦwww.easternairways.com
Easyjet ⓦwww.easyjet.com
Flybe ⓦwww.flybe.com
Ryanair ⓦwww.ryanair.com
Thomsonfly ⓦflights.thomson.co.uk

Getting to the Isle of Wight

Three **ferry companies** serve the Isle of Wight
on three different routes. **Wightlink** runs the
Lymington to Yarmouth car ferry, a high-
speed catamaran from Portsmouth to Ryde
(foot passengers only), and a car ferry from
Portsmouth to Fishbourne. **Red Funnel** runs
a high-speed catamaran for foot passengers
from Southampton to West Cowes and a car
ferry from Southampton to East Cowes, while
Hovertravel runs a hovercraft from Southsea
in Portsmouth to Ryde for foot passengers
only. For full details of routes, journey times
and frequencies, see p.253.

Isle of Wight ferry contacts

Hovertravel ☎023 9281 1000 or 01983 811000,
ⓦwww.hovertravel.co.uk
Red Funnel ☎0844 844 9988, ⓦwww.redfunnel
.co.uk
Wightlink ☎0871 376 1000, ⓦwww.wightlink.co.uk

Getting around

The most practical way of getting around the region in this Guide is by car, though
congestion in some towns and on the main routes to and from the coast can be
a problem. Train or coach is feasible if you are travelling to one of the main towns
in the region, but if you want to explore the rural areas, car or bicycle is pretty
much the only way to get around. Travelling around the Isle of Wight is feasible
without a car as the island has a reasonable public transport network and plenty
of cycle routes. The Traveline website (☎0871 200 2233, ⓦwww.traveline.org.uk)
gives timetables and routes for all public transport, directing you to the relevant
company for your journey.

By train

Dorset, in particular, is poorly served by
trains, as during the Industrial Revolution

three of the most powerful landowning
families clubbed together to prevent train
lines from crossing their land. The result is

one main line along the coast, one skirting the northern edge of the county, and one minor route towards the western edge of the county between Dorchester and Yeovil, continuing on to Bristol; trains run every couple of hours or so (contact First Great Western for details; ⓦ www.firstgreatwestern .co.uk).

Hampshire is better served: as well as the main-line trains (see p.19 for details), some smaller branch lines are also operated by South West trains, such as the Brockenhurst to Lymington line, which runs along a jetty to connect with the Isle of Wight ferry; and the south coast line which connects Brighton with the main line at Eastleigh, near Southampton, and runs to Fareham, Portsmouth Harbour, Southsea and Havant.

The **Isle of Wight** has one main train route, the Island Line (ⓦ www.island-line.co .uk), which runs from Ryde Pier Head to Shanklin (see p.255 for details). If you plan to use the train several times during your visit, it may be worth buying a season ticket: a weekly season ticket giving unlimited travel on the line costs £15.30.

In addition, the region has three independently owned **steam train** lines: The Watercress Line between Alton and Arlesford (see p.211); the Swanage Railway to Norden (see p.76); and the Isle of Wight Steam Railway, which runs from Wootton to connect with the Island Line at Smallbrook Junction (see p.264). All three run through picturesque countryside, and tend to have seasonal services only.

By bus

While National Express provides coach links between the main towns in the area and the main UK cities (see p.19 for details), there are also several smaller regional bus companies. **Wilts and Dorset** (ⓦ www .wdbus.co.uk) is the main company in East Dorset: based in Bournemouth, it serves Poole, Christchurch, Ringwood, Fordingbridge, Wimborne, Blandford Forum and the Purbecks. West Dorset is served mainly by **First Bus** (ⓦ www.firstgroup.com), with services around Dorchester, Beaminster, Weymouth and Portland, Bridport and Lyme Regis. The area around Portsmouth and Southampton is also served by First Bus,

while **Stagecoach** (ⓦ www.stagecoachbus .com/south) also serves the Portsmouth area, as well as Winchester, Alton and Basingstoke. **Bluestar** (ⓦ www.bluestarbus.co.uk) serves the south Hampshire region, with services to Southampton, Romsey, Winchester, Totton and Hythe. Buses on the Isle of Wight are run by **Southern Vectis** (ⓦ www.islandbuses.info) and **Wightbus** (ⓦ www.iwight.com): see p.255 for further details.

In several towns, there are guided **bus tours** of the surrounding countryside, which can be a useful way of seeing all the attractions in the area if you are short of time. Most will pick up from your hotel and they can usually be booked through the local tourist offices. A good example is the Bournemouth-based. Discover Dorset (ⓦ www.discover dorset.co.uk), which collects from hotels and language schools around Bournemouth, and runs half-day tours (£15) to the Jurassic Coast and Stonehenge, as well as a full-day Deepest Dorset tour (£28).

By car

Most people **drive** around the region, with main routes to and from the coast suffering from congestion in the summer, particularly on Friday afternoons heading south and on Sunday afternoons heading north; see p.18 for details. Bottlenecks also form around the coastal towns of Swanage, Bournemouth, Poole, Weymouth and Bridport, as well as inland around Dorchester, Wareham and Lyndhurst in the New Forest. The queues too, for the Studland ferry can be horrendous on sunny weekends heading south in the mornings and north in the evenings. Once you are off the main roads, however, the tiny rural country lanes can be a pleasure to drive down, particularly in the northern section of the New Forest, central Hampshire and northern Dorset.

Parking is not particularly problematic, except in peak summer holiday season: most of the big towns have ample car parks or on-street pay-and-display machines. Most towns charge around 70p–£1 an hour for parking.

Car rental companies

Avis ⓦ www.avis.com
Europcar ⓦ www.europcar.com

Top drives

Here are the seven top drives around the area:

Studland to Corfe Castle Head up past the golf course for Poole Bay vistas and down until the amazing ruins of Corfe Castle come into view. See p.81.

Cerne Abbas to Milton Abbas Take the narrow back roads to enjoy Dorset scenery little changed from Hardy's "Wessex". See p.108.

Burton Bradstock to Abbotsbury This fantastic road passes high above the coast with stupendous views of the Fleet Lagoon. See p.133.

Shaftesbury to Tollard Royal Full of loops, twists and turns, the B3081 winds through the beautiful woods and hills of Cranbourne Chase. See p.154.

Linford to South and North Gorley This narrow country lane takes you through archetypally picturesque New Forest scenery – watch out for ponies meandering along the road. See p.171.

Rhinefield to Bolderwood Another classic New Forest stretch, this one through ancient woodland. See p.179.

St Catherine's Point to Freshwater Hugging the cliff-top, this road takes in the best coastal scenery along the unspoilt south of the Isle of Wight. See p.277.

Hertz Ⓦ www.hertz.com
Thrifty Ⓦ www.thrifty.com

By bicycle

Cycling round the region is a pleasure once you are off the main road. Good areas to cycle are the New Forest, the Purbecks, north Dorset, central Hampshire and the Isle of Wight. Most towns have bike rental outlets: we have listed them in the guide. See p.32 for further details on cycling.

On foot

With stunning coastal routes, plenty of inland footpaths and bridleways through beautiful rural scenery, the region is a pleasure to walk in. Following the **South West Coast Path** is the most popular way to explore the coast, with reasonable transport links and good accommodation options en route; the website Ⓦ www.southwestcoastpath .com provides detailed maps and route descriptions for the entire route and suggestions for shorter walks. The unofficial **South Downs Way** website Ⓦ www.southdowns way.co.uk provides similar information for the region's second long-distance footpath, including useful transport advice for accessing sections of the path. For more information see p.32.

Accommodation

A quiet revolution has taken place in the quality of English seaside accommodation over the last few years. Most South Coast resorts now have at least one boutique-style B&B or guest house, but more importantly their advent has led to a serious improvement in the quality of all accommodation. Whilst you will still find a few swirly carpeted, fusty-smelling, chintzy-decored traditional B&Bs, the vast majority have really improved their game, and even simple B&Bs now tend to provide clean rooms, modern light decor, comfy beds and decent-quality breakfasts. Of course, there are still some that think by adding a flat-screen TV to a dingy run-down room, they can claim to be boutique-style, but most really have cleaned up their act and you shouldn't find it too difficult to get reasonably priced accommodation of a decent standard.

Hotels, guest houses and B&Bs

There's a lot of overlap between small **hotels**, **guest houses** and **B&Bs**, all of which can offer a wide variety of accommodation and facilities. A farmhouse or manor house B&B in the country, for example, may have a pool, grand dining room and large grounds, whilst a town hotel may be more basic with less facilities. **Prices** are not always an accurate guide either to the quality of the accommodation – in high season a fairly simple place on the coast will charge a lot more than somewhere more comfortable and luxurious inland. As very few places in this Guide are more than an hour's drive from the coast, you're often better off opting for a delightful country B&B, and driving to the seaside. Out of high season, however, and with the current financial climate, it's always worth negotiating a good rate.

Country inns and gastropubs

Inland Dorset and Hampshire have some lovely **country inns** and **gastropubs** with rooms. Often in the middle of nowhere, these places tend to have highly regarded restaurants specializing in local, seasonal food with a few rooms upstairs. They vary tremendously in terms of how luxurious they are – some have flat-screen TVs and all mod cons, other are simpler and more rustic in style – but the ambience is usually friendly, with the emphasis on a good meal and a comfortable room to stay the night.

Hostels

There are only seven YHA **youth hostels** in the area covered in this Guide – two in the Isle of Wight, one in the New Forest, and the other four along the Dorset coast. They vary from lively seaside townhouses, such as at Swanage, to basic, rural, walkers' shelters, such as Litton Cheney. You don't have to be a member to stay at a YHA hostel, though the annual membership of £16 per person will get you a reduced rate of up to £3 a night; for details, contact ☎01629 592700, ⍟www.yha.org.uk.

In the larger coastal towns, such as Bournemouth, Southampton, Portsmouth

---

Accommodation price codes

Throughout this guide, the accommodation is listed on a scale of ❶ to ❾, according to the cheapest room for two people in high season:

❶ £60 and under	❹ £81–90	❼ £121–150
❷ £61–70	❺ £91–100	❽ £151–200
❸ £71–80	❻ £101–120	❾ £201 and over

Top places to stay

There are some great places to stay in the region – here are some of the more unusual ones.

Mudeford beach huts No power, no running water, barely room to swing a cat, but you can't beat a night out on the sandspit in one of the best located beach huts in the UK. See p.58.

Purbeck Vineyard Look out over the vines on this working vineyard with a steam railway at the bottom of the garden. See p.77.

Lighthouse cottages, Durlston Stay on a remote cliff-top below a working lighthouse. See p.81.

Clavell Tower, Kimmeridge Spend a night in this Victorian tower perched on the cliff-top with great views. See p.88.

Summer Lodge, Evershott In the heart of Hardy's "Wessex", you can stay in this lovely country house, part of which was designed by Hardy himself. See p.141.

Onion Store, Romsey Choose from one of the eclectic former fruit and vegetable stores – including one with a tree growing in it – for an unforgettable night. See p.234.

Xoron, Bembridge This converted World War II gunboat, moored in Bembridge harbour on the Isle of Wight, makes a cosy and atmospheric B&B. See p.269.

and Weymouth, you'll also find some **independent hostels**. These usually provide basic quality dorm-bed accommodation from around £14 a night. In rural areas, **walkers' barns** provide simple, hostel-style dorm-bed accommodation, usually on farms or campsites, for around £8 a night.

Camping

There is no shortage of **campsites** in the region, many in the most spectacular locations, and in the summer camping can be one of the best ways to visit the region.

The **New Forest campsites** are an experience in themselves (see p.173), with ponies peering into your tent in the morning and vast tracts of traffic-free tracks to cycle down safely. Head along the coastal path, and you can't fail to notice that some of the most **dramatic cliff-top locations** are topped by campsites. While this may be disappointing for walkers, it's great for campers and if you're staying at one of the campsites, the views from your tent may be stunning. In addition, there are a series of **farm campsites** in idyllic rural locations where children can collect the eggs for breakfast, and enjoy the atmosphere of a working farm. For those that prefer more comfort, several places have yurt camping, while upmarket Featherdown Farms (ⓦ www.featherdownfarms.co.uk) has three

sites in the region, one in rural Hampshire, one in rural Dorset, and one in Purbeck, with comfortable ready-erected tents on working farms.

Several companies in the region rent out **camper vans** for touring the area, including Isle of Wight Campers (ⓣ 01983 852089, ⓦ www.isleofwightcampers.co.uk), and Dub-days in Whitely near Portsmouth (ⓦ www.dubdays.co.uk), both of which have traditional VW camper vans; or Kamperhire (ⓣ 0845 226 7869, ⓦ www.kamperhire.co .uk), which has more modern models, based just outside Southampton.

Self-catering

There's an enormous array of **self-catering accommodation** available in the region, from converted lighthouses on cliff-tops to remote, rural farmhouses, to high-tech architect-designed houses. There are also many cottages on working farms that vary from simple farm cottages to luxurious barn conversions with a pool and all mod cons. Prices start from about £200 a week in low season to well over £1000 in high season, depending on the size, facilities and location.

The companies below all rent out properties in the region or, for private rentals, tourist boards and small ads can help.

Self-catering agencies

Dorset Coastal Cottages ☎0800 980 4070, ⓦwww.dorsetcoastalcottages.com. Has a huge array of cottages of all shapes and sizes, some in rural Dorset, others right by the coast.

Dorset Cottage Holidays ☎01929 553443, ⓦwww.dhcottages.co.uk. Specializes in cottages in Purbeck, but also some further afield in Weymouth, Christchurch and Ferndown.

Farm and Cottage Holidays ☎01237 459888, ⓦwww.holidaycottages.co.uk. A wide range of accommodation throughout the region, from barn conversions to modern bungalows.

Farmstay UK ☎02476 696909, ⓦwww.farmstayuk.co.uk. Provides a variety of accommodation on working farms in the region, some organic.

Halcyon Holiday Cottages ☎07515 881329, ⓦwww.halcyonholidaycottages.co.uk. For larger groups, Halcyon has several properties in the New Forest that sleep up to 36.

Isle of Wight Farm and Country holidays ☎01983 551368, ⓦwww.wightfarmholidays.co.uk. A good selection of cottage and barn conversions around the Isle of Wight.

Island Cottage Holidays ☎01983 481555, ⓦwww.islandcottageholidays.com. Rents out some more unusual properties, including the Indian Summer House, built by Queen Victoria on the Osborne House estate.

National Trust Cottages ☎0844 8002070, ⓦwww.nationaltrustcottages.co.uk. Rents out some lovely properties in prime National Trust land, including the only holiday cottage on Brownsea Island, the old tennis pavilion in Studland, and the former coastguard's cottage on The Needles in the Isle of Wight.

New Forest Cottages ☎01590 679655, ⓦwww.newforestcottages.co.uk. An enormous variety of places to rent in all regions of the New Forest, from traditional thatched cottages to modern family homes.

Rural Retreats ☎01386 701177, ⓦwww.ruralretreats.co.uk. Has several cottages in the area including converted former lighthouses in stunning locations, such as St Katherine's Point on the Isle of Wight and Anvil Point near Swanage.

Food and drink

At the forefront of the local, seasonal food movement, Dorset, Hampshire and the Isle of Wight have no shortage of decent places to eat and drink. The region's restaurants harbour several well-known Michelin-starred chefs, though you're just as well off choosing one of the smaller independent restaurants and cafés that specialize in simple dishes made from local ingredients. And probably the best way to experience the region's specialities is to head to one of many farm shops, delis or farmers' markets and pick up some of the delicious local produce on offer for a picnic.

Restaurants

There are a scattering of well-known chefs with **restaurants** in the region – Gary Rhodes runs two restaurants in Christchurch (see p.191); Mark Hix has his oyster house in Lyme Regis (see p.138); Britain's youngest Michelin-starred chef, Robert Thompson, runs *The Hambrough* in the Isle of Wight (see p.276); and, of course, Hugh Fearnley-Whittingstall's River Cottage is on the Devon/Dorset border, near Lyme Regis (see p.133).

But there also some very well-regarded local establishments, whose chefs are less well known but who produce food of an equally high standard, often at much lower prices. Along the coast, fish is the mainstay and there are several places that serve reasonably priced, locally caught **fish and seafood** in great coastal locations: some of the best are the *Hive Beach Cafe*, right on the beach in Burton Bradstock (see p.133); the *Crab House Café* in Portland (see p.122) for oysters from the Fleet Lagoon; West Beach in Bournemouth (see p.59) for great sea views and fresh fish; *Pebble Beach* on the cliff-top at Barton-on-Sea (see p.193); the *Priory Hotel* on the Isle of Wight (see p.268) for Bembridge lobster and great views; and *Wheelers Crab*

The chain gang

Despite the increase in independent places offering local seasonal food, Dorset, Hampshire and the Isle of Wight are not immune from the ubiquitous chain restaurants that seem to have taken over high streets around the country. Having said that, they are not all bad, and there are certainly some towns in the region where they could well be your best bet for a good-value meal in a lively atmosphere, especially if you have children with you. We have listed some of the best chains below, which are represented in the area.

Ask Pizzeria Often in beautiful old buildings that have been converted or restored, they have a good selection of reasonably priced pasta and pizza dishes.

Café Nero The best of the chain cafés serving authentic Italian coffee and decent pastries.

Café Rouge French-style bistros serving traditional brasserie dishes, such as *moules marinières* and Toulouse sausages.

Pizza Express Lively, buzzy restaurants, with a contemporary stylish decor. Their pizzas are the most authentically Italian of all the chains.

Prezzo Also often in converted historical buildings, they serve pizzas and pasta, but the rotisserie chicken is the dish to opt for, especially if there are two or more sharing.

Shed on the Isle of Wight, for great home-made crab pasties served warm on the beach (see p.276). Inland, too, many restaurants and gastropubs make use of **local wild produce**, such as venison, game, rabbit and mushrooms: some good places to try are Sienna in Dorchester for local meat and cheeses (see p.102); *Hotel du Vin* in Winchester for local pheasant and cosy dining rooms (see p.207); *La Fosse* in Cranborne (see p.158) for local meat and game; and the *White House Hotel* in Charmouth (see p.139) for using its own fruit, veg, herbs and eggs.

Regional specialities

Covering a predominantly rural area, Dorset, Hampshire and the Isle of Wight enjoy plenty of **locally grown** fruit, vegetables and herbs, as well as organic and free-range farms selling pork, chicken and beef and lamb. Game is also widely available, as is **wild produce** such as nettles, wild garlic, mushrooms and, of course, fish and seafood.

In addition, there's an increasing number of artisan products, such as cheeses and bread, ice cream, chutney, pickles and jams made in the area. The best-known **bakery** is Long Crichel (see p.158), outside Wimborne, whose organic breads and pastries are renowned across the country: there's also the Town Mill Bakery, which makes organic bread, pizzas and pastries in the centre of Lyme Regis.

The best-known local **cheese** is the Dorset Blue Vinney, a delicious Stilton-like cheese that is made throughout the county. Denhay Cheddar is made at Denhay Farm near Bridport, while Woolsery goat's cheese comes from Up Sydling near Dorchester. Lyburn Farm in Hamptworth in the New Forest makes a range of delicious cheeses, including a garlic and nettle cheese and a full-flavoured Old Winchester: you can sample them at various pubs in the area, such as the *Royal Oak* in Fritham (see p.172), or buy them from local farmers' markets or their farm shop (Tues–Fri 11am–4pm).

There are several highly regarded companies whose **ice creams** – made using local milk, cream and other ingredients – can be found around the region. New Forest ice creams, based in Totton, near Southampton, is the largest, while Purbeck ice creams, based in Kingston, near Wareham, produces some unusual flavours, such as chilli and liquorice ice creams. Barford Farmhouse, near Sturminster Newton produces sorbet from locally grown blueberries: it has its own shop and ice cream garden (Easter–Oct Tues–Sun 11.30am–5.30pm) or can be sampled at Gary Rhodes' Christchurch restaurants (see p.191). Minghella produces the best-known ice cream on the Isle of Wight (see box, p.267).

The best place to sample local regional produce is at a **famers' market**. Most small towns in the region have one at least once a month, with Winchester hosting the country's largest farmers' market every other Sunday. For dates and details of famers' markets in Hampshire and Dorset, check ⓦ www.hampshirefarmersmarkets.co.uk, and ⓦ dorsetfarmersmarkets.co.uk.

In the Isle of Wight, markets are held every Friday morning in Newport and every Saturday morning in Ryde; see ⓦ www.islandfarmersmarket.co.uk for more details.

Drink

Some of the best **pubs** in the country are in Dorset, Hampshire and the Isle of Wight, from welcoming, rural places with cosy bars, low beams and open fires to vast, bustling pubs whose crowds spill out onto the seashore on a sunny afternoon. Many serve a good range of local ales – some even have their own on-site breweries – as well as food of all descriptions, varying from home-made pies and local cheese ploughman's, to Thai curries and full-blown Michelin-standard restaurant meals.

Local beer

There are three main local long-established **breweries** in the region, all brewing their own individual award-winning beers and ales. **Ringwood Brewery** produces a variety of different beers from its brewery in Ringwood, ranging from the light, summery ale, Boondoggle, to the strongest offering, Old Thumper. **Hall and Woodhouse**, based in Blandford Forum, brews a huge range of ales, including the gingery Blandford Fly and the floral-flavoured bitter, Tanglefoot. It also produces some seasonal beers, such as the organic dandelion ale, Lemony Cricket with lemongrass and the River Cottage Stinger, produced using nettles from Hugh Fearnley-Whittingstall's HQ (see p.133). Look out, too, for beers brewed by **Palmers** in Bridport, such as the light Dorset Gold and the darker full-strength Tally Ho. The three breweries above all offer tours and tasting sessions; see the relevant chapters in the Guide for details.

There are also some smaller, newer independent breweries worth looking out for, such as the **Dorset Piddle Brewery** (ⓦ www.dorsetpiddlebrewery.co.uk) in Piddlehinton, producer of the light, fruity Jimmy Riddle and the stronger Silent Slasher; the **Dorset Brewing Company** (ⓦ www.dbcales.com) in Weymouth – check out their lager-type Chesil or the Durdle Door bitter; and the **Itchen Valley Brewery** (ⓦ www.itchenvalley.com) in New Arlesford, which produces a fine Winchester ale.

On the Isle of Wight, the local breweries to look out for are Goddards (ⓦ www.goddards-brewery.co.uk) in Ryde, with its award-winning Fuggle-Dee-Dum and Yates (ⓦ www.yates-brewery.co.uk) in Ventnor.

Several pubs in the region have their own **microbreweries** attached, including the *Bankes Arms* in Studland (see p.85) and the *Flowerpots Inn* in Cheriton (see p.209), both well worth a visit.

For a roundup of the best pubs in the region, see the box on p.9.

Wine

With their mild climates, Dorset, Hampshire and the Isle of Wight now have several **vineyards** producing wines and sparkling wines of a reasonable quality. While they still have a long way to go to compete with the more traditional wine-producing countries – particularly on price, as many are more expensive than the French equivalent – they are improving rapidly. Several of the vineyards also provide bed and breakfast accommodation and tours: some worth looking out for are the **Purbeck Vineyard** near Corfe Castle (see p.77), **Adgestone** (ⓦwww.adgestonevineyard.co.uk) and **Rosemary** vineyards (ⓦwww.rosemaryvineyard.co.uk) in the Isle of Wight, **Setley Ridge** (ⓦwww.setleyridge vineyard.co.uk) and **Marlings** vineyards (ⓦwww.newforestwine.co.uk) in the New Forest, and the **Wickham Vineyard** (ⓦwww.wickhamvineyard.com) in Shedfield, between Southampton and Portsmouth.

Festivals

There are plenty of events and festivals in the region, which take place throughout the year – ranging from Southampton's Asian Mela to the British Beach Polo championships, via the World Nettle-eating competition. In July and August, in particular, every small town and resort has its own festival or carnival – we've picked out some of the best, listed below. Music festivals are on p.31.

Festivals and events calendar

February

Rallye Sunseeker Bournemouth (last week of Feb). The south's largest car rally runs from Bournemouth's seafront up into the forests round Wareham and Ringwood. ⓦwww.rallyesunseeker.co.uk.

March/April

Lambing weekend Kingston Maurward (usually the middle two weekends in March). Pretty much the closest you can get to a sheep giving birth – you can also help to bottle-feed the young lambs. ⓦwww.kmc.ac.uk.
Giant Easter Egg Hunt Lulworth Castle. Go home with plenty of free eggs – if you can find them round the grounds of the castle first. ⓦwww.lulworth.com.

May

International Beach Kite Festival Weymouth (early May). Huge festival of kites on the beach, culminating in impressive fireworks. ⓦthekitesociety.org.uk.
Christchurch Food Festival (mid-May). Stalls and restaurants celebrating international flavours – cookery demonstrations from celebrity chefs, tastings and special menus. ⓦchristchurchfoodfest.co.uk.
Walk the Wight Isle of Wight (mid-May). The UK's largest walking festival, including a cross-island trek for those who like a challenge. ⓦisleofwightwalkingfestival.co.uk.
Evolution Rocks Charmouth and Lyme Regis (end of May). Talks and fossil hunts on the famous Jurassic Coast, together with performance artists and family entertainment. ⓦwww.evolutionrocks.net.
Beaulieu Trucks and Troops Beaulieu (end of May). Festival of all things military in the fine grounds of Beaulieu, including mock battles, fly-pasts and parades. ⓦwww.beaulieu.co.uk.
Old Gaffers Festival Yarmouth, Isle of Wight (end of May). Named after the gaff sailing boats that come from all round the country to participate in three days of events and entertainment round Yarmouth. ⓦwww.yarmoutholdgaffersfestival.co.uk.
Dorset Art Weeks Dorset (end of May). Biennial event in which over 300 artists across the region open up their studios to the public. ⓦwww.dorsetartweeks.co.uk.

June

World Stinging Nettle-Eating Competition *The Bottle Inn*, Marshwood, Dorset (mid-June). Annual competition to see who can eat the longest stinging nettles, helped along by the pub's fine selection of ales. ⓦwww.thebottleinn.co.uk.
Dorchester Festival (mid-June). Innovative ten-day festival of acts and performances based around Dorchester's history. ⓦdorchesterfestival.co.uk.
Round the Island Race Isle of Wight (end of June). The world's top sailors take part in this

challenging round-the-island race to and from Cowes. ⓦwww.roundtheisland.org.uk.

Portsmouth Festivities Portsmouth (end of June). The town holds ten days of music, shows, films and special events around the city. ⓦwww .portsmouthfestivities.co.uk.

Tankfest Bovington, Dorset (end of June). The annual outing for the tank museum's working beasts, with mock battles and plenty of gunfire. ⓦtankmuseum.org.

Bridport Food Festival (end of June). Local suppliers and producers display their wares round town at stalls, cafés and restaurants. ⓦbridportfoodfestival.org.uk.

July

British Beach Polo Championships Sandbanks, Poole (early July). Two days of beachside competition featuring the top names in this exclusive sport – followed by a giant beach party with top name DJs. ⓦwww.sandpolo.com.

Gold Hill Fair Shaftesbury (early July). Foodstalls and live entertainment around the famous "Hovis" hill. ⓦshaftesburydorset.com.

Winchester Hat Fair Winchester (early July). The longest running street arts festival in the UK, with fun and innovative acts from round the world performing round town. ⓦwww.hatfair.co.uk.

Aldershot Army Show Aldershot (early July). The home to Britain's army shows off its talents during a weekend of spectacular events including motorcycle display teams, parachute displays and parades. ⓦwww.armyshow.co.uk.

Bourne Free Pride Bournemouth (mid-July). Parades, live shows and street parties celebrating the gay community. ⓦwww.bournefree.co.uk.

Wareham Carnival (mid-July). A weekend of live music and various events round town. ⓦwareham -carnival.org.uk.

Southampton Mela Southampton (mid-July). Vibrant festival celebrating the town's Asian community with dance, music and arts. ⓦwww.artasia.org.uk.

Farnborough Air Show Farnborough (mid-July). Biennial air spectacular, with planes of all sorts zooming overhead. ⓦwww.farnborough.com.

New Forest Show New Park, Brockenhurst (end of July). Giant agricultural show displaying the best of the New Forest's livestock along with equestrian shows, stunts and pig races. ⓦwww.newforestshow.co.uk.

Swanage Carnival and Regatta Swanage (end of July). Various events in and around the seaside resort, including races and firework displays. ⓦwww .swanagecarnival.com.

Sandown Carnival (end of July). Lively parades, events and fireworks at the Isle of Wight's principal south coast resort. ⓦwww.sandowncarnival.com.

August

Bournemouth Carnival (early Aug). The south coast resort gets in the party mood with floats and various events round town. ⓦbournemouthcarnival .org.uk.

Cowes Week Cowes, Isle of Wight (first week in Aug). One of the world's largest sailing events (see box, p.258). ⓦskandiacowesweek.co.uk.

Garlic Festival Newchurch, Isle of Wight (mid-Aug). Celebration not only of garlic but also arts and crafts from the island, together with live music, food-stalls, beer tents and more. ⓦgarlic-festival.co.uk.

Bournemouth Air Festival (mid-Aug). The Red Arrows provide a spectacular flying display over three days along the length of the seafront. ⓦbournemouth.co.uk.

Hampshire Open studios Hampshire (last 2 weeks in Aug). Artists around the county exhibit their work to visitors in their houses and studios.

September

Great Dorest Steamfair Tarrant Hinton, Blandford Forum (early Sept). Huge an d lively show celebrating steam engines of all sorts – the largest of its kind in the world – together with stalls and entertainment. ⓦgdsf.co.uk.

Southampton Boat Show Southampton (mid-Sept). Giant exhibition of the latest boats available to aspiring sailors, Roman Abramovich's and the like. ⓦwww.southamptonboatshow.com.

The Isle of Wight Cycling Festival (mid-Sept). Various trails for people of all ages and abilities – including the Hills Killer mountain bike challenge. ⓦwww.sunseaandcycling.com.

Cheese Festival Sturminster Newton (mid-Sept). Sample some of the finest local cheeses round town. Also cheese-making demonstrations and children's entertainment. ⓦcheesefestival.co.uk.

International Charity Classic Car Show Newport/Ryde, Isle of Wight (mid-Sept). Classic and retro cars and bikes descend over a weekend. ⓦisleofwighttouristguide.com.

Wessex Heavy Horse Show and Country Fayre Shaftesbury (last weekend of Sept). Rare breeds of horse together with ferret racing, bird displays and traditional entertainment. ⓦwessexheavyhorsesociety .org.uk.

October

Southampton Film Week (early Oct). Various talks, screenings and events held throughout the city. ⓦsouthampton.gov.uk.

Pumpkin Competition and Beer Festival *Square and Compass*, Worth Matravers (early Oct). An extraordinary assembly of giant pumpkins vie for attention with fantastic local ales at this classic Dorset pub. Ⓦsquareandcompasspub.co.uk.

Exbury Ghost Train (mid-Oct). A special ghoulish train ride is laid on in the lead up to Halloween, along with other events in Exbury Gardens. Ⓦexbury.co.uk.

Purbeck Film Festival Isle of Purbeck (last 2 weeks in Oct). The UK's largest rural film festival with screenings in village halls and historic buildings including Corfe Castle. Ⓦpurbeckfilm.org.uk.

November

Bonfire Night (around Nov 5). Various displays are held throughout the region – some of the best are at the Beaulieu National Motor Museum, Fort Nelson near Portsmouth and Stanpit in Christchurch.

Dorset Food Week (last week in Oct). Regional celebration of Dorset delicacies, with restaurants, shops and local farms laying on special events throughout the region. Ⓦdorsetfoodweek.co.uk.

December

Winchester Christmas Festival (all month). Inner Close, Winchester. Wooden stalls and an ice rink transform the area into a winter wonderland round Winchester's cathedral in the run up to Christmas. Ⓦvisitwinchester.co.uk.

Music

For a relatively small area, a huge selection of **music festivals** takes place in the region over the summer season. As well as the big-hitters, The Isle of Wight Festival, Bestival and Camp Bestival, there's a wide range of smaller, independent festivals – they may not attract the really big names, but often provide excellent bands, a more chilled-out vibe and a lower ticket price.

Music festivals

April

Isle of Wight Jazz Festival (usually early April). Local and international performers in and around Ventnor. Ⓦiowjazzfestival.co.uk.

May

Mayfest Winchester (mid-May). Three days of music in pubs and squares around the town, including folk, jazz, blues, ceilidhs and children's entertainment. Ⓦwinmayfest.co.uk.

June

Wimborne Folk Festival Wimborne (second weekend in June). A weekend of live folk round the Dorset town. Ⓦwimbornefolkfestival.co.uk.

Isle of Wight Festival Seaclose Park, Newport, (mid-June: see box, p.262). The biggest and best-known festival attracting major bands: from Neil Young to the Ting Tings, The Prodigy to July Collins, it's an eclectic mix of talent. Ⓦisleofwightfestival.com.

July

Blissfields Bradley Farm, Alresford (early July). Small, intimate festival with comfy yurts featuring up-and-coming bands, fuelled by local food and drink. Ⓦwww.blissfields.co.uk.

Camp Bestival Lulworth Castle, East Lulworth (end of July). 2008's best new festival provides good music, good food and drink and plenty of family-friendly entertainment – including jousting sessions and comedians – in a lovely setting. Ⓦcampbestival.co.uk.

Glade Matterley Bowl, Winchester (mid-July). Four days of electronic music in a natural amphitheatre. Ⓦgladefestival.com.

Lakeside Magic Kingston Maurward (mid-July). Four-day festival of tribute bands by the lake, with impressive fireworks. Ⓦlakesidemagic.biz.

Swanage Jazz Festival Swanage (mid-July). Various big and up-and-coming traditional jazz, blues and contemporary jazz performers around town. Ⓦswanagejazz.org.uk.

Larmer Tree Larmer Tree Gardens, Dorset/Wiltshire borders (end of July). Family-orientated festival with storytelling, art installations and plenty of music – Jooles Holland is an annual performer. Ⓦwww.amertreefestival.co.uk.

August

Endorse it in Dorset Sixpenny Handley (early Aug). A quirky, independent festival featuring comedy, scrumpy and bands such as Sham 69, Dreadzone and the Tofu Love Frogs.

Summer Gathering Gaunts House, Dorset (early Aug). Hippy-ish festival with plenty of yoga and t'ai chi together with music, dance and entertainment. Ⓦgauntshouse.com.

September

Bestival Robin Hill Country Park, Isle of Wight (mid-Sept). Alternative music festival hosted by Radio 1 DJ Rob da Bank, featuring acts such as Kraftwerk, Massive Attack, Lilly Allen and Elbow. Ⓦbestival.net.

End of the Road Larmer Tree Gardens, Dorest/Wiltshire borders (mid-Sept). Celebrates the end of the festival season with a folksy, hippy crowd squeezing out corporate names. Ⓦendoftheroadfestival.com.

Sports and outdoor activities

The big draw in this region is the coast, which offers tremendous opportunities for swimmers, sailors and watersports enthusiasts, though the rural inland areas also offer great walking and cycling. The region's rivers, too, provide excellent fishing, particularly in Hampshire. Spectator sports are plentiful, and range from one of the world's most famous sailing events to watching cricket at its birthplace.

Walking

All three counties boast superb **walking** terrain, across rolling downs, through river valleys and along a dramatic coastline, and though there are no mountains to tackle, there are plenty of challenging hills and extremely steep sections of coastline. The whole of the **Isle of Wight** is well equipped for walkers, with its series of marked trails, as is **Purbeck** in Dorset and the **New Forest** in Hampshire. Two long-distance paths cross the region, the most famous being the **South West Coast Path** (see p.83), which begins at Poole Harbour, as well as the **South Downs Way**, which starts in Winchester (see p.208).

We've highlighted the best local walks throughout the Guide. These aim to provide a cross section of the regions' varied landscapes. Most of these routes are straightforward to follow and can be enjoyed easily in a day or less, but it goes without saying that even for short hikes you need to be properly equipped with an OS map; see p.38 for details of the OS maps that cover this region. Even with a map, always follow local advice and listen out for local weather reports – British weather is notoriously variable and conditions on some of the coastal paths in particular can be hazardous. Along with the walks in this book, we list some of the best walking guidebooks, which are reviewed on p.296. Local tourist offices are also excellent resources. As well as having walk leaflets, sometimes for a small fee, many of the regional offices organize regular guided walks that are perfect for inexperienced walkers or those who want on-the-ground information: see ⓦwww.westdorset.com, ⓦ www3.hants.gov.uk/guidedwalks.htm and ⓦwww.islandbreaks.co.uk for details.

Cycling

Particularly geared up to **cyclists** are the Isle of Wight – with several well-signed cycle routes – and the New Forest. The latter has several bike hire outlets and even a bus to take cyclists to the start of routes: see p.170 for details. But there are plenty of other cycling possibilities in the region. You're never very far from one of the numbered routes that make up Britain's **National Cycle Network**, 10,000 miles of

Top five walks

Studland to Swanage (Dorset), p.83. This cliff-top trail offers fantastic views over Old Harry Rocks.

Langton Matravers to Worth Matravers (Dorset), p.86. A bracing coastal walk encompassing archetypal Purbeck scenery.

Ashurst New Forest walk (Hampshire), p.174. An easy walk through a range of New Forest scenery, from open heath to ancient woodlands.

Beaulieu to Buckler's Hard (New Forest), p.185. This tranquil riverside walk joins two of the region's traditional villages.

Tennyson Down (Isle of Wight), p.280. No wonder Tennyson was inspired: far-reaching views, towering cliffs and The Needles vie for your attention.

signed cycle route, a third on traffic-free paths (including disused railways and canal towpaths), the rest mainly on country roads: all the routes are detailed on the Sustrans website (℡0845 113 0065, ⓦwww .sustrans.org.uk), a charitable trust devoted to the development of environmentally sustainable transport.

Most local tourist offices and good bookshops stock a range of **cycling guides** (many of which we review on p.296) with maps and detailed route descriptions. You can also get maps and guidance from Sustrans and from the Cyclists Touring Club (℡0870 873 0060, ⓦwww.ctc.org.uk). For **cycling holiday operators**, see p.35.

Watersports

With hundreds of miles of coastline and inland waterways, the whole region offers excellent watersports opportunities. Conditions for **sailing** around the Isle of Wight and the Solent are renowned, the waters celebrated for their double tides and challenging conditions. Not surprisingly, the area has spawned some of the globe's best sailors, many of whom return to take part in the **Cowes Week** sailing regatta on the Isle of Wight, one of the most famous sailing events in the world (see p.258). The UK Sailing Academy (℡01983 294941, ⓦwww.uk-sail.org.uk) in Cowes is England's finest instruction centre for windsurfing, dinghy sailing, kayaking and kitesurfing and offers non-residential and residential courses. **Weymouth** and **Portland**, too, have first-rate watersports facilities, being the sailing venue for the 2012 Olympics. But though offshore conditions are not for the faint-hearted – the English Channel being the busiest shipping lane anywhere, crisscrossed by container ships as well as giant cross-Channel ferries – there are also plenty of opportunities for less experienced sailors and other watersports' enthusiasts. For beginners, the shallow waters of **Poole Harbour** are excellent for windsurfers, kayakers and kitesurfers, who can use the dedicated areas away from commercial craft. **Christchurch Harbour** is also extremely shallow and good for beginner sailors and watersports – it has hosted international youth windsurfing competitions. Equipment hire is available from all of the places mentioned above as well as from most major resorts, with prices for windsurf hire starting at around £15 an hour and kayaks around £10 an hour, while tuition for watersports varies from around £30–50 an hour.

Surfing has long been popular around Bournemouth and the south coast of the Isle of Wight, but the Bournemouth suburb of Boscombe (see p.56) has grabbed the spotlight since the creation of Europe's first artificial surf reef. This has attracted quite a stir amongst the surfing community, but though surf hire shops and extremely expensive "surf pods" (glorified beach huts) have appeared around the reef, the actual surf area is relatively small and conditions far less appealing than, say, Newquay. That said, the beach at Boscombe is as fine as anywhere and the region is certainly good for non-full-time surfies. For the latest details, visit ⓦwww.bournemouthsurfreef .co.uk. Bournemouth Surf School (ⓦwww .bournemouthsurfschool.co.uk) offers surf lessons starting at around £30 (for 2–3hr sessions) with board hire from around £2.50 an hour – the website also gives the latest surf conditions.

Watersports hire and lessons

ⓦ**www.harbourchallenge.co.uk** Sailing, kayaking and watersports instruction for children and adults in Poole Harbour.

ⓦ**www.h2o-sports.co.uk** Various watersports lessons and equipment hire in Poole Harbour.

ⓦ**www.paracademyextreme.co.uk** Kitesurfing and power-kiting lessons and equipment rental in Portland Harbour.

ⓦ**www.pooleharbour.co.uk** Offers lessons in kayaking, windsurfing and kitesurfing in Poole Harbour.

ⓦ**www.sckitesurfing.co.uk** Kitesurfing lessons and equipment hire in Bournemouth.

ⓦ**www.x-is.co.uk** Watersports training and accommodation on the Isle of Wight.

Diving and rock climbing

The area is known for its excellent **diving**, especially around Lulworth and Portland where there are several dive schools (see p.126). Along with clear water, the chief appeal is a series of old wrecks that are easily accessible from the shoreline. See ⓦwww.ukdiving.co.uk for further information. The Isle of Portland is also something of a magnet for rock climbers, with around 900 climbing routes around its craggy shoreline, long sculpted by years of quarrying which has led to steep climbs with few overhangs. Note, however, that certain parts of the coast are off-limits during nesting seasons for some sea birds – always obey the signs or check with the local tourist office on ⓦwww.visitweymouth.co.uk. Purbeck, too, has some challenging climbs, most on sea cliffs, many with overhangs. Dancing Ledge near Worth Matravers (see p.85) is particularly popular.

Fishing

There are many first-rate fishing rivers in the region, but none better than the **Avon**, **Itchen** and **Test**, all in Hampshire. These are rated three of the top fly-fishing rivers in the country thanks to the chalky substrata. Alkaline water filters up through the chalk, creating clear river water with a consistent year-round temperature. This is perfect for plant and marine life, with salmon, grayling and trout in particular flourishing along with freshwater shrimps. The fish are well supplied with native stoneflies, caddis flies and other insects, which all makes for excellent fly-fishing conditions. Note, however, that most of the rivers are carefully managed so fishermen will need to find out about obtaining local permits. See ⓦwww.fishingnet.com for details. Sea fishing is also popular in the area and Bournemouth beach is often lined with fishermen landing sea bass. Most of the main resorts' harbours, such as Mudeford, Swanage, West Bay, Lymington and Lyme Regis also offer fishing trips, usually to catch mackerel.

Spectator sports

You can catch top-quality **cricket** throughout the region, with a plethora of competitions and matches between the 18 "first-class" English counties taking place in summer. If the four-day County Championship matches or the five-day **Test matches** seem like too much of a commitment, there are also various one-day matches. The small town of Hambledon in Hampshire is regarded as the birthplace of modern cricket (see p.250), but these days it is the county of Hampshire itself which is the cricket powerhouse. The club is based at the modern Rose Bowl, Botley Road, Southampton (☎0870 243 0291, ⓦwww.rosebowlplc.com), where you can also see occasional test matches. The county cricket season runs from around May to September, though for the full English cricketing experience, you may prefer to seek out a local match at a village green.

Football is, of course, the national sport, though the south of England is not really a soccer hotbed. The top club is Premier League **Portsmouth**, winners of the FA Cup in 2008. They play at the atmospheric but ageing Fratton Park (☎0844 8471898, ⓦwww.porsmouthfc.co.uk), one of the Premier League's smallest grounds. As a result, tickets are hard to come by, though the club hopes to redevelop their ground in the next few years. **Southampton**, too, have had FA Cup success, reaching the final in 2003 and famously winning it in 1976. They play at the modern St Mary's Stadium (☎0845 6889448, ⓦwww.saintsfc.co.uk). In recent years, the cash-strapped team has sunk into the third tier which means tickets are relatively easy to come by, with matches usually on Saturday afternoon. Tickets are also generally easy to obtain at lower-league **Bournemouth** (℡01202 726300, ⓦwww .afcb.co.uk), who play at Dean Court in King's Park; and Hampshire club **Aldershot**, who play at the EBB Stadium (℡01252 324347, ⓦwww.theshots.co.uk). Tickets tend to be graded according to the opposition, with prices starting at around £15.

See also p.29 for a list of the annual one-off sporting events throughout the regions.

Activity holiday operators

Most operators offering **activity holidays** are likely to have two types of trip: escorted (or guide-led) and self-guided, the latter usually slightly cheaper. On all holidays you can expect luggage transfer each night, pre-booked accommodation, detailed route instructions, a packed lunch and backup support. Some companies offer budget versions of their holidays, staying in hostels or B&Bs, as well as hotel packages.

Boating and sailing

Classic Sailing ℡01872 580022, ⓦwww .classic-sailing.co.uk. Hands-on sailing holidays on traditional wooden boats and tall ships, departing from Southampton and Portsmouth.

Cycle tour operators

Country Lanes ℡01425 655022, ⓦwww .countrylanes.co.uk. Ranging from day-trips to week-long outings, mainly in the New Forest and the Isle of Wight.

Saddle Skedaddle ℡0191 265 1110, ⓦwww .skedaddle.co.uk. Biking adventures and classic road rides – includes guided and self-guided tours in the New Forest.

Walking

Contours Walking Holidays ℡01768 480451, ⓦwww.contours.co.uk. Short breaks or longer walking holidays and self-guided hikes in the Isle of Wight and along the South West Coast Path.
Footscape ℡01300 341792, ⓦwww.footscape .co.uk. Dorchester-based walking company offering a range of self-guided or guided walks around the Jurassic Coast, from two nights to a week or more.
HF Holidays ℡0845 470 7558, ⓦwww .hfholidays.co.uk. Guided week-long walking holidays in the Isle of Wight and Purbeck.
Hidden Britain Tours ℡023 8028 2269, ⓦwww .hiddenbritaintours.co.uk. Gentle and low-key guided day walks in and around the New Forest.
Ramblers Countrywide Holidays ℡01707 386800, ⓦwww.ramblersholidays.co.uk. Sociable guided walking tours (scenic, themed or special interest) around Dorset, graded from "leisurely" to "challenging".
The Discerning Traveller ℡01865 515618, ⓦwww.chycor.co.uk. Self-guided graded walking holidays, mostly in Dorset, based in B&Bs and guest houses.
Walking Women ℡0845 644 5335, ⓦwww .walkingwomen.co.uk. Popular, year-round women-only walking breaks in Purbeck and the South Downs.

General activity

YHA ℡0870 770 8868, ⓦwww.yha.org.uk. Huge range of good-value hostel-based activity weekends and holidays, from walking, climbing and biking to surfing, kayaking and caving.

Travel essentials

Costs

The south of England is one of the priciest parts of the country, due to its relative affluence and proximity to the capital. Even if you're camping or hostelling, using public transport, buying picnic lunches and eating in pubs and cafés your minimum expenditure will be around £40–50 per person per day. Couples staying in B&Bs, eating at unpretentious restaurants and visiting a fair number of tourist attractions, are looking at £60–100 per person, while if you're renting a car, staying in hotels and eating well, budget for at least £120 a day. This last figure, of course, won't even cover your accommodation if you're staying in stylish or grand country-house hotels.

Many of the region's **historic attractions** – from castles to stately homes – are owned and/or operated by the **National Trust** (☏0870 458 4000, ⓦwww.nationaltrust.org .uk) whose properties are denoted in the Guide with "NT". Most of the other historic sites are operated by **English Heritage** (☏0870 333 1181, ⓦwww.english-heritage .org.uk), whose properties are labelled with "EH". Both organizations charge entry fees for some of their sites (usually £4–8), though many others are free. If you plan to visit more than half a dozen places owned by either, it's worth considering an annual membership (NT £47.50; EH £43), which allows unlimited entry to each organization's respective properties – and you can join on your first visit to any attraction.

There are also many **stately homes** that remain privately owned, in the hands of the landed gentry, who tend to charge £8–12 for admission to edited highlights of their domain. Other old buildings are owned by local authorities, which generally charge lower admission charges or allow free access.

Municipal art galleries and museums across the region often have free admission, while private museums and other collections usually charge for entrance, but rarely more than £6. **Cathedrals** and some of the larger churches charge admission – of around £4 – but most ask for voluntary donations.

The admission charges given in the Guide are the full adult rate, unless otherwise stated. **Concessionary rates** for senior citizens (over 60), under-26s and children (from 5 to 17) apply almost everywhere, from fee-paying attractions to public transport, and typically give around fifty percent discount; you'll need official identification as proof of age. The unemployed and full-time students are often entitled to discounts too, and under-5s are rarely charged.

Crime and personal safety

Covering a largely rural area, Dorset, Hampshire and the Isle of Wight are relatively crime-free and visitors will feel pretty safe in all but a few small inner-city areas of the larger cities, such as Portsmouth and Southampton. Your only contact with the **police** is likely to be If you are robbed – If this happens, you'll need to report it to the police, not least because your insurance company will require a **crime report number** – make sure you get one.

The **emergency numbers** for the Police, Fire Brigade, Ambulance, Mountain Rescue and Coastguard are ☏999 or 112.

Electricity

In the UK, the current is 240V AC. North American appliances will need a transformer and adaptor; those from Europe, Australia and New Zealand only need an adaptor.

Entry requirements

EU citizens have the right of free movement and residence throughout the UK, with just a passport or identity card. US, Canadian, South African, Australian and New Zealand citizens can stay here for up to six months without a visa, provided they have a valid passport. Most other nationalities – but not citizens of Switzerland or EEA countries like

Norway – require a visa, obtainable from the British consular office in the country of application. For current details about entry and visa requirements, consult the UK's Foreign and Commonwealth Office's visa website ⓦwww.ukvisas.gov.uk.

Health

Citizens of all EU and EEA countries are entitled to free medical treatment within the UK's National Health Service (NHS), which includes the vast majority of hospitals and doctors, on production of their **European Health Insurance Card** (EHIC) or, in extremis, their passport or national identity card. The same applies to those Commonwealth countries that have reciprocal healthcare arrangements with the UK – for example Australia and New Zealand. If you don't fall into either of these categories, you will be charged for all medical services, so health insurance is strongly advised.

All small towns in the region have a **pharmacy**, which is open standard shop hours, though in large towns some stay open until 10pm – local newspapers carry lists of late-opening "duty" pharmacies, and the information will also be posted on pharmacy doors. For generic, off-the-shelf pain-relief tablets, cold cures and the like, it's usually cheaper to go to the local supermarket.

Minor complaints and injuries can be dealt with at a **doctor's (GP's) surgery** or call NHS Direct (☏0845 4647, ⓦwww .nhsdirect.nhs.uk) which provides 24-hour medical advice by phone. For complaints that require immediate attention, you can turn up at the 24-hour casualty (A&E) department of the local **hospital** (see below). In an **emergency**, call an ambulance on ☏999 or 112.

Main hospitals

Basingstoke and North Hampshire Hospital Aldermaston Rd, Basingstoke ☏01256 473202, ⓦwww.northhampshire.nhs.uk.
Dorset County Hospital Williams Ave, Dorchester ☏01305 251150, ⓦwww.dch.org.uk
Poole Hospital Longfleet Rd ☏01202 665511, ⓦwww.poole.nhs.uk.
Queen Alexandra Hospital Southwick Hill Rd, Cosham, Portsmouth ☏023 9228 6000, ⓦwww .porthosp.nhs.uk.

Royal Bournemouth Hospital Castle Lane East ☏01202 303626, ⓦwww.rbch.nhs.uk.
Royal Hampshire Hospital Romsey Rd, Winchester ☏01962 863535, ⓦwww.wehct.nhs.uk.
Southampton General Hospital Tremona Rd ☏023 80 777222, ⓦwww.suht.nhs.uk.
St Mary's Hospital Parkhurst Rd, Newport, Isle of Wight ☏01983 524081, ⓦwww.iow.nhs.uk.

Insurance

A typical **insurance** policy usually provides cover for loss of baggage, tickets and – up to a certain limit – cash or traveller's cheques, as well as cancellation or curtailment of your journey. Most exclude so-called dangerous sports unless an extra premium is paid, such as most watersports and rock climbing, though hiking and kayaking would probably be covered.

Internet access

There are **internet cafés** in virtually every town and resort in Britain, mainly open only in the daytime. Charges vary wildly, but average around £2–3 an hour. An increasing number of hotels, guest houses, hostels, cafés and tourist offices have internet terminals for public use, and many have a **wi-fi** facility (branches of McDonald's and Starbucks, for example, are wi-fi-enabled). Almost every **public library** in the country also offers internet access, usually for free (though you may be limited to 30min or so) – where there is a charge it's always almost cheaper than the alternative.

Laundry

Coin-operated laundries (launderettes) are commonplace in every large city and town. Most operate extended opening hours – usually about twelve hours a day – and many offer "service washes", with your laundry washed and dried for you in just a few hours; this costs around £6 for a bagful of clothes. Using a hotel laundry service is always far more expensive.

Mail

Virtually all **post offices** are open Monday to Friday from 9am to 5.30pm, and on Saturdays from 9am to 12.30 or 1pm, with smaller branches closing on Wednesday afternoons too. In major cities main offices stay open all day Saturday, while in small and rural communities you'll find sub-post offices operating out of general stores, though post office facilities are only available during the hours above even if the shop itself is open for longer.

Stamps are on sale at post offices, though if you know which ones you want, you can avoid queues by buying them instead at newsagents and other stores advertising them. The **Royal Mail** website (℡0845 774 0740, ⓦwww.royalmail.com), details postal services and current postage costs, and can help you find individual post offices.

Maps

The most detailed **maps** of the area are produced by Ordnance Survey (OS; ⓦwww .ordnancesurvey.co.uk), whose maps are vital if you intend to do any walking in the region. Their 1:50,000 (pink) Landranger series shows enough detail to be useful for most walkers and cyclists, and there's more detail still in the full-colour 1:25,000 (orange) Explorer series. There are three areas in this guide covered by the Explorer series: OL29 covers the Isle of Wight; OL22 covers Bournemouth, Southampton and the New Forest; and 0L15 covers Purbeck and South Dorset. Of the Landranger maps, 195 covers Bournemouth and Purbeck; 119 covers Portsmouth and East Hampshire; 132 covers Winchester and around; 144 covers Basingstoke and North Hampshire; 118 covers Shaftesbury and Blandford Forum; while 117 covers West Dorset.

The **National Cycle Network** of cross-country routes along country lanes and traffic-free paths is covered by a series of excellent waterproof maps (1:100,000) published by Sustrans (ⓦwww.sustrans.org .uk): the OS Tour 7 covers Hampshire, including the New Forest and the Isle of Wight.

Otherwise, for general route-finding the most useful resources are the **road atlases** produced by AA, RAC, Geographers' A–Z and Collins, among others, at a scale of around 1:250,000.

Most of these maps are available from large bookshops or **specialist map and travel stores**, such as Stanfords (ⓦwww .stanfords.co.uk), in London or Bristol.

Online maps include ⓦwww.multimap.com, which has town plans and area maps with scales up to 1:3600, plus address search, traffic info and more, and ⓦwww.visitmap .com, with clickable A–Z maps covering cities and large and small towns.

Money

Britain's currency is the **pound sterling** (£), divided into 100 pence (p). Coins come in denominations of 1p, 2p, 5p, 10p, 20p, 50p and £1 and £2. Notes are in denominations of £5, £10, £20 and £50. Scottish and Northern Irish banknotes are legal tender throughout Britain, though some traders may be unwilling to accept them.

Every sizeable town and village has a branch of at least one of the main high-street **banks**: Barclays, Halifax, HSBC, Lloyds TSB and NatWest. The easiest way to get hold of cash is to use your **debit card** in an **ATM**; there's usually a daily withdrawal limit of £250. You'll find ATMs outside banks, at all major points of arrival and motorway service areas, at most large supermarkets, some petrol stations and even in some pubs, rural post offices and village shops (though a charge may be levied on cash withdrawals at small, stand-alone ATMs). Depending on your bank and your debit card, you may also be able to ask for "cash back" when you shop at supermarkets.

Outside banking hours, you can change cheques or cash at **post offices** and **bureaux de change** – the latter tend to be open longer hours and are found in most city centres, at airports, ferry ports and train stations.

Finally, **credit cards** can be used widely either in ATMs or over the counter. Master-Card and Visa are accepted in most hotels, shops and restaurants in Britain, American Express and Diners Club less so. Plastic is less useful in rural areas, and smaller establishments all over the country, such as B&Bs, will often accept cash or cheques only.

Opening hours and public holidays

General **business hours** for most businesses, shops and offices are Monday to Saturday 9am to 5.30 or 6pm, although the **supermarket** chains tend to stay open until 8 or 9pm from Monday to Saturday, with larger ones staying open round the clock. Most major stores and supermarkets **open on Sundays**, too, usually from 11am or noon to 4pm, though some provincial towns still retain an **early-closing day** (usually Wed) when most shops close at 1pm. **Banks** are usually open Monday to Friday 9am–4pm, with some branches also open Saturday mornings.

Banks, businesses and most shops close on **public holidays**, though large supermarkets, small corner shops and many tourist attractions don't. However, nearly all museums, galleries and other attractions are closed on Christmas Day and New Year's Day, with many also closed on Boxing Day (Dec 26).

Phones

There are few remaining public **phone boxes** in the region: those that do still exist usually take debit and credit cards and coins (with a minimum charge of 40p). Most people however, rely on the **mobile phone** network, which has decent coverage in all the major towns and cities and most of the countryside. There are occasional blind spots, and coverage can be patchy in rural and hill areas, but generally you should have few problems: note, however, that in some coastal areas of the Purbecks, your phone may ping to a French network, which obviously has a stronger signal than the British one.

Time

Greenwich Mean Time (GMT) is used from late October to late March, when the clocks go forward an hour for British Summer Time (BST). GMT is five hours ahead of the US Eastern Standard Time and ten hours behind Australian Eastern Standard Time.

Tipping

Although there are no fixed rules for **tipping**, a ten to fifteen percent tip is anticipated by restaurant waiters and expected by taxi drivers. Some restaurants levy a "discretionary" or "optional" **service charge** of 10 or 12.5 percent. If they've done this, it should be clearly stated on the menu and on the bill. However, you are not obliged to pay the charge, and certainly not if the food or service wasn't what you expected. It is not normal to leave tips in pubs, but the bar staff are sometimes offered drinks, which they may accept in the form of money. The only other occasions when you'll be expected to tip are in taxis, and in upmarket hotels where porters, bellboys and table waiters expect and usually get a pound or two.

Public holidays

Britain's public holidays, also known as bank holidays, are:

January 1
Good Friday
Easter Monday (not Scotland)
First Monday in May
Last Monday in May
Last Monday in August
November 30 (or nearest Mon if weekend; Scotland only)
December 25
December 26

Note that if January 1, December 25 or December 26 falls on a Saturday or Sunday, the next weekday becomes a public holiday.

Tourist information

Most towns in the region have **tourist offices** (also called Tourist Information Centres, or "TICs" for short), though some may only be seasonal kiosks, staffed by volunteers, and others have fairly erratic opening hours; full details are in the Guide. Most can provide information about accommodation, local attractions, facilities such as boat trips and bike rental, and many sell or give away maps of local walking routes. They can also provide lists of local cafés, restaurants and pubs, though they aren't supposed to recommend particular places. The official national website, ⓦwww.enjoyengland.com, has coverage of Dorset, Hampshire and the Isle of Wight, including everything from local accommodation to festival dates, and the area number of useful regional websites too (see below).

Useful tourist websites

ⓦwww.islandbreaks.co.uk Ferry crossings, accommodation, festivals and activities on the Isle of Wight.
ⓦwww.thenewforest.co.uk Campsites, activities and maps in the New Forest.
ⓦwww.purbeck.gov.uk Information about Purbeck, including detailed maps of cycling and walking routes in the area.
ⓦwww.visit-dorset.com Provides information on accommodation, attractions, markets and events in the county.
ⓦwww.visit-hampshire.co.uk Farmers' markets, shopping and activities in the county.
ⓦwww.visitsoutheastengland.com Tourism South East official website that covers Hampshire, including the New Forest, and the Isle of Wight.
ⓦwww.visitsouthwest.co.uk Website of the official South West Tourism board: covers Dorset, including Poole and Bournemouth.
ⓦwww.westdorset.com Accommodation and information in West Dorset, including Lyme Regis, Bridport, Dorchester and Sherborne.

Travellers with disabilities

In many ways, the UK is ahead of the field in terms of facilities for travellers with disabilities. All new public buildings – including museums, galleries and cinemas – are obliged to provide wheelchair access, train stations and airports are generally fully accessible, many buses have easy-access boarding ramps, while dropped kerbs and signalled crossings are the rule in every city and town. The number of accessible hotels and restaurants is also growing, and reserved parking bays are available almost everywhere in the regions, from shopping malls to museums.

Travelling with children

The region covered in this Guide is particularly suited to **holidaying with children**, with safe, sandy beaches, lovely campsites, traffic-free cycle routes, farms to visit, castles to clamber around and plenty of wet-weather attractions. Older children, too, are well catered for with watersports such as sailing, surfing and windsurfing, available all along the coast, while the larger resorts, such as Bournemouth, Weymouth and Southampton provide good clubbing opportunities. There's also, of course, the festivals – the Isle of Wight and Bestival are good for teenagers, while Camp Bestival and the Larmer Tree are aimed at younger kids.

Most **pubs and restaurants** nowadays welcome families: some have specific family rooms or beer gardens, others are happy for children to eat in the bar/dining area. Many **B&Bs and hotels** have family rooms, though some won't accept children under a certain age (usually 12); where this is the case, we have detailed it in the Guide. There's also no shortage of good-quality self-catering accommodation in the region (see p.25), which is often the most practical way to holiday with children.

Under-5s generally travel free on public transport and get in free to attractions; 5- to 16-year-olds are usually entitled to **concessionary rates** of up to half the adult rate/fare. Note that at attractions aimed specifically at children, such as theme parks and adventure farms, the children's rate is usually only a couple of pounds cheaper than the adult's.

Guide

Guide

www.roughguides.com

Bournemouth and Poole

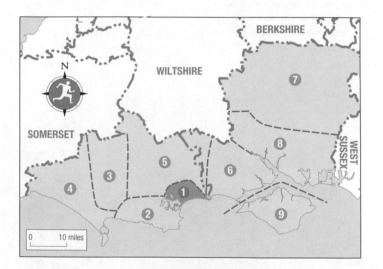

CHAPTER 1 # Highlights

✳ **Bournemouth beach** Relax on the seven-mile stretch of sandy, south-facing shore that runs from Bournemouth to the Sandbanks peninsula in Poole. **See p.51**

✳ **The Russell-Cotes Museum** Check out the eclectic collection of Victoriana at this beautiful cliff-top museum. **See p.52**

✳ **Surfing at Boscombe** Europe's first artificial reef, plus designer surf pods make Boscombe the cool place to surf. **See p.56**

✳ **Walking on Hengistbury Head** Take in the views over Christchurch harbour, Mudeford beach huts, the Isle of Wight and across to the Purbecks. **See p.57**

✳ **Sandbanks** Hang out at *Café Shore* on the Sandbanks peninsula and watch the jet set at play on their yachts. **See p.65**

✳ **Boat trip to Brownsea Island** Spot the red squirrels on this idyllic island in the middle of Poole Harbour. **See p.66**

▲ The Russell-Cotes Museum

Bournemouth and Poole

ournemouth is one of Britain's most famous seaside resorts, long famed for its mild climate and immaculate sandy beaches. It's a relatively new town, founded around two hundred years ago and originally the playground of wealthy Victorians such as Gladstone, Charles Stewart Rolls (of Rolls Royce fame), and the future Edward VII and his mistress, Lillie Langtry. Its beautiful setting – soft sandstone cliffs above golden sands looking out to the Isle of Wight to the east and Purbeck to the west – has long inspired writers, such as Robert Louis Stevenson and J.R.R. Tolkien, amongst others. There are still relics of its Victorian heyday in the form of its solid **pier**, its churches, lush gardens and especially the **Russell Cotes Museum**, a fine mansion packed with Victoriana. Since World War II, Bournemouth has expanded to become Dorset's largest town, with its current population standing at over 160,000. Fortunately, only on a hot day in high summer do the sands get truly packed, and the town has enough shops, gardens and sights – including a tethered **balloon** and an **Oceanarium** – to occupy visitors and residents alike. Poole is also known for its lively nightlife, while the artificial **surf reef** at Boscombe has put the town firmly back in the cool-place-to-go category.

Bournemouth's suburbs now merge with neighbouring Poole to the west to form a coastal conurbation of around a third of a million people. **Poole** has a very different feel, however. Set inside an almost landlocked, giant natural harbour, it is an ancient port with a long history of trade and boat building. This is still evident today along its quay, where inns and fishermen's cottages overlook the comings and goings of cross-Channel ferries, fishing boats, yachts and pleasure cruisers. The town's history is superbly encapsulated in its **Waterside Museum**, the town's main sight. From opposite the museum you can take various boat trips to local attractions including **Brownsea Island**, an uninhabited refuge for the red squirrel and a great destination for a picnic. The island sits in the middle of Poole Harbour, whose southern extremities are separated from the sea by the sandspit of **Sandbanks**, famed for having some of the most expensive real estate in the world. Its golden beaches, however, are accessible to anyone, as are the superb landscaped gardens of **Compton Acres** that run across the hills overlooking the harbour.

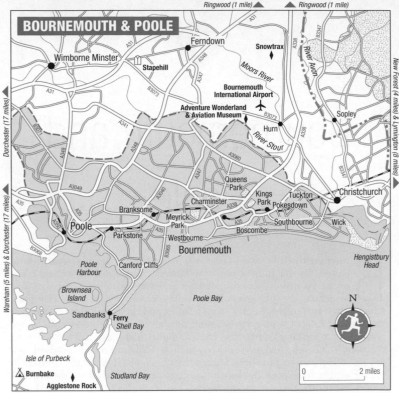

Bournemouth and around

With seven miles of clean, sandy beach, a lively pedestrianized shopping centre and pleasant gardens, **Bournemouth** has plenty for families, while its nightlife attracts clubbers from all over the country. Once known largely for its retirement homes, the town now has a much younger, more vibrant air, abetted by its university and language schools, while weekenders down for stag and hen nights give the town centre a raucous atmosphere in the summer. By day, however, its quaint cliff railways, pier and plethora of well-tended public gardens lend Bournemouth an undeniably genteel feel, while its sands form the best town beach on the south coast. To the west is the suburb of **Westbourne**, where a couple of Victorian arcades house some upmarket shops, while the eastern cliff leads to the suburb of **Boscombe**, traditionally a rather run-down area, but now experiencing a resurgence following the construction of Europe's first artificial surf reef. Beyond Boscombe, the residential suburb of **Southbourne** leads to the end of Bournemouth's beach at the dramatic **Hengistbury Head**.

Some history

Less than 200 years old, Bournemouth was a purpose-built holiday resort from its inception, unlike older resorts which grew up around industries such as fishing or shipping. It was open **heathland** until 1811, when **Captain Lewis Tregonwell** built a holiday home on the site of what is now the *Royal Exeter Hotel* in the town centre. An army officer, Tregonwell had spent most of his career guarding this wild stretch of coast from invasion and the activities of smugglers, and set about building a series of holiday villas after he retired. He also planted hundreds of pine trees and a garden walkway to the beach known as **Invalids' Walk**, which was expanded in the 1860s to become today's Pleasure Gardens.

During the nineteenth century Bournemouth developed as a resort for the wealthy, and because of its mild climate, it became popular with invalids, particularly those suffering from tuberculosis. The roll call of famous **Victorians** who visited the resort for their health included Robert Louis Stevenson, Charles Darwin, whose wife recuperated here from scarlet fever, and Disraeli, who came here for his gout on the recommendation of Queen Victoria. This royal approval, combined with the endorsement of Dr Granville, a leading spa expert of the era who announced that the town was superb for the treatment of consumption, sealed Bournemouth's status as an upmarket resort, and by the 1890s it was attracting such visitors as the Empress of Austria, Empress Eugenie of France and the King of the Belgians.

Wealthy landowner **Sir George Tapps-Gervis** influenced Bournemouth's development throughout the nineteenth century: keen to develop it into a resort to rival Brighton and Weymouth, he had Westover Villas, Westover Gardens and the *Bath Hotel* built in 1837, and under his guidance the first real hotels began to appear while villas to rent started to line the cliff-top. Bournemouth's **pier** was built in 1880, and the arrival of the **railway** in 1900 further boosted the town's popularity as a seaside resort.

Bournemouth's **population** grew dramatically too, from 692 in 1851 to 59,000 by 1900 and by the 1920s it had become a major south coast resort, with facilities such as cliff lifts to take people to the beach, electric trams and buses, a theatre and a resident symphony orchestra. It continued to thrive until the postwar period, but by the 1970s suffered the same fate as most British seaside resorts as cheap air travel attracted holiday-makers abroad. With tourism in decline, **financial service industries** such as building societies, insurance companies and banks took over as the mainstay of its economy, and by the end of the twentieth century the town had reinvented itself as a **clubbers' paradise**. In the first decade of the twenty-first century, however, Bournemouth also hopes to attract a more laid-back surfer crowd with Europe's first artificial surf reef, while the credit crunch, combined with a strong euro is bringing Bournemouth's core visitors, families, back to the town, after decades of holidaying abroad.

Arrival and information

Strung out over a series of hills and dips, central Bournemouth can be confusing for drivers, with its one-way systems and pedestrianized areas: your best bet is to head for the seafront, where you'll find plenty of pay-and-display car parks, and walk from there along the gardens into the centre. The **train** and **bus station** are next to each other about a mile inland, by the main Wessex Way bypass. Frequent buses (£1.20) connect the station to the seafront and town centre, or it's a 15–20 minute walk. The **tourist office** is on the centrally located Westover Road (Oct–May Mon–Sat 10am–5pm; June daily 10am–5pm; July–Sept Mon–Sat 9.30am–6pm & Sun 10am–5pm; ℡0845 0511700, ⓦwww .bournemouth.co.uk) and can help with accommodation. Despite its many hills,

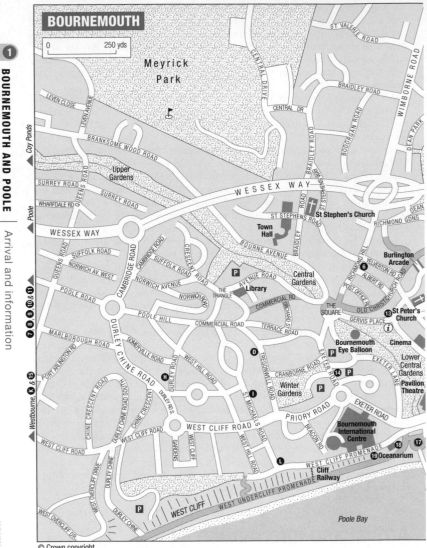

© Crown copyright

central Bournemouth is easily explored on foot, while its suburbs are well connected by **bus** (see p.68).

Accommodation

A 2009 international survey rated Bournemouth's accommodation as the best value in the world and, indeed, there is no shortage of hotels and guest houses to suit all budgets. With so much competition, there are some extremely good deals, particularly in low season when rooms can be found for £40 or less a night.

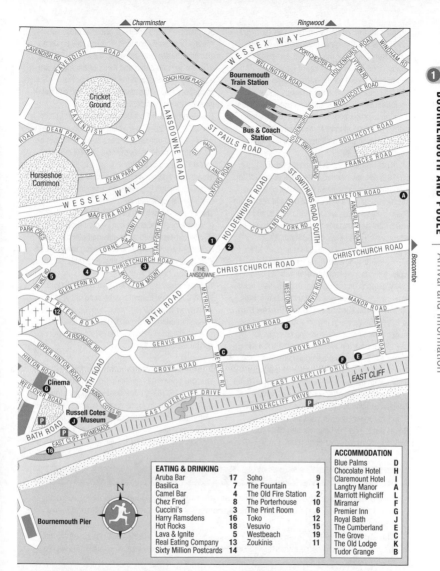

EATING & DRINKING

Aruba Bar	17	Soho	9
Basilica	7	The Fountain	1
Camel Bar	4	The Old Fire Station	2
Chez Fred	8	The Porterhouse	10
Cuccini's	3	The Print Room	6
Harry Ramsdens	16	Toko	12
Hot Rocks	18	Vesuvio	15
Lava & Ignite	5	Westbeach	19
Real Eating Company	13	Zoukinis	11
Sixty Million Postcards	14		

ACCOMMODATION

Blue Palms	D
Chocolate Hotel	H
Claremount Hotel	I
Langtry Manor	A
Marriott Highcliff	F
Miramar	L
Premier Inn	G
Royal Bath	J
The Cumberland	E
The Grove	C
The Old Lodge	K
Tudor Grange	B

Central Bournemouth

Blue Palms 26 Tregonwell Rd, West Cliff ☏01202 554986, ⍟www.bluepalmshotel.com. A small but friendly hotel in a quiet street a short walk from the centre. Rooms are a good size and there is a comfortable communal living area and small garden. ❸

Chocolate Hotel 5 Durley Rd, West Cliff ☏01202 556857, ⍟www.thechocolatehotel.co.uk. Boutique hotel whose name refers largely to the decor, as well as to the weekend chocolate-making workshops. Modern rooms in the attractive nineteenth-century building are all decently sized with flat-screen TVs – it helps if you like brown. ❹

Claremount Hotel 89 St Michael's Rd ☏01202 290875, ⍟www.claremounthotelbournemouth .co.uk. The best of a row of guest houses a short walk from the seafront, with its own small piano bar and well-priced rooms, each with neutral decor. Family rooms cost £10 extra. ❸

Langtry Manor 26 Derby Rd, East Cliff ☎01202 290550, 🌐www.langtrys-restaurant.co.uk. Not particularly handy for the seafront, but a highly atmospheric former hideaway of Edward VII, who had the place built for his mistress Lillie Langtry in 1877. Standard doubles are spacious and well equipped, though less grand (and expensive) than the King's former bedroom. It also hosts theme nights, including Murder Mystery weekends, and Edwardian banquets on Saturdays in its highly rated restaurant. **❼**

Marriott Highcliff 85 St Michael's Rd ☎01202 557702, 🌐www.marriott.co.uk. This large cliff-top four-star has superb views from most of the substantial rooms and a decent bar and restaurant. There's also a great pool with sea views, and a small front garden. Look for low-season special offers, which can be very good value. **❻**

🏃 Miramar East Overcliff Drive ☎01202 556581, 🌐www.miramar-bournemouth .com. Built as a diplomat's home with its own lovely gardens on the cliff-top, this pleasant hotel, where J.R.R. Tolkien was a regular, has a friendly atmosphere and good-sized rooms. Doubles start at £120, but it's worth paying £10 extra for a sea view or, even better, a sea-facing balcony. **❻**

🏃 Premier Inn Westover Rd ☎0870 423 6462, 🌐www.premierinn.com. In a 1930s Art Deco building where the cover of a Beatles album, With the Beatles, was shot, this chain hotel is very central and offers good-value rooms – all rooms, including family rooms, are the same price (£85), so request one with sea views. **❹**

Royal Bath Bath Rd, Bournemouth ☎01202 555555, 🌐www.devere-hotels.com. Once Bournemouth's top hotel – a favourite of Oscar Wilde – with lovely gardens, fine sea views and an attractive health club. However, it's all now looking a bit shabby and dated and some of the rooms are a bit poky and not up to the standard of the communal areas. Reasonable value if you can get a good out-of-season deal. **❺**

The Cumberland East Overcliff Drive, East Cliff ☎01202 290722, 🌐www.cumberlandbournemouth .co.uk. This sumptuous Art Deco building is right on the seafront, and has its own substantial outdoor pool on decking in the front garden. It also has a leisure club and stylish bar. Rooms are more standard, though bag one with a sea view and you won't be disappointed. **❼**

The Grove 2 Grove Rd, East Cliff ☎01202 552233, 🌐www.grovehotel.net. Set in elegant grounds, this slightly old-fashioned and rambling hotel has rooms of varying sizes, the best facing the gardens. There's also a lounge bar and sun terrace. Good low-season rates. **❹**

Tudor Grange 31 Gervis Rd, East Cliff ☎01202 291472, 🌐www.tudorgrangehotel.co.uk. If Tudor-style decor is your thing, you'll love the dark wooden interior and period furniture of this hotel set in substantial grounds. It also has its own decent restaurant. **❸**

The western suburbs

The Old Lodge 92 Alumhurst Rd, Alum Chine ☎01292 757763. On the western fringes of town, but a short walk from the superb beach below Alum Chine, this picture-book lodge dates from 1850 – and has just one self-contained room, so it's best to book in advance. **❶**

Annual Bournemouth events

Rallye Sunseeker The south's largest car rally races along Bournemouth's seafront; much of the town is cordoned for this spectacular annual race. End of Feb; 🌐www .rallyesunseeker.co.uk.

Classic Cars on The Prom Classic cars from 1915 to the early 1980s gather along the seafront from the pier stretching up West Cliff. Sun April–Sept; 4–6.30pm; 🌐www .ccotp.co.uk.

Bournemouth Carnival A week of activities, such as duck-racing, sand-castle building and floats around town. July or Aug; 🌐www.bournemouthcarnival.org.uk.

Friday Night Fireworks Free firework display from the pier. Fri 10pm July–Aug.

Flowers by candlelight Children gather from dusk in the Central Gardens to light more than 15,000 candles. Wed night Aug.

Bournemouth Air Festival Hugely popular event with spectacular fly-pasts and stunts over the seafront by planes old and new, including the Red Arrows. Aug; 🌐www.bournemouthair.co.uk.

Christmas Market Traditional wooden chalets fill Bournemouth Square, selling crafts and cuisine. Nov–Dec.

The eastern suburbs

🏃 **Mory House** 31 Grand Ave, Southbourne
☎ 01202 433553, 🌐 www.moryhouse
.co.uk. A friendly family-run guest house in a leafy
tree-lined road, a few minutes' walk from the sea.
The spotlessly clean rooms in this Edwardian house
are all light and airy and decorated in a contemporary style, and the breakfasts are great. ❷
Urban Beach Hotel 23 Argyll Rd, Boscombe
☎ 01202 301509, 🌐 www.urbanbeachhotel.co.uk.

A short (but steep) walk from Boscombe's surf
beach, and close to Boscombe's shops, this
old Victorian townhouse has been given a
boutique makeover. There are a variety of
rooms, the least expensive with shower
cubicles, but most are en-suite and stylish
with designer furniture, comfy beds and DVDs.
The downstairs bar-restaurant is also recommended (see p.60). ❺

The seafront

Bournemouth's golden sands are the obvious magnet for most visitors to the
town. These spread either side of the Victorian **pier**, itself stuffed with the usual
arcades and amusements. Built in 1980, then extended in 1894 and 1909 to
more than 1000 feet long, the pier was used as a landing stage for steamers
travelling along the south coast – more than 10,000 people landed on it one
bank holiday in 1901. Today, various boat trips still run from here in summer
to Swanage, Poole, Sandbanks and the Isle of Wight, as well as high-speed, high-
adrenaline excursions along the coast (see p.68).

Come on a hot day in the school holidays and the **beach** is inevitably heaving
– it is best to head west towards Westbourne or east to Southbourne to escape
the crowds (see p.56). Bournemouth's pedestrianized promenade runs all the
way to Hengistbury Head to the east and Sandbanks to the west – you can cycle
the whole seven miles outside July and August, when cycling is restricted to
before 10am and after 6pm. From Easter to October, you can also catch a toy
train, which trundles from the pier east to Boscombe or Southbourne (see p.56)
and west to Westbourne (see p.55).

▲ Bournemouth pier

Marconi in Bournemouth

Towards the end of the nineteenth century, Bournemouth played a key part in the fledgling communication industry when **Guglielmo Marconi** (1874–1937) constructed a 30m-high radio mast at the *Madeira Hotel* on Bournemouth's West Cliff, in order to carry out experiments with radio transmission. It wasn't until the winter of 1898, however, that the full impact of Marconi's work was realized. Close to death, the ailing former Prime Minister Gladstone had gone to Bournemouth for his health, followed by the country's newspaper reporters. When a heavy snowstorm knocked out all the telegraph lines between London and Bournemouth, Marconi stepped in to relay news of Gladstone's rapid decline back to London by wireless, via a mast that he had set up at the *Needles Hotel* in Alum Bay, on the Isle of Wight (see p.280), four and a half miles away. This proved invaluable publicity for Marconi and his work, and on June 3, 1898 the world's **first commercial radio message** was sent from the *Needles Hotel* to the *Maderia Hotel*. Marconi later moved his experiments to the *Haven Hotel* in Sandbanks, Poole, which became a field headquarters for his company for 28 years and from where he succeeded in transmitting radio messages to and from passing shipping.

Just west of the pier is the brown stone of the **Bournemouth International Centre (BIC)**, the town's main venue for concerts, events and political party conferences: in winter, it has a popular indoor ice rink.

Oceanarium

Just west of the pier on the seafront, the **Oceanarium** (daily 10am–5pm, last admission 4pm; £8.50; ☎01202 311 993, ⓦwww.oceanarium.co.uk) houses an impressive collection of sea creatures from round the world, including brightly coloured angelfish and corals, terrapins, stingrays and giant turtles. The creatures are housed in themed areas, such as the Jolly Tropics, the Mediterranean (complete with Greek music) and the very dark Deep-sea Abyss. The highlight is walking along a tunnel that passes through a huge tank, with sharks and stingrays passing over you as they swim. There are also various talks and feeding sessions throughout the day.

Russell-Cotes Museum

One of the south coast's most unusual museums lies up the cliff to the east of the seafront. The **Russell-Cotes Museum** (Tues–Sun and bank hols Mon 10am–5pm; free; ☎01202 451 858, ⓦwww.russell-cotes.bournemouth.gov.uk) houses the artworks and oriental crafts collected by the wealthy Russell-Cotes family in the nineteenth century. The eclectic collection was bequeathed to Bournemouth in 1922 after the death of one of the town's most influential mayors, Sir Merton Russell-Cotes, who set up Bournemouth's first library and the seafront promenade. The museum is housed in his ornately decorated mansion, which sits on the top of the cliff in attractive landscaped gardens with spectacular views over the sea. It displays a treasure-trove of Victorian artefacts, furniture and art from the family's travels in Russia, Japan and the East, including Siamese swords and Italian paintings, such as Rossetti's *Venus Verticordia* (1864). Look out, too, for curios such as a table belonging to Napoleon and the axe that supposedly beheaded Mary Queen of Scots. The museum also houses the country's most important collection of Victorian nudes, which scandalized much of society at the time. There is a room dedicated to the actor Sir Henry Irving, who was much admired by the Russell-Cotes and a frequent visitor to Bournemouth, containing a selection of his theatrical relics. The museum also puts on various temporary exhibitions and activities for children, and there's a great café, serving open sandwiches, home-made soup and quiche and tasty salads.

The town centre

From the seafront, head under the low flyover and you can follow the **Lower Gardens** inland to the town centre. These neatly tended lawns and flowerbeds line the narrow channel of the River Bourne and were laid out in Victorian times, when the fresh sea air made the town popular for those recovering from illness. War poet Rupert Brookes described walking here "with other decrepit and grey-haired invalids", though these days the gardens are usually filled with groups of language students or families playing on the crazy golf courses. In summer the gardens also host outdoor concerts, free children's activities and launch the **Bournemouth Eye Balloon** (Easter–Sept daily 7.30am–11pm, depending on the weather; £10, children under 14 £6; ℡01202 314359, Ⓦwww.sdlballoon.com) a tethered balloon, which rises to 150m above the gardens. Go on a clear day; views stretch some 30km, right across the town and coast beyond, while at night the lights are equally impressive.

Just east of the gardens sits the **Pavilion Theatre**, opened in 1929 as a ballroom. The middle of the gardens rise to **Bournemouth Square**, the neatly paved plaza off which most of the town's largely pedestrianized shopping streets radiate upwards. There is still an elegant Victorian arcade between Westover Road and Old Christchurch Road, though modern chain stores are the norm. Just east of the square, on Hinton Road, **St Peter's Church** graveyard is the

Bournemouth by the book

Bournemouth has been the home and inspiration for some of Europe's greatest and most imaginative writers. **Thomas Hardy** (see box, p.105) called Bournemouth "Sandbourne" in many of his books, describing it as "a fashionable watering place... like a fairy place suddenly created by the stroke of a wand": the pier is described in *The Hand of Ethelberta*, while Tess kills Alec in a fictional Bournemouth boarding house in *Tess of the D'Urbervilles*. **Mary Shelley**, author of *Frankenstein*, is buried in St Peter's Church along with the heart of her husband, **Percy Bysshe** (see p.56) and her parents, William Godwin and feminist **Mary Wollstonecraft**.

In 1876–77, French Symbolist poet **Paul Verlaine** taught French at a Westcliff school after being released from prison for shooting fellow poet and teenage lover Rimbaud. **Oscar Wilde**'s early years were also spent teaching at a Bournemouth prep school and he later spent weekends at the *Royal Bath Hotel*, which still has an *Oscar's Bar*. A frail **Robert Louis Stevenson** was in Bournemouth from 1884–87, initially undergoing treatment with a partly hallucinogenic drug – which may have influenced his writing of *The Strange Case Of Dr Jekyll And Mr Hyde*. He also wrote *Kidnapped* at his house in Alum Chine Road while his friend, **Henry James**, based his 1893 short story, *The Middle Years*, on Boscombe spa after several visits. **J.R.R. Tolkien** holidayed for 30 years in the same room of the *Hotel Miramar* (see p.50), and in the 1960s retired to Bournemouth to be near the sea, which inspired some of the descriptions in *Lord of the Rings*. He died here in 1973. **Rupert Brookes** also took holidays in Bournemouth before World War I, ironically predicting that "I shall expire vulgarly at Bournemouth, and they will bury me on the shore near the bandstand."

final resting place of Mary Shelley, author of *Frankenstein* (see box, p.56). The church, built in 1879, was where Britain's PM William Gladstone took his last communion in 1898. The nearby **St Stephen's Church** on St Stephen's Road is of more interest architecturally: built by master Victorian church builder J.L. Pearson, it has an Italian-style campanile added in 1907, and a beautifully vaulted interior.

Back in the town square, the **Central Gardens** follow the Bourne stream north through the Upper Gardens to Coy Pond Gardens. They pass in front of the **town hall**, formerly the luxurious *Mont Dore Hotel*, which housed one of England's first telephones – its number was 3. In front of the town hall is Bournemouth's **war memorial**, erected in 1921 and flanked by two stone lions. It's a pleasant two-mile urban walk along the stream, through gardens that get progressively less formal and landscaped the further north you walk.

The suburbs

The suburbs of **Westbourne**, **Boscombe Spa** and **Southbourne-on-Sea** all grew up as competing resorts in the nineteenth century, each with its own rival attractions facing extensions of Bournemouth's superb beach. Surprisingly, Boscombe was considered the smartest – possibly due to its spa – a

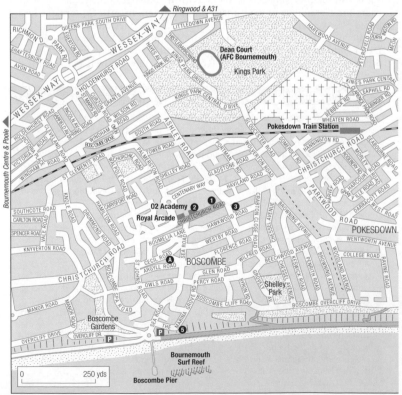

© Crown copyright

contrast to today, with Westbourne the most upmarket. Throughout the twentieth century, however, development spread along the coast from Bournemouth subsuming the four resorts into one linear conurbation, but each retains its own distinct atmosphere, with beautiful beaches usually free of the central area's crowds.

Westcliff and Westbourne

Bournemouth's beach becomes progressively less busy as you head towards its affluent western suburbs. Here, the sandstone cliffs are interspersed with narrow gulleys known as **chines**, originally cut by streams but now mostly neat grass-banked approach roads or footpaths. Many of the town's hotels (see p.48) are strung out along and inland from the cliff-top along these stretches. At **Westcliff**, you can access the cliff-top via one of Bournemouth's ancient funicular railways. Robert Louis Stevenson (see box, p.53), author of *Treasure Island*, set up home above the lovely beach at neighbouring **Alum Chine**, backed by exotic gardens and where one of the leafiest chines makes a fine walk up to Westbourne. History could have altered its course here – a young Winston Churchill fell off one of the bridges on this walk and nearly died. While it boasts few specific sights, **Westbourne** has some of Bournemouth's most upmarket fashionable shops and restaurants gathered round a fine Victorian arcade.

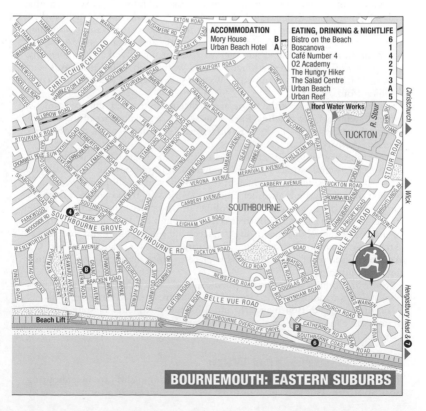

BOURNEMOUTH: EASTERN SUBURBS

Bournemouth and Boscombe have long been pilgrimage sites for fans of **Mary Shelley**, author of *Frankenstein*, and her husband, the poet **Percy Bysshe Shelley**. Mary Shelley's son, Sir Percy, bought Boscombe Manor in 1849 in the hope that Bournemouth's sea air would help his ailing mother, but she was to die two years later. Mary is buried in Bournemouth's St Peter's Church (see p.54), close to the heart of Percy Bysshe. In typically ghoulish Victorian fashion, Sir Percy then exhumed Mary's parents from a cemetery in London, so that the remains of William Godwin and the feminist Mary Wollstonecraft – author of *A Vindication of the Rights of Women* – could rest with their daughter in Bournemouth. For much of the twentieth century, Boscombe Manor was a Shelley shrine and museum, and it now sits at the top of a flourishing park named after the family.

Boscombe

Just over two kilometres east of Bournemouth pier, **BOSCOMBE** has Britain's first artificial surf reef, putting it firmly in the spotlight after years of being in the doldrums. Set below craggy cliffs, Boscombe's beach is every bit as good as Bournemouth's, and it even has its own pier, originally built in 1889, though its recent renovation has left merely a truncated walkway from which to admire the sea. East of the pier lies the **surf reef**, built in 2009 with sand-filled geotextile bags dumped offshore to create regular breakers. The surf reef was part of a redevelopment plan that has included a giant residential complex, a reworked plaza and the remodelling of the leafy Boscombe Gardens that run up another wooded chine past children's play areas, cycle paths and a crazy golf course – a toy train runs from here in summer to save the uphill hike. The formerly run-down seafront has received a face-lift too, with the so-called **surf pods** – in reality, 1950s beach huts revamped by Wayne Hemingway of Red or Dead fame – selling from £64,000.

On the opposite side of the chine are further neatly tended cliff-top gardens, which extend as far as **Shelley Park**. This was all originally part of the Shelley estate, whose Boscombe Lodge – now converted into flats – sits in the northern edges of the park (see box above).

Boscombe was originally known for its spa water, which bubbled up from the foot of its cliffs, attracting health-concious visitors from the 1870s. By the 1890s, it was considered an upmarket resort, with a smart shopping arcade and its own theatre on the high street. But after World War II, Boscombe's fortunes dipped and it became synonymous with bedsits and petty crime. Around a mile inland, its pedestrianized high street is lively enough by day, with a good range of shops and cafés, but remains slightly seedy after dark. The renovated **Royal Arcade** is splendid, however, and the former Grand Theatre, now the **O2 Academy** (see p.60) is the fashionable place to go at night, hosting big-name gigs and club nights.

North of the high street lies the open expanse of **King's Park**, which has its own athletics stadium and the Fitness First Stadium, home to Bournemouth FC – originally called Bournemouth and Boscombe Athletic. Despite its poor performance in recent years, it's still a fun afternoon out watching Bournemouth play (for fixtures and tickets see ⓦ www.afcb.co.uk).

Southbourne and Wick

The beach east of Boscombe runs below sandstone cliffs to neighbouring **Southbourne**. This stretch tends to be relatively quiet even in summer, partly because recent anti-erosion works have left the beach here controversially mingled with shingle. But though the sand is poor for beach games and sand castles, this stretch does catch the last of the day's sun, and the views towards the Isle of Wight are superb. Southbourne's main drawback is lack of tourist facilities – its own Victorian pier was dismantled in 1900, while Southbourne High Street is largely shut up and deserted after dark – eating and drinking options are restricted to a handful of pubs and cafés.

The suburb's main historical claim to fame is as the site of Britain's first ever fatal plane crash in 1910, which killed pioneer pilot Charles Stewart Rolls. The man behind Rolls Royce took part in one of England's first ever air shows on the flat grassland above Southbourne beach, crashing his plane while attempting to land.

Apart from the beach and Hengistbury Head, the best local walks are along the River Stour, which divides this part of Bournemouth from neighbouring Christchurch. A riverside path leads south from the bridge at **Tuckton** through parkland to the attractive hamlet of **Wick**; regular boats run from the *Tuckton Tea Gardens* (Easter–Oct; Ⓦ www.bournemouthboating.co.uk) to Christchurch and Hengistbury Head, while in Wick itself there is a small passenger ferry over the river to Christchurch (see p.187). Beyond Wick lies a nature reserve known as **Wick Fields**: once a rubbish tip, this area now consists of verdant wetlands and grassy meadows, some of it grazed by cattle and with fine views back over Christchurch Priory. A path continues out to Hengistbury Head, popular with dog walkers and twitchers who often spot herons, egrets and other wading birds. Just north of Tuckton, the former **Iford Waterworks** is where Tolstoy's novels, then illegal in Russia, were first published by Count Vladimir Tchertkov and his Free Age Press.

Hengistbury Head

Southbourne's bungalows peter out on the fringes of **Hengistbury Head** (approach road closed 10pm–7am), a low nature reserve set around a 37m-high headland that offers superb views over the coast and Christchurch harbour. There are various footpaths running up and over the scrubby headland; you can also walk out along the sand and shingle beach below crumbling cliffs, or round the inner harbour which is usually bustling with yachts or windsurfers. Cycling is restricted to a paved track running through deciduous woods parallel to the inner harbour.

A **land train** (daily except Christmas day; £1.20) also runs this route, out to the end of the head which narrows to a narrow sandspit known as **Mudeford**

Beach living

The sandspit at Mudeford Sandbank shelters a sizeable colony of colourful beach huts, which are credited as being Britain's priciest, and the only ones that allow overnight stays (Feb–Oct). They don't come cheap, either to rent or to buy – indeed they often change hands for six-figure sums, making them about as expensive per square foot as the illustrious Sandbanks (see p.65) on the other side of Bournemouth. But with stupendous outlooks and a secluded position, many feel that is a price worth paying. You can rent the huts for the week, or weekend off season (look out for advertisements in the hut windows or on the notice board at the café), or stay in a little more comfort in one of the four self-catering apartments in the former smugglers' haunt, **The Black House** (Ⓦ www.theblackhouse.co.uk; from £350 a week for four people).

▲ Southbourne beach from Hengistbury Head

Sandbank. Flanked largely by tidal mudflats on one side and a sandy beach on the other, this spit has one café-restaurant (see below) and various beach huts (see box, p.57). Regular ferries also connect the sandspit to Mudeford Quay, on the other side of the harbour (see p.191 for details).

The land train leaves and arrives by the *Hungry Hiker* café (see opposite) and information centre, just by the main car park. Alongside this are fenced off **double dykes**, a pair of defensive ditches built in 1 BC to protect a port which once traded with Europe – various coins and amphorae have been found on this spot. Evidences of Iron Age settlements have also been found on the Head which until the last century was a flourishing centre for smugglers. For a time, the Head was owned by Gordon Selfridge of the shopping fame, and only World War I prevented his plan to build a giant castle on the top.

Eating, drinking and entertainment

With a steady flow of year-round visitors, Bournemouth's restaurants don't have to try too hard to keep going – and with a few exceptions, the result is a motley collection of fairly average eateries. It also has a severe shortage of decent pubs, though there are more than enough bars and clubs to keep a vibrant nightlife pulsing until the small hours. Detailing local restaurant reviews, gigs, clubs and the like, *Listed* magazine comes out once every two months – pick it up from bars, clubs and restaurants.

Cafés and restaurants

Many of central Bournemouth's most cheap and cheerful restaurants and cafés are along the Old Christchurch Road, while the more adventurous should head north of town to Charminster Road, where there a range of good-quality ethnic restaurants, including Lebanese, Thai, Persian, Turkish, Spanish and Japanese.

The seafront and the town centre

Cuccini's 218–220 Old Christchurch Rd ☎01202 780882. Attractive restaurant serving authentic Italian dishes, such as Vitello Milanese (breaded veal escalope served with spaghetti), plus the usual pizzas and pasta. Service is friendly and the weekday lunch menu is good value at £8 for two courses.

Harry Ramsdens Pier Approach ☎01202 295818. Famous chain specializing in fish and chips, served here with panache in a splendid chandeliered dining room overlooking the beach, where waiter service and white sliced bread go hand in hand. There's also a takeaway outlet down below. Daily until 7pm, Fri–Sat until 9pm, July–Aug to 10pm.

Hot Rocks Pier Approach ☎01202 555559. Surf-themed restaurant, with a downstairs cocktail bar and great first-floor dining room overlooking the sea. Good for families or large groups, the menu features mid-priced burgers, Cajun chicken and other Tex-Mex-influenced mains.

Real Eating Company Gervis Place ☎01202 556920. Entered through the Steamer Trading shop, this upstairs café has great coffee and decently priced sandwiches, soups and daily special lunches, as well as selling a range of organic preserves, coffees and chocolates. Closed eves.

The Fountain First floor 10–15 Holdenhurst Rd ☎01202 294191. In the centre of town, this good-value all-you-can-eat Chinese restaurant is great for large groups. For £15 a head, the friendly staff produce a nonstop stream of delicious dishes such as crispy duck and spicy squid.

The Print Room Richmond Hill ☎01202 789669. One of Bournemouth's top dining spots, in the superbly converted Art Deco former *Daily Echo* press rooms, this lively restaurant has great 1920s-style decor with wooden booths and chandeliers. The menu features brasserie classics, such as steak, wild sea bass, oysters and lobster, while breakfast includes eggs Florentine and pancakes, and there's a good-value afternoon tea.

West Beach Pier Approach ☎01202 587785. This award-winning seafood restaurant has a prime position on the beach, with decking out on the promenade. It's smart and stylish, and you can watch the chefs work in the open kitchen, or admire the sea views through huge floor-to-ceiling windows. Fish dishes, around £20, feature strongly on the menu, with locally caught daily specials.

Westcliff and Westbourne

Basilica 73 Seamoor Rd, Westbourne ☎01202 757722. Cosy café-restaurant on two levels, serving delicious breakfasts and a short but good-value evening menu featuring salads, soups and daily fish specials. Closed Sun.

Chez Fred 10 Seamoor Rd, Westbourne ☎01202 761023. Top-quality fish and chips at this sit-down restaurant and takeaway, which regularly wins awards and is popular with locals and visiting celebs – hence the queues at peak times.

Vesuvio Seafront, Alum Chine ☎01202 759100. Bright and airy beachside Italian, with a range of generous pizzas, pasta and chippy meat dishes. The outside terrace is only for drinks and cake-eating. Expect to queue for a table in high season.

Zoukinis 18 Seamore Rd, Westbourne ☎01202 766797. This serves the best, freshest vegetarian and vegan food this side of Bournemouth, with fabulous falafels, vegetarian burgers, salads and burritos. There's also a small paint-your-own pottery section at the back. Closed Mon.

Boscombe and Southbourne

Bistro on the Beach Solent Promenade, Southbourne ☎01202 431473. A great position right on the beach with a superb outlook over the waves, though service can be poor in the summer. Dishes up cooked breakfasts, simple café meals and sandwiches throughout the day, and stays open later at the weekend when it becomes a pricey restaurant, serving some good fish dishes from local suppliers. Winter closes Mon & Tues.

Boscanova 650 Christchurch Rd, Boscombe Pedestrian Precinct ☎01202 395596. Boscombe's most bohemian café, with plenty of bare brick, works of art and a very good-value Mediterranean-influenced menu. The food is all freshly cooked and the Middle Eastern meze are superb, as are the soups, noodle salads and fresh juices. Closed eves.

Café Number 4 4 Southbourne Grove ☎01202 424687. Serves a good range of inexpensive meals such as Thai curries, salads, soups and great breakfasts. Uses local organic ingredients where possible, and has a few tables in the garden at the back. On Thurs, Fri & Sat eves it serves more of a restaurant menu, often with live music. Closed Sun afternoon & Sun–Wed eve.

The Hungry Hiker Broadway, Hengistbury Head ☎01202 428552. Bright and airy café with outdoor tables by the land train departure point. Food is all fresh and very good value, with hearty and filling breakfasts, grills, soups, sandwiches and cakes. Closed eves.

The Salad Centre 667 Christchurch Rd, Boscombe ☎01202 393673. Inexpensive vegetarian, wholefood daytime canteen serving excellent daily specials, fresh salads, juices and cakes.

Urban Reef Undercliff Drive, Boscombe ☎01202 443960. New Art Deco-style restaurant/bar/café in a fabulous position on the seafront. Designed to give great views from all three floors with quirky decor such as a mock-up beach hut hanging on the wall, and a terrace for drinks on the front. Food varies from eggs Florentine (£6) and porridge (£3) for breakfast, through sandwiches (£6–7) and mussels (£7.50) for lunch, to steaks (£18.50) and line-caught sea bass (£16) for dinner.

Bars and clubs

Aruba Bar Pier Approach ☎01202 554211. This stylish Caribbean-themed bar sits above the entrance to Bournemouth pier: its outdoor terrace has comfy swing seats and overlooks the beach. Inside, its soaring ceilings, palm trees, resident parrot, giant central bar area and various alcoves make it a great place to hang-out, play scrabble or watch the beach activity below.

Camel Bar 174 Old Christchurch Rd, Bournemouth ☎01202 291420. Egyptian-style bar where you can chill out with a shisha, belly dancers and bongos, or dance the night away till 6am.

Lava & Ignite Firvale Rd, Bournemouth ☎01202 311178, ⓦwww.lavaignite.com/bournemouth. Bournemouth's largest nightclub with four rooms, each playing a different style of music – sounds vary from Latin & salsa, R&B, garage, cheese and, of course, disco.

O2 Academy (formerly the Opera House) 570 Christchurch Rd, Boscombe ☎01202 399922, ⓦwww.operahouse.co.uk. Great music, regular club nights with top DJs such as Judge Jules, and themed events such as retro roller discos. Recent acts have included Pete Doherty, Isaac Hayes and the Mighty Boosh.

Sixty Million Postcards 19 Exeter Rd ☎01202 292697. One of Bournemouth's best bars, attracting an unpretentious but trendy student crowd. There are board games, various alcoves for cosy chats and lounge areas for larger groups. Offers a good range of beers, drinks and inexpensive snacks and occasional live music.

Soho 100–102 Poole Rd, Westbourne ☎01202 759000. Fashionable Westbourne café-bar serving decent breakfasts and lunchtime snacks, and attracts a young, moneyed crowd after dark.

The Old Fire Station 36 Holdenhurst Rd, Bournemouth ☎01202 963889, ⓦwww .oldfirestation.co.uk. DJs, such as Rob da Bank, club nights, including Hed Kandi, live bands – Scouting for Girls, Pigeon Detectives and Zane Lowe among others – and comedy in this popular venue in a converted fire station. Also hosts Bournemouth Uni's student nights, so drinks are cheap.

The Porterhouse 113 Poole Rd, Westbourne ☎01202 768586. A small, friendly local pub with a good selection of local ales and ciders and plenty of board games.

Toko 33–39 St Peter's Rd, Bournemouth ☎01202 318952 ⓦwww.toko-bar.co.uk. Regular club and party nights with resident and visiting DJs in this glitzy club with large fish tanks, VIP areas and a good-sized dancefloor.

Urban Beach 23 Argyll Rd, Boscombe ☎01202 301509. This hotel bar-restaurant has become the social hub of Boscombe thanks to its hip decor, fantastic cocktails and regular live music sessions (usually Thurs). In summer, most people spill onto the decking at the front.

Listings

Airport Bournemouth's international airport (ⓦwww.bournemouthairport.com) is a short drive northeast of the centre at Hurn, just off the A338. An airport shuttle bus runs to and from the town centre hourly from 7am–7pm (15min; last departure from centre 6pm; £4).

Bike rental On Yer Bike, 88 Charminster Rd (☎01202 315855, ⓦwww.onyerbike.co.uk) hires bikes from £8 a day or £12 a week.

Boat trips Dorset Belle Cruises (☎01202 558550, ⓦwww.dorsetcruises.co.uk) run speedboat rides and cruises from Bournemouth Pier to Poole, Swanage, and along the coast, starting from around £6 for a 30min round-the-bay cruise.

Bus information Local services are run by Yellow Buses (☎01202 636000, ⓦwww.yellowbuses .co.uk) with single fares starting from £1.10. All-day travelcards, available from the driver on the bus, are good value at £3.70. In summer, Yellow Buses runs an open-top double-decker along the coast between Bournemouth and Boscombe piers every 20min. Buses to other local towns, such as Salisbury, Ringwood and Lymington, are run by Wilts & Dorset bus company (☎01202 673555, ⓦwww.wdbus .co.uk). Long-distance buses are operated by National Express (☎08705 808080, ⓦwww .nationalexpress.com).

Bus tours Discover Dorset (☎ 01202 557007, ⓦ www.discoverdorset.co.uk) runs full- (£29) and half-day (£22) minibus tours to nearby places such as Stonehenge, Bath and the Jurassic Coast, picking up from hotels and language schools throughout Bournemouth and Poole.

Car rental Auto-Europe (☎ 0800 358 1229, ⓦ www.auto-europe.co.uk); Avis (☎ 0844 5446040, ⓦ www.avis.co.uk); Budget (airport ☎ 01202 577429, ⓦ www.budget-carrental.co.uk); Hertz (☎ 0870 507190, ⓦ www.hertz.com); and Thrifty (☎ 01202 291231, ⓦ www.thrifty.co.uk).

Cinemas The Odeon (35–43 Westover Rd (☎ 0871 224 4007) and ABC (27–28 Westover Rd) are both centrally located and show the latest big-name films (both on ☎ 0871 224 4007, ⓦ www.odeon.co.uk).

Gay and lesbian The area around The Triangle is the centre of Bournemouth's gay life with *The Xchange* at no. 4 (☎ 01202 294321, ⓦ www.xchangebar.co.uk), *Rubyz* drag club at 29–30 (☎ 01202 552553, ⓦ www.rubyz.co.uk); *The Branksome* 152–154 Commercial Rd (☎ 01202 552544), and *2930 The Triangle* slightly further up on Poole Hill (☎ 01202 589069, ⓦ www.2930thetriangle.com). For further info and listings check ⓦ www.gaybournemouth.net.

Hospital Royal Bournemouth Hospital, Castle Lane East ☎ 01202 303626, ⓦ www.rbch.nhs.uk.

Police 5 Madeira Rd ☎ 01202 222222 (24hr).

Surf hire Sorted Surf Shop ☎ 01202 309638, ⓦ www.sortedsurfshop.co.uk) in Boscombe rents out boards and wet suits from £15 a day.

Taxi There are taxi ranks at the station, along Westover Rd, and outside the BIC; fares from the station to anywhere within the town are around £5. Try United Taxis (☎ 01202 556677).

Trains Bournemouth is on the Weymouth to London line: train details on ☎ 08457 484950, ⓦ www.nationalrail.co.uk.

Poole and around

Arranged around the second largest natural harbour in the world, **Poole** is best approached by sea, when its magnificent position overlooking the wooded slopes of Brownsea Island can really be appreciated. The town has a reputation as being a millionaire's playground, largely because of the phenomenal prices of properties on the sandspit peninsular known as Sandbanks; the luxurious reputation is reinforced by the fleet of Sunseeker pleasure boats that frequent the marina – they are built in a shipyard opposite the town quay and feature in several James Bond films. Entering by road, however, gives a very different impression: Poole's outskirts consist largely of distinctly unglamorous 1970s tower blocks, shopping complexes and bypasses. But head down the atmospheric High Street to the old quays and Poole's real charm becomes evident as an ancient and historic port long colonized by fishermen, merchants and pirates.

Arrival and information

Poole **train station** is north of the town centre on Serpentine Road, while **buses** pull in nearby, in front of the Dolphin Centre. From both, it's about a fifteen-minute walk down the High Street to Poole Quay, where you'll find the **tourist office** (May, June, Sept & Oct daily 10am–5pm; July & Aug daily 9.15am–6pm; Nov–April Mon–Fri 10am–5pm, Sat 10am–4pm; ☎ 01202 253253, ⓦ www.pooletourism.com).

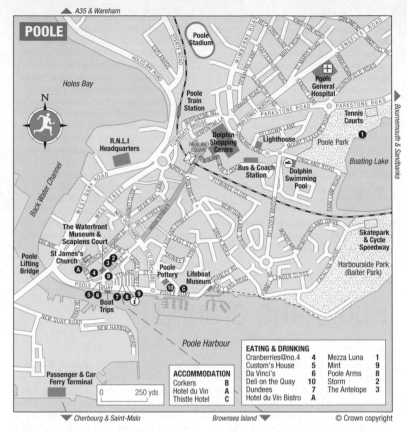

© Crown copyright

Accommodation

Poole's accommodation is in two distinct clusters: **the town** itself, which is convenient for shops and restaurants; and the **Sandbanks** peninsula, which lacks any budget places, but is handy for the beach. There are a few cheaper B&Bs along the roads around the harbour, but, without your own transport, these are too far to walk to either the town or the beach.

The Town

Corkers 1 High St ☎01202 681393, ⓦwww.corkers .co.uk. Above a lively café-restaurant, this B&B offers some of the best-value rooms in town – especially if you bag one of the two superb front rooms with their own harbour-facing balconies, one of which sleeps three. Parking offered for a small fee. **②**

Hotel du Vin Thames St ☎01202 685666, ⓦwww.hotelduvin.com. Inside a fine old mansion house with a double staircase, this stylish hotel houses plush rooms, a superb restaurant (see p.67) and wine cellar, and a very cosy bar – great in winter, with its own log fire. **⑧**

Thistle Hotel The Quay ☎01202 666800, ⓦwww.thistle.com. In an enviable position facing the harbour, it is worth paying the extra £20 for the front sea-view rooms at this modern but low-rise hotel – back rooms overlook the car park. Rooms are well equipped if on the small side, most with sofa beds for those with children. Good low-season rates. **⑦**

Around Sandbanks

Luminiere 78 Haven Rd, Sandbanks ☎01202 707868, ⓦwww.luminiere.co.uk. This boutique B&B in a tastefully converted Edwardian townhouse has its own leafy garden and conservatory, though you'll need a car to get here. Rooms are of various sizes – including a huge Art Deco room with a walk-in bathroom and a downstairs studio with its own patio. **⓻**

The Haven Hotel Sandbanks, Poole ☎01202 707333, Ⓦwww.fjbhotels.co.uk. At the far end of the peninsula overlooking the chain ferry, this four-star hotel is owned by the same company as the *Sandbanks*, but is aimed more at adults, with a good restaurant, a spa, indoor and outdoor pools and the usual luxury facilities. **⓽**

Milsoms 47 Haven Rd, Canford Cliffs ☎01202 609000, Ⓦwww.milsomshotel.co.uk. Eight stylish

rooms above the *Loch Fyne* restaurant (see p.67). Reasonably priced for the location, only a few minutes' walk from the beach, though the rooms can be noisy and hot. **⓹**

The Sandbanks Hotel Sandbanks, Poole ☎01202 707377, Ⓦwww.fjbhotels.co.uk. In a prime position right on the beach, most of the rooms at this four-star hotel have views over the harbour on one side or the sea on the other. It's particularly suitable for children, with family rooms, an indoor pool, plus various watersports on offer, such as windsurfing, kayaking and yachting. **⓼**

The old town and Quay

Apart from the usual high-street shops, there is little of interest in central Poole, and you're best off heading down the largely pedestrianized High Street to the **old town** gathered round Poole Quay. Developed in the thirteenth century, this area was successively colonized by pirates, fishermen and timber traders and still contains over a hundred historic buildings. **The Quay** itself is an atmospheric strip of pubs, cafés and bars overlooking fishing boats, pleasure cruisers and the Sunseeker boatyard, along with the giant cross-Channel ferries that rumble out daily from the headland opposite. In summer, the central part of the Quay is closed off to traffic and hosts frequent events, including regular Thursday night concerts and firework displays and Tuesday night motorbike meets. Various kiosks sell tickets for **boat trips** up and down the coast, upriver to Wareham and to Brownsea Island (see p.68).

Towards the eastern end of the Quay is **Poole Pottery** (☎01202 668681, Ⓦwww.poolepottery.co.uk; free), the remaining outlet of the town's once-thriving ceramics industry. Although it is no longer independent and the bulk of the pottery is made in Stoke-on-Trent, there are still a few potters here; you can watch them at work, and there's also a section where children can paint their own pots.

The Waterfront Museum and Scaplens Court

If you want to see more examples of Poole Pottery, from early samples to the brightly coloured contemporary designs, the **Waterfront Museum**, at the bottom of Old High Street (April–Oct Mon–Sat 10am–5pm, Sun noon–5pm; Nov–March Tues–Sat 10am–4pm, Sun noon–4pm; free; Ⓦwww.poole.gov.uk /museums) has a whole floor dedicated to local ceramics. The industry grew up in the region in the nineteenth century due to a combination of good clay deposits and the harbour providing excellent transport links for the finished products. Other displays in the museum trace Poole's development over the centuries, with the ground floor housing an Iron Age long boat that was dug out of the harbour in 1964: carved out of a single tree trunk, the 10m-long boat dates from around 300 BC. Look out, too, for the fascinating footage of the Poole flying boats that took off from the harbour during the 1940s for the Far East and Australia. The museum's design successfully combines a very contemporary entrance with an eighteenth-century warehouse, and the medieval Town Cellars behind, which house the local history centre. On the top floor is a great outdoor terrace with views over the old town and harbour.

Next door to the museum, **Scaplens Court** (free; ☎01202 2626000) is a fine example of a medieval house, with a Tudor herb and physic garden. Used as an education centre for school groups for most of the year, it is open to the public in August, when it puts on demonstrations of domestic life, exhibitions and events.

The Lifeboat Museum and the parks

From the Quay you can walk all the way along the waterfront to the broad **Harbourside Park**, aka Baiter. En route you'll pass the small former lifeboat station which now serves as a tiny **Lifeboat Museum**, complete with a real lifeboat and memorabilia: it's manned by volunteers so opening hours are erratic, but in summer it aims to open daily 11am–4pm. Poole is also home to the RNLI headquarters, which now sits on the waterfront just west of the railway station – though closed to the public, you can view the practice capsize sessions most Wednesdays from 2.30–4pm from a raised viewing deck above the practice pool.

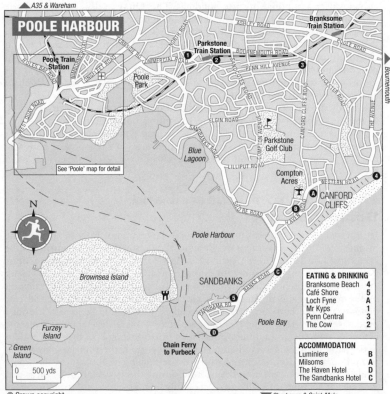

© Crown copyright

Poole Harbour

Formed during the last Ice Age, **Poole Harbour** is the second largest natural harbour in the world after Sydney. Its surrounding heath and wetlands contain eighteen designated sites of Special Scientific Interest, and most of the coastline is remarkably unspoilt, despite the sprawl of Poole and the well-hidden oil-pumping station at Brands Bay. It is also extremely shallow, with an average depth of just 50cm, making it ideal for a range of bird- and sea life. The same conditions also make it great for **watersports**; kite- and windsurfing events are regularly held here, including the Animal Poole Windfest (Ⓦwww.animalwindfest.co.uk) in September. Cross-Channel ferries use a specially dredged, 7.5m-deep channel to negotiate the harbour, though patrols frequently have to rescue smaller boats caught by the deceptive tidal shallows. In all, the harbour consists of sixty miles of coastline, and shelters eight islands – mostly uninhabited – of which Brownsea Island is the largest.

The harbour has long been a busy waterway – the discovery of an Iron-Age longboat here (see p.63) shows that there was water traffic as far back as 300 BC – but during the 1940s it also doubled as an airstrip, becoming the UK base for both military and commercial **flying boats**. Run by the newly formed BOAC, the flying boats took off from the harbour to carry mail and passengers to the colonies, even travelling as far as Australia.

▲ Poole Harbour

Just north of Harbourside Park is the more interesting **Poole Park**, a pleasant space gathered round a substantial boating lake. As well as a large children's playground, there are tennis courts, a small ice rink (for times and sessions see Ⓦwww.centralparkpoole.co.uk/ice-skating.php); £5, under-12s £4 and a mini-train that trundles round a leafy duck pond daily.

Sandbanks and the beaches

The enviable position of **Sandbanks** – the flat, curved sandspit that protects Poole Harbour from the sea – has propelled house prices on this narrow peninsula to being the fourth highest in the world. Many of the properties back onto the soft sand **beach** (winner of a European Blue Flag for cleanliness and water quality more times than any other UK beach), while others boast private moorings directly on the harbour. Unless you are visiting a celebrity resident, such as football manager Harry Redknapp, you will mostly likely be here for the beach and **watersports** – the shallow harbour makes it excellent for learning windsurfing and kitesurfing (see p.33) – as the peninsula itself is little more than a glorified one-way system with very little in the way of shops or cafés, and even the inflated prices of its property cannot disguise the poor architecture. But the location is stunning, its cafés are great for people-watching, and it is definitely worth catching the annual **beach polo** each July (Ⓦwww.sandpolo.com; see p.39). At the far end of the peninsula, a **chain ferry** (daily every 20min from 7am–11pm return from 7.10am–11.10pm; 90p single, cars £3; Ⓦwww.sandbanksferry.co.uk) crosses the entrance of Poole Harbour to the superb beaches at the eastern end of the Isle of Purbeck (see p.84): the short ride is great fun, especially when giant cross-Channel ferries pass by in the surprisingly deep channel.

Sandbanks' beach extends east to join the sands of Bournemouth, most of it linked by a seafront promenade. The superior village-like high street of **Canford Cliffs** sits above some of the best, softest sands of the entire coast.

Brownsea Island

From Poole Quay (40min; £8.50 return) or from near the chain ferry on the Sandbanks peninsula (30min; £5 return), ferries (ⓦ www.brownseaisland ferries.com & ⓦ www.greensladepleasureboats.co.uk); run every thirty minutes from 10am to the beautiful **Brownsea Island** (daily: mid–March to late July & Sept 10am–5pm; late July–Aug 10am–6pm; Oct 10am–4pm; £4.90; NT). It's known for its red squirrels, wading birds and other wildlife, which you can spot along themed trails that reveal a surprisingly diverse landscape – much of it heavily wooded, though there are also areas of heath and marsh, and narrow, shingly beaches. Brownsea was largely self-sufficient until World War I – it is said that incomers could only work on the island if they could play a musical instrument to entertain the residents. In 1927, the island was purchased by Mary Bohham Christie, who let much of the previously farmed land revert to natural heathland. When she died in 1961, the National Trust took over, backed by the John Lewis Partnership, who still maintains the castle. There has been a **castle** (closed to the public) here since the reign of Henry VIII, though the current structure was largely built in the eighteenth century and remodelled in Victorian times.

The island is also known for being the birthplace of the **Scout movement**. In 1907, Robert Baden-Powell took 22 working-class boys from Poole and Bournemouth to set up camp on the south coast of the island, an event that kicked off the now widespread Scouting movement. Aside from John Lewis, whose partners can stay at the castle, and one National Trust cottage that's available to rent (ⓦ www.nationaltrustcottages.co.uk), Scouts are the only people allowed to stay overnight on the island at a specially designated campsite – which is something of a magnet for Scouts and Guides from around the world. The National Trust also lays on **events** during the year, such as guided walks and nature trails, but otherwise the only public facilities are a harbourside shop, visitor centre and **café-restaurant** inside the former coastguard station. Look out, too, for the fabulous summer Shakespeare performances at the **Open Air Theatre** (see ⓦ www.brownsea-theatre.co.uk).

Compton Acres

One of Dorset's most famous gardens lies on the outskirts of Canford Cliffs at **Compton Acres** (daily: April–Oct 9am–6pm; Nov–March 10am–4pm; £6.95), signposted off the A35 Poole road, towards Bournemouth (buses #150 & #151). Spectacularly sited over ten acres on steep slopes above Poole Harbour, the gardens were laid out in the 1920s by a wealthy entrepreneur. They are divided into seven garden areas, each with a different theme, including a formal Italian garden and the elegantly understated Japanese Garden, whose meandering streams crossed by stone steps and wooden bridges make it a peaceful wander. Keen gardeners won't mind the pricey admission fee, but it's rather overpriced for the casual visitor. There is, however, a good deli and café, a children's play area and a small model railway centre (£1.50 entry).

Eating, drinking and entertainment

Poole has a much better selection of good-quality restaurants than neighbouring Bournemouth, with lots to choose from in the **old town** and along the **Quay**. It also has some decent old-fashioned pubs, though its nightlife is more low-key and laid-back than in Bournemouth. For information on restaurants, theatres, clubs and festivals, check out *Listed* magazine, free from bars, clubs and restaurants.

Cafés and restaurants

Branksome Beach Branksome Chine ☎01202 767235. In a 1930s Art Deco building, that used to house a swimming pool, this restaurant is right on the beach with a great outdoor terrace. The menu is predominantly modern British, with main courses (£12–20) particularly of fish and local produce, such as smoked haddock with poached egg, and venison sausages. Closed Sun eve; Sept–June closed Sun–Tues eve.

Cranberries @no.4 4 Sarum St, Poole ☎01202 660670. It's hard to resist beginning with a fine cocktail at this good-value and intimate bar-restaurant with a small sunny garden. Inside is all bleached wood with a menu featuring very fresh, largely locally caught fish and seafood (bream, bass, mussels) along with tasty meat dishes.

Da Vinci's 7 The Quay ☎01202 667528. Set in an old warehouse facing Poole Quay, this is an old-fashioned Italian serving inexpensive pizza and pasta downstairs, and upmarket Italian cuisine upstairs.

Deli on the Quay D17 Dolphin Quays, The Quay ☎01202 660022. Bright, light harbourfront café-deli with floor-to-ceiling shelves stacked with delicious preserves, wines and the likes. The café is a great breakfast or lunch stop, serving fresh croissants and sandwiches and decent coffee.

Hotel du Vin Bistro Thames St ☎01202 785570. A lovely dining room with open kitchen, serving classic European dishes using local produce, such as Dorset pork loin, or roast partridge – the cheese board is heavenly. Most mains are around the £15–17 mark.

Loch Fyne 47 Haven Rd ☎01202 609000. A light, airy colonial-style building with a bustling atmosphere. It serves excellent fresh fish, including more unusual dishes such as salmon with a whisky, shellfish and mushroom sauce (£13), as well as the classic shellfish platters.

Mezza Luna Poole Park ☎01202 742842. Classic Italian dishes, such as veal *milanese*, and excellent crispy pizzas in this attractive building overlooking the lake in Poole Park. Closed Sun eve from Oct–June.

Penn Central Penn Hill Ave, Poole ☎01202 710888, ⊛www.pennnow.co.uk. Lively bar and bistro serving informal bar meals, including tapas. The smarter restaurant upstairs is pricier, with the starters including seafood such as scallops and mussels (Wed–Sat eve only). The bar area, in a former bank, has live music most Thursdays. Also sometimes offers a pay-what-you-think-your-meal-is-worth menu on Wed and Thurs, but phone first or check the website.

Storm 16 High St, Poole ☎01202 6749701. Owned by a chef/fisherman, this restaurant, unsurprisingly, specializes in locally caught seafood. The menu changes daily according to what is available, but expect such delights as sole or plaice from Poole Bay and lobster and scallops from the Purbeck coast. Closed Sun lunch; Nov–April closed Sun & Mon eve, phone for irregular lunchtime hours.

Bars and pubs

The Antelope 8 High St ☎01202 672029. Cheerful high-street pub set round an internal courtyard, with frequent live music and theme nights, including karaoke. It also offers reasonable rooms from £100 B&B.

Café Shore 10–14 Banks Rd, Sandbanks ☎01202 707271. This is *the* café-bar to be seen in affluent Sandbanks. There's a restaurant here too, though the food is no great shakes, so on a summer evening settle back with a cocktail on one of the comfy sofas or on the small outdoor terrace, and watch the jet set at play.

The Cow 58 Station Rd, Parkstone ☎01202 74956. It is worth heading outside Poole town centre to seek out this award-winning gastropub, with fine wines and a stripped wood interior. The backroom restaurant is spacious with good-value, quality food.

Customs House The Quay ℡01202 676767. The historic Georgian Customs house – complete with double staircase outside – has a great outdoor terrace overlooking the harbour that catches the last of the day's sun. Inside is very different, with an upstairs restaurant and a fashionable bar with flat-screen TV. The bar menu is also good value – the steaks are recommended.

Dundees The Quay ℡01202 661491. Wall-to-wall screens show sports most nights, though resident

DJs and karaoke takes over when the sports are done; brash and lively Aussie bar right on the front. Closed Mon–Tues unless a sports event is on.

Mr Kyps 8a Parr St, Ashley Cross, Lower Parkstone ℡01202 748945. Poole's premier live music venue, with a stream of mostly tribute bands but the occasional big name or up-and-coming star.

Poole Arms The Quay ℡01202 673 450. Completely covered with green tiles, this wonderfully atmospheric historic pub is reassuringly old-fashioned, with prints of old Poole on the walls, decent beers and an average pub menu.

Listings

Arts Centre The South's largest art centre, The Lighthouse, 21 Kingland Rd (℡0844 406 8666, Ⓦwww.lighthousepoole.co.uk) has an excellent calendar of live music, theatre, films, dance, art exhibitions and children's shows.

Bike rental The Water Sports Academy, Banks Rd, Sandbanks (℡01202 708203, Ⓦwww.thewater sportsacademy.com) rents out mountain bikes for £20 a day, or £12.50 for half a day.

Boat trips Numerous boats leave from Poole Quay on trips round the harbour, to Swanage, out to Old Harry Rocks and upriver to Wareham. Companies include Brownsea Island Ferries (℡01929 462383, Ⓦwww.brownseaislandferries.com), Greenslade Pleasure Boats (℡01202 631828, Ⓦwww .greensladepleasureboats.co.uk), Dorset Belle Cruises (℡01202 558550, Ⓦwww.dorsetcruises .co.uk) and Blue Line Cruises (℡01202 467882, Ⓦwww.bluelinecruises.co.uk).

Bus information Local services are run by Wilts & Dorset buses (℡01202 673555, Ⓦwww.wdbus .co.uk) and Yellow Buses (℡01202 636000, Ⓦwww.yellowbuses.co.uk). Further information on Ⓦwww.poole.gov.uk/transportation.

Bus tours see p.22.

Car rental Alamo (℡0870 400 4562, Ⓦwww .alamo.co.uk); Europcar (℡01202 667300,

Ⓦwww.europcar.co.uk); Sixt (℡0844 2486611, Ⓦwww.sixt.com).

Cinemas The multi-screen Empire is in the Tower Park complex on the bypass into town (℡0871 4714714, Ⓦwww.empirecinemas.co.uk), while The Lighthouse (see above) shows more art-house films.

Hospital Poole Hospital, Longfleet Rd (℡01202 665511, Ⓦwww.poole.nhs.uk).

Police Sandbanks Rd (℡01202 667766, Ⓦwww .dorset.police.uk).

Taxi Try Poole Taxis (℡01202 377020, Ⓦwww .taxispoole.co.uk) or Poole Radio Cabs (℡01202 666333, Ⓦwww.pooleradiocabs.com).

Waterpark Splashdown (℡01202 716123, Ⓦwww.splashdownpoole.co.uk) at Tower Park on the Poole bypass has waterslides, rapids and flumes, both in and outdoor, plus splash pools and jacuzzis.

Watersports The Water Sports Academy, Banks Rd, Sandbanks (℡01202 708203, Ⓦwww .thewatersportsacademy.com) rents out equipment and provides training for all sorts of watersports, including kayaking, sailing, windsurfing, wakeboarding and waterskiing.

The Isle of Purbeck

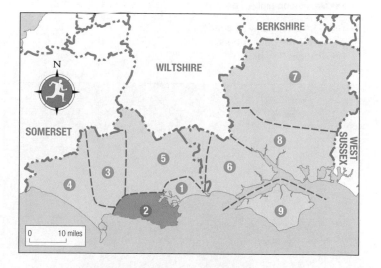

CHAPTER 2 # Highlights

✳ **Corfe Castle** These fairy-tale ruins form one of England's most spectacular castles. See p.75

✳ **Swanage to Norden railway** Hop on a steam train for a gentle chug through beautiful countryside. See p.76

✳ **Durlston Country Park** A great cliff-top reserve with its own castle, café and giant Purbeck stone globe. See p.81

✳ **Shell Bay** Superb, soft sands make this the perfect beach destination. See p.83

✳ **The Square and Compass** The best pub in Dorset looks like something out of a Hardy novel. See p.86

✳ **Tyneham**This village was evacuated in World War II and has remained eerily empty ever since. See p.88

✳ **Durdle Door** Dorset's iconic geographical landform is one of the highlights of the Jurassic Coast. See p.89

▲ A world away: Durlston Country Park

The Isle of Purbeck

Though the **ISLE OF PURBECK** is far from being an island, its geographical inaccessibility makes it feel like one, especially if you approach it by ferry from Poole. It also has the timeless quality of an island, with **Wareham** and the amazing castle ruins of **Corfe Castle** seemingly rooted in past centuries. Its coast is remarkably unspoilt, largely thanks to the MOD's ownership, and only **Swanage** has anything approaching resort status. Cliffs and inaccessible coves make this stretch of the South West coastal footpath truly spectacular, especially round **Lulworth Cove**, and the iconic **Durdle Door**. Its other coves, such as **Kimmeridge**, **Worbarrow Bay** and **Chapman's Pool**, have their own allure, though beach lovers should head for the **Studland** peninsula and its glorious sands round Shell Bay. There are also plenty of wet-weather attractions, including the **Monkey World** rescue centre, T.E. Lawrence's home at **Clouds Hill** and the **Tank Museum** at Bovington.

Though only quite small – about fifteen miles by ten miles – Purbeck has a lot to see in it, which means that it can get very busy on summer weekends, particularly around the traffic bottlenecks of Corfe Castle and Wareham. Most people drive, as local buses are fairly limited, and the steam train is a pricey, if fun, way of getting around. However, the best way to explore the area is by bike or on foot: there are some wonderful footpaths and country lanes that head across Purbeck, as well, of course, as the coastal path that skirts the region.

Wareham and around

Gateway to the Isle of Purbeck if you arrive by road or train, **WAREHAM** is a small, pretty market town that makes a good base for exploring the surrounding countryside, with the **Arne Nature Reserve** being a great spot for local walks and birdwatching. There are plenty of attractions nearby that will appeal to children in particular, such as an excellent local farm park, **Farmer Palmers**, and the **Margaret Green Animal Sanctuary**.

Arrival and information

Wareham is on the main London to Weymouth train line; the **station** is around fifteen minutes' walk north of town. It is also served by regular **buses** from Poole and Swanage. Drivers will find the approach road from Poole something of a bottleneck, especially during school holidays. There is plenty of parking along the approach roads into Wareham, or pay-and-display parking on the

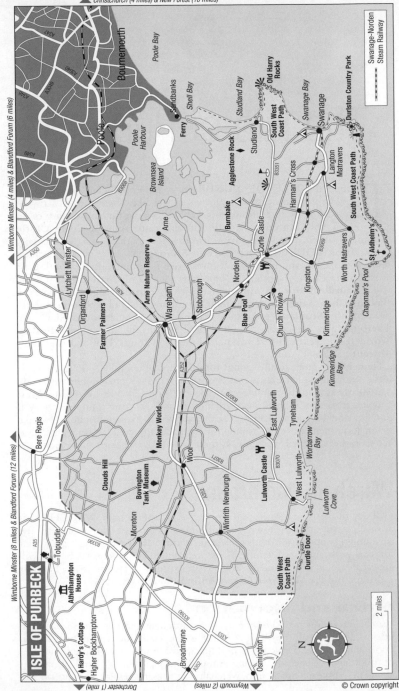

ISLE OF PURBECK

Christchurch (4 miles) & New Forest (10 miles)

Wimborne Minster (4 miles) & Blandford Forum (6 miles)

Wimborne Minster (8 miles) & Blandford Forum (12 miles)

Dorchester (1 mile)

Weymouth (2 miles)

Swanage–Norden
Steam Railway

Bournemouth
Poole Bay
Poole
Poole Harbour
Sandbanks
Shell Bay
Ferry
Brownsea Island
Studland Bay
Old Harry Rocks
Studland
South West Coast Path
Swanage Bay
Swanage
Durlston Country Park
Agglestone Rock
Burnbake
Corfe Castle
Harman's Cross
Langton Matravers
South West Coast Path
Arne
Arne Nature Reserve
Lytchett Minster
Organford
Wareham
Stoborough
Norden
Blue Pool
Church Knowle
Kingston
Worth Matravers
St Aldhelm's
Chapman's Pool
Farmer Palmers
Kimmeridge
Kimmeridge Bay
Bere Regis
Clouds Hill
Bovington Tank Museum
Monkey World
Wool
Winfrith Newburgh
East Lulworth
Tyneham
Worbarrow Bay
Lulworth Castle
West Lulworth
Lulworth Cove
Durdle Door
South West Coast Path
Tolpuddle
Athelhampton House
Hardy's Cottage
Higher Bockhampton
Moreton
Broadmayne
Osmington

A347
A338
A35
A31
A351
A350
A352
A353
A354
A3030
A3070
A3071
A3391
A3390
B3390
B3066
B3075
B3351
B3069
B3070

N

0   2 miles

© Crown copyright

Quay. The **tourist office** (Easter–Oct Mon–Sat 9.30am–5pm; Nov–Easter Mon–Sat 10am–4pm; ☎01929 552740, ⓦwww.purbeck.gov.uk) is in Holy Trinity Church at the bottom end of South Street.

Accommodation

Anglebury 15–17 North St ☎01929 552988, ⓦwww.angleburyhouse.co.uk. Simple if rather faded and old-fashioned rooms above a restaurant in a fine sixteenth-century building decked out in dark wood. The restaurant serves traditional English mains from around £8 along with all-day breakfasts and cream teas. **②**

🏃 **North Mill** off Shatters Hill ☎01929 555142, ⓦwww.northmill.org.uk. The best budget option in town, this lovely B&B is in a Grade II listed, sixteenth-century former mill overlooking the River Piddle (and the bypass beyond). There is one double and one twin room, but guests can use a large communal lounge with a log fire in winter. Breakfast includes eggs from the resident hens and other local produce. **③**

The Priory Hotel Church Green ☎01929 551666, ⓦwww.theprioryhotel.co.uk. This former priory building dating back over 500 years is now a luxury hotel, with beautifully tended gardens, running down to the river. The rooms in the main house are traditional and luxurious, but the more modern rooms in the boathouse are the best, with terraces overlooking the river and their own jacuzzis. A three-course menu in the rather formal restaurant costs around £40, though in fine weather you can have a cheaper lunch outside on the terrace. **⑨**

Trinity 32 South St ☎01929 556689, ⓦwww.trinitybnb.co.uk. By the tourist office, this homely B&B has charming rooms in a sixteenth-century townhouse, some en suite. **①**

The Town

The best approach to **Wareham** is from the south across the River Frome, from where the town's skyline has little changed from medieval times. Indeed, the grid pattern of its streets indicates its Saxon origins and much of the old town is still ringed by grassy mounds that formed defensive ramparts dating back to the tenth century – the tourist office (see above) has leaflets detailing a fine walk following the walls' circuit. Today, Wareham is a pleasant market town with a bustling Thursday market. Its main sight is the **Lady St Mary's Church**, which contains the marble coffin of Edward the Martyr, murdered at Corfe Castle in 978 by his stepmother, to make way for her son Ethelred. **St Martin's Church**, at the north end of town, dates from Saxon times and holds a faded twelfth-century mural of St Martin offering his cloak to a beggar. The church's most striking feature, however, is a romantic effigy of T.E. Lawrence in Arab dress, which was originally destined for Salisbury Cathedral, but was rejected by the dean there who disapproved of Lawrence's sexual proclivities. The small **museum** next to Wareham's town hall in East Street (Easter–Oct Mon–Sat 10am–4pm; free) displays some of Lawrence's memorabilia, though those interested in his life should head to nearby Clouds Hill (see p.92) where he lived. Otherwise, Wareham's main focal point is the Frome riverside, especially around The Quay – there are delightful walks in either direction following its course, or you can take a **boat trip** (Easter–Sept, weather permitting; 45min; £5; ⓦwww.warehamboathire.co.uk). Boats also come up here from Poole when tidal conditions allow (ⓦwww.greenslade pleasureboats.co.uk & ⓦwww.brownseaislandferries.com). Film buffs should take a peek inside **The Rex Cinema** on West Street (ⓦwww.therex .co.uk), one of the oldest cinemas in Dorset – it dates back to 1927 and has many of its original fittings; there is also a bar so you can enjoy a drink with the film.

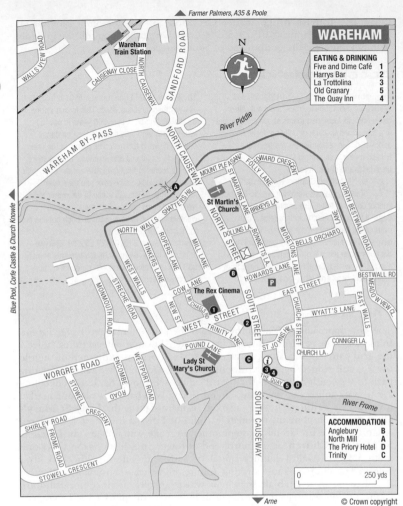

▲ Farmer Palmers, A35 & Poole

▼ Arne   © Crown copyright

Eating and drinking

Five and Dime Café The Rex Cinema, West St.
A cosy little café attached to the cinema serving a
good selection of sandwiches, soups, light lunches
and veggie meals. Closed evenings.

Harrys Bar 20 South St ☎01929 551818.
Fashionable bar-restaurant on the main street, with
good-value breakfasts and food ranging from tapas
and wraps to mains such as fish pie, from around
£4–7. Also does delicious coffees and has a small
patio garden. Closed Sun.

La Trottolina The Quay, South St ☎01929
551662. Traditional Italian trattoria right on the
quay, serving good-value pizzas at around £6, and

pasta dishes, such as *linguine al cartoccio* –
seafood in tomato sauce, baked in the
oven – for £6–7.

Old Granary The Quay ☎01929 556689. Stylishly
renovated gastropub with a series of bleached-
wood rooms and a great riverside terrace on two
levels. As well as decent breakfasts and teas, you
can have classy mains such as monkfish wrapped
in prosciutto, steaks, salads and pasta dishes
from £8–15.

The Quay Inn The Quay ☎01929 552735.
No-nonsense pub grub at reasonable prices, with a
few sunny outdoor tables facing the quay.

Around Wareham

Three miles north of Wareham at Organford, **Farmer Palmers** (daily: Feb, March, Nov & Dec 10am–4pm; April–Oct 10am–5.30pm; closed Jan; £6.95 for adults and children) is a great destination for anyone with younger children. It's a working farm, where you can pet various animals, watch cows being milked and enjoy tractor rides round the grounds; there are also go-karts and wet-weather attractions such as a haybarn and soft play area, as well as a café serving reasonably priced snacks. The farm is run by the Palmer family, who are very much in evidence, giving friendly and informative talks on aspects of farming, such as milking and lamb-feeding, throughout the day.

Around three miles south west of Wareham at Furzebrook lies the **Blue Poole** (daily March–Nov 9.30pm–dusk; £5; ⓦ www.bluepooltearooms.co.uk), a clay pit whose waters are famed for their remarkable colours, varying from bright green to blue – or grey if you catch it on a dull day. It's rather overpriced, but the tearooms (from 10am) and surrounding woodlands are a pleasant enough place to spend an hour or so. Continue on the road beyond to wind up over a steep ridge – this makes a dramatic alternative approach to Corfe Castle (see below).

After a couple of miles, the road passes through **Church Knowle**, a typical, tiny Purbeck village, enveloped by lovely walking countryside. It's also home to the **Margaret Green Animal Sanctuary** (daily except Christmas Day 10am–4pm), where you can wander around the attractive grounds and view the animals that have been rescued and are waiting to be re-homed: they usually have lots of domestic animals – from cats and dogs to gerbils and guinea pigs – as well as larger animals, such as horses, goats and sheep. It's free to enter, though donations are welcome. There's a pleasant **pub** next door, the *New Inn* (☎01929 480357), which serves good, if slightly pricey, food and has a beer garden. There's a lovely rural **campsite** just over a mile away at *East Creech Farm* (☎01929 480519, ⓦ www.eastcreechfarm.co.uk) with a good children's play area and great views of Poole Harbour.

Arne

Around five miles southeast of Wareham, **Arne Nature Reserve** encompasses woodland and tidal mudflats next to Poole Harbour and Long Island. There are several marked trails around the reserve and along its shingle beaches, where you can spot rare wading birds as well as deer. **Arne** itself is a pretty little hamlet with a beautiful thirteenth-century church of St Nicholas. The rest of the village was largely evacuated in World War II, when the area was used as a decoy site – flares and smoke were sent up from here to distract bombers away from an explosives factory across the bay at Holton Heath. The village is also home to a small toy museum, **The World of Toys** (July–Aug daily 10.30am–5.30pm; Sept & April–June Tues–Sun 1.30–5pm; £3.50, children £2.50; ☎01929 552018), which contains a motley collection of historical bears, boats and musical boxes.

Corfe Castle and around

The first sighting of the towering ruins of **CORFE CASTLE** (daily: March & Oct 10am–5pm; April–Sept 10am–6pm; Nov–Feb 10am–4pm; £5.40; NT) never fails to impress, particularly if you approach from Church Knowle – the castle's hilltop position makes it look impregnable. The castle defends virtually

▲ Arne Nature Reserve

the only gap in a ridge of low, steep hills that stretch for fourteen miles, all the way from Ballard Down on the coast near Swanage to Worbarrow Bay.

The castle was first built in the eleventh century by William the Conqueror and expanded in the thirteen century by King John, who used it as both a prison and royal residence. Later monarchs were less taken with it, however, and Queen Elizabeth sold it to her chancellor before it passed into the hands of Sir John Bankes, Attorney General to Charles I. As a Royalist stronghold, the castle withstood a Cromwellian siege for six weeks, and was gallantly defended by Lady Bankes. It fell only after one of her own men, Colonel Pitman, eventually betrayed the castle to the Roundheads, who set about demolishing much of the structure with gunpowder. Apparently the victorious Roundheads were so impressed by Lady Bankes's courage that they allowed her to take the keys to the castle with her when she was turfed out – they can still be seen in the library at the Bankes's subsequent home, Kingston Lacy (see p.149). You can still clamber round its towers and ramparts, which command superb views over the surrounding countryside as well as the Norden to Swanage steam

Norden to Swanage steam railway

Corfe is the first main stop on the atmospheric Norden to **Swanage steam railway** (April–Oct daily, Nov, Dec & March weekends only, Feb half-term only; £9 return, children £7; ⓦwww.swanagerailway.co.uk). The line dates back to 1885, though British Rail closed it down in 1972 and took up all the track. Since 1975, it has been run by volunteers, who have worked over the decades to gradually replace the track and re-open the line. It's a lovely route, chuffing mostly through fields and woods with stops at the tiny stations of Harman's Cross and Herston Halt. The full run from Norden, just under a mile north of Corfe, to Swanage takes just twenty minutes. Services run roughly hourly from around 9am–5pm, but check the website for a full timetable which varies depending on the type of train: they also run special events, including Santa Specials and Thomas the Tank Engine days. Volunteers have now succeeded in clearing the tracks as far as Wareham, where it joins the main line to London and in April 2009 the first passenger service from Waterloo to Swanage since 1972 ran along the whole line, though a regular service has yet to be implemented.

railway (see box, p.76). Look out, too, for screenings of films in the castle grounds during the summer, as part of the Purbeck Film Festival (Wwww .purbeckfilm.org.uk), England's largest rural film festival.

The village of Corfe Castle is very pretty, its low cottages built with soft Purbeck stone (see box, p.86). It's worth a quick peer inside the town **museum**, housed inside England's smallest town hall: it contains historical artefacts and photographs of the village in days gone by. Young children will enjoy the **Model Village** opposite (April–Oct daily except Fri 10am–5pm; Nov–March Fri–Sun 10am–4pm; £3.25, children £2; Wwww.corfemodelvillage.co.uk): it's a quirky place with a model of the village in attractive gardens, an enchanted fairy garden, and a selection of giant outdoor games.

There are also some fine **walks** around Corfe: to the east, you can pick up the Purbeck Way, which eventually joins the coastal path between Swanage and Studland (both around seven miles from Corfe); alternatively head west up West Hill opposite the castle, where you can join a great ridge walk, cutting down to the attractive neighbouring village of Church Knowle (see p.75), a three- to four-mile round walk.

Practicalities

As well as the Swanage steam railway (see box opposite), Corfe is served by hourly buses from Swanage, Wareham and Poole. There's comfortable **accommodation** at the *Bankes Arms Hotel* (☎01929 480206, Wwww.dorset-hotel.co.uk; ❷), which has a range of rooms, not all en suite, above a sixteenth-century inn on the main East Street, though if your budget allows, first choice is just beyond on the same road at *Mortons House* (☎01929 480988, Wwww.mortonshouse.co.uk; ❼). A sixteenth-century manor house with a beautiful walled garden and log fires in winter, this award-winning small hotel has snug rooms, some with four-poster beds and stone fireplaces. The **restaurant** offers three courses of fine dining for £30. Another great option is two miles southeast of Corfe Castle at Harman's Cross where the ⭐ *Purbeck Vineyard* (☎01929 481 525, Wwww.vineyard.uk.com; ❺) has plush, contemporary rooms with their own terraces overlooking a working vineyard – and the Swanage steam railway in the distance. Non-residents can also visit – tasting trips include a guided tour of the vineyard, wine tasting and lunch for £20, while in autumn, you can join the local villagers who all muck in for the grape harvest. The vineyard also has its own excellent restaurant which serves top-quality contemporary British cuisine (around £20–30 a head).

Corfe Castle is well stocked with **tearooms** and gift shops and has a couple of good **pubs** too: *The Fox* on West Street, and, on the main square, *The Greyhound*, one of England's oldest coaching inns. It has a pleasant garden out the back with fine views of the castle, and serves local specialities, such as Lyme Bay scallops and venison casserole (£11). The *National Trust Tearooms*, by the entrance to the castle has a lovely garden and serves light lunches and afternoon teas, with delicious home-made cake. The Model Village also has a decent café serving inexpensive lunches.

Swanage and around

SWANAGE, Purbeck's largest and only real resort, is idyllically set in a natural sandy bay surrounded by green rolling hills. It originally grew up as a port for the local quarrying trade, but thrived with the arrival of the railway, which turned it into a popular Victorian seaside town. There are some great **walks** in

Enid Blyton

The Isle of Purbeck was the favourite holiday destination for **Enid Blyton** in the 1930s. She mostly stayed in Swanage, swimming each morning around both piers with her husband, who later owned the local golf club. Purbeck's heathlands and castles were the inspiration for many of her *Famous Five* children's stories, while most of the Famous Five's holidays begin on the steam train, which still runs from Swanage to Norden (see p.76). Blyton turned Corfe Castle into "Kirrin Castle" for her children's adventures and Brownsea Island, then privately owned by an eccentric recluse, is the mysterious Whispering Island in her *Five Have a Mystery to Solve*. For more on Blyton, visit the Ginger Pop shop in the Square in Corfe Castle (daily except Fri end March to Oct; Ⓦwww.gingerpop.co.uk), which organizes Enid Blyton tours and sells Blyton-style souvenirs, such as a kit for brewing your own ginger beer and toys without batteries.

the countryside around the town: head north along the beach and you'll see steps up the cliff which joins the **coastal path to Studland** via Ballard Down (see p.81), and south from the town the path continues along the coast through **Durlston Country Park**.

Arrival and information

The town's station is the southern terminus of the **Swanage Steam Railway**, which runs as far as Norden, just north of Corfe Castle (see p.75). Regular **buses** pull in here from Poole via Wareham and Corfe Castle, and in season (usually around Easter–Oct; weather dependent) **boat trips** arrive at the town pier from Bournemouth and Poole (Ⓦwww.bluelinecruises.co.uk, Ⓦwww.brownseaislandferries.com & Ⓦwww.dorsetcruises.co.uk). Out of season, there is plenty of **parking** along the main seafront road, though the middle section of this is closed in the summer, when drivers are best off heading for one of the central car parks. Swanage's **tourist office** is by the beach on Shore Road (Easter–Oct daily 10am–5pm; Nov–Easter closed Sun; ☏0870 442 0680, Ⓦwww.swanage.gov.uk). This can give details of local accommodation and various summer events, including the lively Swanage Carnival (Ⓦwww.swanagecarnival.com) in late July.

Accommodation

As well as the places listed below, the town's numerous accommodation options include a YHA **hostel**, in a Victorian house on Cluny Crescent (☏0845 3719346, Ⓦwww.yha.org.uk; £16) with lovely views across the bay. and a cluster of B&Bs on King's Road near the train station. There are also several **campsites** in the vicinity, including the *Swanage Coastal Park* (☏01929 648331, Ⓦwww.shorefield.co.uk/swanage), a mile out of town on the Priest's Way, and the *Ulwell Cottage* on the Ulwell road (☏01929 422823, Ⓦulwell.users30.donhost.co.uk), with an indoor pool and children's play area.

Bella Vista 14 Burlington Rd ☏01929 422873. Fantastic views from most of the bedrooms and a great garden that overlooks the beach. The rooms are clean and comfortable, and there's a spacious family room on the top floor. ❹

Clare House 1 Park Rd ☏01929 422855, Ⓦwww.clare-house.com. A Grade II listed Victorian town house in a central location on the western side of

town. The rooms are spacious and the owners friendly. ❸

Purbeck House Hotel 91 High St ☏01929 422872, Ⓦwww.purbeckhousehotel.co.uk. Once the private home of George Burt, who also owned Durlston Castle (see p.81), this amazing Victorian pile is quite a sight, with soaring ceilings, dark wood and acres of floral wallpaper, not to mention the original bellrings for servants (including ones for the Dressing Room and Ladies Room). There's a cosy bar, a formal dining room and substantial grounds that include a modern annexe, though rooms in both buildings have contemporary facilities. ⑥

The Grand Hotel Burlington Rd ☎01929 423353, ⓦwww.grandhotelswanage.co.uk. Dating from 1898, this classic Victorian seaside hotel has lovely grounds leading down to its own private beach, and great views from the public rooms. The bedrooms have been updated with wi-fi and TVs and there's an indoor pool, jacuzzi and the usual health club facilities. ⑧

The Swanage Haven 3 Victoria Rd ☎01929 423088, ⓦwww.swanagehaven.com. Billing itself as a boutique guest house, this pleasant B&B is in a good location, with cosy rooms with all mod cons. The breakfasts are organic and the decked garden has a great outdoor hot tub. Good value. No children. ②

The White Horse 11 High St ☎01929 422469. A good budget option, with simple double rooms above this pub on the High St, though be warned that front rooms can be very noisy especially when there's live music downstairs. ①

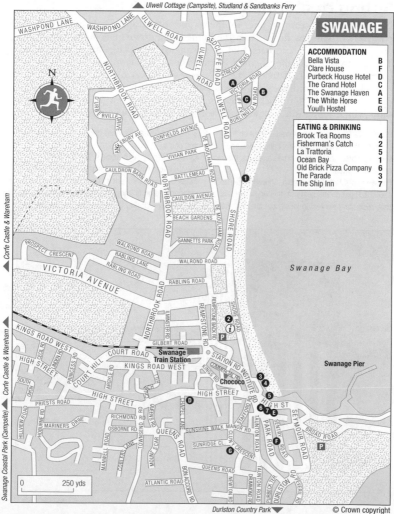

▲ Ulwell Cottage (Campsite), Studland & Sandbanks Ferry

SWANAGE

ACCOMMODATION
Bella Vista	B
Clare House	F
Purbeck House Hotel	D
The Grand Hotel	C
The Swanage Haven	A
The White Horse	E
Youth Hostel	G

EATING & DRINKING
Brook Tea Rooms	4
Fisherman's Catch	2
La Trattoria	5
Ocean Bay	1
Old Brick Pizza Company	6
The Parade	3
The Ship Inn	7

Swanage Bay

Swanage Pier

◄ Corfe Castle & Wareham
◄ Corfe Castle & Wareham
Swanage Coastal Park (Campsite) ▲

0   250 yds

Durlston Country Park ▼

© Crown copyright

The Town

Swanage has plenty of fine Victorian townhouses, though its most ornate structure is the Town Hall; its facade was actually designed by Christopher Wren but dismantled and moved here after its original London home, Mercers Hall in Cheapside, was demolished. But though the old town is pleasant enough, Swanage's real appeal lies in its **beach** – a fantastic swathe of soft sand that stretches from the town centre east under Ballard Down – as you'd expect, it gets progressively quieter as you head away from town, especially the eastern stretches below high cliffs. In summer the eastern section has areas where you can hire pedaloes and jet skis and there are also a couple of seasonal beach café kiosks. Peak season sees large crowds and traditional Punch and Judy shows on the beach, but for much of the year the town has a decidedly laid-back and sleepy feel.

Eating and drinking

In summer the seafront and southern end of Swanage's High Street are positively heaving, with the latter the home to the town's late-night action in a series of lively pubs and bars. Out of season, a lot of places are firmly closed. Tucked away in an alley behind Station Road, the wonderful Chococo on Commercial Road (ⓣ01929 421777, ⓦwww.chococo.co.uk), sells its own chocolates made with local ingredients, such as cream, lavender and honey – the dark chocolate chilli truffles are heaven: you can watch them being made in the shop window opposite, or have a go yourself during workshops.

Brook Tea Rooms 15 The Parade. Right on the seafront, this pleasant café has good views and serves up breakfasts, sandwiches and pies, all reasonably priced.

Fisherman's Catch The Cabin, Shore Rd ⓣ01929 426222. Right on the seafront, this unpretentious café-restaurant serves up locally caught fresh fish and seafood and also does decent takeaway fish and chips.

La Trattoria 12 High St ⓣ01929/423784. Evenings-only traditional Italian restaurant with a range of moderately priced pasta and pizza; good seafood and grills, though these push the prices up to expensive. During the day, cappuccinos and

▲ Swanage beach

baguettes are served next door at the attached *Forte's Caffe.*

Ocean Bay 1–7 Ulwell Rd, Swanage ☎01929 422222, ⓦoceanbayswanage.com. In an enviable position facing the beach, with outdoor tables on a narrow terrace, this is the best place for a top-quality meal. Mains (around £10–15) use mostly local produce such as Swanage Bay crab risotto and Purbeck venison sausages. It also does moderately priced sandwiches and salads for lighter lunches.

Old Brick Pizza Company 23 High St ☎01929 422620. Spacious and modern pizzeria that also serves delicious pasta and salads from £7. Closed at lunchtime from Oct–April.

The Parade The Parade ☎01929/422363. Cheap and cheerful fish and chip restaurant with a few indoor tables and a fine upstairs dining room (April–Sept only). As well as the usual battered fare, it serves fine locally caught fresh fish such as red mullet and trout.

The Ship Inn 23a High St ☎01929 423855. A nice, old pub with contemporary decor inside and a few tables out the front. Serves pub grub, such as fish in Ringwood Ale batter (£9), and local sausages, cheese and fish.

Durlston Country Park

Heading south from Swanage, you can pick up the coastal path round to **Durlston Country Park**, around a mile out of town. Set in 280 acres of coastal woodland and crisscrossed with cliff-top paths, it is a great place for a picnic or for wind-blown walks. There is a small visitor centre (Easter–Oct daily 10am–5pm; Nov–March weekends and school holidays 10.30am–4pm; free) detailing the local wildlife – giant turtles and a resident school of dolphins can sometimes be spotted from the cliffs, which also shelter sea birds such as a puffin colony – and a great café, *The Lookout.* The café's location and views are fantastic and it serves reasonably priced local breads, cheeses and home-made cakes: it also makes a dramatic venue for films, shown as part of the Purbeck Film Festival (see p.31).

The Lookout is situated below **Durlston Castle**, a Victorian folly built by wealthy local George Burt, and is currently being renovated into a new visitor centre and exhibition space. He also built the Great Globe that sits south of the castle, a huge carved globe made from Portland limestone. From here, the cliff path below skirts round to the entrance to the **Tilly Whim Caves**. These were once limestone quarries – named after a quarryman, Tilly, and a basic crane called a whim – and later became a popular visitor attraction, but you only have to look at the cracks around the entrance to see why they were closed for safety reasons. A further ten minutes south brings you to **Anvil Point Lighthouse**, opened in 1881 by Neville Chamberlain's father, then Minister of Transport. You can look round the lighthouse on a guided tour (for dates and times, see ⓦwww.trinityhouse.co.uk/events_and_leisure /visitor_centres/anvil_point.html; £2), or to really appreciate the stunning location and views, you can rent one of two cottages below it, *Rowena* and *Veronica* cottages (ⓦwww.ruralretreats.co.uk). Beyond the lighthouse, the coastal path continues beyond the park towards Dancing Ledge and Worth Matravers (see p.86).

Studland and around

Around four miles north of Swanage lies pretty **Studland**, a well-to-do village spread out above a lovely stretch of coast that makes a fine alternative base to Swanage. From the bottom of the hill below the *Bankes Arms* pub, a footpath leads down to Studland's small but appealing South Beach. Managed by the National Trust, the beach is being left to face natural coastal erosion,

Studland at war

One of England's most important World War II relics is tucked away behind the beach huts at Middle Beach. During the war, the whole of the Studland peninsula was evacuated so that the bay could be used as a rehearsal ground for the Normandy D-day Landings. A 90-foot-long bunker, known as **Fort Henry**, was built by Canadian troops in 1943, with concrete walls almost three feet thick, and an 80-foot recessed observation slit from where the troops' activities in the bay below could be viewed in safety. Winston Churchill, King George VI and Generals Eisenhower and Montgomery all sheltered in this pillbox, watching the rehearsals and discussing tactics for the forthcoming invasion of France. In April 1944, six amphibious tanks sank in the bay during rough weather, with the loss of six lives: this tragic accident, however, had a positive result in that it was then realized that the tanks were not seaworthy in rough conditions and should drive into shallow water, thus ensuring the success of the Landings in June. You can go inside the bunker and peer through the observation slit, or clamber on the remains of the protective dragon's teeth and pillboxes on the beach below.

with a decision to abandon coastal defence plans. This means the whole lot will probably soon disappear – so make the most of the narrow sandy strip backed by beach huts. The sea shelves gently here so swimming is generally very safe, though occasional seaweed deposits can leave a pungent aroma in the summer.

Arrival and information

There are fairly regular Wilts and Dorset **bus** services to Studland from Swanage, though the best approach is on the hourly (two-hourly on Sun) #50 bus from Bournemouth, which comes over on the Sandbanks ferry and passes the turnings to the main beaches. If you're **driving**, there are pricey National Trust car parks by the ferry, at Middle Beach and Knoll Beach, and beside the *Bankes Arms* (see below) for South Beach.

Accommodation

Accommodation is fairly limited in the Studland area, with a few upmarket hotels, some self-catering cottages and one **campsite**, the lovely rural *Burnbake* at Rempstone (Easter–Sept; ☎01929 480570, Ⓦwww.btinternet .com/~burnbakecampsite), with rope swings in the woods and a small shop: to get there, take the right-hand fork to Corfe Castle beyond Studland village, and it's signed to the right off the road.

The Bankes Arms Studland ☎01929 450225, Ⓦbankesarms.com. Attractive rooms, some en suite with sea views, in this lovely old pub (see p.85). ❹

Knoll House Studland Bay ☎01929 450450, Ⓦwww.knollhouse.co.uk. This pricey, traditional family hotel is a child-friendly option, with indoor and outdoor pools, and lovely grounds that lead down to the sea: note, it only offers weekly full board in high season.

Manor House Studland Bay ☎01929 450288, Ⓦwww.themanorhousehotel.com. If you fancy splashing out, this eighteenth-century manor house has a fantastic location with lovely gardens leading down to the sea, and its own tennis courts: it has an old-fashioned air about it, but the rooms are comfortable, some with four-posters and sea views. ❾, includes four-course dinner.

Seaview next to the *Bankes Arms* in Studland Ⓦwww.nationaltrustcottages.co.uk/south_west /dorset/seaview/99. The National Trust rents out this characterful three-bedroomed cottage in an old tennis pavilion: it's in a wonderful location with sea views from the veranda which leads onto a large garden. Sleeps six; £400 a week in low season, up to £1500 in high season.

Old Harry Rocks

South of Studland village, just beyond the path down to the beach – or joined by a separate path up from the beach – is the start of the coastal path to **Old Harry Rocks**. It's around a twenty-minute walk to this dizzy and spectacular landform – a series of chalk stacks rising sheer out of the sea, some tunnelled with arches and caves. You can walk right up to the cliff edge – take great care as this section is unfenced. Indeed until the late eighteenth century, you could walk right onto Old Harry itself before erosion led to its current position. Eventually it will befall the fate of so-called Old Harry's Wife – a sad chalk stump alongside that collapsed in 1896.

The **coastal path** continues west from here all the way to Swanage – a lovely walk of around an hour over soaring cliffs, the coast path eventually dropping steeply down to join the eastern end of Swanage's sandy beach. Alternatively, you can walk to the top of the hill above Old Harry Rocks and then turn right to skirt back to Studland over Ballard Down.

Agglestone Rock

From the village of Studland, a signed path leads up to **Agglestone Rock**, part of the Godlingston Heath National Nature Reserve. This peculiar sandstone ball looks like it has been dropped on the open heathland from outer space – there are various legends as to how it got here, including that it was thrown by the devil in an attempt to knock down the "skittles" of Old Harry. The scientific explanation is that it is an eroded pedestal rock that has fallen on its side. It's a steep walk from the village to the rock – an easier approach is to drive along the road through Studland, then take the right-hand fork signed to Corfe Castle, which leads along the top of a ridge with dramatic views back over Poole Harbour. Before you reach the golf club, once owned by Enid Blyton and her husband (see box, p.78), you'll see a signed path leading off the road down to Agglestone Rock.

To Shell Bay

Heading north from Studland, the road passes along a narrow isthmus of land, most of it forming the Studland Heath Nature Reserve, which faces Poole Harbour on one side and the sea on the other. It's a lovely walk along the coast from Studland's narrow **South Beach**, through **Middle Beach**, and the lively **Knoll Beach**, with its watersports facilities and naturist section, which leads into **Shell Bay**, a magnificent stretch of icing-sugar sand. This whole stretch of coast is backed by a remarkable heathland ecosystem that's home to all six

---

The South West Coast Path

The **South West Coast Path**, Britain's longest footpath, begins its 630-mile coastal route from Shell Bay to Minehead in Somerset via Land's End. Originally conceived in the 1940s, the path was fully opened in the 1970s, much of it thanks to the National Trust through whose land many miles of the route pass. Check Ⓦ www .explorethesouthwestcoastpath.co.uk for detailed descriptions of sections of the walk or the South West Coast Path Association (Ⓦ www.swcp.rg.uk), who can estimate timings and recommend which bits are most suited to your fitness levels. We describe sections of the walk in the chapter below, but before you set off, always check local weather conditions as footpaths can be steep and slippery, and get a copy of the OS map OL15 (Purbeck and South Dorset).

British species of reptile – adders are quite common, so be careful – and it's also the only place in the UK to have breeding populations of both the native species of **sea horse**. They breed in the offshore seagrass meadows, and boats are currently banned from anchoring off South Beach, in order to protect their population. The beach gets packed in summer, though the central stretch – a bit of a walk from any of the car parks – is quieter. At the top end of the beach is

▲ An essential stop in Studland

a chain **ferry** (see p.65) connecting the Isle of Purbeck with Sandbanks in Poole, though in summer and at busy weekends there are queues of over an hour to get across.

Eating and drinking

Bankes Arms Studland ☎01929 450225. The best place for inexpensive food, as well as a great range of real ales, some from local independent breweries and others from its own on-site microbrewery, the Isle of Purbeck Brewery. It serves a good range of pub food, slightly more pricey than average, but the portions are big, and frankly it's worth it for the joy of sitting in the substantial lawned garden at the front with fantastic bay views, or in the cosy Purbeck stone interior, where log fires roar. On sunny summer days, the place is heaving.

Joe's Café on South Beach. Little more than a wooden shed on the beach, this laid-back café serves fair-trade filter coffee and superb simple lunches such as couscous and Greek salads, as well as organic soup and sandwiches.

The Knoll Beach Café Knoll Beach. A pleasant café run by the National Trust, serving the usual good-quality sandwiches, light lunches and cakes.

The Shell Bay Seafood Restaurant at the top end of the beach, right by the chain ferry ☎01929 450363, ⓦ www.shellbay.net. In a lovely location, right on the harbour: it specializes in fish dishes, with main courses for around £15 in the evening, though lighter lunches are cheaper and come with the same great views.

The South Purbeck Coast

Part of the world Heritage Jurassic Coast, the segment of the Dorset coast that runs from Swanage to Lulworth is truly spectacular, although most of it traces along steep cliffs, which means access to the sea is somewhat limited. Here, the idyllic villages of **Langton** and **Worth Matravers** are both good bases for some great coastal walks. The western stretches between **Kimmeridge** and **Lulworth**, known as the Ranges, are owned by the Ministry of Defence, and are often closed to the public during military exercises, when through-roads are also barred: these usually take place during the week – rarely at weekends and holidays – and there are plenty of signs on all the approach roads to warn of this, as well as red flags flying over the area. The upside of MOD-ownership is that the entire vicinity is remarkably unspoilt, with no modern development. Many rare species of flora and fauna thrive here, while several of the villages were evacuated during World War II and have remained empty since, notably the ghost village of **Tyneham**.

Langton Matravers and around

Some two miles out of Swanage and just inland from the South West coastal path (see p.83), the small village of **Langton Matravers** is a pleasing medley of Purbeck stone houses. If you want to **stay**, the best option is the wonderfully sited and well-run *Tom's Field Campsite* (☎01929 427110, ⓦ www .tomsfieldcamping.co.uk), which also lets out bunks in a converted Nissen hut – *The Walker's Barn* – or a converted pigstyle called *The Stone Room* (both ❶). The campsite has its own shop, but only takes reservations for longer stays – for short stays, especially on sunny weekends, you'll need to turn up early to bag a pitch. Langton Matravers has a couple of decent **pubs** on the main through-road: the *King's Arms* on the High Street serves inexpensive pub grub and has a small beer garden.

From the car park at Langton House, or from the path alongside *Tom's Field* campsite, there's a lovely 1.5-mile walk over the downs to the coast and

Purbeck stone

Purbeck stone gives the warm, greyish tint to the local villages of Swanage, Worth Matravers, Kingston and Corfe Castle, while Purbeck marble – actually a limestone that can be polished to look like marble – has also been used extensively for slab flooring in many of England's cathedrals. The stone has been quarried since Roman times, much of it along the coast so that the heavy stones could be carried away by boat; like Portland (see p.124), Swanage largely grew up round the quarrying trade. Miners traditionally worked in metre-high galleries that plummeted steeply down, following the natural dip in rock that was sandwiched between ridges of clay. The clay was removed from above and below before the stone could be carted out in blocks – an extremely hazardous occupation. Today, open-cast quarrying continues in Purbeck, though many of the quarries have closed: you can visit or see the disused quarries around **Tilly Whim Caves**, **Dancing Ledge** and **Winspit**, which supplied the stone for Lulworth and Durlston castles. These days the disused mines have become the home to several species of bats – but keep clear of the entrances, which can be dangerously unstable.

Dancing Ledge, a low rock ledge washed over by the sea at high tide, which Victorian quarrymen blasted into a natural bathing pool for local school children to swim in. It remains a popular bathing spot to this day, though be warned that to reach it involves a fairly steep scramble down rocks for the last stretch. The cliffs around the ledge are also popular for local climbers.

Tom's Field campsite is also the starting point of a great three-hour **walk** to Worth Matravers via the coast and back again inland. Start at the footpath on the Langton side of the campsite, from where you head uphill through fields. You will soon cross the route back (on the Priest's Way), but continue straight on (towards Dancing Ledge) across more fields before a steep slope takes you down towards the coast. It's a short detour to Dancing Ledge (see p.85) or you can continue west along the coastal path. This stretch, above high cliffs, is relatively flat all the way to the inlet of Seacombe, above ledges cut into the cliffs by quarrymen. Take the path up Seacombe Bottom (signed Worth Matravers), a fairly steep climb up a delightful valley. To return, head out of Worth Matravers on the road towards Langton Matravers, and after 200m you will pick up a path signed Swanage, off to the right. This soon joins the dirt path of the Priest's Way. It's about one and a half miles back on this, past a couple of working quarries, before you pick up the path you started on above *Tom's Field*.

Worth Matravers

A couple of miles up the coast from Langton Matravers, **Worth Matravers** is the quintessential Purbeck village, complete with a picturesque church, duck pond and dazzling views over the surrounding downs, which are best enjoyed from one of England's finest pubs, the ✱ *Square and Compass*. This doubles as a **museum**, housing a fine collection of local fossils; it also puts on various exhibitions throughout the year, including one for local sculptors, and in autumn there's a pumpkin festival, when the garden is laid out with pumpkins the size of tables. The bar is a tiny hatch, the interior is a winter fug of log fires, walkers, families and dogs (and the occasional live band), and outside you may have to move the odd chicken to sit on a motley collection of stone seats and wooden benches. Regularly winning CAMRA awards for its local ales and ciders, it also serves delicious home-made pies and pasties.

Worth Matravers has one of the oldest churches in Dorset, **St Nicholas Church**, which is also home to the grave of **Benjamin Jesty**, the first recorded person to be vaccinated against smallpox, some twenty years before Edward Jenner. Jesty was a farmer who noticed that those people who had caught the milder disease of cowpox and recovered from it were usually immune to the more serious smallpox. In 1774, during a bad outbreak of smallpox, Jesty took his pregnant wife and two sons, aged three and two, to a nearby farm and deliberately infected them with cowpox, by wiping the infected pus from a cow's udder onto a darning needle and scratching his wife's arm with it, then inserting the pus. He repeated the procedure on his two sons, who both suffered a mild case of cowpox for a couple of days, but stayed free of the more serious smallpox. Jetsy's wife, however, became ill with a bad fever, which the local doctor was called in to treat – she recovered and lived another fifty years, but Jesty's secret was out and the first documented case of vaccination against smallpox became public. Jesty, however, was scorned for his actions: local accounts state he was "hooted at, reviled and pelted whenever he attended markets in the neighbourhood. He remained undaunted and never failed from this cause to attend to his duties." In 1797, Jesty and his family moved to Worth Matravers, where he carried on his pioneering work, though the medical establishment never accepted that Jesty's work had pre-empted theirs by twenty years. Jesty, however, freely admitted that local farmers had been using similar techniques for years before his documented work, and the inscription on his gravestone reads that Jesty was "the first person (known) that introduced the Cow Pox by inoculation".

There are a couple of great walks from Worth Matravers. One of the best is to take the signed footpath from Worth's little pond down to **Winspit**. It's about a mile and a half down a steep valley path to a series of eerie former quarries and ruined quarrymen's homes – the quarry caves look incredibly unstable, though there are no fences and most people happily wander around them. You can then continue along the coast path southwest for another mile and a half to St Aldheim's head, where there is a tiny lifeguard station and the ancient **St Aldheim's Chapel**. Possibly Norman in origin, legend has it that it was built as a warning to other sailors by a father, whose son drowned in a storm in 1140. From the chapel, take the footpath inland and the well-signed footpath returns to Worth Matravers via Weston Farm (around a further two miles).

Chapman's Pool and Kingston

From just beyond the church in Worth Matravers, you can pick up a fine walk to **Chapman's Pool** (two miles), with a fairly steep final descent to a semicircular bay. The beach is a mixture of mud and gravel, but as it can only be reached on foot or by boat, it is especially popular in summer with walkers and yachties.

Two miles northwest of Worth Matravers is another attractive stone village at **Kingston**, whose hilltop position commands superb views down towards Corfe Castle. There are some great walks from here too, either south to the coast at Chapman's Pool (two miles), or on the Purbeck Way down to Corfe Castle – take the path that leaves from the eastern edge of the village or pick up the well-signed path off the B3069, around a mile east of Kingston. There's an excellent **pub** here, too, *The Scott Arms* (☎01929 480270), an old inn with a warren of cosy rooms at the front and a large, modern-looking back room that doubles as its restaurant. But the biggest draw is its garden, which commands a stupendous view over Corfe Castle in the valley below, a scene that can have changed little in five hundred years. The food is substantial and varied and good value at around £9 for mains.

Kimmeridge

Five miles by road east of Kingston lies a lovely Dorset cove, **Kimmeridge Bay**. It's part of the Smedmore Estate, so you have to pay to park your car here, or you can park for free at the small quarry car park a ten-minute walk above the bay. The beach here is not particularly appealing, an almost-black mixture of limestone ridges and fossil-rich clay, so rich in oil that you can literally set fire to it. BP has exploited this area which happens to be the largest onshore oil field in the country – though it's so well landscaped you'd hardly believe it; evidence is a nodding donkey that's been extracting oil from the ground since the 1950s.

Despite the oil, the row of fishermen's cottages and idyllic location make the bay well worth a visit. It forms part of the Purbeck Marine Wildlife Reserve and you can find details of a marked snorkelling trail (bring your own equipment) at the small marine centre at the east end of the bay – the limestone ridges that jut out to sea make the area particularly rich in marine life; dolphins, Portuguese man-of-war, spider crabs and brittlefish have all been spotted around here.

Sitting on the hillside to the east of Kimmeridge Bay is the **Clavell Tower**, built in 1830 as an observatory and folly by a local reverend – 25m from its current position. In 2007/8 the whole structure was moved inland as it was getting perilously close to the eroding cliff edge. In Victorian times the tower was visited often by Thomas Hardy, and also inspired the P.D. James novel, *The Black Tower*. Today it is run by the Landmark Trust, who rents it out for holiday lets (☎01628 825925, ⓦwww.landmarktrust.org.uk; £470 a week in low season, up to £880 in high season).

Tyneham and Worbarrow Bay

Five miles by road east of Kimmeridge, nestled in a remote valley reached via the army ranges (open most weekends and at other times as signed), **Tyneham** was a thriving rural community until it was taken over by the army during World War II when the entire population was evacuated, never to return. Most of the village is now in ruins, but you can wander around and get a good idea of what life would have been like in prewar rural Dorset. Some of the buildings, such as the church, have been restored and maintained to their original condition: the school room is still laid out as it would have been in the 1940s, with desks, samples of work and textbooks, a teacher's blackboard and little coat hooks with the children's names.

A mile south, reached via a rough track, **Worbarrow Bay** is a crescent-shaped sand-and-shingle beach overlooked by the distinctive hillock of Worbarrow, which you can climb up. It's not the nicest beach on this stretch, but is good for beachcombing and to admire the remarkably blue water thanks to its chalky substrata. Like Tyneham, there was once a thriving community here, though the fishermen were also moved out during the war and little is left to show their time here.

Tyneham also marks the starting point of a great **two-hour round walk** via Flower's Barrow, which embraces superb coastal views from the top of a ridge, part of the South West Coast path and an Iron Age hillfort. Start at the track that leads uphill behind Tyneham's church. This heads to the top of the ridge; by a communications mast, turn left and follow the track towards the coast for fifteen minutes. As it begins to go downhill, take the clear grassy track on the left – the views over the coast and inland over the ranges and to Lulworth Castle from the top here are absolutely stunning. Within ten minutes you will reach Flower's Barrow, an Iron Age fort in a distinctive concave dip with awesome views over the coast. The fort – probably a protective gateway for coastal routes north – was built by the Durotriges tribe, who also built Maiden Castle. From the fort, join the coastal path east, which heads down a very steep grassy hill to Worbarrow Bay – this is a fifteen-minute walk. From the beach, it's a mile back to Tyneham up a wooded valley, home to various wildlife including badgers and bats.

Lulworth Cove, Durdle Door and around

The quaint thatch-and-stone village of **West Lulworth** forms a prelude to **Lulworth Cove**, a perfect almost-circular bay surrounded by tall cliffs. The bay formed when the sea broke through a weakness in the cliffs and then eroded them from behind, forming a round cave that eventually collapsed to leave a bay enclosed by sandstone cliffs. Sadly, the diminutive and highly picturesque former fishing village at the head of the cove is now dwarfed by a giant car park and its attendant tourist facilities, including the **Lulworth Heritage Centre** (daily: March–Oct 10am–6pm; Nov–Feb 10am–4pm; free) which details the local geology. And it is the geology that pulls in hundreds of school parties as well as tourists. Immediately west of the cove, **Stair Hole** is a roofless sea cave riddled with arches that will eventually crumble to form another cove. Stair Hole is also famous for the so-called Lulworth Crumple – a perfect cross section of folds in the rock.

If you can, come out of season when the cove's magic returns and the surrounding coastal paths are quieter. This is especially true of the footpath to Dorset's other iconic site – the limestone arch of **Durdle Door**. Most people take the uphill route to the arch, which starts from the car park at Lulworth Cove, but you can avoid the steep climb by walking from the *Durdle Door Holiday Park*, on the road to East Chaldon from West Lulworth. The arch itself sits at the end of a long shingle beach (which can be accessed via steep steps), a lovely place for catching the sun's rays and swimming in fresh, clear water. There are other steps to a bay just east of Durdle Door, St Oswald's Bay, with another shingle beach and offshore rocks that you can swim out to.

Arrival and accommodation

There are fairly regular **bus services** to Lulworth from Wool (see p.90) and Dorchester (see p.95). **Drivers** get funnelled into the giant car park by Lulworth Cove, though if you don't mind a short if steep walk, you can usually park up in West Lulworth around the church.

There are several places to **stay** around the cove itself, though in high season these may be full, so you'll have to base yourself up the hill in West Lulworth. **Campers** can pitch up at the superbly positioned *Durdle Door Holiday Park* (☎01929 400200, ⊛www.lulworth.com; closed Nov–Feb) on the cliffs above Durdle Door, while West Lulworth has a very basic YHA **hostel** in a lovely rural location at the end of School Lane (☎0870 3719331, ⊛yha.org.uk; sporadic opening in winter; £13.95), a stone's throw from the Dorset Coast Path.

Cromwell House Hotel Lulworth Cove ☎01929 400253, Ⓦwww.lulworthcove.co.uk. Slightly ageing but homely rooms in this Victorian hotel that enjoys a great position on a bluff just above the cove. Front rooms have a superb outlook and there is also a lovely terraced garden with a small heated outdoor pool. ❻

Gatton House Main Rd, West Lulworth ☎01929 400252, Ⓦwww.lulworthcovebedandbreakfast .com. Attractive early twentieth-century country retreat set back from the main road above West Lulworth. Great views from most of the spotless rooms. Closed Oct–April. ❸

Lulworth Cove Inn Lulworth Cove ☎01929 400333, Ⓦwww.lulworth-cove.com. Comfortable if small rooms above a seventeenth-century inn; the best rooms have little coast-facing terraces. ❹

Tewkesbury Cottage Main Rd, West Lulworth ☎01929 400561. This tiny thatched cottage opens right onto the main road, though luckily there is a pleasant patio garden; it has a couple of cosy doubles, one en suite. ❶

The Beach House Lulworth Cove ☎01929 400404, Ⓦwww.lulworthbeachhouse.com. The first choice in Lulworth itself, especially if you can bag one of the front rooms that come with their own cove-view terraces (❼). Contemporary decor and a fine downstairs restaurant. ❹

Eating and drinking

Castle Inn Main Rd, West Lulworth. Up in the village, this sixteenth-century thatched pub has a lovely terraced garden, a good range of local ales and a selection of traditional pub games. The bar meals consist of high-quality pub grub, with dishes such as home-made steak and ale pie and beef bourguignon. It also has a few rooms (❸).

Lulworth Cove Inn Decent pub food, local Blandford ales, and a pleasant garden. Specializes in local seafood and game, with dishes such as wild boar and apple faggots, and traditional pies: main courses £8–12.

Pebbles *The Beach House*. The delightful garden with views of the cove is a perfect spot for a meal or drink. The menu, unsurprisingly, is fairly fishy, with dishes such as crab and fennel risotto (£11) or fish pie (£10).

Lulworth Castle

Around three miles northeast of Lulworth Cove at East Lulworth is the impressive **Lulworth Castle** (Sun–Fri late Sept to March 10.30am–4pm; April to late Sept 10.30am–4pm; £8.50). Originally built in the sixteenth century by Viscount Bindon to entertain royal hunting parties, the castle has been altered over the centuries and much of the present ornate interior dates from rebuilding work after a fire in 1929. The grounds include a small children's animal farm complete with alpacas, pygmy goats and pot-bellied pigs. The castle also lays on various events, foremost of which is **Camp Bestival**, a three-day music festival with an emphasis on family entertainment: details on Ⓦwww.campbestival.net. For **food**, head opposite to *The Weld Arms*, a great thatched pub dating back to the seventeenth century with decent pub food and a large beer garden backing onto fields. Alternatively, just up the road in the former Catholic school, *The Old School* does café food and has its own gift shop and internet access.

Wool and around

There is little of interest in **Wool**, whose main claim to fame is the residency of the D'Urbervilles in Hardy's *Tess of the D'Urbervilles*. However, you may well pass through it, as it is on the main rail line and gives easy access to a number of local attractions. Best of these, around 1.5 miles north of Wool at Longthorns, is **Monkey World** (daily: Sept–June 10am–5pm; July–Aug 10am–6pm; £10.50, children £7.25; ☎01929 462537, Ⓦwww.monkeyworld.co.uk) a well-run

▲ Rescued chimps at Monkey World

primate sanctuary in 65 acres of attractive Purbeck countryside, that's home to 240 animals, including the largest collection of chimps outside Africa. Most of the animals have been rescued from laboratories, zoos or circuses around the world and include gibbons, orang-utans, macaques and woolly monkeys along with an array of very cute smaller beasts such as lemurs, squirrel monkeys and marmosets. All the enclosures have loads of swings, ropes, trees and ladders for the monkeys to play on, and at the end of the park, there's a great adventure play area for children, with similar rope ladders and climbing frames. You can watch the animals being fed at various stages in the day.

West of here, around two miles to the north of Wool, at the rather bleak Bovington Camp, lies the impressive **Bovington Tank Museum** (daily 10am–5pm; £11 annual pass, which allows unlimited re-entry for a year; ☎01929 405096, ⓦwww.tankmuseum.org). Recently renovated, the centre contains the world's biggest collection of tanks and is one of the most important collections of military vehicles in the world, from the earliest armoured vehicles to the latest models available to the British army. You can scramble around inside the vehicles, practise driving them in simulators and learn about various military operations, including the recreation of life in the trenches in the eerie and hard-hitting World War I experience. Dramatic displays of the tanks in action are also held during the school holidays in the outdoor tank arena.

Just by the exit to the Museum lies **Clouds Hill** (mid-March to Oct Thurs–Sun noon–5pm or dusk; £4.50; NT; ☏01929 405616), one-time home to Thomas Edward Lawrence aka Lawrence of Arabia (1888–1935), who spent his retirement here after being stationed at Bovington. He had just completed the *Seven Pillars of Wisdom*, his classic account of his campaigns in World War I to unite Arab forces against the Ottoman Turks – allies of the Germans – and their successful war of attrition. After the war, Lawrence joined the RAF, working on speedboats. He was also a motorbike fan, and it was in 1935 that Lawrence died after a motorbike accident on the road from Bovington. Today you can look round his simply furnished cottage, peppered with photos of his life; there is also a pleasant three-mile round walk around the cottage to a hilltop picnic spot.

Central Dorset

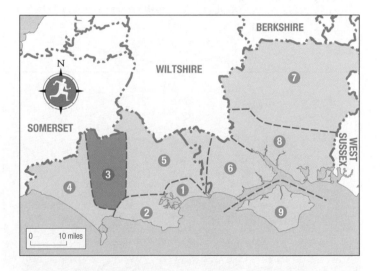

CHAPTER 3 # Highlights

* **Maiden Castle** One of Europe's greatest hillforts, partly dating back to the Stone Age. See p.103

* **Kingston Maurward** The manor and gardens of what is now an agricultural college represent the best of rural English opulence. See p.104

* **Hardy's Cottage** Even if you've never read his books, you'll enjoy the atmospheric walk to his tiny birthplace near Dorchester. See p.105

* **Cerne Abbas** It is hard not to be impressed by the chalk giant, though the village of Cerne Abbas is also a delight. See p.107

* **Sherborne New Castle** Once the home of Sir Walter Raleigh, with fantastic lakeside walks. See p.111

▲ The Cerne Abbas giant

Central Dorset

Central **Dorset** embodies the county at its most rural, traditional and mystical. This was the area that inspired Thomas Hardy, who used many of its ancient sites in his evocative novels of Victorian England. Hardy's birthplace can be visited at the tiny village of **Higher Bockhampton**, as can his later home in **Dorchester** where he spent most of his life. The country town is steeped in history: it's home to a Roman villa, the ancient **Maumbury Rings** and the even older hillfort of **Maiden Castle**. Dorchester is also where the Tolpuddle Martyrs were tried in the nineteenth century – a museum in the nearby village of **Tolpuddle** details the plight of these brave campaigners for workers' rights. The area is dotted with grand country mansions, too, including **Athelhampton House** and **Kingston Maurward**, both are surrounded by elaborate grounds. A little north brings you to the idyllic village of **Cerne Abbas**, best known for its mysterious chalk figure carved into a hillside and as a wonderful area for walks. North of here is another historic town, **Sherborne**, the ancient capital of Wessex and home to a magnificent abbey and two castles.

There are limited bus services in this rural area, and it's a pleasure to drive along the pretty country lanes, so a car is the best way to get around the region. It's also ideal cycling and walking country, peppered with country pubs and thatched villages. But be aware, there are some steep hills and valleys. Dorchester is the busiest town in the region, though even this is not very touristy as most visitors head south to the coast in the summer, and in the countryside north of Dorchester, you're really off the beaten track here.

Dorchester

DORCHESTER, Dorset's county town, is forever associated with local author **Thomas Hardy**, who called it "Casterbridge" in his novels. At first sight it is disappointing – a workaday county town with the usual ubiquitous chain stores and traffic-ridden high street – but stick around to explore its backstreets, and you'll discover more of the town's ancient and distinctive character. Stone Age relics can still be seen at Maumbury Rings, and dotted around town are the remains of Roman walls and a villa, while the names of several of its pubs and cafés hark back to the time of Judge Jeffrey's "Bloody Assizes" and to the local Tolpuddle Martyrs. For most visitors, however, this is essentially **Thomas Hardy**'s town: he spent much of his life here in **Max Gate**, to the south of town; his statue now stands on High West Street; and there is a recreation of his

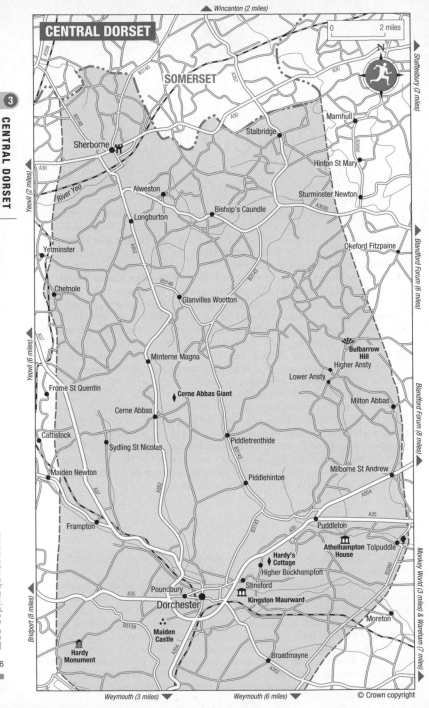

CENTRAL DORSET

▲ Wincanton (2 miles)

SOMERSET

0   2 miles

N

▶ Shaftesbury (2 miles)

Sherborne

Marnhull

Stalbridge

Hinton St Mary

◀ A30

◀ Yeovil (2 miles)

River Yeo

Alweston

Sturminster Newton

Longburton

Bishop's Caundle

Yetminster

Okeford Fitzpaine

▶ Blandford Forum (6 miles)

Chetnole

Glanvilles Wootton

◀ Yeovil (6 miles)

Minterne Magna

Bulbarrow Hill

Higher Ansty

Frome St Quentin

Lower Ansty

Cerne Abbas Giant

Cerne Abbas

Milton Abbas

▶ Blandford Forum (8 miles)

Cattistock

Sydling St Nicolas

Piddletrenthide

Maiden Newton

Piddlehinton

Milborne St Andrew

Frampton

Puddleton

Athelhampton House

Tolpuddle

▶ Monkey World (3 miles) & Wareham (7 miles)

Hardy's Cottage

Higher Bockhampton

Poundbury

Stinsford

Kingston Maurward

Dorchester

Moreton

Maiden Castle

Hardy Monument

Broadmayne

▲ Weymouth (3 miles)   ▲ Weymouth (6 miles)

© Crown copyright

study in the **Dorset Country Museum**. The modern town has a pleasant central core of mostly seventeenth-century and Georgian buildings, with some grand Victorian additions, notably the mock medieval keep, now the **Military Museum**. There are also an unusually large number of museums for a town this size, including some surprising recreations of history at the **Tutankhamun Exhibition** and the **Terracotta Warriors Museum**, as well as the family-oriented **Teddy Bear** and **Dinosaur museums**. The best time to visit the town is on a Wednesday, when the **market** is in full swing.

Some history
The **Maumbury Rings**, to the south of the town, are evidence that this was an important site in Stone Age times (around 2500 BC), though they were later adapted by the Romans, who held vast gladiatorial combats here. In around 60 AD, the Romans established a settlement called Durnovaria that, by the second century AD, was large and important enough to have its own aqueduct, public baths and forum. Remnants of their stay are apparent in the form of the **Roman Town House** (see p.100) and the old Roman Wall at the end of Princes Street, though most of these were replaced in the eighteenth century by tree-lined avenues called "Walks" (Bowling Alley Walk, West Walk and Colliton Walk). After the Romans left, Dorchester became a provincial agricultural town known for its wool and breweries. In the Middle Ages it held three weekly markets and entertainment, including bear-baiting, took place at the Maumbury Rings. Much of the town was destroyed in a series of fires in the seventeenth century (resulting in a ban on thatched cottages in 1776). Around this time, Dorchester became associated with the notorious **Judge Jeffreys**, who, after the ill-fated rebellion of the Duke of Monmouth against James II, held his "Bloody Assizes" on Cornhill in 1685. A total of 292 men were sentenced to death, though most got away with a flogging and transportation to the West Indies, while 74 were hung, drawn and quartered, their heads stuck on pikes throughout Dorset and Somerset. Some were executed at Maumbury Rings – used then for public hangings.

Throughout the nineteenth century, Dorchester flourished as a **market town** – it was at this time (1834) that the **Tolpuddle Martyrs** (see p.107) were tried in Dorchester for attempting to improve workers' rights. The railway arrived in 1847, in a flurry of great social change. This was the Dorchester that Thomas Hardy regularly visited from his home at nearby Higher Bockhampton before he moved here in 1885. Today, the town remains a thriving market town with a population of around 16,000, swelled by the modern extension of **Poundbury** to the east. This modern town, built in a traditional style, was begun in 1993, largely thanks to the support and ideas of HRH Prince Charles (see p.101).

Arrival and information
Dorchester has two **train stations**, both of them to the south of the centre: trains from Weymouth and London arrive at Dorchester South, while Bath and Bristol trains use the Dorchester West station. Most **buses** stop around the car park on Acland Road, to the east of South Street. The **tourist office** is in Antelope Walk (May–Sept Mon–Sat 9am–5pm, Sun 10am–3pm; Nov–March Mon–Sat 9am–4pm; ☎01305 267992, ⊛www.westdorset.com): it has some useful free leaflets detailing various **historical walks** around town, such as the Thomas Hardy Walk and the Roman Town walk, which vary from thirty to ninety minutes. There are plenty of short or long stay **car parks** round the centre. **Bike rental** is available from Dorchester Cycles, 31 Great Western Rd (☎01305 268787) for around £12 a day.

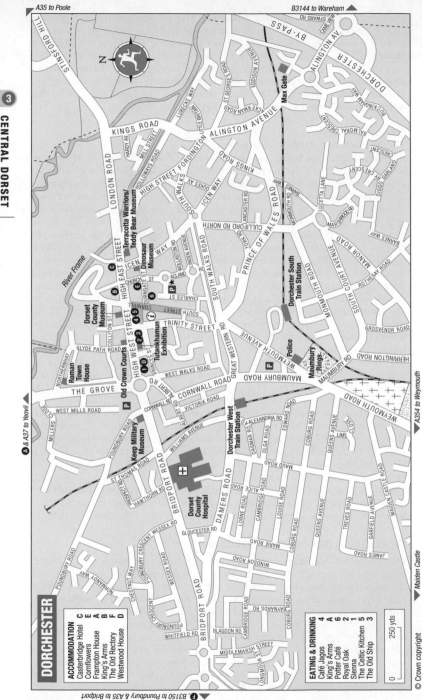

DORCHESTER

ACCOMMODATION
Casterbridge Hotel	C
Cornflowers	E
Frampton House	A
King's Arms	B
The Old Rectory	F
Westwood House	D

EATING & DRINKING
Café Jagos	4
King's Arms	A
Potter Café	6
Royal Oak	2
Sienna	1
The Celtic Kitchen	5
The Old Ship	3

0 — 250 yds

© Crown copyright

A35 to Poole

B3144 to Wareham

STINSFORD HILL

KINGS ROAD

LONDON ROAD

River Frome

Dorset County Museum

Roman Town House

THE GROVE

Old Crown Courts

Keep Military Museum

Tutankhamun Exhibition

Terracotta Warriors/ Teddy Bear Museum

Dinosaur Museum

HIGH EAST STREET

HIGH WEST STREET

TRINITY STREET

WEST WALKS ROAD

CORNWALL ROAD

Dorchester West Train Station

Dorset County Hospital

BRIDPORT ROAD

DAMERS ROAD

HIGH STREET FORDINGTON

KINGS ROAD

ALINGTON AVENUE

Max Gate

PRINCE OF WALES ROAD

Dorchester South Train Station

Police

Maumbury Rings

WEYMOUTH AVENUE

MAUMBURY RD

GROSVENOR ROAD

MONMOUTH ROAD

MANOR ROAD

DORCHESTER BY-PASS

ALINGTON AV

A & A37 to Yeovil

A354 to Weymouth

Maiden Castle

B3150 to Poundbury & A35 to Bridport

Accommodation

There are a few reasonable places to stay in Dorchester itself, but you may well be tempted to stay in some of the picturesque surrounding villages, many of which have excellent overnight options.

In town

Casterbridge Hotel 49 High East St ☎01305 264043, ⓦwww.casterbridgehotel.co.uk. Friendly hotel on the main through-road with small but homely rooms. There's a relaxing communal lounge and small patio garden, with some rooms off it, including a family room (£150). ❻

Cornflowers 4 Durngate St ☎01305 751703, ⓦwww.cornflowers.biz. Cosy B&B in a seventeenth-century townhouse a short walk from the centre. Just three double rooms, two en suite. ❹

King's Arms 30 High East St ☎01305 265353, ⓦwww.kingsarmsdorchester.com. Spacious rooms above a Georgian inn with its own bar and restaurant (see p.102). Rooms at the front can be noisy. ❻

Westwood House 29 High West St ☎01305 268018, ⓦwww.westwoodhouse.co.uk. Comfortable townhouse on the busy high street, with well-furnished rooms, and a good breakfast. ❸

Out of town

Frampton House Frampton ☎01300 320308, ⓦwww.frampton-house.co.uk. In a small village five miles northwest of Dorchester, this grand Grade II listed eighteenth-century manor house has played host to the likes of Thomas Hardy and Landseer. It has three very comfortable bedrooms, one with a four-poster bed, and a tennis court in the grounds, next to a park laid out by "Capability" Brown. ❹

The Old Rectory Winterbourne Steepleton ☎01305 889468, ⓦwww.theoldrectorybandb .co.uk. A lovely former rectory in the tiny, pretty village of Winterbourne Steepleton, four miles west of Dorchester. Dating from 1850, the B&B has four comfortable en-suite rooms, one with a four-poster, and attractive well-kept gardens. ❷

Dorset County Museum and Old Crown Courts

The best place to learn about Dorchester's history is the impressive **Dorset County Museum** on High West Street (July–Sept daily 10am–5pm; Oct–June Mon–Sat 10am–5pm; £6.50; ⓦwww.dorsetcountymuseum.org). Founded in 1846 to record the county's social and environmental history, the Victorian building, complete with balconied galleries, is quite a sight. Inside, there is a rich hotchpotch of archeological and geological displays tracing Celtic and Roman history, including a section on Maiden Castle; some fine paintings including works by Thomas Gainsborough; and some evocative historical photos of the region. There's also a Jurassic Coast gallery divulging the history of the local coastline, with the help of animated flying dinosaurs, as well as fossils and treasures found along its 95-mile length. Pride of place goes to the re-creation of Thomas Hardy's study, where his pens are inscribed with the names of the books he wrote with them.

Just west of the museum are the **Old Crown Courts**, also known as Shire Hall (court Mon–Fri 10am–noon & 2–4pm; free; guided tour of court and cells Mon–Fri at 2pm, 2.45pm & 3.30pm; £2). It was here, in 1834 that six men from the nearby village of Tolpuddle, known as the Tolpuddle Martyrs, were sentenced to transportation. While the council buildings are still in use, the room in which the Martyrs were tried has been preserved as a memorial, and you can visit it, sit behind the judge's desk and bang his gavel or ponder their fate from the juror's bench. There's more information about the martyrs in the Tolpuddle Martyrs Museum in nearby Tolpuddle (see p.107).

▲ Dorchester's charming backstreets

Roman Town House and the Keep Military Museum

Tucked away behind the County Hall is the country's best-preserved **Roman Town House** (open access, free; Ⓦ www.romantownhouse.org). Discovered in 1937 almost by chance (while workers were digging the foundations for a new council building), the remains date from the fourth century and were almost certainly the home of an important Romano-British family involved in the governing council of Durnovaria. The only example in the country of a fully exposed Roman townhouse, it's a fine Roman villa with a well-preserved mosaic floor: the mosaics and some of the rooms, including the remains of a hypocaust, are protected beneath a covered roof, while others are open to the elements. Picture boards around the site make it easy to imagine the villa in its heyday, and give a good idea of how the Romans would have used each room.

Five minutes' walk southeast of here rise the impressive battlements of **Keep Military Museum** (April–Sept Mon–Sat 10am–5pm; Oct–March Tues–Sat & school half-term Mon 10am–4.30pm; £6; Ⓦ www.keepmilitarymuseum.org), on Bridport Road. Though resembling an impressive medieval fortress, the building is actually a Victorian replica built in 1879, and traces the fortunes of the Dorset and Devonshire regiments over three hundred years, showcasing uniforms and weapons. You can also see one of the original cells beneath the fortress, which has been reconstructed to give an idea of what life was like in a military prison. While the military history in the museum is of fairly specialist interest, most people will find the highlight a trip up the narrow spiral staircase to the battlements, from where you get sweeping views over the town and surrounding countryside.

Other town museums

If you find yourself here on a wet day or with restless children, there are several museums that warrant a visit. It seems rather incongruous to have a reconstruction of Tutankhamun's tomb in a converted church in Dorset, but the **Tutankhamun Exhibition**, High West Street (daily: April–Oct 9.30am–5.30pm; Nov–March Mon–Fri 9.30am–5pm, Sat–Sun 10am–5pm; £6.95, children £5.50; ⒲www .tutankhamun-exhibition.co.uk) is just that. It houses many of the recreated artefacts from the British Museum's original exhibition on Egypt's most celebrated pharaoh, with a replica of his tomb as it would have been on its discovery in 1922, copies of his treasures and a model of the mummy itself. Hoping to follow on its success is the **Terracotta Warriors Museum** (daily: April–Oct 10am–5pm; Nov–March 10am–4.30pm; £5.75, children £4; ⒲www .terracottawarriors.co.uk) on the corner of High East Street and Salisbury Street. Impressive replicas of the warriors line up alongside interactive displays on the history of why they were made, certainly enough to whet your appetite to see the real things in China. The museum shares the premises of the **Teddy Bear Museum** (same hours and price or combined ticket to both museums; £8.55, children £6; ⒲www.teddybearmuseum.co.uk) with a cute collection of bears throughout the ages, including human-sized bears and celebrity bears such as Paddington. It will certainly appeal to younger children, as will the **Dinosaur Museum** (daily: April–Oct 10am–5pm; Nov–March 10am–4.30pm; £6.75, children £4.95; ⒲www.thedinosaurmuseum.com) on the corner of Durngate Street and Icen Way. There are some fine life-size models of T-Rex, various fossils, skeletons and inter-active displays packed with dinosaur facts and figures.

Maumbury Rings and Max Gate

Around ten minutes south of town, near the Railway Station South, a series of grassy ridges mark the **Maumbury Rings**, where many of Dorchester's less savoury historical events were carried out, including gladiator fights, bear-baiting and public executions (see p.97). In the first century AD, the Romans converted the Neolithic site here into one of the largest amphitheatres in the country by removing earth from the centre of the rings and using it to make a bank round the edge. The Rings were further re-modelled in 1642–43 to become an artillery fort, built to protect Dorchester's southern edge during the English Civil war. Today, the site is used by the local youth as a skateboard park, and hosts the odd band, play and firework display. Fifteen minutes' walk west of here, near the junction of the Wareham road and the A35, lies **Max Gate**, on Arlington Avenue (April–Sept Mon, Wed & Sun 2–5pm; £3; NT), the former home of Thomas Hardy. You can only visit the hall, dining room and drawing room, but anyone who has also been to Hardy's Cottage where he was born (see p.105) will realize how much his social standing had improved by the time he moved here in 1885. You can admire the spot where he wrote *Tess, Jude the Obscure* and *The Mayor of Casterbridge*, as well as some of the furniture in a house that he also helped design.

Poundbury

Welded onto the western suburbs of Dorchester is Prince Charles' "eco-community" of Poundbury, part of the Duchy of Cornwall's estate. *A Vision of Britain*, Prince Charles' book, published in 1989, set in motion the principals behind a pioneering development; begun in 1993, the village isn't set to be completed until around 2025. The principals are sound: a traditional community of houses, mostly modelled on country cottages and Georgian houses, built in a series of wending streets, squares and crescents unblighted by unnecessary street furniture, with local work opportunities on their doorstep. The results, however, are somewhat mixed. Some residents like the

Hardy's Wessex

Thomas Hardy set many of his novels in "Wessex", an ancient name he used for an area that embraced much of southwest England, and in particular in "South Wessex," which is modern-day Dorset. Hardy used fictional names for his towns, such as "Sandbourne" and "Casterbridge" which, although they have changed hugely since his day, still obviously refer to Bournemouth and Dorchester respectively. Some rural communities that Hardy described in detail are little changed today: Beaminster, for example, is easily recognized as Hardy's "Emminster" in *Tess of the D'Urbevilles*, which ends in "Wintoncester" prison – based on Winchester. The riverside setting of Sturminster Newton, where Hardy also lived, is called "Stourcastle" in *The Return of the Native*. Below is a list of some of Hardy's better-known fictional names and the real-life places they represent:

Abbot's-Cernel	Cerne Abbas	**Marlott**	Marnhull
Abbotsea	Abbotsbury	**Mellstock**	Stinsford and Higher
Anglebury	Wareham		& Lower Bockhampton
Budmouth	Weymouth	**Port Bredy**	Bridport
Chaseborough	Cranborne	**Shaston**	Shaftesbury
Evershead	Evershot	**Isle of Slingers**	Isle of Portland
Havenpool	Poole	**Solentsea**	Southsea
Kingsbere	Bere Regis	**Stoke Barehills**	Basingstoke
Knollsea	Swanage	**Street of Wells**	Fortuneswell
Lulwind Cove	Lulworth Cove		

peaceful and spacious streets where parking is rarely a problem, while others consider it a boring enclave where nothing much goes on apart from continuing building work. There are certainly few facilities, and cars seem to dominate the environment, but it is worth a wander or drive round to experience a very different urban landscape from anywhere else in Dorset. It is around fifteen minutes' walk west of town; the Dorchester tourist office sells a map of it, which may come in handy as there are virtually no signposts.

Eating and drinking

Café Jagos 8 High West St ☎01305 266056. Good-value salads and sandwiches come in large portions at this pleasant café with contemporary decor – the fresh tuna salad, paninis and grills are all tasty.

King's Arms 30 High East St ☎01305 265353. This eighteenth-century coaching house has its own restaurant area and bar with a selection of moderately priced pub food and daily specials, most made from locally sourced ingredients. Main courses from £8.

Potter Café 19 Durngate St ☎01305 260312. Very appealing café-restaurant with its own log fire in winter and small garden. A range of inexpensive dishes such as fish soups, tiger prawns and curries from £6–9. Closed eves Sept–April.

Royal Oak 20–21 High West St. Inexpensive pub grub, such as scampi and chips and burgers, for around £6–7, at this old pub with a small patio behind.

Sienna 36 High West St ☎01305 250022. Small, upmarket restaurant specializing in modern British cuisine like duck with root vegetables and poached saddle of West Country venison. Lunch menus start at around £20 for two courses up to £37 for three courses at dinner. Closed Sun & Mon.

The Celtic Kitchen Antelope Walk. Home-made West Country pasties make great picnic food – try some of the more unusual fillings such as Stilton, apple and walnut.

The Old Ship 16 High West St. Dorchester's oldest pub dates from the 1600s, but has a contemporary feel inside, with wooden floors and comfy sofas. It has a good selection of real ales, with different guest beers each month, and serves the usual pub staples as well as some more unusual South American dishes.

Around Dorchester

Though Hardy would struggle to recognize many aspects of modern-day Dorchester, much of the countryside around it is little changed from his time, and the area is well worth exploring. Hardy's birthplace can be visited in **Higher Bockhampton**, while the nearby village of **Tolpuddle**, famed for its trade union martyrs, is highly attractive in its own right. There are also some grand estates at **Athelhampton House** and **Kingston Maurwood**, the latter with superb grounds and adjacent to pretty **Stinsford**, where Hardy's heart lies buried in the church graveyard. Finally, one of Europe's greatest Iron Age hillforts is a must-see at **Maiden Castle**.

Maiden Castle and the Hardy Monument

Though it is only just over a mile southeast of Dorchester, and approached through residential suburbs, the spectacular hillfort of **Maiden Castle** nevertheless whisks you back thousands of years in time. It's a fairly steep – but lovely – climb up grassy paths to the top, where you begin to get an idea of the scale of the defences. The site, which covers a total area of 47 acres, is made up of concentric earthen ramparts enclosing a grassy plateau the size of 50 football pitches. This was once home to several hundred of the Durotriges tribe who would have been protected by the vast ramparts – some rising to 20 feet in height – topped then by wooden fences and staggered gates to hinder enemy attacks. The Durotriges tribe built all this in around 450 BC on the site of an even older Stone Age settlement dating back to around 3000 BC. There is evidence that the Stone Age dwellers built a defensive ditch of 545m in length; they also left various burial mounds. The site was finally conquered by the Romans in 43 AD, when the residents were either killed or moved out to what was to become Dorchester. In the fourth century, the Romans built a temple here (its foundations survive), but shortly afterwards the site was abandoned. Today it is grazed by sheep, but there are various footpaths around the ramparts; there is nothing to stop you finding one with a good view for an afternoon picnic.

▲ Maiden Castle

Visible from miles around on an exposed hilltop near Portesham, the **Hardy Monument** (NT) is not dedicated to the well-known author associated with the region, but to his distant relative, Vice Admiral Thomas Masterman Hardy of "Kiss me, Hardy" fame. The 72ft-high monument commemorates Hardy, who served aboard Nelson's ship HMS *Victory* (see p.242) during the Battle of Trafalgar in 1805. The monument, built of Portland Stone, is currently closed to the public, due to serious erosion caused by its exposed location. When it does re-open, check the National Trust website (⬤ www.nationaltrust.org) for the latest situation – the views from the top are stunning.

Kingston Maurward

The **Kingston Maurward** estate (daily 10am–5.30pm; closed for a couple of weeks over Christmas; £3), two miles northeast of Dorchester, is made up of a classic Palladian house, built in 1720, surrounded by attractive gardens. The estate is now used by an agricultural college, so the main house is not open to the public, but the grounds, gardens and animal park, which are also used for teaching purposes, are fine attractions. The grounds encompass various types of garden, from the "Capability" Brown-style rolling lawns leading down to a lake and a temple, to the more formal Arts and Crafts-style series of Edwardian garden rooms, to a tranquil Japanese garden. The animal park is great for children, being home to pigs, ducks, chickens, ponies, goats, guinea pigs, donkeys and emus, many of which can be cuddled and fed. Because it's part of the agricultural college, there are regular keeper talks about the animals' welfare, and there are also an entertaining children's play area, and sometimes tractor rides round the estate. Highlight of the year at Kingston Maurward is the **lambing weekends** – the dates vary according to the weather, but they usually take place over two or three weekends in March – where you can get right up close to the lambing pens and watch the lambs being born. There are always informative agricultural staff on hand to answer questions, and you can even bottle-feed the lambs. You can stay on the estate at the privately owned Elizabethan *Old Manor* house (☎ 01305 261110, ⬤ www.kingston-maurward.co.uk; ⬤), built in the 1590s. It offers **B&B** in grand Tudor style: all the bedrooms have views over the grounds and parkland, and one has a four-poster bed.

Stinsford

Just behind the walls of the Kingston Maurward estate, St Michael's Church in **Stinsford** (Hardy's "Mellstock" in *Under the Greenwood Tree*) is an attractive little country church dating from the early thirteenth century. For such a small building – its average congregation is thirty – it has a surprisingly large number of eminent residents: buried in its churchyard are Thomas Hardy's heart, his two wives, his parents, his brother and two sisters, his grandparents, aunt, uncle and cousin, as well as the Poet Laureate Cecil Day-Lewis, father of the actor Daniel Day-Lewis. The Hardy family connections began with Hardy's grandfather, father and uncle who all played instruments in the church choir. Hardy himself was baptized here, after which he attended, then taught at, the Sunday school. It was Hardy's specific wish to be buried at Stinsford, but it was decided that he should be honoured with a place in Poet's Corner in Westminster Abbey. On 16 January, 1928 his ashes were buried in Westminster Abbey at the same time as his heart was buried here in the grave of his first wife, Emma, where they were later joined by his second wife, Florence. Inside the church you can see the Norman font where Hardy was baptized, and the beautiful stained-glass memorial window, designed by Douglas Strachen in 1930, and dedicated to

Thomas Hardy (1840–1928) was born in the village of Higher Bockhampton, just outside Dorchester, and was the oldest of four children. He spent much of his childhood exploring the rural countryside that was to have such a great influence on his later books – some of the most charming of his descriptions of the village he was born and grew up in can be found in *Under the Greenwood Tree* (see p.295). But he was no slouch – a keen reader, he studied Latin, Greek and French, played the violin and helped his father, a stonemason and builder, with various building projects. At the age of sixteen, he was apprenticed to an architect in Dorchester, later moving to London in 1862 to work with architect Arthur Blomfield. Though successful, Hardy never felt comfortable in London and returned to Dorset with an ambition to be a writer.

He married **Emma Lavinia Gifford** in 1874, shortly after he had begun to make money through his writing *Under the Greenwood Tree* (1872), *A Pair of Blue Eyes* (1873, based on his courtship of his wife) and *Far From the Madding Crowd* (1874). The latter was successful enough for him to give up his work as an architect and he began to write full time. The Hardys moved briefly to Sturminster Newton, where he wrote *The Return of the Native* (1878). In 1885, Hardy designed his own "cottage", Max Gate in Dorchester, where he wrote some of his finest works: *The Mayor of Casterbridge* (1876), *The Woodlanders* (1887), *Tess of the D'Urbervilles* (1891) and *Jude the Obscure* (1895). The latter two books were seen as extremely risqué, with *Tess of the D'Urbervilles* based on a true-life murder, and the "explicit" *Jude the Obscure* dealing with issues such as illegitimacy, fratricide and suicide amongst others. The controversy placed a great strain on his wife, and though they were soon estranged, Hardy was greatly depressed by her sudden death in 1912. They had no children. Hardy then turned to writing poetry, his greatest love, though his poems were never as successful as his novels.

In 1914, he married his secretary, **Florence Emily Dugdale** (1879–1937) who was nearly 40 years his junior. Hardy died at his home Max Gate in Dorchester on 11 January, 1928; his remains lie in Poet's Corner in Westminster Abbey, though his heart was removed and lies in the church at Stinsford (see p.104), alongside his wives Emma and Florence.

Hardy: it features the colours of Egdon Heath, and the storm and tempest from Hardy's favourite Bible lesson, 1 Kings, chapter 19, which is read here on June 1 each year to celebrate the author's birthday.

Higher Bockhampton

The attractive hamlet of **Higher Bockhampton**, three miles northeast of Dorchester is known for one thing, **Hardy's Cottage** (mid-March to Oct Sun–Thurs 11am–5pm; £3.50), where the famous author was born and lived until the age of 34, with his two sisters and brother. A lovely path winds from the car park through the ancient woodland of Thorncombe Woods to the cottage – a fitting approach that gives a sense of the rural isolation that Hardy writes about so frequently in his books. The cottage itself is a simple cob and thatch affair, built in 1800 by Hardy's grandfather and surrounded by a small, pretty garden. It is little altered since the author's days, and has been furnished simply with period furniture. Downstairs, the parlour is the main room – a larger version of it features as the parlour where the villagers dance in *Under the Greenwood Tree* – while next door is the tiny office where Hardy's father and grandfather did their accounts. Upstairs are three bedrooms, the first belonging to Hardy's two sisters, the second to his parents, and the third to Hardy himself, which he later shared with his younger brother Henry: it was here that he wrote

▲ Hardy's Cottage

Under the Greenwood Tree and much of *Far From the Madding Crowd*. From his window, he could then gaze out at the Hardy Monument, commemorating his distant relative (see p.103), though the view today is obscured by trees.

A small lane leads from the cottage through the hamlet back to the car park, where you'll find *Greenwood Grange* (☎01305 268874, Ⓦwww.greenwoodgrange .co.uk; from £300 a week), sixteen beautifully furnished **self-catering cottages** in converted barns and farm outbuildings, some built by Thomas Hardy's father. The complex aims to be eco-friendly with an organic vegetable garden, and also has an indoor pool on site, plus lovely gardens with a trampoline, and tennis courts.

Athelhampton House

Five miles east of Dorchester, **Athelhampton House** (March–Oct Sun–Thurs 11am–4.30pm, Sun 11am–4.30pm all year round; £8.75; Ⓦwww.athelhampton .co.uk) is a striking fifteenth-century manor house, surrounded by attractive walled gardens dotted with fountains and interesting topiary pyramids. Thomas Hardy's father, a builder, was involved in the restoration of the house in the nineteenth century, while Hardy himself set his story, *The Waiting Supper*, here and painted a fine watercolour of the house. The rooms inside are furnished with suitable grandeur and finery, many housing an interesting collection of antiques that the house was bought to display. The Tudor Oak Hall, built by Sir William Martyn in 1485, is the most impressive room, with its hammer-beam ceiling, original fireplace and oriel window. Outside, the gardens, laid out in 1891, are worth exploring; and there's a lovely riverside walk tracing the banks of the River Piddle. The *Topiary Restaurant* inside the house (from 10am) serves good-value sandwiches, light lunches – such as smoked trout and Blue Vinney cheese salad – and a few more substantial main courses, all from local, sustainable and seasonal ingredients.

If you fancy revelling in the gardens for longer, the pretty thatched *River Cottage* (☎01305 848363) in the grounds is available for **rent** from £615 a week. Alternatively, there's B&B just down the road at *The White Cottage* (☎01305 848622, Ⓦwww.white-cottage-bandb.co.uk; ❷) a gorgeous 300-year-old thatched cottage in three acres of grounds. With a family room and welcoming atmosphere, it's very child-friendly; the rooms are comfortable, and some have views over the grounds and river; breakfast usually involves eggs from their own chickens.

Tolpuddle

Some eight miles east off Dorchester, just off the A35, is the village of **Tolpuddle**, a delightful little Dorset village of interest principally because of the **Tolpuddle Martyrs**. In 1834, six villagers, George and James Loveless, Thomas and John Standfield, John Brine and James Hammett, were sentenced to transportation for banding together to form the Friendly Society of Agricultural Labourers, in order to petition for a small wage increase on the grounds that their families were starving. After a public outcry the men were pardoned, and the Tolpuddle Martyrs passed into history as founders of the trade union movement. Six memorial cottages were built in 1934 to commemorate the centenary of the martyrs' conviction, and the middle one has been turned into a little **museum** (April–Oct Tues–Sat 10am–5.30pm, Sun 11am–5.30pm; Nov–March closes at 4pm; free), which charts the story of the men, from their harsh rural lives before their conviction to the horrors of transportation in a convict ship and the brutal conditions of the penal colonies in Australia. Only one of the martyrs, James Hammett, remained in Tolpuddle after their pardon: he worked as a builder's labourer on his return and died in the village aged 80 in 1891. He is buried in the graveyard of the twelfth-century church of St John the Evangelist, in front of which the Martyrs' Tree still stands, where the Friendly Society meetings often took place. The village pub, *The Martyrs Inn*, serves good real ales and delicious, if pricey, food.

North of Dorchester

The countryside north of Dorchester is a rolling rural idyll scattered with thatched villages. Designated an Area of Outstanding Natural Beauty, it's criss-crossed with footpaths, and it's a pleasure just to take a meandering drive down the winding country lanes that wend their way through farmland and valleys, passing villages with improbable names such as Plush, Droop and Melbury Bubb. However, there are also two sites of interest that most visitors head for, the **Cerne Abbas Giant** and the historic abbey and gardens of **Milton Abbas**.

Cerne Abbas and the Giant

Nestled into a deep valley six miles north of Dorchester, **CERNE ABBAS** is one of the most historic and prettiest villages in Dorset. It is also the most visited site in the county, principally because of the famous **chalk giant** that stands on a hillside just outside the village. The best place to see the giant is to follow signs to the car park and viewpoint on the hillside opposite. Here you can see the 55m-high man carved out of chalk in all his priapic glory, flourishing a club over a disproportionately small head. No one knows when it was carved, but it dates back to at least Roman times and is almost certainly a fertility symbol – it was long believed that childless women could bear children after lying on his crotch.

You can walk right up and round the giant, though the carving is now fenced off to avoid erosion and, in fact, you can barely make it out from close up. A better option is to follow the well-signed **Giant's Walk**, a one hour thirty minutes trail round and over the Giant's hill, returning via a ridge across fields, with great views back across the valley.

The village, too, warrants an hour or two's exploration. The picturesque high street boasts some fine old pubs and an attractive church, though its most historic site is the former **Abbey**, founded in 987 and later visited by various royals including King John and Henry III. Nowadays its remains are privately owned (70p donation in box outside). You approach it up Abbey Street, once the heart of the medieval town with its row of ancient cottages. Many of the monastic visitors stayed in the Guest House, a rare surviving example, dating from 1470, which is the first building you come to as you enter the site. Beyond here is a small exhibition area in the Abbey Porch, once the entrance to the Abbey Hall.

Cross the churchyard opposite the abbey and you'll see **St Augustine's Well** – actually more of a spring – where St Augustine is said to have offered shepherds beer or water. When they opted for the latter, St Augustine rewarded them with a brewery.

Practicalities

There are two daily (Mon–Fri only) bus services to Cerne Abbas that run between Dorchester to Sherborne. Of the lovely **pubs** in the village, the best option is the sixteenth-century *The Royal Oak* on 23 Long St (☎01300 341797), next to the church, with a cosy wooden-beamed interior embellished with hanging jugs and horse brasses, and a charming beer garden. The food is moderately priced and portions are generous – the home-made soups are excellent. If you want to **stay** in Cerne Abbas, *Abbots* at 7 Long St (☎01300 341349, ⓦwww.abbotsbedandbreakfast.co.uk; ❸) has five decent rooms above a bright teashop right on the High Street.

Milton Abbas

From Cerne Abbas, it's a wonderful cross-country drive along winding lanes to the village of **MILTON ABBAS**, nine miles east. A mile south of the village is **Milton Abbey**, founded in 938 by King Athelstan: it burnt down after being hit by lightning in 1309 and the present Abbey Church was started soon after. The choir and transept were built by the end of the fourteenth century though the nave was never finished, leaving the church looking rather incomplete. A sizeable town grew up around the abbey, with more than a hundred houses, a grammar school and many taverns. After the Dissolution of the Monasteries, the estate was sold off to a succession of families until in 1752, it was bought by John Damer, who knocked down the old monastic buildings and built the present mansion house on the site: it was arranged around a quadrangle, making it particularly suitable for its current use as a school. He also had the impressive grounds landscaped by "Capability" Brown. Once the house and gardens had developed into a grandiose estate, Damer, now Lord Milton, decided that the squalor of the nearby town was lowering the tone of the place and, with the high-handedness typical of many eighteenth-century landlords, had it destroyed and rebuilt a mile away up the hill – out of sight and earshot of the manor. The church and gardens are now owned by a public school, but they will usually permit visitors to have a look round the Abbey (usually weekdays 10.30am–5pm). You can walk from the Abbey, along a footpath known as the Monk's Path, which leads to the bottom of the village.

Built in 1780 by Sir William Chambers, the current village of **Milton Abbas** was England's first planned village, and is comprised of sturdy thatched houses on either side of a wide road, and lawns in front. It's easy to see how this planned village, so regimented in style, differs from nearby villages with their narrow winding lanes and higgledy-piggledy cottages of varying ages. Today it's an extremely pretty place, made up of a row of cottages, almshouses, a church

and the thatched *Hambro Arms* **pub** (☎01258 880233, Ⓦwww.hambroarms
.com). With low beams and a log fire, the pub serves local ales, and dishes up
good food, such as steak and Dorset ale pie: it also has a few rooms (❹).
Alternatively, *The Old Bank* (☎01258 880520, Ⓦwww.theoldbankmiltonabbas
.co.uk; ❸), towards the bottom of the main street at no. 56/57, offers **B&B** in
one of the thatched cottages with white cob walls: the rooms are snug and
comfortable, and breakfast comes with home-produced eggs and home-made
bread and jams. A couple of miles northwest of Milton Abbas, the *Fox Inn*
(☎01258 880328, Ⓦwww.anstyfoxinn.co.uk; ❷) at Ansty is another good
option for food and lodging: a 200-year-old pub that was formerly a family
home, it has restful, recently refurbished rooms, a lovely garden and cosy bar
serving local real ales. The food is reasonably priced with dishes such as duck
cassoulet with chorizo, butter beans and asparagus for around £11.

Sherborne

In the far northwest corner of Dorset, ten miles north of Cerne Abbas, the
pretty town of **SHERBORNE** was once the capital of Wessex, its church
having cathedral status until Old Sarum usurped the bishopric in 1075. Its
golden days are behind it, but with an exclusive public school and handsome

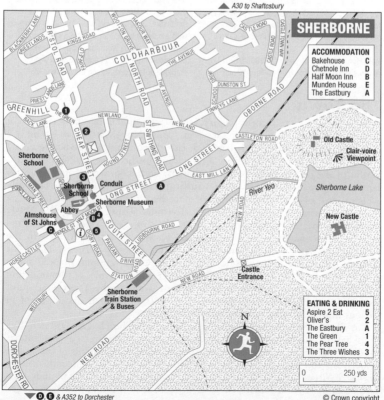

© Crown copyright

architecture, it retains a sense of both affluence and importance, not to mention oodles of history that make it a must-visit in anyone's Dorset itinerary.

Arrival and information

The **train station** is in the south of the town, about a five-minute walk from the centre, and is served by hourly trains between London and Exeter, with some services continuing on to Plymouth. **Buses** from Dorchester, Yeovil and Blandford Forum also pull in outside the station. The **tourist office** is at 3 Tilton Court, Digby Rd (Mon–Sat: Easter–Oct 9am–5pm; Nov–Easter 10am–3pm; ☎01935 815341, ⓦwww.westdorset.com).

Accommodation

Bakehouse 1 Acreman St ☎01935 817969, ⓦwww.bakehouse.me.uk. A friendly and relaxed B&B in an eighteenth-century bakehouse with some rooms overlooking the abbey. ❷

Chetnole Inn 7 miles southwest of Sherborne, in the village of Chetnole ☎01935 872337, ⓦwww.thechetnoleinn.co.uk. Lovely traditional country pub with log fires, local ales and an attractive garden filled with ducks waddling free. The comfortable rooms overlook the village church and are well decorated with Egyptian cotton sheets and flat-screen TVs. The food is good quality too – reasonably priced home-made pub grub as it should be. ❹

Half Moon Inn Half Moon St ☎01935 812017, ⓦwww.marstonsinns.co.uk. This friendly pub in a central location has clean, well-equipped rooms with free wi-fi and digital TV – some also have views over the Abbey. ❸

Munden House ☎01963 23150, ⓦwww.mundenhouse.co.uk. A couple of miles southeast of town in the village of Alweston, this B&B has well-decorated rooms and lovely views over the gardens and surrounding countryside. ❺

The Eastbury Long St ☎01935 813131, ⓦwww.theeastburyhotel.co.uk. In a fine Georgian house, this is the smartest choice in town, with its own restaurant, bar and lovely walled gardens complete with a croquet lawn. Front rooms (£125) are on the small side and it is worth paying the £20 extra for an executive room, which are spacious and boutique in feel, overlooking the gardens. ❼

The Town

Sherborne's former historical glory is best embodied by the magnificent **Abbey Church** (daily: April–Oct 8am–6pm; Nov–March 8am–4pm; £2 donation), which was founded in 705, later becoming a Benedictine abbey. Most of its extant parts date from a rebuilding in the fifteenth century, and it is one of the best examples of Perpendicular architecture in Britain, particularly noted for its outstanding **fan vaulting**. The church also has a famously weighty peal of eight bells, the heaviest in the world, led by "Great Tom", a tenor bell presented to the Abbey by Cardinal Wolsey. Among the Abbey Church's many tombs are those of Alfred the Great's two brothers, Ethelred and Ethelbert, and the Elizabethan poet Thomas Wyatt, all located in the northeast corner. The **almshouse of St John's** (May–Sept Tues & Thurs–Sat 2–4pm; £2) on the opposite side of the Abbey Close was built in 1437 and is a rare example of a medieval hospital; another wing provides accommodation for Sherborne's well-known public **school**, one of the finest (and most expensive) in the country – founded in 1550 and which has appeared in various films, including *Goodbye Mr Chips* (1969).

The **Sherborne Museum** near the abbey on Church Lane (March–Oct Tues–Sat 10.30am–4.30pm; £2; ⓦwww.sherbornemuseum.co.uk) includes a model of the Old Castle before it was ruined, along with exhibits of Edwardian underwear. You can also see photographs of parts of the fifteenth-century *Sherborne Missal*, a richly illuminated tome weighing nearly fifty pounds, now housed in the British Library. Another fine old relic is the **conduit**, an arched former washhouse moved here after the dissolution of the monastery in 1539, which has since been used as the town's water supply and later as a police station and a bank. The attractive **Cheap Street** – pedestrianized from noon–4pm Mon–Sat – runs through the heart of town, and is worth browsing for its interesting antique and quirky gift shops.

Sherborne castles

The town boasts no less than two "castles", both associated with Sir Walter Raleigh (see box below) and both around fifteen minutes' walk from the centre. Queen Elizabeth I first leased, then gave, Raleigh the twelfth-century **Old Castle** (Tues–Thurs, Sat & Sun: Easter–June & Sept 10am–5pm; July & Aug 10am–6pm; Oct 10am–4pm; £2.50; EH), but it seems that he despaired of feudal accommodation and built himself a more comfortably domesticated house in the adjacent deer park in 1594. The Old Castle was pulverized by Cromwellian cannon fire for the obstinately Royalist leanings of its occupants and now lies in ruins – you can wander round its old walls, though it's best to view it for free from the adjacent **Sherborne New Castle** (Easter–Oct Tues–Thurs & Sun 11am–4.30pm, Sat 2–4pm; castle & gardens £9, gardens only £4.50, children under 15 free).

The Digby family acquired Raleigh's former house and have lived there ever since, remodelling the original structure to provide comforts for visitors like Prince William of Orange (who stayed in 1688), the poet Alexander Pope (1724) and George III (1753). But you can still make out parts of the original Raleigh house in the Solarium, with its Tudor ceiling; in the entrance hall, which has a pipe given to Raleigh by American Indians (and subsequently damaged in the Blitz of 1941); and in the splendid kitchens, with the original ovens. Elsewhere, priceless furniture, ceramics and books are displayed in a whimsically Gothic interior, remodelled in the nineteenth century. Don't miss the fabulous painting of *Elizabeth I in Procession*, by Robert Peake the Elder; the ornate panelled Oak Room; the upstairs photos showing the house's use as a Red Cross hospital in World War I and as HQ for the D-day landings in World War II; and the basement museum, housing archeological remains from the old castle. Outside there are alluring tearooms with tables on the lawn and lovely lakeside walks in the grounds laid out by "Capability" Brown in 1753 – you can see over the Old Castle from the Clair-Voire viewpoint, signed from the gardens.

Sir Walter Raleigh

Famed for his explorations of the New World – he helped the English colonize Virginia in the 1580s and is often credited with introducing potatoes and tobacco to the UK – **Sir Walter Raleigh** was one of the Elizabethan era's most flamboyant and controversial figures. A writer, poet and explorer, he became a favourite of Queen Elizabeth I, helping put down rebellions in Ireland and allegedly laying down cloaks over puddles for the queen. He blotted his copybook in 1591, however, when he secretly married one of the royal ladies-in-waiting without the queen's permission, and both were sent packing to the Tower of London for their sins. When they were released, they retired to the New Castle in Sherborne in 1594. The gardens still contain Raleigh's Seat, where he liked to smoke his newly discovered tobacco. It is said a passing servant was so surprised at this novel sight that he threw a jug of beer over him, believing that Raleigh was on fire. After Elizabeth's death, Raleigh was framed for a plot against the recently crowned King James, and sentenced to prison again in Winchester's Great Hall. His estate in Sherborne was forfeited to the king, who handed it to Sir John Digby in 1617, a year before Raleigh's beheading, after being accused of further machinations.

Eating and drinking

Aspire 2 Eat Opposite the tourist office on Digby Rd ☎01935 389666. A smart bistro with its own bar area, serving quality daily specials from around £12, including some vegetarian options. Closed Sun pm & Mon.

Oliver's 19 Cheap St. With long wooden benches laid out in a former butcher's, adorned with the original tiles, this friendly café-deli serves great cakes and coffee, accompanied by oodles of atmosphere.

The Eastbury *The Eastbury Hotel*, Long St ☎01935 813131. Upmarket restaurant; three courses of locally sourced seasonal delicacies, such as West Country fillet of beef from a local farm, costs £33.

The Green 3 The Green ☎01935 813821. A small, friendly family-run restaurant specializing in local seasonal produce: the lunch menu features delights such as pan-fried breast of wood pigeon with almond potatoes for £8. Closed Sun & Mon.

The Pear Tree Half Moon St. The place to come for a light lunch, this café-cum-deli serves delicious soups, sumptuous salads and sandwiches, as well as selling local produce to put together a fine picnic.

The Three Wishes 78 Cheap St ☎01935 817777. With a lovely walled garden at the back, this bistro, owned by the *Eastbury* (see p.110), serves tasty coffee, pasta dishes (around £9) and lunches during the day: on Fridays and Saturday evenings, it serves more substantial meals, such as local lamb and seafood main courses for £11–16.50.

Coast

The coasts of Dorset, Hampshire and the Isle of Wight are astonishingly varied, and take in some of the country's finest beaches, as well as the UNESCO World Heritage Jurassic Coast. Within a few miles you can enjoy remote bays, gently sloping sandy beaches and dramatic cliffs, with most of the coast linked by footpaths, including Britain's longest, the South West Coast Path.

Fossils at Lyme Regis ▲

Sailing on Poole Harbour ▼

Great conditions for windsurfing ▼

Remains of the day

The region is one of the best anywhere for finding **fossils**. The sea has eroded Dorset's 200-million-year-old Jurassic Coast, exposing a vast number of fossils especially around Lyme Regis and Charmouth – there are plenty of organized fossil hunts hereabouts if you're unsure of where to look. The Isle of Wight, too, shares the Jurassic Coast's geology and over twenty species of **dinosaur** have been identified on the island: many of their bones can be seen in Dinosaur Isle in Sandown.

Take a bow

The Solent's famous **double tides** have made it renowned for **sailing**, with major yachting centres at Lymington, Christchurch and Poole. There's the country's most famous sailing event at Cowes, though Weymouth will take centre stage for watersports during the 2012 Olympics. **Grander boats** reside at the great naval docks at Portsmouth, where the *Mary Rose* set off from on its final voyage and *Victory* came to rest. For much of the last century, neighbouring Southampton was the departure point for ships to America, including the *Titanic*.

Surf's up

The region is a heaven for watersports enthusiasts. Hayling Islanders even claim to have invented **kitesurfing** – conditions are superb here for both kite- and windsurfing, as are the sheltered Christchurch and Poole harbours, the latter being the second-largest natural harbour in the world. Meanwhile Boscombe has become the new kid on the block for **surfing**, with Europe's first **artificial surf reef** guaranteeing breakers for much of the year.

Rock on

Much of Dorset is formed from the hard Portland and Purbeck stone with dramatic former **quarries** and spectacular **cliffs** making it ideal for climbers especially on the isles of Portland and Purbeck. The dramatic Portland headland is still heavily quarried for a stone that graces some of the world's finest buildings (see p.86), while you can visit the atmospheric, disused Purbeck stone mines around Tilly Whim Caves, Dancing Ledge and Winspit, which supplied the stone for Lulworth and Durlston castles.

Marine life

The warm waters off the south coast are particularly rich in marine life. The cliffs of Durlston Country Park are the best place to spot **dolphins**, **porpoises**, the odd **whale**, and the occasional **giant leatherback turtle** on the hunt for jellyfish. Also native to the shores is the spiny **seahorse**, which is relatively common around Shell Bay – Britain's largest colony of the beautiful creatures lives off South Beach.

The missing link

The **Needles** are chalk stacks formed over 60 million years ago by an upheaval in the earth's crust. They are the western end of a chalk ridge that runs across the Isle of Wight, then continues beneath the sea floor to emerge in Dorset at Ballard Down, Swanage. At one time the Island was connected to mainland Britain by this chalk ridge before sea levels rose and erosion took place: by standing on top of the Needles or on Ballard Down, you can clearly see how the two land masses, now fifteen miles apart, were once linked. A fourth Needle, known as "Lot's Wife", disappeared during a storm in 1764.

▲ Rock climbing, Portland

▲ A marine visitor

▼ The Needles

CHAPTER 4 # Highlights

✳ **Abbotsbury Swannery** May to June is the time to walk amidst the squawking, fluffy cygnets – you can even see the eggs hatching. See p.128

✳ **Hive Beach Café, Burton Bradstock** On a sunny lunchtime, you can't beat overlooking the beach eating fresh, locally caught seafood, accompanied by a cold bottle of white. See p.133

✳ **Lyme Regis** A pretty seaside town with excellent restaurants and cafés, great coastal walks and a lovely beach. See p.134

✳ **Fossil tours at Charmouth Heritage Centre** Informative, fascinating and incredibly satisfying when you come home with your pockets filled with fossils plucked on the beach. See p.139

✳ **Climb the Golden Cap** It's a bracing, steep walk up the south coast's highest cliff with far-reaching coastal views. See p.140

✳ **Evershot** An unspoilt thatched village that remains pretty much as it was in Thomas Hardy's time. See p.141

▲ The Golden Cap

4

Western Dorset

T he coastline of **WESTERN DORSET** is one of the most varied and
dramatic in the country. From the Regency resort of **Weymouth**, with
its jutting peninsula of **Portland**, to the pretty town of **Lyme Regis**
– so beloved of Jane Austen – the coast combines history with stunning
unspoilt beaches and cliffs. The eastern section is dominated by the eighteen-
mile-long pebble bank of **Chesil Beach**, which ends near the picture-postcard
village of **Abbotsbury**, with its six-hundred-year-old swannery. From here,
sandstone cliffs take over to the lively market town of **Bridport** and beyond
via **Golden Cap**, the south coast's highest point. The far western stretch
around **Charmouth** and Lyme Regis is rich in fossils, and has thrown up
some of the country's most important geological finds.

Inland too, western Dorset is a bucolic idyll dotted with quaint villages,
winding country lanes and unexpected hills boasting far-reaching views, such
as **Pilsdon Pen**, site of an Iron Age hillfort. With only one main town, the
modest **Beaminster**, and one in road, the A35, the inland area is a joy to
explore. The area is also at the forefront of the local food renaissance – Hugh
Fearnley-Whittingstall's River Cottage is nearby – and a visit to one of the
thatched country pubs serving seasonal food and real ales, followed by a walk
along pretty much any country footpath, will rarely disappoint.

The coast is fairly easy to explore by public transport, with buses connecting
the main towns, and trains serving Weymouth and the region inland of Lyme
Regis, though to reach the more out-of-the-way spots, it's best to have a car.

Weymouth and around

An elegant and bustling town, **Weymouth** has one of the best beaches in
western Dorset and some fine Georgian buildings. Its name is inextricably linked
with "mad" King George III, who visited the town to recuperate from illness in
1789. Part of his remedy was to take to the sea in a bathing machine while a
band played "God Save the King". It's said he then drank the sea water and ate
cuttlefish and earwigs for good measure. Amazingly, his physical – if not mental
– health actually improved after the experience. A likeness of the monarch on
horseback is now carved into the chalk downs northwest of the town. Weymouth
has continued to be a popular seaside resort ever since, and received a giant boost
to its self-esteem by being chosen to host the sailing events at the 2012 Olympics.
Not surprisingly, Weymouth harbour is great for windsurfing and kiting, and
hosts the Speed Week watersports festival in October.

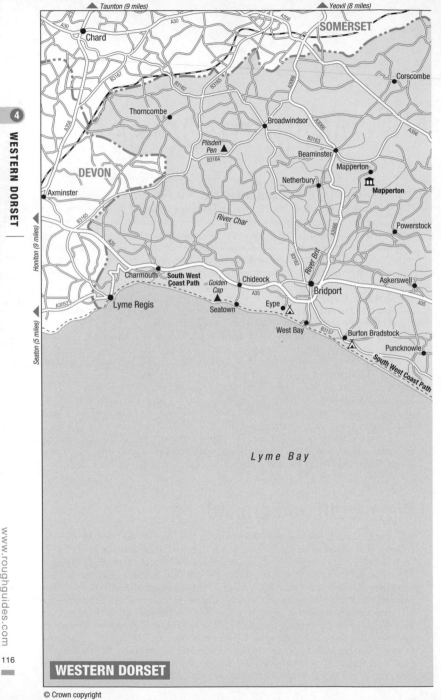

Taunton (9 miles)

Yeovil (8 miles)

SOMERSET

A30

A30

A356

Chard

A30

B3167

Corscombe

B3162

B3165

A3066

Thorncombe

Broadwindsor

A356

A3066

B3163

A358

Pilsden
Pen

Beaminster

B3164

Mapperton

DEVON

Netherbury

Mapperton

Axminster

River Char

A3066

Powerstock

B3165

B3162

River Brit

A35

Charmouth   South West
Coast Path

Chideock

Askerswell

Golden
Cap

A35

Lyme Regis

Seatown

Eype

Bridport

A35

A3052

West Bay

B3157

Burton Bradstock

Honiton (9 miles)

Seaton (5 miles)

Puncknowle

South West Coast Path

Lyme Bay

© Crown copyright

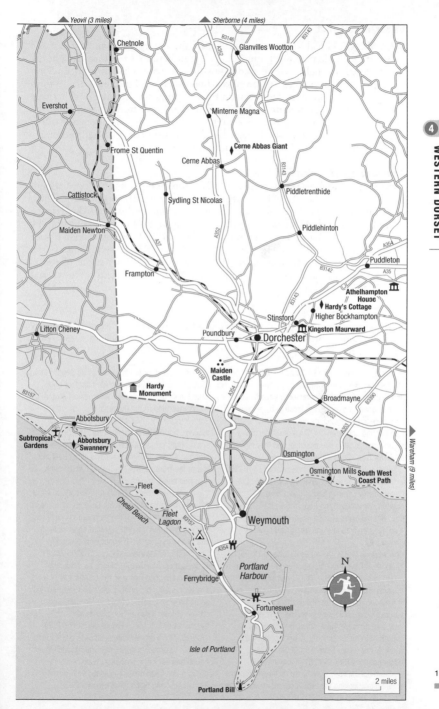

Yeovil (3 miles)

Sherborne (4 miles)

Chetnole

B3146

Glanvilles Wootton

B3143

A352

Evershot

Minterne Magna

Cerne Abbas Giant

Frome St Quentin

Cerne Abbas

B3143

Piddletrenthide

Cattistock

Sydling St Nicolas

Piddlehinton

A354

Maiden Newton

A37

A352

Puddleton

A35

B3142

Frampton

B3143

Athelhampton House

Hardy's Cottage

Higher Bockhampton

Stinsford

Litton Cheney

Poundbury

Kingston Maurward

Dorchester

B3159

Maiden Castle

A354

Broadmayne

B3390

Hardy Monument

B3157

A352

A353

Wareham (9 miles)

Abbotsbury

Subtropical Gardens

Abbotsbury Swannery

Osmington

Osmington Mills South West Coast Path

Fleet

Chesil Beach

Fleet Lagoon

B3157

A354

Weymouth

A354

Portland Harbour

Ferrybridge

N

Fortuneswell

Isle of Portland

www.roughguides.com

0   2 miles

Portland Bill

Weymouth

WEYMOUTH had long been a port before the Georgians popularized it as a resort. It's possible that a ship unloading a cargo here in 1348 first brought the Black Death to English shores, and it was from Weymouth that John Endicott sailed in 1628 to found Salem in Massachusetts. A few buildings survive from these pre-Georgian times, but Weymouth's most imposing architectural heritage stands along the **Esplanade**, a dignified range of bow-fronted and porticoed buildings gazing out across the graceful bay. The more intimate quayside of the **Old Harbour**, linked to the Esplanade by the main pedestrianized thoroughfare St Mary's Street, is lined with waterfront pubs.

Arrival and information

Weymouth is well served by **trains** from London, Southampton, Bournemouth and Poole (at least hourly), plus less regular services from Bristol and Bath, which arrive at the station on King Street, a couple of minutes' walk back from the seafront. **Buses** from Dorchester (every 30min or so) pull in at the bus stops by King George III's statue. **Ferries** from the Channel Islands and St Malo in France arrive at the terminal on The Quay (☎01305 763003, ⊛www.condorferries .com). The **tourist office** is on the Esplanade by the King's statue (☎01305 785747), and sells a series of leaflets detailing local walks around the town and surrounding area (10p).

Accommodation

There's no shortage of reasonably priced **guest houses** in Weymouth, many of them along the Esplanade with sea views, though there are no really upmarket **hotels**.

B&B Weymouth 68 The Esplanade ☎01305 761190, ⊛www.bb-weymouth.com. Weymouth's first boutique B&B with contemporary rooms and all mod cons. The rooms are clean and spacious, and there's a lovely lounge with a sea view and free tea and coffee on tap. The breakfasts are organic and local where possible, and they lend out bikes for free. ❹, or ❺ with a sea view.

Bay View House 35 The Esplanade ☎01305 782083, ⊛www.bayview-weymouth.co.uk. Clean, friendly and well-kept guest house. A comfortable room at the front of the house with a bay window overlooking the sea costs just £60. Also has family rooms and free private garage parking. ❶

Chatsworth Hotel 14 The Esplanade ☎01305 785012, ⊛www.thechatsworth.co.uk. Lovely guest house in a great location. The furnishings are modern and all the rooms have either harbour or sea views. There's a terrace overlooking the harbour where breakfast is served on fine days: they also do meals here, specializing in local fish caught daily by the friendly owner's brother. ❺

Glenthorne Castle Cove, 15 Old Castle Rd, Weymouth ☎01305 777281, ⊛glenthorne -holidays.co.uk. Former Victorian rectory, in a prime position overlooking the sea. Three rooms, one with a sea view, and large gardens leading directly to Castle Cove beach, with a heated outdoor pool, table tennis and trampoline. Also has self-catering accommodation in the grounds. ❺

Ocean Hotel 15 The Esplanade ☎01305 782012, ⊛www.theoceanweymouth.co.uk. The *Ocean Hotel* has a bright breakfast terrace overlooking the harbour: all the rooms have views either over the sea at the front or over the harbour at the back. Also has family rooms. ❷

Old Harbour View 12 Trinity Rd ☎01305 774633, ⊛www.oldharbourview.co.uk. Cosy guest house in a great location right on the harbourfront. Only has two rooms, but it's worth paying a bit extra for the one at the front with a harbour view (£88). ❸

The Seaham 3 Waterloo Place ☎01305 782010, ⊛www.theseahamweymouth.co.uk. Attractive Georgian terraced house at the quieter end of town. The rooms are comfortable and well furnished and some have sea views: breakfast includes a good choice of local free-range products. ❷

Wilton Guest House 5 Gloucester St ☎01305 782820, ⊛www.thewiltonguesthouse.co.uk. Once home to George III's butler, this child-friendly guest house has several reasonably priced family rooms (£85). It has been newly renovated with modern furnishings, and has a small terrace. ❶

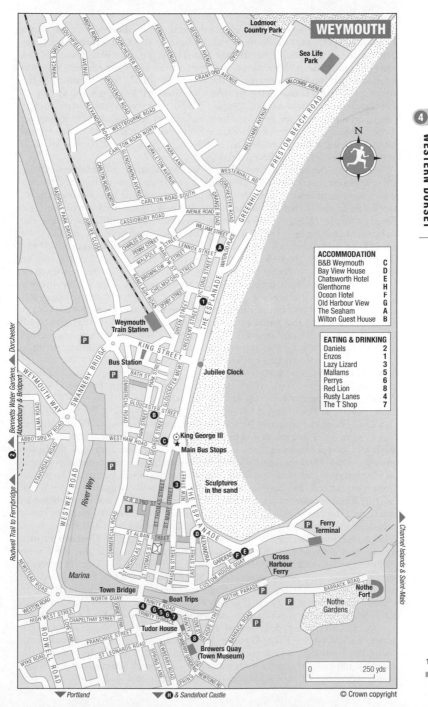

WEYMOUTH

Lodmoor
Country Park

Sea Life
Park

N

Weymouth
Train Station

Bus Station

Jubilee Clock

King George III
Main Bus Stops

Sculptures
in the sand

Ferry
Terminal

Cross
Harbour
Ferry

Nothe
Fort

Nothe
Gardens

Marina

Town Bridge

Boat Trips

Tudor House

Brewers Quay
(Town Museum)

River Wey

Bennetts Water Gardens;
Abbotsbury & Bridport

Dorchester

Rodwell Trail to Ferrybridge

Channel Islands & Saint-Malo

Portland

& Sandsfoot Castle

0   250 yds

© Crown copyright

4

WESTERN DORSET

www.roughguides.com

119

The Town

Weymouth's main attraction is its lovely long, sandy **beach**, but it's also a pleasant town to explore. A good place to start is the **Old Harbour**, on the eastern side of the lifting Town Bridge. From here, the main drag, Trinity Road, runs alongside the harbour, lined with restaurants and cafés on one side and boats offering **harbour cruises** on the other (see p.122). At the bottom of the street is **Tudor House** (May to mid-Oct Tues–Fri 1–3.45pm; Nov, Dec & Feb–April first Sun of month 2–4pm; £3.50; Ⓦ www.weymouthcivicsociety .org), formerly the home of a merchant and one of Weymouth's few remaining Tudor buildings. Built around 1600, the house has been restored to its original condition and a tour round gives good insight into the domestic life of a seventeenth-century middle-class family.

Round the corner, the lively Hope Square is home to **Brewers Quay** (Ⓦ www.brewers-quay.co.uk), a converted Victorian brewery now containing a hotchpotch of craft and souvenir shops, museums and wet-weather attractions. Inside, the **Town Museum** (daily 10am–4.30pm; free) is worth a look for its eclectic collection of Weymouth-related memorabilia, including the original mechanism of the Town Hall clock and various displays on smuggling and maritime matters. For further historical background, the **Timewalk** (daily 10am–5.30pm; £4.50, children £3.25) takes you on an atmospheric, forty-minute trip through various events in the town's past, such as the Black Death, probably bought to England on ships via Weymouth; children will enjoy travelling past the lively tableaux on moving escalators and being guided by talking cats. Upstairs the **Discovery** exhibition (Jan & Feb Wed–Sun opening hours vary; March–Dec daily 10am–4.30pm; open till 8pm in Aug; £4.50, children £3.50; Ⓦ www.discoverdiscovery.co.uk) houses a collection of interactive displays illustrating various scientific processes, such as a bike that can be pedalled to produce electricity.

From Hope Square, a pleasant fifteen-minute walk leads along the harbourfront, past the town ferry (50p), which crosses the harbour to the Esplanade, out to **Nothe Fort** (Easter, May–Sept & Oct half-term daily 10.30am–5.30pm; Oct, Nov, March & April Sun 11am–4.30pm; £6, under-14s £1). Sitting on a headland beside the attractive Nothe Gardens, this well-preserved Victorian fort was built in 1872 to protect Weymouth from coastal attack. It was constructed with the lowest magazine level designed to store gunpowder and shells; the middle level housed the cannons and the soldiers, while the top level consisted of the ramparts and platform from where weapons could be fired. Despite all these precautions, the fort didn't actually witness any fighting until World War II, when it came under air attack. The fort is worth a visit, not only for its interesting displays of World War II memorabilia – children can clamber inside a tank in the courtyard – but for also for its fantastic location and views.

Back over Town Bridge, on the Georgian side of Weymouth, **Custom House Quay** runs alongside the harbour facing Trinity Road and is also lined with cafés, restaurants and B&Bs. Behind here is a grid of narrow shopping streets to explore; some, such as the atmospheric St Alban Street, are pedestrianized and home to interesting independent art and craft shops; the others house the usual mainstream high street chains. This part of town also has the town's main facilities, such as cinemas, supermarkets, department stores, bus and train stations and the tourist office. The pedestrianized St Mary Street leads up to the centre of the town, marked by the **King George III statue** and the **Jubilee Clock**, both along the Esplanade, which runs the full length of the beach. In summer, the **beach** is the focus of activity, with watersports and beach activities of all descriptions, including the UK's longest-running Punch and Judy show (the first

Sculptures in the sand

Towards the western end of the beach, look out for the quirky **sand sculptures** that have been created here since the 1920s, first by Fred Darrington, and now by his grandson Mark Anderson. During the winter, Mark models sculptures for international festivals and clients, such as the Ministry of Sound and Selfridges, and in the summer he can often be found on Weymouth beach. Past sand sculptures made by Fred and Mark include a full-size mini, Tutankhamun and the Empire State Building: see Ⓦwww.sculpturesinsand.com for more examples.

recorded puppet show here was in 1881, with breaks only during the two world wars), donkey rides, firework displays, sand sculpting (see above) and kite festivals.

A **land train** (Easter–Sept; £1) runs the length of the Esplanade from the tourist office to **Lodmoor Country Park** at its eastern end, where you'll find some low-key amusements, such as mini-golf, a model railway, a skate park and the excellent **Sea Life Park** (daily 10am–6pm; winter sometimes closes earlier, phone for exact times; last admission 1hr before closing; £17, children £13.50 on the door; £12, children £8.50 online; ℡01305 761070, Ⓦwww.sealifeeurope.com), home to sharks, turtles, penguins, otters, caymans and seals. As well as indoor aquariums, there's a sea-horse breeding centre, the crocodile creek log flume ride, plus outdoor water-jets and splash pools for children to play in on hot days.

Eating and drinking

Daniels 159 Abbotsbury Rd. A recent winner of the best fish and chip shop in the south of England, this immaculate takeaway serves the freshest fish and tastiest chips in the area – a standard cod and chips will set you back £4.25. It also has good veggie options, such as pea fritters. It's about a mile out of the Centre and also has branches in the Littlemoor shopping centre, and in Fortuneswell on Portland.
Enzos 110 The Esplanade ℡01305 778666. Traditional Italian restaurant, but with clean, contemporary decor, tiled floors and modern furnishings; it's right on the seafront, but slightly away from the hubbub of the main drag. It serves authentic freshly made pizzas (around £7), a range of pasta dishes (£7–8), as well as daily local specials, such as sea bream. Excellent value.

Lazy Lizard 52–53 The Esplanade. Light and airy place with wooden floors and quirky wooden furniture overlooking the beach. With a lively but laid-back atmosphere, it serves reasonably priced fish and chips, burgers and all-day breakfasts, and hosts live music and DJs in the evenings.
Mallams 5 Trinity Rd ℡01305 776757. In a great location overlooking the harbour – ask for a window seat – this cosy restaurant has a two-course menu for £24, featuring dishes such as Portland crab cakes and local hand-dived scallops. Also has a flat upstairs that can be rented by the night (from £85), with great harbour views.
Perrys 4 Trinity Rd ℡01305 785799. Next door to *Mallams* with the same great views, *Perrys* is an unpretentious restaurant serving good-quality food,

The Rodwell Trail

Running from Abbotsbury Road, near the centre of Weymouth, to Ferrybridge, the **Rodwell Trail** is a leafy two-mile cycle- and walkway along the old Great Western railway line. Originally built in 1865 to carry passengers and Portland stone between Weymouth and Portland, the rail line later served the factory at Ferrybridge where torpedoes were invented by Robert Whitehead in 1891 and tested in the harbour: the factory at Ferrybridge continued to make the weapons up until 1993. The train line was closed in 1965 and the track taken up – in 2000, it was re-opened as a cycle- and walkway. The bottom end of the trail runs alongside the harbour, giving wonderful views of Portland and the coast: it is well signposted, but if you want a map, pick one up from Weymouth tourist office (see p.118).

with main courses around £12–18 and daily changing fish specials. The fish soup (£5.50) is great, and they do a good-value two-course set-lunch menu for £15.

Red Lion Hope Square. Opposite Brewers Quay, this bustling pub is a good place for a drink with outdoor tables on the square and a cosy interior. It serves a good choice of local real ales and reasonable pub grub.

Rusty Lanes 19 Trinity Rd ℡ 01305 772023. Atmospheric and lively bar-restaurant with

harbour views and barrels for tables. Serves reasonably priced tapas-style dishes (£4–5), such as Spanish chorizo in cider; some come with a more local twist, such as Portland crab on rocket and a selection of Dorset cheeses. Main courses are also good value – try the veggie paella (£7).

The T Shop 11a Trinity St. Traditional teashop with tables on the waterfront; serves delicious home-made cakes, cream teas, plus sandwiches and light lunches.

Listings

Bike rental Weymouth Bike Hire, 10 Bowleaze Coveway (℡ 01305 834951, ⊛ www.weymouth bikehire.com) rents out bikes for £15 a day.

Boat trips Cruises and boat trips of all descriptions leave from the harbour alongside Trinity Rd; Weymouth White Water (℡ 07899 892317, ⊛ weymouth-whitewater.com) offers high-speed RIB trips round the harbour and out to Portland (from £15 for 1hr trip); White Motor Boats (℡ 01305 785000, ⊛ www.whitemotorboat.freeuk .com) runs boat trips to Portland castle (£7.50) and along the Jurassic Coast (£12). The Fleet Observer

(℡ 01305 759692, ⊛ www.thefleetobserver.co.uk) runs a glass-bottomed boat on the Fleet Lagoon from the jetty being the *Ferry Bridge Inn* at Ferrybridge (£7 for a 1hr trip).

Buses Local buses are run by Sureline Buses (℡ 01305 823039, ⊛ www.surelinebuses.co.uk) and First Bus (℡ 0780 0106 022, ⊛ www.firstgroup.com).

Post office Main branch is at 67 St Thomas St ℡ 0845 7223344.

Taxis Weymouth Station Taxis, Weymouth Station, King St (℡ 01305 788888); Weymouth Taxis, The Esplanade (℡ 01305 777000).

Osmington and around

Six miles east of Weymouth, the charming thatched village of **Osmington** has little to it save a couple of campsites and an excellent **pub**, *The Smugglers Inn*, at Osmington Mills, which serves real ales and decent pub food. Nestled in a valley, this thatched thirteenth-century pub has a lovely garden with a children's play area and a stream running through it, and a path leading down to the beach. From here the coastal path snakes eastwards to the pretty beach at Ringstead Bay, and west back towards Weymouth via the seasonal ⚑ *Eweleaze Farm* **campsite** (Aug only; ℡ 01305 833690, ⊛ www.eweleaze.co.uk). With seven fields – some car-free – and fantastic sea views, this spectacular cliff-top campsite has solar-powered showers, and an on-site shop selling local organic produce: it also has access to its own shingle beach.

Bennetts Water Gardens

Two miles west of Weymouth, in the village of Chickerell, **Bennetts Water Gardens** (daily except Sat 10am–5pm; £6.95) is an eight-acre garden planted with lilies from the very same nursery in France that supplied Monet's garden in Giverny. Laid out round a series of ponds – including one with a Japanese bridge to recreate Monet's famous painting *Water-Lily Pond 1899* – the gardens hold an impressive collection of water lilies that flower from late spring through to autumn. There's also a tropical greenhouse here, a nursery where you can buy some of the lilies, and a decent café.

Ferrybridge and Sandsfoot Castle

A couple of miles south of Weymouth, the mainland "bridge" to Portland begins by the workaday town of **FERRYBRIDGE**, home to the superb *Crab*

▲ The Smugglers Inn

House Café on the Portland Road (☎01305 788867; closed Mon, Tues & Jan & Feb). This upmarket beach shack by the Fleet Lagoon is renowned for its superb, locally caught fresh fish and seafood, including oysters from the Fleet and Portland crab. The menu changes daily according to the catch, but expect dishes such as skate wing with chorizo (£16). There are tables outside, and reservations are advised for the restaurant, though you may be lucky to squeeze into the café area. Alongside, the Fathom and Blues Dive Centre offers PADI diving courses (ⓦwww.fathomandblues.co.uk). The area is particularly good for diving thanks to rich marine life and various sunken wrecks, including the *Aeolian Sky*, a Greek freighter that sank twelve miles off Portland in 1979. Ferrybridge also marks the start/finish of some fine local walks. Head beyond the *Crab House Café*, and you can pick up the coastal path from Ferrybridge to Littlesea caravan site. It's about an hour's walk along the edge of the Fleet Lagoon (see p.128), skirting the local military camp – the last section has superb views over Chesil Beach. The energetic can then continue another eight miles to Abbotsbury (see p.128).

Heading the other way, opposite the *Ferry Bridge* pub is the start of the Rodwell Trail (see box, p.121) to central Weymouth via **Sandsfoot Castle** (free access), about twenty minutes' walk from Ferrybridge. Now in ruins but surrounded by fine gardens, this was one of a pair of sea defences built by Henry VIII (the other being Portland Castle opposite; see p.126). Fearing attack from the continent after his dissolution of the monasteries, Henry built it partly using stones from Bindon Abbey near Wool, which he had had dismantled. The castle was later occupied by parliamentary forces during the English Civil War and used as a mint, but coastal erosion has caused the structure to slowly collapse.

Heading over the land bridge to Portland gives the easiest access from Weymouth to **Chesil Beach** (there's a large car park on the right halfway across). This extraordinary geological "tombolo" is a two-hundred-yard-wide, fifty-foot-high bank of 100 million tonnes of pebbles that extends for eighteen miles. Its component stones gradually decrease in size from fist-like pebbles at Portland to "pea gravel" at Burton Bradstock in the west – during fog, fisherman can tell where they are by the size of the shingle. This sorting is an effect of the powerful coastal currents, which make it one of the most dangerous beaches in Europe – churchyards in the local villages display plenty of evidence of wrecks and drownings, so swimming is not recommended. It is also slowly being pushed inland by the sea, by about 5m every one hundred years or so.

Enclosing the Fleet Lagoon, where oyster beds have flourished since the eleventh century, Chesil is also popular with sea anglers, and its wild, uncommercialized atmosphere makes an appealing antidote to the south coast resorts. But think carefully before you consider walking down it – in *Notes from a Small Island*, Bill Bryson describes his walk down the beach as "the most boring walk I've ever had" as the pebbles "are nearly impossible to walk on since you sink to your ankle-tops with each step." Other authors, however, have been more inspired: Ian McEwan took various pebbles from the beach to gain inspiration for his award-winning *On Chesil Beach* – when this fact became known, the local council threatened to fine him £2000 as removing the pebbles is an offence. An apologetic McEwan duly returned them to their rightful place.

The Isle of Portland

A giant lump of largely treeless land jutting out from the sea and connected to the mainland by a narrow causeway, the **ISLE OF PORTLAND** is a strange place. Labelled the "Gibraltar of Wessex" by Thomas Hardy, it's best known for its hard white limestone, which has been quarried here for centuries (see box, p.126) – as testified by the ragged, broken cliffs around its shorelines and its various exposed quarries dotting the top. First impressions are not appealing – with an industrial port and quarries, a bleak prison, and towns as hard and unforgiving-looking as the rocks themselves – but head for the far side of the island and linger awhile and you may well acquire a taste for the strange landscape.

Accommodation

There's a variety of accommodation on the Isle of Portland, with more being built in preparation for the Olympics. The area's **youth hostel** in an Edwardian house in Fortuneswell, with views over Chesil Beach (☏0845 3719339, ⓦwww.yha.org.uk; £18).

Brackenbury House Fortuneswell ☏01305 826509, ⓦwww.brackenburyhouse.co.uk. This small B&B on the main through-road has five comfortable rooms – good value. ❶

Church Ope Studio Church Ope ☏01305 860428, ⓦwww.churchopestudio.com. Tiny, self-catering studio that's the only place to stay in Church Ope: it's well furnished and right on the coast path (£350 a week).

Heights Hotel Yeates Rd, at the top of the hill ☏01305 821361, ⓦwww.heightshotel.com.

A rather old-fashioned place with plain rooms, but it does have a heated outdoor pool and fabulous views over the coast. ❻

Old Bill House Portland Bill ☏01305 822449, ⓦwww.oldbillhouse.com. This little B&B has three cosy en-suite rooms with sea views – one with its own balcony – in an old coastguard's cottage (facing the lighthouse, turn left opposite the *Pulpit Inn*). ❶

Portland Spa Hotel Southwell Park ☏01305 826000, ⓦwww.theportlandspa.com. The smartest option on the Isle of Portland. Built from Portland

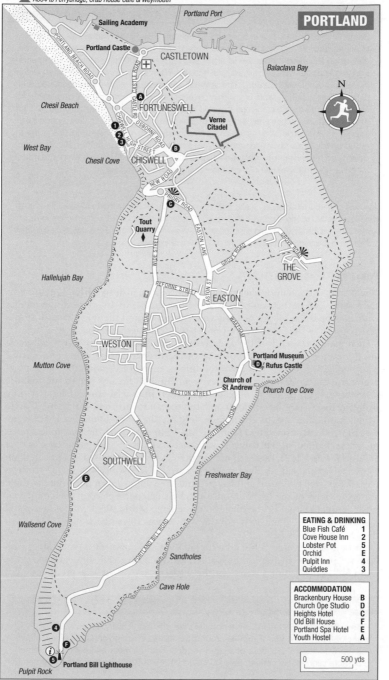

PORTLAND

A354 to Ferrybridge, Crab House Café & Weymouth

Portland Port

Sailing Academy

Portland Castle

CASTLETOWN

Balaclava Bay

N

Chesil Beach

FORTUNESWELL

Verne Citadel

West Bay

Chesil Cove

CHISWELL

NEW ROAD

PRIORY ROAD

Tout Quarry

EASTON LANE

GROVE ROAD

THE GROVE

Hallelujah Bay

WIDE STREET

REFORNE STREET

EASTON ST

EASTON

WESTON

Mutton Cove

Portland Museum

Rufus Castle

Church of St Andrew

Church Ope Cove

WESTON STREET

SOUTHWELL ROAD

AVALANCHE ROAD

SOUTHWELL

Freshwater Bay

Wallsend Cove

PORTLAND BILL ROAD

Sandholes

Cave Hole

Pulpit Rock

Portland Bill Lighthouse

EATING & DRINKING
Blue Fish Café	1
Cove House Inn	2
Lobster Pot	5
Orchid	E
Pulpit Inn	4
Quiddles	3

ACCOMMODATION
Brackenbury House	B
Church Ope Studio	D
Heights Hotel	C
Old Bill House	F
Portland Spa Hotel	E
Youth Hostel	A

0   500 yds

Portland stone

Some of the world's finest buildings – including St Paul's Cathedral, the British Museum and the UN headquarters in New York – have been constructed from the distinctive **Portland stone**. It was also used for the 6000ft breakwater that protects Portland Harbour – the largest artificial harbour in Britain, which was built by convicts in the mid-nineteenth century. The stone is of unusually high quality because it is extremely hard and durable but with an even structure, which means it can be cut in any direction without cracking. It was formed in the Jurassic Period, around 135 million years ago when the Purbeck coast would have been a shallow, warm sea. Minute structures known as ooliths developed when limestone particles formed round grains of sand or shell as they were rolled round the sea floor. Slowly these developed into layers of limestone which built up into the distinctive even structure, a bit like cod roe. The Isle of Portland is still quarried to this day.

stone and formerly a MOD building, it's an odd place – part of the building is still used by various businesses – but there's no denying the luxurious well-designed rooms, great spa facilities and fantastic location, a short walk along the coastal path from Portland Bill: just make sure you ask for a sea view, or you'll be overlooking the old defence buildings. **⑦**

North Portland

The largest settlement on the Isle of Portland is **Fortuneswell**, located immediately at the end of the causeway as you enter the island. Its western side merges with the appealing village of **Chiswell**, tucked behind the huge bank of stones that constitutes the southern end of Chesil Beach (see p.124).

Turn east at the end of the causeway road to **Castletown** and you'll get a good view of the huge harbour, one of the deepest in the world and a naval base since 1872, which will form the hub of many of Weymouth's watersports events in the 2012 Olympics. Development has already begun around the Castletown area, currently a rather run-down industrial zone of interest only really to divers (see box below) and for the Tudor fortress, **Portland Castle** (daily: April–June & Sept 10am–5pm; July & Aug 10am–6pm; Oct 10am–4pm; £4; EH), commissioned by Henry VIII in 1540 to protect the two-mile stretch of water known as Portland Roads, between here and its sister castle at Sandsfoot (see p.123). Besieged during the Civil War, later used as a prison, then a private home, and finally a military base during World War II, the castle is remarkably well preserved and has an attractive garden. From the ramparts, there are great views of the harbour, once the best defended place in the country: it was a frequent target for German bombs during World War II, and you can still see sections of the Mulberry harbour, which was towed back here after use in the D-day landings (see p.291).

Just beyond the castle, behind the Ocean View development, a (signposted) path leads steeply up to the top of the island. This was once a cliff railway employed to transport Portland stone down to the harbour, and is now a precipitous but

Diving in Portland

The waters around Portland are a popular **dive site**, particularly because of the many wrecks from World War II that lie around the island. Castletown is the island's dive centre with several outfitters offering dive trips, boat charters and equipment rental. For more information, contact Dive Dorset (☎01305 860269, ⓦ www.divedorset.com).

rewarding twenty- to thirty-minute walk up to the 150m summit of Verne Hill. The castle at the top, **Verne Citadel**, was built in Victorian times as a fortress: convicts sentenced to hard labour carried out much of the construction work on the building, which is now used as a working prison – not surprisingly, visitors are discouraged from getting too near.

The main road through Portland leads steeply up then splits, as the western fork leads past **Tout Quarry**. Opened in 1983, this huge, open-air sculpture park has animals, figures and shapes carved out of the quarried rock face. Sadly it's all rather run-down and unkempt and many of the sculptures have been damaged: also, there's no signage, so you'll be lucky to find specific works, such as Anthony Gormley's dramatic *Still Falling* figure. Despite this, it's worth just wandering around seeing what you can find, and clambering up through the arches for fantastic views down the western edge of the island and along Chesil Beach. Regular stone-carving workshops are held at the quarry, when you can carve your own sculptures out of the native stone; for more details, contact ☏01305 826736, ⓦlearningstone.org.

South Portland

The eastern fork of the main road leads through the town of Easton towards the south of the island at the pretty hamlet of **Church Ope Cove**, where you'll find Portland's only beach and the **Portland Museum** (11am–4.30pm: May, June, Sept & Oct Fri–Tues; July & Aug daily; £2.20), in two thatched seventeenth-century cottages with a pretty garden. Inside is an assorted collection of displays on all things related to Portland, including stone-carvings, fossils and information on birth control pioneer Marie Stopes, who lived in the Old Lighthouse on Portland and founded the museum. There's a lovely round walk (about 30min) from the museum down a steep path that leads to the pebbly beach: en route, you'll pass beneath an archway belonging to the Norman **Rufus Castle**, built for William II, who was known as Rufus because of his red hair; the island's oldest castle, it is now privately owned and closed to the public. After visiting the beach – with its collection of beach huts with strange rock-gardens – backtrack a short way up the steps to where a path leads off to the left to the ruined **Church of St Andrew**, Portland's oldest surviving building. Thought to date from the twelfth century, the tumbledown church and overgrown graveyard make a great place to wander. From here a small path winds up through woods to join the main road and car park near the museum.

From Church Ope, it's a couple of miles south through fairly bleak landscape that improves greatly at **Portland Bill**, the southern tip of the island. This blowy headland is a great place for scrambling over rocks, flying kites and windswept coastal walks. It's capped by a lighthouse which has guarded the promontory since the eighteenth century: you can climb the 153 steps of the present one, dating from 1906, for fabulous views (Easter–Sept Mon–Fri & Sun 11am–5pm; £2), and it also houses Portland's **tourist office** (Easter–Sept daily 11am–5pm; ☏01305 861233).

Eating and drinking

Blue Fish Café Chiswell. Friendly, laid-back restaurant serving excellent food, such as scallops with black pudding (£10), and *moules frites* with a glass of wine or beer (£10); it has a nice garden outside beneath the shadow of the Chesil bank.

Cove House Inn Chiswell. The best place for food and drink on the island, *Cove House Inn* serves fresh local fish, such as mackerel (£6), fish pie (£8) and scallops (£10): it's cosy inside with a wood-burner and big windows with sea views, while the outside tables look over Chesil Beach.

The Fleet Lagoon

The largest tidal lagoon in Britain, the **Fleet Lagoon** is separated from the sea by the eighteen-mile-long Chesil Beach, creating a unique home for marine and birdlife. Some 150 types of seaweed and sea grasses thrive in its waters, giving shelter and food to 25 species of fish, including sea bass and mullet. This in turn attracts thousands of birds throughout the year. Winter visitors include Brent Geese from Siberia and wigeon from Russia, while spring sees southern migrants from Africa including little terns and grey herons. Its most famous birds are the giant population of mute swans at Abbotsbury (see below). During the seventeenth century, there were attempts to drain the entire lagoon to create agricultural land. Fortunately for today's wildlife, the system of dams and sluices that were built failed miserably, with salt water constantly percolating through the shingle. The plan was abandoned and the lagoon has been kept intact ever since. Long associated with smuggling, the lagoon was immortalized in the children's adventure story *Moonfleet* by J. Meade Falkner, which was set in the nineteenth century at *Moonfleet Manor*, now a lovely, upmarket and child-friendly hotel (℡01395 786948, ⓦwww.moonfleetmanorhotel .co.uk; ⑧). The lagoon also played an important role during World War II, when Barnes Wallace's bouncing bombs were tested here in September 1942, before being used against the Germans, as immortalized in the film *The Dambusters*.

Lobster Pot Portland Bill. This place enjoys a great position right on the headland by the lighthouse, with outdoor tables on the cliff-top. Head here for light lunches and tasty cream teas.
Orchid In the Portland Spa (see p.124). Large modern-style restaurant with great views across the island, serving a good-value three-course dinner of modern British food, including local fish, for £20.50.
Pulpit Inn Portland Bill. Busy and lively pub that does reasonably priced local fish and seafood as well as pub staples in a great location right near the headland.
Quiddles A short walk south of *Cove House Inn* (see above). By day *Quiddles* is a pleasant café serving cakes, ice creams and sandwiches; by night (Thurs–Sun) it stays open till 9pm for dinner, serving local seafood such as *Coquille St Jacques* (£9.25) and an alfresco paella on warm Thurs eves.

Abbotsbury

Eight miles west of Weymouth, the pretty village of **Abbotsbury** has a surprising number of attractions for such a small place. First and foremost is the **Swannery** (late March to Oct daily 10am–5 or 6pm; £9, children £6; ℡01305 871858) established over six hundred years ago by Benedictine monks, who built an abbey here in the 1040s, and bred the swans for their lavish banquets. Ballerina Anna Pavlova visited here in 1920 to gain inspiration for her movements in *Swan Lake*, and scenes from the 2009 film *Harry Potter and the Half-Blood Prince* were filmed here. Today, the swannery is the only place in the world where you can get so close to a colony of nesting mute swans; you can walk around their nests, and along pretty paths through reed beds. Feeding time (twice daily, noon & 4pm) is spectacular, with up to 600 birds squabbling and flapping over the food. The best time to visit is when the cygnets hatch (May–June), when the whole site is studded with neat nests, cracking eggs and extremely fluffy cygnets. It can get very busy at this time, particularly during school holidays, though the swans themselves seem fairly oblivious to the crowds. A tractor trip runs from the entrance down to the nesting sites, and there is also a maze, where you can get lost in rows of twisted willows laid out in the shape of a swan.

Abbotsbury's second attraction is the large **Subtropical Gardens** (daily 10am–5 or 6pm; closed Christmas and New Year and at 4pm in winter; £9; ☎01305 871387), sitting in a sheltered wooded valley whose mild climate allows exotic and unusual plants to thrive. Established in 1765 by the Countess of Ilchester as a kitchen garden, the grounds now house a mixture of formal and informal areas, with walled gardens, valley walks and coastal views. In spring, the magnolias and camellias are particularly impressive, followed by colourful rhododendrons and hydrangeas in the summer.

Abbotsbury is also home to England's largest Tithe barn, built by Benedictine monks in the 1390s. It has been fully restored and now holds a **Children's Farm** (late March to Sept daily 10am–5 or 6pm; Sept to late Oct Sat & Sun 10am–5pm; Oct half-term daily 10am–5pm; £7.50, children £6; ☎01305 871817), where kids can watch goat-racing, then cuddle guinea pigs, ride tractors, and play in the barn on a soft-play area with slides and swings. If you want to visit more than one of the attractions above, it's worth buying a **passport ticket** (£15, children £10; ⓦwww.abbotsbury-tourism.co.uk), which gives admission to all three sites, and can be bought at any of the sites.

Near the tithe barn, on the site of the original abbey from which Abbotsbury took its name, is the wonderful, ⚔ *Abbey House* **tearooms** and **guest house** (☎01305 871330, ⓦwww.theabbeyhouse.co.uk; ❷), parts of which date from the fifteenth century. With over an acre of grounds and lovely views down to the coast, the pretty gardens are the perfect spot for a delicious cream tea, cake or light lunch, while the comfortable rooms are traditionally decorated with views over the gardens and the barn. They even host outdoor operas and theatre in the gardens in summer; see ⓦwww.abbmusic.org.uk for details of productions.

From opposite the *Abbey House* car park, a path leads steeply uphill to the fourteenth-century **St Catherine's Chapel**, a local landmark which can be seen from miles around, and has even inspired a song by P.J. Harvey, *The Wind*. Built from local stone, it has immensely thick walls, which make it tiny inside despite its solid exterior appearance. The walk up to the chapel is lovely and views from the top are fantastic.

Bridport, West Bay and around

Situated slightly inland on the main A35, many people regard historic **Bridport** as an inconvenient traffic hold-up on their way further west. But it has a lively, slightly alternative feel, good cafés and restaurants and a vibrant twice-weekly market, so a longer stay is certainly worthwhile. With its beach just south of town at **West Bay**, it also makes a good base for exploring the nearby coastal villages of **Eype** to the east and **Burton Bradstock** to the west.

Bridport and West Bay

Founded on land between the rivers Asker and Brit, **BRIDPORT** was mentioned in the Domesday Book of 1086 and was an important port before the rivers silted up in the early 1700s. But its fine buildings mostly date from the time it was a major rope-making centre – the pleasant old town of solid brick buildings has unusually wide streets, a hangover from when cords were stretched between the houses to be twisted and dyed (see box, p.131). It's a twenty-minute walk from the centre of Bridport, along a path behind the church in South Street, to the town's nearest bit of sea, a mile or so south at

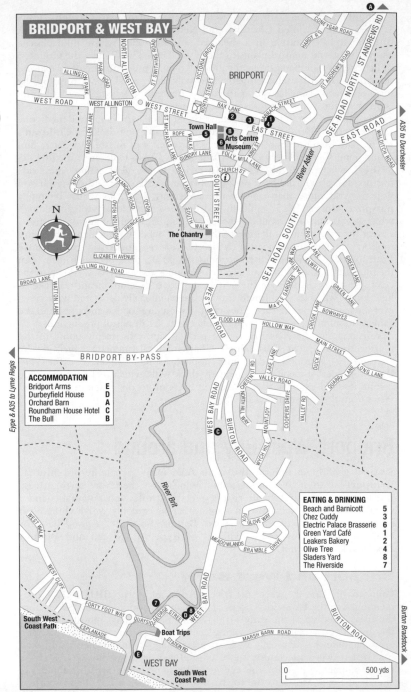

BRIDPORT & WEST BAY

BRIDPORT

CONEYGAR ROAD

HARDY RD

ST ANDREWS RD

A35 to Dorchester

EAST ROAD

WALDITCH ROAD

SEA ROAD NORTH

ST ANDREWS ROAD

COANE ROAD

NORTH ALLINGTON

ALLINGTON PARK

PARK ROAD

NORTH ALLINGTON

ST SWITHINS ROAD

VICTORIA GROVE

NORTH STREET

RAX LANE

BARRACK STREET

WEST ROAD

WEST ALLINGTON

WEST STREET

WEST STREET

EAST STREET

Town Hall **5**

B Arts Centre
Museum **6**

2 **3** **4**

River Asker

MAGDALEN LANE

ST MICHAELS LANE

ROPE WALKS

GUNDRY LANE

PRIORY LANE

KING ST

FOLLY MILL LANE

CHURCH ST

ℹ

EAST ROAD

SEA ROAD SOUTH

CROOK LANE

GREEN LANE

PINE VIEW

ALEXANDRA ROAD

CORONATION ROAD

PRINCESS ROAD

SOUTH STREET

SOUTH WALK

The Chantry

ELWELL

PAST

MAPLE GARDENS

GREEN LANE

ELIZABETH AVENUE

SKILLING HILL ROAD

BROAD LANE

WATTON LANE

WEST BAY ROAD

FLOOD LANE

HOLLOW WAY

CROOK LANE

MAIN STREET

DUCK ST

BOWHAYES

QUARRY LANE

LONG LANE

BRIDPORT BY-PASS

Eype & A35 to Lyme Regis

WEST BAY ROAD

BURTON ROAD

VALLEY ROAD

CHESTNUT RD

NORTH HILL WAY

WITCH HILL

MOUNTJOY

COOPERS DRIVE

VALLEY RD

C

LAKE LANE

River Brit

WEST WALK

WEST CLIFF

FORTY FOOT WAY

ESPLANADE

FOX GLOVE WAY

MEADOWLANDS

BRAMBLE DRIVE

WEST BAY ROAD

GEORGE STREET

STATION RD

7

Quayside

8 **D**

Boat Trips

MARSH BARN ROAD

BURTON ROAD

Burton Bradstock

South West
Coast Path

E WEST BAY

South West
Coast Path

0	500 yds

© Crown copyright

WEST BAY, which has a fine sandy beach sheltered below majestic red cliffs – the sheer East Cliffs are a tempting challenge for intrepid walkers.

Arrival and information

Bridport is well served by **buses** from Lyme Regis and Dorchester. On Wednesdays and Saturdays, a shuttle bus runs between West Bay Road car park and East Street in Bridport every 15 minutes from 9.30am to 3pm (late July to Sept only; £1 return). Bridport's well-stocked **tourist office** is at 47 South St (Mon–Sat: April–Oct 9am–5pm; Nov–March 10am–3pm; ☎01308 424901, ⓦwww .westdorset.com) and can provide information on local accommodation.

Accommodation

Bridport Arms West Bay ☎01308 422994, ⓦwww.bridportarmshotel.co.uk. Right on the seafront, this unusual thatched pub has big rooms with big views, either of the harbour or the sea. There is also a suite with its own jacuzzi. ❻
Durbeyfield House 10 West Bay ☎01308 423307, ⓦwww.durbeyfield.co.uk. Decent if simple rooms in an attractive Georgian townhouse next to the *Quarterdeck Tavern*, a short walk to the harbour. ❶
Orchard Barn Bradpole, near Bridport ☎01308 455655, ⓦlodgeatorchardbarn.co.uk. Comfortable and friendly two-bedroomed B&B, a mile or so north of Bridport. Guests have use of a private sitting room with a log fire and French windows onto the lovely, large south-facing garden that leads down to the banks of the River Asker. ❻

Roundham House Hotel Roundham Gardens, off West Bay Rd ☎01308 422753, ⓦwww.roundham house.co.uk. Set just off the main road to West Bay, a 15min walk to either Bridport or the beach, there are airy rooms of varying sizes in this fine Edwardian house with its own bar, gardens and dining room. Service is courteous and friendly. ❺
The Bull 34 East St ☎01308 422878, ⓦwww .thebullhotel.co.uk. Friendly, boutique-style hotel in a former seventeenth-century coaching inn in the centre of town. The individually designed rooms are comfortable with all mod cons and Neal's Yard toiletries: it's child-friendly with family rooms too. The restaurant and bar are good: Wednesday is currently the very popular *moules frites* night – mussels, chips and a beer or wine for £10. ❹

The Town

Arranged around a crossroads where North, South, East and West streets meet, Bridport has long been a lively market town. In the past, the streets had very distinct characters; the East and West streets were home to the wealthy travellers and merchants, while South Street was populated by sailors and poor people. In the 1800s, the town had several inns – it is said that every other house in South Street sold beer to cater to visitors. It retains its brewing connections to this day, with **Palmers Brewery**, founded in 1794, still producing beer from its original site in West Bay Road – indeed part of the brewery is still thatched: two-hour

---

In the net: Bridport's rope-making

Bridport has been a major centre for **rope-making** probably since Roman times, thanks to the top-quality hemp and flax that grew in the surrounding countryside. The town became famous for naval rope-making – Henry VII once decreed that all hemp within five miles of the town was for exclusive use of the navy. The expression "to be stabbed by a Bridport dagger" was a popular one and referred to being hanged, for nooses were also made using the tough Bridport rope. When naval rope-making switched to Portsmouth in the 1800s, Bridport swopped to net-making, predominantly kitting out the fishing fleets that set sail to Newfoundland. The trade continues to this day, though modern nets don't use hemp but synthetics; Bridport nets have been used in the Space Shuttle, for army camouflage, not to mention the nets at Wimbledon and, most famously, for the Wembley nets when England won the World Cup in 1966.

tours run on Monday to Friday at 11am from Easter to September (book in advance on ☎01305 427500, ⓦwww.palmersbrewery.co.uk; £7.50), ending with a tasting session.

Bridport is best visited on a Wednesday or Saturday, when East, West and South streets fill with **market** stalls selling an assortment of local produce, arts and crafts, antiques, bric-a-brac and junk. The town also has a thriving artistic community – its **Arts Centre** (ⓦwww.bridport-arts.com), also on South Street, puts on contemporary theatre and hosts a farmers' market on the second Saturday of every month in a former Victorian Methodist chapel.

The unremarkable **town museum** (April–Oct Mon–Sat 10am–5pm; £2.50; ⓦwww.bridportmuseum.co.uk) is set in a fine Tudor building on South Street, and has models of how ropes were stretched across Bridport's streets (see box, p.131), together with other aspects of the town's history. Other notable buildings are the Georgian **town hall**, at the top of South Street, and a fourteenth-century **chantry** (closed to the public) at the bottom of the same street, whose upstairs pigeon loft was once used to supplement the resident priest's diet.

West Bay

Clustered round a working fishing harbour squeezed between concrete piers – built in the 1860s to protect the river estuary from storms – **West Bay** can at best be described as atmospheric. Its motley collection of ugly seaside flats, fishermen's cottages and souvenir stalls make it possibly the least attractive resort in Dorset, though you may not care once ensconced on the beach to the east, or up on the superb coastal paths in either direction. There are plenty of **boat tours** and mackerel **fishing trips** from the harbour, too, from around £10 per person for thirty minutes (ⓦwww.lymebayseaschool.co.uk or www.lymebayribcharter .co.uk for details), or you can try diving to one of the local wrecks (see ⓦwww .westbaydiving.com).

Eating and drinking

Bridport has a good selection of **restaurants** and **cafés**, many selling local produce, as championed by Hugh Fearnley-Whittingstall at his nearby River Cottage (see p.133). Look out, too, for the Bridport Food Festival, held each June. In West Bay, the best-value food is from the colourful wooden huts along the harbour – they sell delicious, fresh fish and chips.

Beach and Barnicott 6 South St ☎01308 455688. Distinctive bar-restaurant in a Georgian building with several dining rooms on three floors each decorated in a different style. The menu changes daily using local food where possible, such as steaks and mussels (£12). Tapas night on Wed, with tapas for £2–3 a portion.

Chez Cuddy 47 East St, Bridport ☎01308 458770. Small, modern brasserie with superb dishes produced by the former chef of the *Atlantic Bar and Grill* in London. Seafood is the speciality, with reasonably priced dishes including mussels, local scallops and seafood ragout. Tues–Wed 10am–3pm, Thurs–Sat 10am–3pm & 6–11pm.

Electric Palace Brasserie 35 South St, Bridport ☎01308 426336. Atmospheric café in the lobby of this great 1920s cinema, serving drinks, soups, salads and daily special lunches at around £6 for a main course. Daily 9.30am–3pm.

Green Yard Café 4–6 Barrack St, Bridport ☎01308 459466. A good spot for breakfast, tea or lunch, with a good range of veggie dishes. Soups are fresh and filling, as are the quiches, salads and sandwiches. Tues–Sat 9am–5.30pm.

Leakers Bakery 29 East St. The place to stock up for a picnic with organic breads, pastries and cakes made in the on-site kitchen using local, seasonal produce. Choose from savouries such as cheese and cider bread or curry-filled naans, or sweeter treats like ginger and date scones and almond croissants, all baked daily.

Olive Tree 59 East St, Bridport ☎01308 422882. Not particularly cheap but good for families with a range of well-prepared pasta dishes, such as rigatoni with fennel, courgette and tomato sauce, and stone-baked pizzas. Tues–Sat noon–2pm & 6–9pm.

Sladers Yard West Bay Rd, West Bay. This taste-fully converted warehouse gallery showcases works by local artists and has a small downstairs café, a great spot for a coffee or snack. Wed–Sat 10am–5pm Sun 11am–5pm.

The Riverside West Bay ☎01308 422011. Reservations are recommended for this renowned restaurant which offers fresh sumptuous fish and seafood and fine views over the river. There is a daily changing menu, but expect the likes of Thai-style fried prawns, grilled sea bass with mango along with a vegetarian option. Mains from around £16. Mid-Feb to Dec Tues–Sat noon–2.30pm & 6.30–9pm; April–Sept also Sun noon–2.30pm.

Burton Bradstock

Three miles east of Bridport, the pretty village of **BURTON BRADSTOCK** is regularly voted Dorset's best-kept village and boasts a lovely stretch of cliff-backed pebble beach – though bathers should be aware of the strong currents here. It's a special spot, with fine coastal walks along the cliff-tops and several places to eat and stay. Top choice for food is the laid-back *Hive Beach Café* (☎01308 897070, ⓦ www.hivebeachcafe.co.uk), on a bluff above the beach, which dishes up top-quality seafood, such as Lyme Bay plaice (£17), local sea trout (£17) and Lyme Bay scallops (£20), as well as delicious home-made cakes, excellent coffee and very friendly service. In the village there are also a couple of popular **pubs** that serve fantastic seafood: the *Three Horseshoes* (☎01308 897269) on Mill Street is a cosy place with a wood-burner, and serves daily specials such as scallops thermidor (£14) as well as good-value pub food; while the *Anchor Inn* (☎01308 897228) on the High Street does reasonably priced local fish, such as scallops and lobster and a superb seafood platter for two. The Edwardian *Norburton Hall* on Shipton Lane (☎01308 897007, ⓦ www.norburtonhall.com; ❻) is the best place **to stay**, with six acres of rolling grounds and three beautifully furnished en-suite bedrooms, one with a four-poster bed: grand without being too formal, it also has several self-catering cottages to rent in the outbuildings. Simpler en-suite double and family rooms are available at *Bridge Cottage*, 87 High St (☎01308 897222, ⓦ www.bridgecottagebedandbreakfast.co.uk; ❶).

The River Cottage effect

The area inland from Bridport and Lyme Regis has been one of the main inspirations behind the resurgence of interest in **local, seasonal food** in the UK. Chef **Hugh Fearnley-Whittingstall** moved here to the original **River Cottage** in 1998, bringing with him an infectious enthusiasm for growing and catching all his own food. He caught fish and seafood from West Bay, grew his own fruit and vegetables, promoted local artisan food producers, and raised his own animals, cooking delicious meals with parts of the animal that many would throw away, such as the offal. He even produced his own beer from local, organic nettles, the River Cottage Stinger, brewed by Hall & Woodhouse, based in Blandford Forum (see p.151). His campaigning for the welfare of poultry led to his attempt to convert the entire nearby town of Axminster, just over the border in Devon, to buying free-range chicken; while the campaign was not wholly successful, it highlighted the plight of intensively farmed chickens and led major supermarket chains to re-think their policies towards using higher welfare farming. While Fearnley-Whittingstall still lives in Dorset, the River Cottage headquarters has now moved just across the border to Devon, where it runs pricey workshops on fishing, cooking with seasonal produce, bread-making, bee-keeping, growing your own vegetables, and foraging for free food (ⓦ www .rivercottage.net). It's also worth detouring into Devon to the excellent *River Cottage Store and Canteen* on Trinity Square in nearby Axminster, to pick up supplies or sample the delicious local, seasonal, sustainable meals, such as white onion and cider soup, or gurnard and chips.

Eype

A couple of miles southwest of Bridport and accessed by an incredibly narrow, roller coaster of a road, the tiny, picturesque village of **EYPE** – whose name aptly means "steep place"– spreads across hills that dip down to a pretty pebble beach. The *Eype House* **campsite** (☎01308 424903, ⓦwww.eypehouse.co.uk) enjoys a lovely location near the beach: its camping field has great cliff-top views over the sea. Alternatively, the *Eype's Mouth Country Hotel* (☎01308 423300, ⓦeypesmouthhotel.co.uk; ❹), a little further up the lane, has friendly service and an outdoor terrace with splendid sea views shared by some of the comfortable rooms; others look inland over the countryside.

Lyme Regis and around

Dorset's most westerly town, **LYME REGIS**, is also its most alluring. It shelters snugly between steep hills, just before the grey, fossil-filled cliffs lurch into Devon. Its intimate size and highly photogenic qualities make it a popular and congested spot in high summer, though the town still lives up to the classy impression created by its regal name, resulting from a royal charter granted by Edward I in 1284. It also has some upmarket literary associations – Jane Austen summered in a seafront cottage and set part of *Persuasion* in Lyme, while novelist John Fowles lived here until his death in 2005, and set his best-known book here, *The French Lieutenant's Woman*. Austen's description of Lyme is still pretty accurate today: "the Cobb itself…with the very beautiful line of cliffs, stretching out to the east of the town, are what the stranger's eye will seek, and a very strange stranger it must be who does not see charms in the immediate environs of Lyme, to make him wish to know it better."

The coast either side of Lyme is spectacular, with great walks heading west into Devon and east to the tiny hamlet of **Seatown**, via the towering **Golden Cap** and the appealing village of **Charmouth**, another favourite of Jane Austen.

Arrival and information

Lyme's nearest **train station** is in Axminster, five miles north (served by regular bus #31), while First buses runs a daily **bus** service from Exeter, Bridport, Weymouth and Poole every couple of hours (ⓦwww.firstgroup.com). Drivers will find the central stretch hard to park in, though there are plenty of car parks just uphill. The **tourist office** is on Church Street (April–Oct Mon–Sat 10am–5am, Sun 10am–4pm; Nov–March Mon–Sat 10am–3pm; ☎01297 442138, ⓦwww.lymeregistourism.co.uk).

John Fowles and the French Lieutenant's Woman

On a windswept day, it's hard to resist standing on The Cobb staring moodily out to sea, knowingly recreating the iconic image of Sarah Woodruff, played by Meryl Streep in *The French Lieutenant's Woman*, the romantic film based on John Fowles' 1969 book. Fowles lived in Lyme from 1968 until his death in 2005, writing many of his best-known novels here, but had an ambivalent relationship with the town. On the one hand, he was very involved with the community as curator of the museum for several years and an active chronicler of its historical society: on the other hand, he was a reclusive figure, whose *Journals* suggest a brooding darkness about the town and make clear that he found the place stifling and remote.

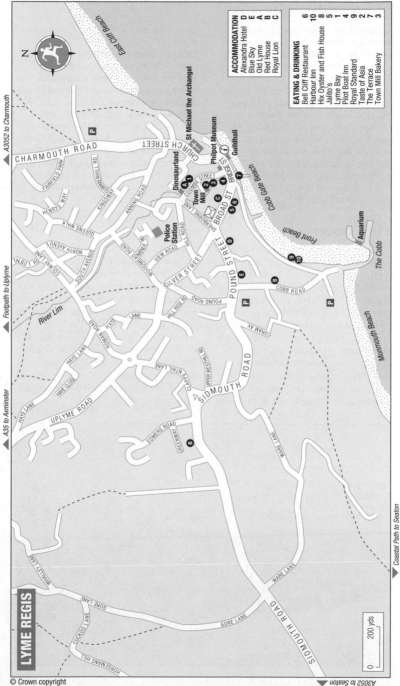

LYME REGIS

ACCOMMODATION
Alexandra Hotel   D
Blue Sky   E
Old Lyme   A
Red House   B
Royal Lion   C

EATING & DRINKING
Bell Cliff Restaurant   6
Harbour Inn   10
Hix Oyster and Fish House   8
Jalito's   5
Lyme Bay   1
Pilot Boat Inn   4
Royal Standard   9
Taste of Asia   2
The Terrace   7
Town Mill Bakery   3

East Cliff Beach

A3052 to Charmouth

St Michael the Archangel

CHARMOUTH ROAD

FAIRFIELD PARK

WINDMILL RD

KINGSWAY

ANNING ROAD

HENRY'S WAY

QUEENS WALK

NORTH AVENUE

COLWAY LANE

Footpath to Uplyme

SOUTH AVENUE

WOODMEAD ROAD

CHARMOUTH ROAD

HILL ROAD

SHERBORNE LANE

COOMBE STREET

CHURCH STREET

Dinosaurland

Town Mill

Philpot Museum

Guildhall

BRIDGE ST

BROAD ST

Cobb Gate Beach

Police Station

VIEW ROAD

SILVER STREET

POUND ROAD

POUND STREET

Front Beach

Aquarium

A35 to Axminster

River Lim

HAYE LANE

HILL RISE RD

COBB ROAD

The Cobb

HAYE ROAD

ROMAN ROAD

HAYE LANE

HAYE CLOSE

CLAPPENTAIL LANE

UPPER WESTHILL RD

CORAM AV

Monmouth Beach

UPLYME ROAD

SIDMOUTH ROAD

SOMERS ROAD

GREENWAY

WARE LANE

WHALLEY LANE

GORE LANE

CUCKOO LANE

GORE LANE

HORSEMANS HILL

SIDMOUTH ROAD

WARE LANE

Coastal Path to Seaton

A3052 to Seaton

© Crown copyright

0   200 yds

Accommodation

Alexandra Hotel Pound St ☎01297 442010, ⓦwww.hotelalexandra.co.uk. Eighteenth-century manor house with lovely gardens overlooking the sea. The comfortable rooms are newly refurbished and many have sea views. ❻

Blue Sky 8 Pound St ☎01297 442339, ⓦwww.bluesky-lymeregis.co.uk. Friendly B&B a steep walk uphill from the main high street. The back rooms have good views over town, though the larger family rooms overlook the main road. Good breakfasts, though there's no parking. ❸

Old Lyme 29 Coombe St ☎01297 442929, ⓦoldlymeguesthouse.co.uk. Central guest house close to Dinosaurland (see p.137), in a lovely stone former post office, with six smallish but spruce bedrooms; one is a family room and most en suite. ❸

Red House Sidmouth Rd ☎01297 442055. An attractive 1920s house with three comfortable rooms, two of which have good views over the coast: there's a large garden, but it's a steepish walk back from town; minimum booking two nights. ❸

Royal Lion Broad St ☎01297 445622, ⓦwww.royallionhotel.com. Welcoming seventeenth-century coaching inn on the main street, complete with grandfather clock and a high-ceilinged dining room. There's off-street parking and a small indoor pool. Most rooms have balconies facing the sea, though downstairs spacious family rooms have small outdoor patios. ❻

The Town

Unlike many coastal towns, **LYME REGIS** has an interesting mix of architecture, from thatched cottages to ornate Victorian house fronts. While colourwashed cottages and elegant Regency and Victorian villas line its seafront and flanking streets, Lyme's best-known feature is a briskly practical reminder of its commercial origins: **The Cobb**, a curving harbour wall first constructed in the thirteenth century. It has suffered many alterations since, most notably in the nineteenth century, when its massive boulders were clad in neater blocks of Portland stone. Set in a row of former fishermen's houses out on The Cobb is a **Marine aquarium** (March–Oct plus Feb half-term daily 10am–5pm; £5, children £4.50) – expensive considering its size but its display of local marine life is certainly fun and includes poisonous weaver fish, sea scorpions, sea horses and pipe fish, not to mention bits of old boat and planes recovered by fishermen, including the canopy of a Red Arrow that crashed in 1980.

▲ The Cobb

There's a fine walk inland from Lyme Regis up the River Lyme to **Uplyme**, which is actually in Devon, although virtually a suburb of Lyme Regis – look out for the sign that tells you you have crossed the county border. Start out by heading uphill from the Town Mill, with a brief detour up the street alongside the *Angel* pub, and the riverside path soon heads into woodland and grassy meadows for the one-and-a-half-mile route to the neighbouring village of Uplyme, via various mills and bridges. Once past the thatched water mill, keep to the left, cross the road, ignoring the path to the left after Honeysuckle Cottage, and you will reach Church Street in Uplyme within around forty-five minutes.

Back in the town centre, the excellent **Lyme Regis Philpot Museum** on Bridge Street (Easter–Oct Mon–Sat 10am–5pm, Sun 11am–5pm; Nov–Easter Wed–Sun 11am–4pm, daily in school hols; £3; @www.lymeregismuseum.co.uk) provides a crash course in local history and geology. The fine Victorian town museum was built in 1901 by Thomas Philpot, appropriately on the site of a fossil shop which kick-started the Jurassic Coast brand (see box, p.138). The shop was, until 1826, also the home of Mary Anning, the woman who first saw the significance of Lyme's fossils and sold them to curious visitors – her collecting is believed to have inspired the saying *She sells seashells on the seashore*. The museum not only traces the history of her life and the Jurassic Coast, but also plots Lyme's maritime history and its connections to famous people through time, including Jane Austen, William Pitt and Laurence Whistler, whose engraved glass can be viewed along with famous paintings of the town. Look out, too, for the impressive seventeenth-century **Guildhall**, opposite the museum, and the fifteenth-century parish **church of St Michael the Archangel**, up Church Street, which contains a seventeenth-century pulpit, a massive chained Bible and the grave of Mary Anning.

Partly dating from 1340, the **Town Mill** on Mill Lane, just off Coombe Street, (Easter–Oct Tues–Sun 11am–4pm; Nov–Easter Sat & Sun 11am–4pm; £2, children £1; @www.townmill.org.uk) is a working water-mill complex, with art galleries, craft shops, a pottery, a cheesemonger and a great café (see p.139). You can look round the current mill building, which is largely seventeenth-century, and watch the water wheel turn to power the grinding stones: the excess hydoelectricity produced is sold back to the National Grid. You can buy the flour that's made here from local organic wheat.

A short walk up Coombe Street, **Dinosaurland** (daily 10am–5pm, but sometimes closed on weekdays from Nov–Feb, so call first to check; £4.50, children £3.50; ☎01297 443541, @www.dinosaurland.co.uk) is great for a rainy day, especially for families. This characterful museum, set inside a beautiful, galleried church dating from 1746, has a collection of fossils and models that romps through natural history using the hook of Mary Anning's famous ichthyosaur, found in the bay in 1811. Although the dinosaur skeletons are replicas, there are plenty of real fossilized ammonites and squid-like belemnites along with the skeletons of various contemporary beasties, including a 3.95m-long python skeleton, trays of butterflies and remains of enormous crabs and lobsters.

The Undercliff

As you walk along Lyme's seafront and out towards The Cobb, look for the outlines of ammonites in the walls and paving stones. Hands-off inspection of the area's complex geology can be enjoyed on both sides of town: to the west

The Jurassic Coast

A unique set of factors contributed to a 95-mile stretch of coast straddling Devon and Dorset being awarded UNESCO World Heritage status in 2001. Known as the **Jurassic Coast**, England's only Natural Heritage site was set up with the aim of safeguarding the amazing geological record displayed by the cliffs, coves and beaches along the coastline. It takes its name from Jurassic times, some 185 million years ago, when the south of England was covered by a warm sea called the Tethys Ocean. Over the years, sea levels fluctuated: clays were deposited when the sea was deepest, followed by sandstones and, when the sea level was shallower, layers of limestone. The shallow seas were particularly rich in sea life, the ocean supporting ancient species such as ammonites, plesiosaurs, ichthyosaurs and belemnites. When the animals died, they sank to the sea bed, and their bones became buried in the soft sea floor before being gradually fossilized.

Centuries later, faults in the Earth threw up the sea bed, sometimes vertically, exposing layers of rock. Any hard fossilized bones then became exposed to the sea, often falling onto beaches. The layers of rock on the Jurassic Coast actually represent three historical periods, the Triassic, Jurassic and Cretaceous. The oldest rocks, in Devon, are some 250 million years old, the youngest being at Studland in Dorset. But each layer shows a snapshot of history and geology, recording a changing landscape that has at times been desert, dinosaur-infested swamps and warm ocean. The Dorset section is richest for fossil hunters particularly around Lyme Regis, where the coast is made up largely of unstable blue Lias (a Dorset corruption of "layers", referring to the layers of soft and hard rock) dating back to the Triassic period, which regularly gives up its wealth of petrified animal and plant life.

lies the **Undercliff**, a fascinating jumble of overgrown landslips, now a nature reserve. The cliffs around Lyme are made up of a complex layer of limestone, greensand and unstable clay, a perfect medium for preserving fossils, which are exposed by frequent landslips. In 1811, after a fierce storm caused parts of the cliffs to collapse, twelve-year-old Mary Anning, a keen fossil-hunter, discovered an almost complete dinosaur skeleton, a 30ft ichthyosaurus that's now displayed in London's Natural History Museum. Hammering fossils out of the cliffs is frowned on by today's conservationists, however, and in any case is decidedly hazardous.

Eating and drinking

Bell Cliff Restaurant 5–6 Broad St ☎01297 442459. A quaint seventeenth-century café-restaurant in a prime position at the foot of the high street. As well as afternoon teas and coffees, the menu features cheap and cheerful meals such as roast chicken and salmon from around £7.

Harbour Inn Marine Parade ☎01297 442299. Lively bar-cum-fish restaurant facing the seafront. Fresh fish from around £14 along with fine meat dishes, though veggies are poorly catered for.

Hix Oyster and Fish House Cobb Rd ☎01297 446910. In a lovely location overlooking The Cobb, this light and airy restaurant, owned by acclaimed chef Mark Hix, specializes in local fish and seafood: main courses such as sea bass with fennel can be pricey at £25, though there are cheaper options, like fish pie (£12) and local grilled mackerel (£11).

Jalito's 14 Broad St ☎01297 445008. Primarily a deli serving local and organic cheeses, meats and pizzas (great for a picnic), with a small café area at the back for sit-down snacks and drinks. Closed eves.

Lyme Bay 44–45 Coombe St ☎01297 445371 ⓦ www.lymebaykitchenandbar.com. Neat little pizza and pasta restaurant, open for evening meals only except in high season. Tasty meat and fish dishes, but best for moderately priced pasta and pizzas for around £8.

Pilot Boat Inn Bridge St ☎01297 443157. A lively pub that also serves some of the best-value food in town. Its extensive menu includes fresh fish, fine steaks and a good range of vegetarian options, though you may have to wait for a table in high season.

Royal Standard 25 Marine Parade ☎01297 442637. Beachside inn dating back 400 years, with a log fire in winter, a sea-facing terrace and a long list of bar food, including vegetarian options and some fine fresh fish.

Taste of Asia The Town Mill, Mill Lane ☎01297 445757. Set in a stone-walled room within the old town mill, with tables outside in the summer, this café-restaurant serves drinks and snacks by day – including Japanese bento boxes – and sumptuous Indian food in the evening, including meat or vegetable thalis from £10, and balti dishes from £7.

The Terrace 8–9 Bridge St ☎01297 444110. The café at the back of this shop has superb views, especially from its terrace. A great stop for a good breakfast such as smoked salmon and scrambled egg, or light lunches, including crab baguette or beef in Devon ale, for around £8.

Town Mill Bakery Unit 2, Coombe St ☎01297 444035. A wonderful rustic-chic bakery, café and restaurant with a superb array of freshly baked breads to take away. Also serves a range of local and largely organic produce, including sublime breakfasts – with local preserves and fresh mushrooms – lunches, such as focaccia and Dorset rarebit (with cider) and evening pizzas, which you can enjoy on low wooden benches. Daily 8.30am–7pm, till 8pm in summer; closed weekday eves in winter.

Charmouth

Three miles east from Lyme, set on a steep hillside is the appealing town of **Charmouth**, Jane Austen's favourite resort and another great place for finding fossils. The **Heritage Centre** down on the beach (Easter–Oct 10.30am–4.30pm; free) runs excellent two-hour fossil-hunting tours (check ⓦwww.charmouth.org for times; £7, children £3) and has an interesting display upstairs on the history and geology of the fossils, including a plaster cast of the complete fossilized skeleton of a Scelidosaurus found here in 2000 – a dinosaur that is unique to Charmouth. Beneath the centre, the *Beach Café* (daily in summer) serves sandwiches, cooked breakfasts and local Bridport pies, and there's another seasonal café, the *Soft Rock Café* in a Portakabin at the eastern end of the beach which offers sandwiches and pies and rents out fossil hammers (£3 an hr). The beach here is a mixture of sand and pebbles, with fossil hunters heading to the west of the beach beneath Europe's largest landslip sight – the coast here is very unstable and you should steer clear of the cliffs themselves. Practised eyes can easily find a plethora of fossilized belomnites loose on the beach.

There's a reasonable choice of **accommodation** in Charmouth, with the family-run *Seadown* **campsite** (☎01297 560154, ⓦwww.seadownholidaypark .co.uk) having the best location, alongside the River Char behind the beach. Nearby, *Swansmead* B&B, Lower Sea Lane (☎01297 560465, ⓦwww .swansmead.co.uk; ❷) is clean, comfortable and friendly – with great sea views from its two rooms and direct access to the beach from the large back garden. Up in the town itself, the lovely Regency 🏃 *White House Hotel*, The Street (☎01297 560411, ⓦwww.whitehousehotel.com; ❻), is well run, with a pretty terrace garden and comfortable rooms: the breakfasts are great and its award-winning restaurant uses local and seasonal ingredients. *The Abbots House* (☎01297 560339, ⓦwww.abbotshouse.co.uk; ❼) further along The Street, has a boutique feel. The *Old Bank Café* on The Street is the place for daytime breakfasts, sandwiches and light lunches (closes 5pm), and there are a couple of **pubs** in the town, both also along The Street: *The George* dishes up decent pub staples (such as fish and chips for £7) and has a great garden with a children's play area and miniature goats; while the *Royal Oak* is good for local ales, sandwiches and simple meals with live music in the evenings – check ⓦwww .royaloakcharmouth.co.uk to see who's playing.

Seatown and the Golden Cap

It's a lovely three-mile walk along the steep coastal path from Charmouth to the headland of **Golden Cap**, whose brilliant outcrop of auburn sandstone is crowned with gorse. It's the highest point on the south coast and the views from here are fantastic – as far as Dartmoor on a clear day. Before setting off, check first with the Heritage Centre (see p.139) at Charmouth, as parts of the coastal path are closed periodically due to landslips.

Alternatively, you can access the Cap from the hamlet of **Seatown** (again check the condition of the path before setting off), just under a mile from the A35 (turn off at Chideock). There's little to Seatown, save a pretty beach, some good walks and a great pub, the *Anchor Inn*. Cosy inside with a wood-burner and a garden on the cliff-top with sea views, it serves decent pub grub (fish and chips for £7), real ales, and daily specials such as local lobster (£14).

Beaminster and around

Five miles north of Bridport, **BEAMINSTER** (pronounced "Beminster") is a typical example of a traditional inland Dorset town. There's not a lot to see here, but it's a great place to shop and consume, since it still retains its butcher, baker, fishmonger and deli, not to mention a scattering of decent pubs, strung out along Hogshill Street and the main square. Most of today's town grew up after a fire in the eighteenth century: this was "Emminster" in Thomas Hardy's *Tess of the D'Urbevilles* – take away today's cars and little would have changed since Hardy's day. Much of the town centre is a conservation area, its most important buildings being the fine, honey-coloured **Church of St Mary's** with an impressive 30m-high tower – where local men were hanged during the Bloody Assizes (see p.97) – and the fabulous Tudor **Parnham House**, just south of town and now privately owned. Hardy fans will want to see Beaminster Rectory on Clay Lane, off Hogshill Street, which was "Emminster" Rectory in *Tess*, where Angel Clare's parents lived. You can learn about the town's former rope, sailcloth and shoe-making industries at the small town **museum** (Easter–Sept Tues, Thurs & Sat 10.30am–12.30pm & 2.30–4.30pm, Sun 2.30–4.30pm; £1) on the edge of town on the Dorchester Road, set in a former seventeenth-century Congregational church.

Practicalities

Beaminster is served by regular **buses** from Bridport and Crewkerne, which is on the main rail route from London to Axminster. If you want **to stay**, the best option is *The Walnuts* at 2 Prout Bridge (℡01308 862211, ⊛www.thewalnuts .co.uk; ❷), in a seventeenth-century former doctor's house with a lovely garden, a stone's throw from the main square. More upmarket, *Bridge House* at 3 Prout Bridge (℡01308 862200, ⊛www.bridge-house.co.uk; ❼) has crisp, white rooms in a former priest's house partly dating back to the thirteenth century – the superior rooms come complete with jacuzzi baths and overlook the gardens: there is also a cosy bar, a good bistro and a fine-dining **restaurant**. More affordable is *The Black Cat Bistro* on the main square (closed Sun), serving daily specials, such as Dorset air-dried ham salad and pan-fried sea bass, with mains from around £12. Alternatively, *The Greyhound* and the *Red Lion* **pubs**, both on the main square, serve reasonably priced pub staples: *The Greyhound* is a traditional pub with a log fire, while the *Red Lion* serves real ales and has a beer garden and skittle alley.

▲ Mapperton House

Around Beaminster

Some three miles southeast of Beaminster off the B3163 lies **Mapperton House** (gardens March–Oct Sun–Fri 11am–5pm; house late June–July and summer bank hols 2–4.30pm; £4.50, children £2; Ⓦwww.mapperton.com) whose sumptuous gardens and Jacobean house, with its own church, have featured in the film versions of *Tom Jones* and *Emma*. The Italianate gardens are simply lovely, spreading out along a clefted dell and studded with fountains, fish ponds and statues of herons. They were landscaped in the 1920s (though the fish ponds date from the seventeenth century), with paths winding up to viewpoints over the coast. The house, enlarged in the 1670s, is currently home to the Earl and Countess of Sandwich, and has been restored to its original Tudor glory: its art collection includes paintings by the likes of Joshua Reynolds and Hogarth. There's also the excellent *Sawmill Café* (open to non-garden visitors March–Oct daily Sun–Fri 11am–5.30pm), which serves organic lunches, breakfasts and cakes in a converted sawmill; there are also tables outside on a lawn where chickens and ducks roam.

Seven miles east of Beaminster, through delightful Dorset countryside, the unspoilt village of **Evershot** ("Evershead" in Hardy's *Tess of the D'Urbevilles*) has featured in many a film, such as Jane Austen's *Emma*. Set in the heart of a private estate, the village boasts a series of thatched cottages, a tiny shop and bakery, a deer park and a beautiful church with an unusual pointed clock-tower. *The Acorn Inn* at 28 Fore St (Ⓣ01935 83228, Ⓦwww.acorn-inn.co.uk) has a restaurant serving pricey but quality fish and meat dishes at the front, and a more relaxed bar at the back with a log fire that serves pub food. It also has a few rooms (❻), but if your budget can stretch to it, you're better off staying at the lovely ⚑ *Summer Lodge* just up the road (Ⓣ01935 482000, Ⓦwww .summerlodgehotel.com; ❾). Set in superbly manicured grounds, complete with fountain, tennis courts and giant chess set, it has a pool, spa facilities, luxurious rooms and attentive, friendly service. The west wing of the hotel was designed by Thomas Hardy during his days as an architect – and the bar even boasts an Armagnac dating back to Hardy's time. The award-winning restaurant is second to none, using largely local, seasonal ingredients and there's a highly rated wine cellar.

Five miles west of Beaminster, the Iron Age hillfort at **Pilsdon Pen** is one of Dorset's highest hills at 277m-high. Fourteen Iron Age roundhouses were found here during excavations in the 1960s and the far-reaching views from the top stretch as far south as Lyme Regis. Indeed, Wordsworth, who rented a house near here at the end of the eighteenth century, declared it the finest view in all England, while his sister Dorothy pronounced it "the place dearest to my recollection upon the whole surface of the Island". A couple of miles south of here, the *Bottle Inn* at **Marshwood** hosts the bizarre annual World Nettle-eating Championships each June (see Ⓦwww.thebottleinn.co.uk for details); the rest of the year, it has decent pub grub, real ales and live music.

East Dorset and the Avon Valley

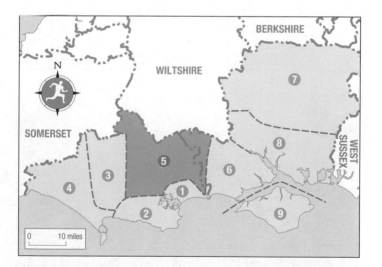

CHAPTER 5

Highlights

✳ **Wimbourne Minster** One of Dorset's finest churches in the heart of a pretty market town. See p.145

✳ **Kingston Lacy** Sumptuous seventeenth-century manor set in extensive grounds. See p.149

✳ **Hambledon Hill** This former Iron Age fort offers great walks and superb views. See p.152

✳ **Gold Hill, Shaftesbury** This idyllic hill is a quintessential slice of England. See p.155

✳ **Cranborne Chase** Former royal hunting grounds and now one of England's least spoilt tracts of land. See p.156

✳ **Go Ape, Moors Valley Country Park** Get wired and hang out in the treetops. See p.162

▲ Gold Hill, Shaftesbury

East Dorset and the Avon Valley

The towns of **EAST DORSET** are small, highly picturesque and historic: an easy excursion from the coast, **Wimborne Minster** is famed for its ancient church while nearby **Blandford Forum** offers a splendid Georgian townscape. The River Avon passes through the attractive market town of **Ringwood** into some of the least spoilt countryside in the whole county. This is particularly true around **Cranbourne Chase** – parts of which appear as almost a void on most maps, with barely a road or town to be seen. Nearby lies the pretty town of **Shaftesbury**, best known for its famous cobbled hill, now forever associated with sliced bread. Less feted but more historic hills include the impressive Hambledon Hill and Badbury Rings, both ancient **Iron Age forts**. It pays to plan your trip round the area carefully though, as many of the local sites are not open daily or year round. But the region's walks and rural scenery are permanent attractions, the highlights of which are the rolling estate at **Kingston Lacy** and the walks around **Fording-bridge**, from where the River Avon begins its approach to the coast along the western edges of the New Forest National Park.

Wimborne Minster and around

On the banks of the Stour, a short drive north from the suburbs of Bourne-mouth, **WIMBORNE MINSTER** is a well-to-do market town best known for its great church, the **Minster of St Cuthberga** (Mon–Sat 9.30am–5.30pm, Sun 2.30–5.30pm; free). Built on the site of an eighth-century monastery, its massive twin towers of mottled grey and tawny stone dwarf the rest of the town, and at one time the church was even more imposing – its spire crashed down during morning service in 1602. What remains today is basically Norman with added later features, such as the Perpendicular west tower, which bears a figure dressed as a grenadier of the Napoleonic era, who strikes every quarter-hour with a hammer. Inside, the church is crowded with memorials and eye-catching details – look out for the orrery clock inside the west tower, with the sun marking the hours and the moon marking the days of the month, and for the organ with trumpets pointing out towards the congregation instead of pipes. The **Chained Library** above the choir vestry (Easter–Oct Mon–Fri 10.30am–12.30pm &

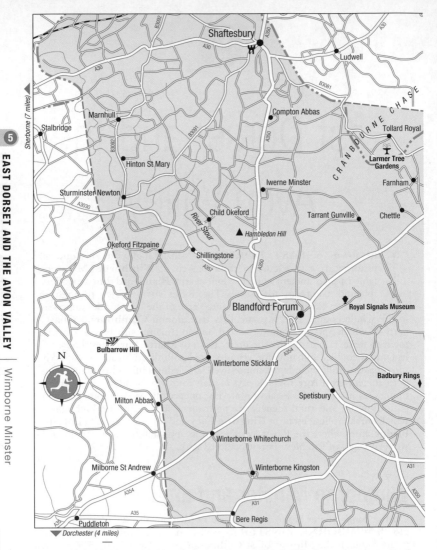

2–4pm, Sat 10.30am–12.30pm), dating from 1686, is Wimborne's most prized possession and one of the oldest public libraries in the country.

Wimborne's older buildings stand around the main square near the minster, and most date from the late eighteenth or early nineteenth century. The **Priest's House** on the High Street began life as lodgings for the clergy, then became a stationer's shop. Now it is a **museum** (April–Oct 10am–4.30pm; also open 2 weeks after Christmas; £3.50), with rooms individually furnished in the style of a different period, such as a working Victorian kitchen and a Georgian parlour. There's also a walled garden at the rear, which is an excellent spot for summer teas.

Also worth seeking out, is the quaint **Model Town** just west of the church (daily: April–Nov 10am–5pm, plus Aug 6.30–10pm; £4.50, children £3.50;

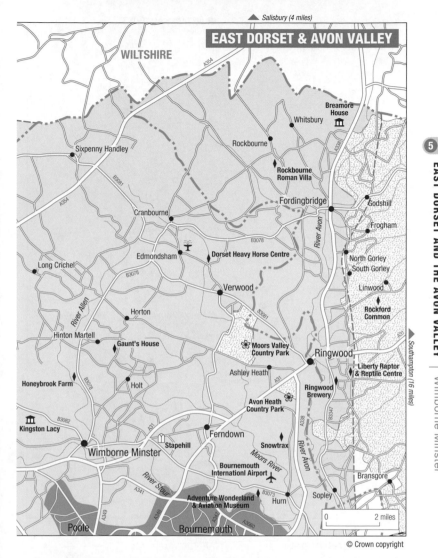

WILTSHIRE

Breamore
House

Whitsbury

Rockbourne

Sixpenny Handley

Rockbourne
Roman Villa

Fordingbridge

Godshill

Cranbourne

Frogham

Edmondsham

Dorset Heavy Horse Centre

River Avon

North Gorley
South Gorley

Long Crichel

Verwood

Linwood

River Allen

Horton

Rockford
Common

Hinton Martell

Gaunt's House

Moors Valley
Country Park

Ringwood

Honeybrook Farm

Holt

Ashley Heath

Liberty Raptor
& Reptile Centre

Avon Heath
Country Park

Ringwood
Brewery

Kingston Lacy

Ferndown

Snowtrax

River Avon

Wimborne Minster

Stapehill

Moors River

Bournemouth
Internationl Airport

Bransgore

River Stour

Adventure Wonderland
& Aviation Museum

Hurn

Sopley

Poole

Bournemouth

0   2 miles

Ⓦ www.wimborne-modeltown.com); this miniature model replicates the town as it was fifty years ago, complete with traditional shops, ringing telephone boxes and a chiming church where a miniature couple are getting married.

About a mile from the town centre, off New Borough Road, **Wimborne Market** (Fri 7am–2pm, Sat 8am–1pm & Sun 9am–4pm) is the largest covered market in the south of England with over 400 stalls, selling a mixture of local produce, plants, antiques, crafts, bric-a-brac, clothes and the usual market junk. Just south of here, you can rent out **rowing boats** (Sat & Sun, public & school hols; £12 an hr; Ⓦ www.dream-boats.org.uk) for a peaceful trip along the river south of town.

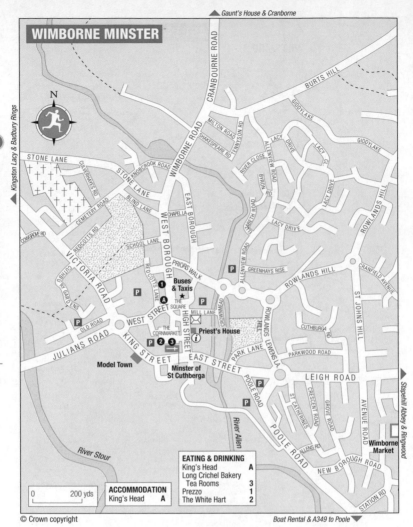

▲ Gaunt's House & Cranborne

◀ Kingston Lacy & Badbury Rings

▶ Stapehill Abbey & Ringwood

© Crown copyright

Boat Rental & A349 to Poole ▼

WIMBORNE MINSTER

N

Buses & Taxis

Priest's House

Model Town

Minster of St Cuthberga

Wimborne Market

River Stour

River Allen

0   200 yds

ACCOMMODATION	
King's Head	A

EATING & DRINKING	
King's Head	A
Long Crichel Bakery	
Tea Rooms	3
Prezzo	1
The White Hart	2

Practicalities

Wimborne is served by **bus** #3 every fifteen minutes from Poole and bus #13 every thirty minutes from Bournemouth; both pull in at The Square. Drivers should head for the central car park by the minster. The **tourist office** is at 20 High St (Mon–Sat 9.30am–5.30pm, until 4.30pm from Oct–April; ☎01202 886116). With the coast so near there is no real reason to **stay**, but if you do, the best option is the nineteenth-century *Kings Head* pub, which has good-value rooms right on the main square (☎01202 880101, ⓦ www.thekingsheadhotel .com; ⑤) as well as parking and its own **restaurant**. There are numerous other **pubs** around the main square, though they only really come to life at weekends when much of the surrounding rural community descend for a night out, or during the Wimborne Folk Festival in June (ⓦ www.wimbornefolkfestival.co.uk).

Best of these is *The White Hart* on Cornmarket, which has a pool table, a small garden and decent pub grub from around £8. There is also a very grand branch of *Prezzos* at 5 West Borough (℡01202 881119), set in a former bank and gentleman's club. The best place for lunch is the *Long Crichel Bakery Tea Rooms* opposite the minster at 7 Cook Row (closed Sun): selling organic bread and pastries from the nearby bakery (see p.158), it also serves home-made soups, inexpensive paninis, sandwiches and a range of tasty cakes.

Around Wimborne

About three miles east of Wimborne, off the Ferndown Road, **Stapehill Abbey** (April–Sept daily 10am–5pm; Oct–March Wed–Sun 10am–5pm; £7.50) was once home to a silent order of nuns. The nineteenth-century buildings are now open to the public, and you can look round the serene cloisters and atmospheric Victorian kitchens. There is also a museum section displaying various farm implements and agricultural machinery from this era. Also worth looking round are the extensive gardens, divided into various styles from round the world – check out the impressive Japanese garden – while there are farm animals, such as pigs, sheep and chickens to keep the children amused.

One of England's finest country houses, **Kingston Lacy** (house: mid-March to Oct Wed–Sun 11am–5pm, grounds: mid-March to Oct daily 10.30am–6pm;

▲ Model Town, Wimborne

Nov–Dec & Feb to mid-March Fri–Sun 10.30am–4pm; house & grounds £10, grounds only £5; NT) lies two miles northwest of Wimborne Minster, in parkland grazed by a herd of Red Devon cattle. Designed in the seventeenth century for the Bankes family, who were exiled from Corfe Castle (see p.75) after the Roundheads reduced it to rubble, the brick building was clad in grey stone during the nineteenth century by Sir Charles Barry, co-architect of the Houses of Parliament. William Bankes, then owner of the house, was a great traveller and collector, and the **Spanish Room**, lined with gilded leather and surmounted by a Venetian ceiling, is a superb scrapbook of his Grand Tour souvenirs. Kingston Lacy is also home to the largest private collection of Egyptian artefacts in the country, while its resident **pictures** are also outstanding, featuring works by Titian, Rubens, Velázquez and many other Old Masters. Be warned that this place gets so swamped with visitors that timed tickets are issued on busy weekends, though you can then devote time to the extensive and attractive **gardens**, complete with woodland walks, a Japanese tea garden and a children's play area.

Like Hambledon Hill (see p.152) and Maiden Castle (see p.103), the **Badbury Rings**, a mile further northwest, mark the site of an ancient Iron Age fort that was used from around 800 BC – though there are also Bronze Age barrows here that date to even earlier (2200–800 BC). The defences – once capped by a wooden fort built at the top of the tree-topped hill – were dug into the chalk, leaving three raised ditches stretching to a height of 15m, though even these hardy defences were not enough to protect the inhabitants from the invading Romans, who successfully took it in around 43 AD. After the Roman occupation, a local monk, Gildas, narrated the tale of how later invaders were repelled from here by a brave warrior called Arthur – who may or may not have been the legendary King Arthur. Whatever the truth, it is a highly attractive and atmospheric spot, the countryside around remaining wild and remote despite once forming a hub of Roman roads that included Ackling Dyke, which once ran from London to Dorchester and beyond.

Around a mile east of here lies **Gaunts House**, named after John of Gaunt (1340–1399), third son of Edward III, who had a home here, though the current building is largely Victorian. Set in superb rolling countryside, the house now runs frequent workshops and retreats (details on Ⓦwww .gauntshouse.com) as well as a couple of fine summer festivals. Also part of the Gaunts estate is **Honeybrook Farm** (Tues–Sun 9.30am–5pm; suggested donation £2.50), a mile or so north of Wimborne on the Cranborne Road. There's a good café that uses local produce, a farm shop, a children's play area and farm animals to pet.

Blandford Forum and around

A quiet market town (cynics call it not only Bland by name), **BLANDFORD FORUM** does have sufficient sights to warrant a half-day detour from the nearby coast. Architecturally it is one of Dorset's most distinctive towns, being almost entirely Georgian, rebuilt in the eighteenth century after a fire destroyed the original town in 1731. Two local brothers – John and William Bastard (pronounced b'stard) set about designing a harmonious townscape on the edges of the gently flowing River Stour, centred round the Town Hall and the **Church of St Peter and Paul**. The church, completed in 1739, has impressive Ionic columns and box pews, though some of the current structure dates from the nineteenth century when the chancel was detached, wheeled out of the way and stuck on a new extension. Blandford's Latin-sounding name was actually a thirteenth-century translation of the old Saxon name *Cheping*, or **market**, which still forms the focal point of the town on Thursdays and Saturdays, as do farmers' markets on the second Friday of each month.

The town's most interesting site is the **Fashion Museum** at Lime Tree House, The Plocks (Easter–Sept Thurs–Mon 11am–5pm, Oct–Nov & mid-Feb to Easter Thurs–Mon 11am–4pm; £3.50; Ⓦ www.cavalcadeofcostume.com), a collection of costumes displayed in a superb example of a Bastard townhouse. With more than five hundred items and accoutrements assembled by local woman Mrs Penny, the museum provides a fascinating take on the development of fashion from 1730 to the 1970s. Opposite the Church of St Peter and Paul in Beres Yard is the small **Town Museum** (Mon–Sat 10.30am–4.30pm; free), charting four hundred years of Blandford's history. Inside, there's an eclectic jumble of everything from a Victorian doll's house to archeological remains, along with a diorama of the Blandford fire, a recreation of a forge, displays on the Bastard brothers and a model railway.

A ten-minute walk or short drive south of town at Blandford St Mary is the **Hall & Woodhouse Brewery** (Mon–Sat 10.30am–5.30pm & Sun Easter to end Sept; £6; visits by appointment only on ☏01258 486004, Ⓦ www .hall-woodhouse.co.uk). This family-run brewery has been based in Blandford since 1899 and now produces the local Badger ales, one of the oldest trademarks on record. The tour shows you how it's brewed and involves a tasting session

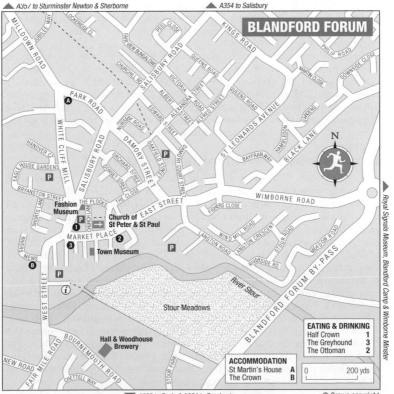

Royal Signals Museum, Blandford Camp & Wimborne Minster

EATING & DRINKING
Half Crown	1
The Greyhound	3
The Ottoman	2

ACCOMMODATION
St Martin's House	A
The Crown	B

0   200 yds

© Crown copyright

A35 / to Sturminster Newton & Sherborne   A354 to Salisbury

A350 to Poole & A354 to Dorchester

at the end (including soft drinks for children or drivers); there is also a decent bar-restaurant in the impressive brewery building.

Finally, a five-minute drive northeast of Blandford (or bus #185) at Blandford Camp is the **Royal Signals Museum** (Feb–Oct Mon–Fri 10am–5pm, Sat–Sun 10am–4pm; Nov–Jan Mon–Fri 10am–5pm; £7, children £5; Ⓦwww.royalsignalsmuseum.com), which traces the history of military signals and communications through the ages. Its chief attraction is one of the ENIGMA code machines and there are plenty of interactive displays, though it is largely of appeal to army enthusiasts.

Practicalities

Blandford Forum is served by regular **buses** #184 from Weymouth or Dorchester, and the hourly #X8 from Poole (Ⓦwww.wdbus.co.uk). The **tourist office** at Riverside House, West Street (Mon–Sat: April–Sept 10am–5pm; Oct–March 10am–3pm; ☎01258 454770) can give you details of local walks along the Stour and the various B&B options. Best of these is *St Martin's House*, White Cliff Street (☎01258 451245, Ⓦwww.stmartinshouse .co.uk; ❷) in a former choristers' house, with period furniture, well-decorated rooms (including a family room) and generous breakfasts. The town's only hotel is *The Crown*, West Street (☎01258 456626, Ⓦwww.innforanight.co.uk; ❸) set in an elegant Georgian coaching inn with its own gardens, bar and restaurant: the rooms are more modest than the communal areas but are still spacious and comfortable. Finding a room is rarely a problem except during the Blandford Georgian Fayre over May Bank Holiday (Ⓦwww.georgianfayre.co.uk) and the five days of the Great Dorset Steam Fair at the end of August (Ⓦwww .steam-fair.co.uk).

There are plenty of places **to eat** around East Street. *The Greyhound*, on Greyhound Yard, does decent pub grub in a former coaching inn, with outdoor tables in the yard. *The Ottoman* at 65–67 East St (☎01258 453207) is a pleasantly old-fashioned Turkish restaurant serving good-value meze, kebabs and vegetarian options from around £7 for mains. For breakfast or a light lunch, the *Half Crown* on Market Place does fine croissants, coffee, quiches and baked potatoes, with comfy sofas inside and a few seats out on the square.

Northwest to Sturminster Newton

The A357 leads northwest of Blandford Forum towards the beautiful, undulating countryside of the Blackmore Vale. Around seven miles northwest of Blandford lies the distinctive hillock of **Hambledon Hill**, best approached from the small village of Child Okeford – follow signs to the village surgery and you'll see a footpath signed off just past it to the right. This was once an Iron Age fort and its terraced grassy flanks are of similar appearance to that of the better-known Maiden Castle near Dorchester (see p.103). It's only around twenty minutes to the top (184m), but it's a steep climb – up which General Wolfe used to train his troops before conquering Quebec in the eighteenth century. In 1645, the slopes also witnessed a battle between Cromwell's New Model Army and some four thousand Dorset rebels, who were easily defeated as Cromwell trampled his way towards Sherborne. These days the hill is a far more peaceful nature reserve, protecting the Adonis blue butterfly that flourishes on the chalkland downs. It's a great spot for a picnic, with dazzling views across rolling fields. Walkers may also want to check out the disused railway track that runs from nearby Shillingstone up to Sturminster Newton.

▲ Hambledon Hill

Four miles northwest of Hambledon Hill, **Sturminster Newton** is an attractive town on the River Stour, with a thatched market square. Thomas Hardy lived here when writing *The Return of the Native*, referring to the town as "Stourcastle" – his house, Riverside, is now a pair of private houses overlooking the river. The town is approached over a six-arched bridge on which a nineteenth-century plaque threatens anyone causing damage with transportation to Australia as a felon. It's a pleasant place for a brief stroll, especially during the Monday market, though its only site of note is seventeenth-century **Sturminster Mill**, just south of town on the A357 (tours mid-March to end Sept Sat–Mon & Thurs 11am–5pm; £2, children 50p; ☏01747 854355, Ⓦ www.sturminsternewton-museum.co.uk), which is still in use and lays on special events, including a September cheese festival. From the mill, there are idyllic walks along the Stour, where otters can frequently be seen. Other local walks are detailed in the leaflets available from the small town **museum** on Bath Road (Easter–Sept Mon, Thurs & Fri 10am–3pm, Sat 10am–12.30pm; free), which has some modest exhibits on the town's history.

Shaftesbury

Perched on top of a hill in the far north of Dorset, with steep gradients on three sides of town, many of **SHAFTESBURY**'s streets enjoy terrific views over the rolling countryside all around. Attracted by the favourable strategic position, it was the legendary King Alfred the Great who, in the ninth century, founded a sturdy, fortified town here, complete with a huge abbey. Little remains of either today, though parts of the former abbey walls form the edge of **Gold Hill**, the town's most famous site.

Arrival and information

Modern Shaftesbury is pretty small and it is easy to walk round the centre. Buses pull into the central High Street close to the **tourist office** on Bell Street (April–Sept Mon–Sat 10am–5pm; Oct–March Mon–Sat 10am–3pm; ☎01747 853514, ⓦwww.ruraldorset.com), which can point you to the start of the well-signed Shaftesbury Heritage Trail. There is a large **car park** just behind the tourist office, though drivers can usually park along the High Street.

Accommodation

Accommodation in the town itself is in fairly short supply and you may want to consider some of the options listed below that are a short drive out of town.

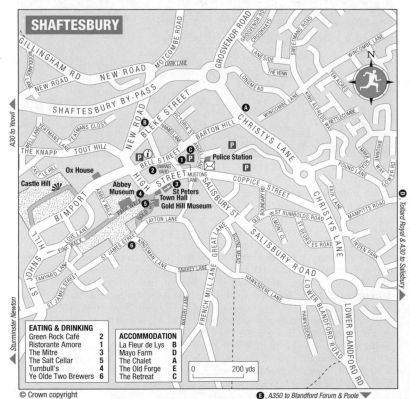

EATING & DRINKING

Green Rock Café	2
Ristorante Amore	1
The Mitre	3
The Salt Cellar	5
Turnbull's	4
Ye Olde Two Brewers	6

ACCOMMODATION

La Fleur de Lys	B
Mayo Farm	D
The Chalet	A
The Old Forge	E
The Retreat	C

0   200 yds

© Crown copyright

ⒺA350 to Blandford Forum & Poole ▼

La Fleur de Lys Bleke St ☎01747 853717, ⓦ www.lafleurdelys.co.uk. The best option in town, which has a range of stylish rooms above a highly rated if pricey restaurant; the back rooms have the best views, the front ones are on a busy through-road. Minimum two nights at weekends in summer. ❼

Mayo Farm Higher Blandford Rd ☎01747 852051, ⓦ www.mayofarmyurts.co.uk. Around a mile or so outside Shaftesbury, this offers something a little different. *Mayo Farm* has a couple of shepherds' huts (£30 a night) and yurts (£60 a night) to rent on a working farm, with chickens, pigs and donkeys for company: you can also pitch your own tent here.

The Chalet Christy's Lane ☎01747 853945, ⓦ www.thechalet.biz. Slightly out of the town centre, about a 5min walk, this is a modern B&B with all mod cons, though it is off a busy road; no credit cards. ❸

The Old Forge ☎01747 811881, ⓦ www .theoldforgedorset.co.uk. Consider heading around four miles south to Compton Abbas where you will find three cosy low-beamed rooms in a converted seventeenth-century forge, or in a restored former gypsy caravan in the grounds. ❹

The Retreat 47 Bell St ☎01747 850372, ⓦ the-retreat.co.uk. A friendly B&B with several large, comfortable rooms on two floors in a Georgian former schoolhouse; good value. ❹

The Town

Everything of note within Shaftesbury is within ten minutes' walk of the main High Street, though most visitors immediately seek out the **Gold Hill**. This ridiculously pretty cobbled hill, lined with thatched cottages and revelling in sublime views from the top was immortalized in the 1970s Hovis advertisement, which was directed by the then little-known Ridley Scott; it's such a classic that it's been recently re-released. Anyone familiar with the ad, showing a boy puffing with his bike up the steep cobbles, will instantly recognize the hill, though in fact it is surprisingly short   a pleasant round walk is to head down it, turning right and then right again, climbing either up through the park or further along up Tanyard and Laundry lanes. These take you up to Park Walk, laid out in the 1760s as a town promenade and commanding more splendid views. The end of here, Love Lane, marks the boundary of the original Saxon town. Heading a little north brings you to **Castle Hill**, a grassy viewpoint with more lovely views over the countryside to the north. Nearby, on Bimport, is the sixteenth-century Ox House, which featured as "Old Grove Place" in Hardy's *Jude the Obscure*.

Pilgrims used to flock to Shaftesbury to pay homage to the bones of Edward the Martyr, brought to the **Abbey** in 978, though now only the footings of the abbey church survive, on Park Walk. The remains now form the **Abbey Museum** (April–Oct daily 10am–5pm; £2.50, joint ticket with Gold Hill Museum £4.50; ⓦ www.shaftesburyabbey.org), which has displays detailing the history of the abbey – where King Canute died – including statuary and illustrated manuscripts, and allows access to the scant abbey ruins around an attractive walled garden. Founded in 888 by Alfred the Great, the abbey was the first religious house in the country to be built solely for women, and Alfred's daughter Aethelgifu was the first abbess. Over the years it became one of the most powerful abbeys in England, with lands stretching as far as Purbeck in the south and Bradford-upon-Avon in the north, until it was dissolved by Henry VIII in 1539. Access to the Abbey Museum can be combined with a visit to the **Gold Hill Museum**, at the top of Gold Hill (April–Oct daily 10.30am–4.30pm; £2.50, joint ticket with Abbey Museum £4.50). Inside is the usual collection of historical artefacts connected with the town, including a wooden fire engine, a mummified cat and a collection of locally made buttons, for which the area was once renowned. However, its real joy is its location, with fantastic views down Gold Hill from the pretty gardens.

Just above Gold Hill lies the grand **town hall**, built in 1827. Alongside, the fourteenth-century **St Peter's Church** is one of the few reminders of Shaftesbury's medieval grandeur, when it boasted a castle, twelve churches and four market crosses.

Eating and drinking

For a relatively small place, Shaftesbury has some excellent places to **eat and drink**, the best of which are listed below.

Green Rock Café Swans Yard. Good veggie dishes, such as vegetable and bean casserole for £4–5, are served at this lively café, as well as the usual sandwiches and baked potatoes (closes 5.30pm & Sun).

Ristorante Amore 6 Mustons Lane ☏01747 855566. An authentic Italian restaurant with a light and airy dining room in a converted chapel complete with frescoes on the walls and ceiling. The service is friendly, the home-made pizzas and pasta such as salmon with asparagus are good value at £7–8, and there are also pricier steak and chicken dishes. Closed Sun.

The Mitre High St. The best pub in town. The terrace at the back has lovely views and inside you'll find a cosy dining room with a wood-burning stove. You can get reasonably priced pub grub, such as steak and ale pie (£8).

The Salt Cellar Gold Hill. Right at the top of the hill itself and with great views, this place serves inexpensive snacks and daily specials from around £7, including home-made pies, in the pillar-lined interior or at outdoor tables on the cobbles (closes at 5pm).

Turnbull's High St. A bustling café and deli round the corner from Gold Hill, selling a fine range of local produce, including fresh hams, cheeses and salads (closed Sun).

Ye Olde Two Brewers St James St. At the bottom of Gold Hill, this pub has an attractive garden with good views, a skittle alley, real ales and decent pub food, including pizzas and tapas dishes from £4–7.

Cranborne Chase

An area of outstanding natural beauty, **Cranborne Chase** became a royal hunting ground during the time of King John (1189–1216), which restricted its cultivation pretty much until the nineteenth century – it now remains one of England's most unspoilt stretches of countryside. In 1714, the monarchs gave the land to the Pitt-Rivers family and today most of it is run by the Kingston Lacy estate. A chalk plateau, it stretches over 380 square miles into Wiltshire and is dotted with ancient hillforts and small villages, many with excellent pubs, as well as some superb gardens.

Madonna and the right to roam

Pop diva **Madonna** – ranked the world's richest female musician in 2008 – and her film-maker ex-husband Guy Ritchie spent the last years of their married life on the 1,130-acre **Aschombe House Estate**, which they purchased for around £9 million. In 2004 they went to court in an attempt to prevent ramblers walking across their property, claiming that their human rights were being infringed. The court largely agreed with them, ruling that walkers were not allowed to go within sight of their home. This hardly ingratiated them to the local community, who weren't overly sympathetic in 2005 when Madonna broke her collarbone and hand after falling from her horse while riding through the estate on her 47th birthday. The case also brought to the fore the whole issue of what constitutes open country – which has "a right to roam" – and what constitutes agricultural land, whose owners can still legally restrict access unless there is a public right of way. Even with the public rights of way, farmers have been known to restrict access by conveniently parking bulls in fields with public footpaths.

Tollard Royal and the Larmer Tree Gardens

The B3081 from Shaftesbury to **Tollard Royal**, seven miles southwest of Shaftesbury, is one of the most enjoyable roads in the region, winding up precipitous slopes, including the aptly named Zig-Zag Hill, with dazzling views over wooded valleys and pretty hamlets. The road passes through the neighbouring county of Wiltshire around Tollard Royal before returning back to Dorset after a mile or two. Tollard Royal takes its name from the royal hunting lodge that was once here – King John is said to have had 22 in the area. It's still very popular with the hunting and shooting set, including Madonna, who lived on an estate nearby with her former husband, Guy Ritchie (see box, p.156). The village also has a smart but friendly gastropub, the *King John Inn* (☎01725 516207, ⓦwww.kingjohninn.co.uk), which serves fine food using local ingredients including Dorset crab and local asparagus; it also lets out comfortable rooms with flat-screen TVs (❺), though it gets very booked up in late August during the start of the shooting season.

A mile or so from here, the superb **Larmer Tree Gardens** (Easter–Aug Sun–Thurs 11am–4.30pm; £3.75) were built as Victorian pleasure gardens by eminent archeologist General Augustus Pitt-Rivers, with the aim to "educate" the local villagers and estate workers, and are some of the finest private gardens in the country. They take their name from an old Wych Elm called the Larmer Tree, where King John would meet his entourage before his hunts. Nowadays there are lawns and walkways through idyllic gardens dotted with peacocks, picnic spots and shelters, together with a teahouse (Sun only). Pitt-Rivers used the gardens for lavish entertainments including illuminated night-time dancing, which visitor Thomas Hardy called "Quite the prettiest sight I ever saw". Fittingly, the gardens continue to host music festivals to this day, including the last one of the season, the chilled-out End of the Road Festival (see p.31).

Farnham, Chettle and Long Crichel

Also part of General Augustus Pitt-Rivers' original estate is the pretty village of **Farnham**, a mile and a half south of the gardens, an idyllic collection of cottages. It also has the fine, thatched *Museum Inn* (☎01725 516261, ⓦwww.museuminn.co.uk), which takes its name from the museum Pitt-Rivers founded before its collection was moved to Oxford. Today it is a smart gastropub, serving top-notch local seasonal and organic food, such as quails' eggs and roast venison (mains from around £14) as well as a good selection of real ales. It also has some smart rooms (❻) if you want to stay, though better value is the nearby *Farnham Farmhouse* (☎01725 516254, ⓦwww.farnhamfarmhouse.co.uk; ❸), with comfortable rooms in a large Victorian building on a working farm surrounded by extensive farmland: it also has its own outdoor pool.

A couple of miles southwest, the delightful thatched village of **Chettle** is home to **Chettle House**, an attractive Queen Anne manor house, built in 1710 by Thomas Archer, whose trademark design can be clearly seen from the outside – all the corners are rounded. The house with its beautifully landscaped gardens has been inhabited by the same family for over 150 years and is only open to the public sporadically (April–Sept first & second Sun of each month 11am–5pm; £4.50). The largely Victorian *Castleman Hotel* nearby (☎01725 8830096, ⓦwww.castlemanhotel.co.uk; ❸) is a quirky place, if rather old-fashioned and fusty-smelling. It has a highly regarded restaurant serving excellent-value meals based around local seasonal produce, such as roast guinea fowl (£13) or venison and mushroom pie (£11): there are also some spacious rooms – those at the back look out over the lovely gardens and verdant countryside.

Drivers may want to detour the three miles or so west to **Tarrant Gunville**, where the *Home Farm* café and shop (closed Mon) is tucked away in the middle of nowhere but offers a diverse array of good-quality local produce; it also has a tearoom selling home-made cakes and light lunches. For picnic supplies, however, you're better off heading three miles south to the charming village of **Long Crichel**, where you'll find another pioneer in the local seasonal food movement: the **bakery** (Tues–Sat 9.30am–5pm; ⓦ www.longcrichelbakery.co .uk) makes it own organic breads in a wood-fired oven, as well as delicious croissants, cakes and savoury pastries, many made with fruit, herbs and vegetables grown in the gardens next door. You can watch the bakers at work in the old stable block, or browse the shop for local cheese and vegetables.

Cranborne, Edmondsham and Horton

Moving southeast, it is another seven miles to the village of **Cranborne**, where you'll find **Cranborne Manor**, home to the Viscount of Cranborne. Originally one of King John's hunting lodges, the current manor was largely rebuilt in 1608 and though closed to the public, you can visit the impressive **gardens** (March–Sept Wed 9am–5pm; occasional Sat in summer; £4; ⓦ www.cranborne .co.uk), a lovely mixture of formal and wild greenery, some of it cultivated for vegetables and orchards. The village of Cranborne is a pretty spot with a village shop selling produce from the Cranborne estate, and the friendly *Fleur de Lys* **pub**, 5 Wimborne St (☎01725 517282), parts of which date back to the eleventh century and which has been a pub since the seventeenth century. Hardy's "Chaseborough" is based on Cranborne, and the barn where Tess danced near the "Flower-de-Luce Inn" is modelled on one of the outbuildings of the *Fleur de Lys*. Recently renovated, the pub serves real ales and good food using local ingredients, as does the highly regarded restaurant, *La Fosse* (☎01725 517604, ⓦ www.la-fosse.com; ⓞ) on The Square. Its menu changes according to what's in season locally, but you can expect dishes such as watercress soup, line-caught bass, and pear, dandelion and burdock sorbet on the three-course £25 menu. There are six stylish rooms upstairs, and a pretty patio at the back.

Just south of Cranborne, the little village of **Edmondsham** has two attractions. Foremost of these, just to the east, is the **Dorset Heavy Horse Centre** (April–Oct daily 10am–5pm; Nov & March weekends only; £7.75, children £5.95), a child-friendly farm park offering wagon and pony rides, play areas and the chance to meet various breeds of horse, from giant shire horses to miniature ponies, as well as smaller animals such as pygmy goats and llamas. There is also a recreated blacksmith, pet shop and café.

Nearby, **Edmondsham House and Gardens** (April–Oct: house Wed only, gardens Wed & Sun 2–5pm; £4, gardens only £2) is a fine Georgian manor house that partly dates back to Tudor times. The owner gives a guided tour of the house and its Victorian dairy on Wednesdays only – much of the appeal is that it is still used as a family home, as well as for the odd wedding; you can also admire the substantial walled gardens, which include a large organic kitchen garden.

A couple of miles south of Edmondsham is **Horton**, home to a good thatched pub, *Drusilla's Inn* (☎01258 840297), with an inglenook fireplace and a pleasant garden. It serves real ales and decent food, including a three-course set menu for £15. From the pub, there's an hour-long round walk to the hexagonal, seven-storey **Horton Tower**, which dominates the landscape hereabouts. Resembling a truncated church spire, the tower was built in the eighteenth century by a local landowner so he could watch the hunts: at the time of its construction, it was the tallest non-religious structure in the country.

The Avon Valley

The **River Avon** runs pretty much due south along the western edges of the New Forest National Park. Much of it is followed by the busy A338, though it doesn't take much to escape the traffic, especially west of pretty **Fordingbridge** where there are some superb walks around the Roman villa at **Rockbourne** and along the Avon itself. To the south, the lively market town of **Ringwood** also has some fine local attractions in the form of two country parks. South of here, Bournemouth's suburbs encroach into the Avon Valley around **Hurn** where there's the fun Adventure Wonderland theme park and a ski centre as well as Bournemouth's International Airport. If you're after a more rural outlook, take the B3347 east of the Avon, which passes through the pretty village of **Sopley**, with its lovely mill.

Fordingbridge and around

FORDINGBRIDGE has to contend with the busy A338, which skirts its flanks, as well as a fair amount of through traffic; sadly, this spoils an otherwise pleasant town on the willow-lined banks of the River Avon. There was a ford here at the time of the Domesday Book, superseded by a medieval seven-arched bridge that forms the focal point of the town today – there are some lovely walks up and down the river, including the **Avon Valley footpath**, which runs south to Christchurch and north to Salisbury in Wilshire, 34 miles in total. The walk can be broken into easily manageable sections, as detailed on ⓦwww3 .hants.gov.uk/walking/longdistance/avon-valley-path.htm.

▲ Fordingbridge

Fordingbridge's only attraction is its small **museum** in King's Yard (Mon–Sat 11am–4pm; free), which contains the usual local bits and bobs, such as a reproduction of an air-raid shelter, a Victorian doll's house, and artefacts from the now-defunct cobblers, ironmongers and blacksmiths. It would be of limited interest were it not for the display upstairs on **Augustus John**, who lived in Fordingbridge from 1927 until his death in 1961 (see box below), and the small collection of portraits of his various children as well as a self-portrait (1931).

Practicalities

Bus #X3 runs from Fordingbridge north to Salisbury and south to Ringwood, Bournemouth and Poole once an hour (every 2hr on Sun). The seasonal **tourist office** is by the museum in King's Yard (☎01425 654560; summer only Mon–Sat 10am–4pm). If you want to **stay**, *The Fig Tree* has decent B&B rooms by the church, though you need to book at the café of the same name at 1 Roman Quay off the High Street (☎01425 655065, ⓦwww.figtreecafe .co.uk; ❶). For longer stays, just west of Fordingbridge at Godshill, is the substantial and superbly named *Sandy Balls* holiday park (☎01425 653042, ⓦwww.sandy-balls.co.uk). It offers a diverse range of accommodation to suit all budgets, including wooden chalets (sleeps 4; around £900 a week), caravans and (May–Sept) ready-erected tents and tepees or simple camping pitches, all set in woodland with its own bar-restaurant, indoor and outdoor pools and spa and bike rental; a three-night minimum let is usually required.

The best place **to eat** is *The George Inn* (☎01425 652040, ⓦwww.georgeat fordingbridge.co.uk), right by the bridge on Bridge Street, with a lovely terrace overlooking the river. It's great inside too, well decorated in a contemporary style with comfy sofas and cosy fireplaces: meals include home-made

Augustus John in Fordingbridge

A unlikely resident of a small and conservative country town, the flamboyant post-Impressionist artist **Augustus John** lived in Fryern Court in Fordingbridge, where he hosted wild parties attended by such guests as Hollywood film star Tallulah Bankhead, author T.E. Lawrence and the Bloomsbury Group. Britain's leading portraitist in the 1920s – he painted figures such as Churchill, Thomas Hardy and George Bernard Shaw – John's bohemian lifestyle did not sit very comfortably with local residents and he made no attempt to disguise his unconventional ways, delighting in upsetting the locals by riding bareback to the local pub, dressing flamboyantly and openly welcoming his many illegitimate offspring to the house. Indeed, John always patted every child he saw in the village on the head, as he said he couldn't be sure whether they were his or not. John had five legitimate children with his first wife Ida, and two with his mistress Dorelia, who lived with John and Ida in a *ménage à trois*, but whom he later married after Ida's death. It was with Dorelia that he lived in Fordingbridge, though his many affairs continued, and up until his death in his eighties he continued to out-drink, out-party and out-flirt those half his age. After his death, the town was divided as to whether to celebrate John, or to play down the connection – eventually the celebrators won out and a statue of him was erected along the riverside by the bridge.

John's sister **Gwen** also lived in Fordingbridge at Burgate Cross for a couple of years. She too was an artist and studied under Whistler and Rodin, becoming the latter's mistress – but she was far more introverted than her younger brother and received much less acclaim than him during their lifetimes. Today, however, she is recognized as being the superior artist, a fact that Augustus John freely acknowledged.

pies, such as game and mushroom (£10), or Thai green curry (£10), plus a good range of daily specials. For a light lunch or snack, *The Fig Tree Café* (see p.160) has wholesome food with veggie options, while *Nelson's Deli*, 71 High St, sells local cheeses and other produce, as well as a good range of tasty baguettes and sandwiches.

Rockbourne Roman Villa and Breamore House

Set in lush countryside around three miles northwest of Fordingbridge are the impressive remains of **Rockbourne Roman Villa** (April–Sept daily 10.30am–6pm; £2.50; Ⓦwww3.hants.gov.uk), once a large estate at the heart of substantial agricultural land. It was discovered by a farmer in the 1940s and its significance was soon recognized as one of the most important villa complexes in the area. The entrance fee includes access to an information centre detailing what the villa would have been like in the fifth century AD and includes finds from excavations – including coins and jewellery – and recreations of the mosaics, while the ruins themselves are sprinkled round the grassy fields and include a bathhouse, farm outbuildings, bedrooms and an impressive series of ceramic pipes that once provided underfloor heating. While here, don't miss a visit to the village of **Rockbourne** itself, around a mile further north, a picturesque row of thatched cottages and the starting point of a great walk (see box, p.162).

A couple of miles east of Rockbourne, just off the main A338 is **Breamore House** (April Tues & Sun; May–Sept Tues–Thurs & Sat–Sun and bank hols house 2–5.30pm, museum 1–5.30pm; £8; Ⓦwww.breamorehouse.com), a sumptuous Elizabethan manor house built in 1583. Still used as a family home, the house is stuffed with ornate tapestries, ceramics, period furniture and paintings, including a rare James I carpet. Highlights include the giant Great Hall and the surprisingly spartan kitchens. There is also a small countryside museum, a collection of agricultural tools and machinery including horse wagons, steam-powered farm machinery and ancient tractors. The house is also pressed into service as a backdrop for films.

Ringwood and around

Despite being dominated by the busy A31, **Ringwood** remains a pleasant market town (Wed morning is market day) with a good range of shops and facilities. Since it has excellent transport links it makes a good base from which to explore the area, including the New Forest to the east. There's a handful of attractions within easy range. Just south of town, on Crow Lane, is the **Liberty's Owl, Raptor and Reptile Centre** (March–Oct daily 10am–5pm; Nov–Feb weekends only 10am–4pm; £7.50, children £4.95) – which, as the name suggests, has an extensive collection of snakes, lizards, tortoises, owls and birds of prey, with various flying displays of the birds through the day. Also south of town on the Sopley road is the **Ringwood Brewery**, an independent family-run brewery that produces some of the best local ales. If you want to find out more about its history, you can take a tour of the brewery (reservations essential on ☏0142 5471177, Ⓦwww.ringwoodbrewery.co.uk; £8).

The other attractions are only conveniently accessible if you have your own transport. Just outside Ringwood, off the A338 Salisbury Road is the **Ringwood Town and Country Experience** (10am–4.30pm, closed Sat from Nov–Easter; £4.75, children £3.95; Ⓦwww.rtce.co.uk), a motley collection of

This easy four-mile (1hr 30min) walk starts at the little car park by the village hall in **Rockbourne** (see p.161) and passes through farmland, lovely woods and a stud farm, via a conveniently situated pub. From the car park, turn left and shortly right into Manor Farm, following the public footpath sign to the side of the farm itself. Keep left into a field and continue straight on, slightly uphill. You then exit the field through a gate into a lovely strip of dense beech woods, particularly beautiful in autumn. As you leave the woods, you continue straight on past the famous Whitsbury stud farm that trained, amongst others, the racehorse Red Rum. Turn right and either continue down the road into **Whitsbury** or take the signed path opposite, which trails round the back of the village via the church. In Whitsbury you can stop in the Cartwheel Inn (℡01725 518362), a traditional country **pub** serving hearty meals, with open fires and a fine beer garden. The return to Rockbourne starts from the road opposite the pub, slightly north back up the hill in the direction you approached. Take the public footpath that skirts a few gardens before crossing fields, with lovely rolling views, on a track which wends back down to the water meadows just southeast of Rockbourne. The path is then signed right just before the stream, which takes you along the back of a few houses before heading back to the road near the village hall where you started.

displays representing Olde England, including recreations of traditional shops, vintage cars, an old-fashioned station and the like – educational for kids though not so gripping for others. From the museum, it is a short drive north along the A338 to **Blashford Lakes**, a series of flooded gravel pits that are now a nature reserve; there are marked tails round the lakes from where you can spot various birds including egrets and kingfishers, and there's also a **watersports** centre, which offers water-skiing and wake-boarding on the lakes; contact ⓦwww .ellinghamwaterski.co.uk for details.

More amusing for people of any age is **Moors Valley Country Park** (daily 8am–dusk, restaurant and visitor centre daily 9am–4.30pm; ⓦwww.moors -valley.co.uk) three miles west at Ashley Heath; note entrance to the park is free if you cycle or come on foot, but car park charges work out around £6–8 a day. Set in coniferous woodland with a large lawned central area encircling a lake, there are numerous trails, picnic spots and play areas as well as bike hire, a tree-top walkway trail and its own golf course. Other paying attractions include a fine narrow-gauge steam train, which skirts the lake and the excellent playground, and **Go Ape**, a fantastic adventure course in which you can test out your Tarzan skills on zip wires and dangling walkways suspended high above the forest floor; book in advance on ⓦwww.goape.co.uk.

Around a mile south of Moors Valley, off the A31 lies the more low-key **Avon Heath Country Park** (daily 8am–dusk; free), the largest country park in the region, with various marked trails through heather and woodland. There are play areas and a visitor centre (daily 11am–4pm), which can point out the various wildlife in the park – sand lizards and smooth snakes are regular visitors.

Practicalities

Ringwood is well served by the hourly #X3 **bus** from Salisbury to Bourne-mouth, via Fordingbridge, and the hourly #36 to Bournemouth. It is also on the fast National Express coach line, which links it with Bournemouth, Heathrow and London. Buses pull in on the main square, The Furlong, where you'll find plenty of parking. The **tourist office** is also on The Furlong (Wed & Fri 10am–1pm & 1.30–3.30pm, Sat 10am–1pm; ℡01425 470896, ⓦwww .hampshire-information.co.uk).

Most of the **accommodation** lies out on the Christchurch Road, signed to Sopley and Winkton. First choice, around fifteen minutes' walk from the centre, is *Moortown Lodge*, 244 Christchurch Rd (℡01425 471404, ⓦwww.moortown lodge.co.uk; ❹); in a pleasant townhouse, the best of the smart rooms are at the back, as front ones can be noisy. A little closer to town, by Ringwood Brewery (see p.161), the *Candlestick Inn*, 136 Christchurch Rd (℡01425 472587, ⓦhotelnew forest.co.uk; ❷) has simple rooms tucked into a quiet annexe behind a thatched bar-restaurant, which also does reasonable pub grub.

The best place to **eat and drink** is *Seven Fish* on Southampton Road (℡01425 480472), a modern friendly canteen-bar that specializes in fish and seafood: it's reasonably priced – scallops with samphire costs £16; feta, watercress and coucous salad is £9.50 – and many of the dishes can be bought in smaller starter portions. *Plummers* on the High Street (℡01425 474563) is a cosy bistro/café with a nice garden at the back: it does light lunches and sandwiches by day and Thurs–Sat, it's open for evening meals, such as poached salmon with spinach (£10.45). *Alisala*, 2 West St (℡01425 478254) is a long-established, consistently pleasing Thai restaurant – try the steamed seafood curry in a banana leaf (£9). For a light lunch, *Frampton Mill*, 15 The Furlong, serves decent sandwiches and cakes outside on the square or inside the former mill building: on Thurs–Sat evenings, it does tapas-style dishes (£3–4), such as chorizo in red wine, or falafels. A mile or so north of Ringwood, just off the A31, the superb *Busy Bee Café* (Mon–Fri 8.30am–4.30pm, Sat 9am–3.30pm) is in a wonderful wooded location. Run by the Lantern Community for people with learning disabilities, the light and airy café serves organic bread and pastries made at the on-site bakery, with delicious quiche, soups and salads made from home-grown organic vegetables: there is also a shop if you want to buy picnic supplies.

Hurn and Matchams

The small village of **Hurn**, five miles south of Ringwood is home to Bournemouth International Airport (ⓦwww.bournemouthairport.com). Right opposite, the **Adventure Wonderland** theme park (April to mid-Sept plus autumn half-term daily 10am–6pm; mid-Sept to mid-Oct Sat & Sun 10am–6pm: mid-Sept to March indoor play area only daily 10am–6.30pm; adults and children over 3 £10) has a series of low-key rides and play areas based loosely around the theme of Alice in Wonderland and most suited to under-12-year-olds. Next door is the **Aviation Museum** (daily 10am–4pm; £3, children £1.50; ⓦwww.aviation-museum.co.uk), with a collection of jet aircraft, a helicopter and a double-decker bus. You can clamber into them all, sit in the cockpits and driver's seat and play with the controls. It's right opposite the airport, so you get a good view of the planes taking off and landing, and you can even attempt to land your own plane at Bournemouth airport, or a selection of other airports around the world, on the flight simulator indoors.

On the other side of the airport, on Matcham's Lane, the year-round **Snowtrax Activity Centre** (daily 10am–10pm; ⓦwww.snowtrax.eu) has the country's widest dry-ski slope. You can hire skis and practise for around £13 an hour, or take ski lessons from around £19 an hour. They also do rubber rings or sledge descents (around £10 an hour), and there's an "Alpine" bar and restaurant and children's play area.

South to Sopley

The B3347 from Ringwood offers a quieter, picturesque approach to the coast, along the lower reaches of the Avon Valley. It follows the river through a series

▲ Sopley Mill

of small hamlets, such as **Bisterne**, home of an annual scarecrow competition. If you drive along the road in August/September, you can't miss the series of imaginative scarecrows and tableaux in front gardens and along the roadside. Around nine miles south of Ringwood is the small village of **Sopley**, part of a private estate, which has kept the village pretty much unchanged for centuries. There's a fine pub here, *The Woolpack*, which has a lovely garden. Even better is *Sopley Mill* on Mill Lane (closed Sun eve & Mon; ☏01425 674196), an idyllic spot right by the Avon. You can watch the river literally flow beneath this former Victorian water mill, now converted into a café-bar-restaurant: it serves good-value bar food and drinks, such as roast beef sandwiches (£5) or roast chicken (£9), in the wooden interior or in the riverside garden dotted with rabbit cages, chickens and goats.

The New Forest

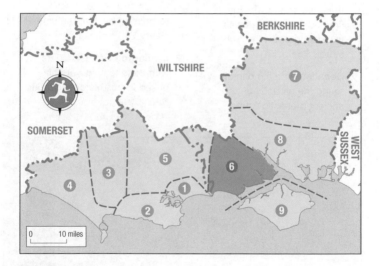

CHAPTER 6 # Highlights

✳ **Walks around Ashurst**
Some of the least spoilt open
countryside lies around this
small town. See p.174

✳ **Hire a bike** Take to one of
the New Forest's well-marked
cycle routes to see the best of
the forest. See p.176

✳ **Brockenhurst** An idyllic New
Forest town, complete with
thatched cottages, a ford,
fine tearooms and ponies
wandering down the high
street. See p.180

✳ **Beaulieu** Ride a monorail
round the grounds of an
ancient monastic estate,
complete with a riverside walk
and the fantastic National
Motor Museum. See p.183

✳ **Christchurch** England's
largest parish church is the
focal point of this ancient
riverside town, now also
gaining a reputation for its
fine restaurants. See p.187

✳ **Hurst Castle** Take a boat out
to this atmospheric coastal
fort dating back to the time of
Henry VIII. See p.192

✳ **Lymington** Rub shoulders
with the yachting fraternity
based in this historic harbour.
See p.194

▲ New Forest ponies

6

The New Forest

Covering about 220 square miles, the **NEW FOREST** is one of the largest medieval forests in western Europe, and dates from 1079, when William the Conqueror requisitioned it as his hunting ground. Declared a National Park in 2005, much of the forest is little changed since the Norman Conquest and some of its trees are more than 400 years old. While parts of the forest consist of dense deciduous woods, most of it is open heathland, dotted with expanses of coniferous plantations. This diverse landscape supports a flourishing wildlife including rare butterflies, woodpeckers and deer, including the tiny **sika deer**, descendants of a pair that escaped from nearby Beaulieu in 1904. It's most well-known animals are, of course, the **New Forest ponies** that roam at will, though they are officially owned by the Forest Commoners, whose rights to the forest date from Saxon times. The ponies are just one of the attractions that have turned the area into one of southern England's main rural playgrounds, pulling in some eight million visitors annually. Traffic bottlenecks, such as the road into Lyndhurst, can spoil its reputation as a country idyll, so it pays to choose your destination – and mode of transport – with care, especially during the summer holidays. The liveliest and most accessible towns are **Lyndhurst** and **Brockenhurst**, the latter is on the main rail route and the most agreeable town in the forest. Not so quaint but also on the rail route and close to some great unspoilt countryside is **Ashurst**, while smaller towns such as **Burley** – with its bizarre white witch connections – can also be rewarding. The northern stretches of the forest around **North Gorley** and **Fritham** are often overlooked by visitors but offer some of its finest walks, while the eastern stretches take in the beautiful **Exbury** gardens and the superb riverside **Buckler's Hard** and **Beaulieu**, famed for its abbey and must-see National Motor Museum.

The forest is also within reach of the coast whose shingle-and-sand beaches lie between the ancient town of **Christchurch** and the buzzy harbour of **Lymington**, where luxurious yachts ply the waters of a natural harbour, alongside ferries to the Isle of Wight.

The two main forest towns, Lyndhurst and Brockenhurst, are pleasant enough places to stay and have some decent accommodation options, though Lyndhurst suffers from heavy traffic, especially in the summer. Indeed on a sunny Sunday in summer, the roads in the southern section of the forest can be very slow and busy. The best way, therefore, to experience the forest is by staying in a countryside B&B or camping in one of the official forest campsites; rough camping is not allowed. From all the campsites, there are plenty of cycle trails and footpaths that take you off the beaten track and deep into the forest.

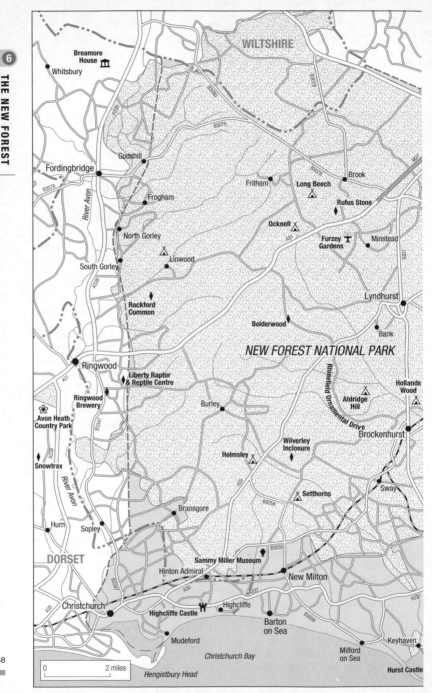

WILTSHIRE

Breamore
House

Whitsbury

Godshill

Fordingbridge

River Avon

Frogham

Fritham

Long Beech

Brook

Rufus Stone

North Gorley

Ocknell

Furzey
Gardens

Minstead

Linwood

Rockford
Common

Bolderwood

Lyndhurst

Bank

South Gorley

NEW FOREST NATIONAL PARK

Ringwood

Liberty Raptor
& Reptile Centre

Ringwood
Brewery

Avon Heath
Country Park

Burley

Rhinefield Ornamental Drive

Aldridge
Hill

Hollands
Wood

Brockenhurst

Snowtrax

River Avon

Holmsley

Wilverley
Inclosure

Setthorns

Sway

Bransgore

Hurn

Sopley

DORSET

Sammy Miller Museum

Hinton Admiral

New Milton

Christchurch

Highcliffe Castle

Highcliffe

Barton
on Sea

Keyhaven

Mudeford

Milford
on Sea

Christchurch Bay

Hurst Castle

0   2 miles

Hengistbury Head

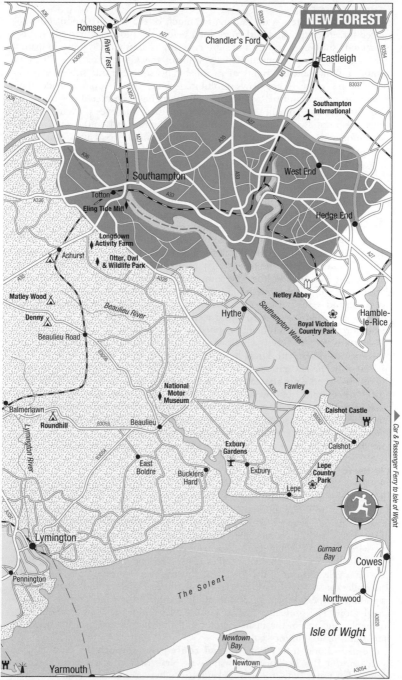

NEW FOREST

Romsey

Chandler's Ford

Eastleigh

B3037

Southampton
International

West End

Southampton

Hedge End

Totton

Eling Tide Mill

Longdown
Activity Farm

Ashurst

Otter, Owl
& Wildlife Park

Netley Abbey

Matley Wood

Beaulieu River

Hythe

Royal Victoria
Country Park

Hamble-
le-Rice

Denny

Beaulieu Road

Southampton Water

Balmerlawn

National
Motor
Museum

Fawley

Roundhill

Beaulieu

Calshot Castle

Lymington River

East
Boldre

Bucklers
Hard

Exbury
Gardens

Calshot

Exbury

Lepe
Country
Park

Lepe

N

Lymington

Pennington

Gurnard
Bay

Cowes

The Solent

Northwood

Isle of Wight

Newtown
Bay

Newtown

Yarmouth

© Crown copyright

Car & Passenger Ferry to Isle of Wight

Some history

The name New Forest is misleading, for much of this region's woodland was cleared for agriculture and settlement long before the Normans arrived, and its poor, sandy soils support only a meagre covering of heather and gorse in many areas. The forest was requisitioned by William the Conqueror in 1079 as a hunting ground, and the rights of its inhabitants soon became subservient to those of his game. Forest laws prohibited fences that would impede the movement of wild animals and terrible punishments were meted out to those who disturbed the animals – hands were lopped off and eyes put out. But in return the forest dwellers were allowed to graze their animals in the open forest. Later monarchs, less passionate about hunting than the Normans, gradually improved the forest dwellers' rights, and today the New Forest enjoys a unique patchwork of ancient laws and privileges, enveloped in an arcane vocabulary dating from feudal times. The forest boundary is the "perambulation", and owner-occupiers of forest land have common rights to obscure practices such as "turbary" (peat cutting), "estover" (firewood collecting) and "mast" (letting pigs forage for acorns and beechnuts, more popularly known as "pannage").

"**Commoning**" has been a recognized way of life since the mid-sixteenth century and basically refers to living off the forest through "rights of common", largely the continuing right to graze livestock. There are still some three hundred commoners in the forest today, exercising their right to graze around six thousand ponies and cattle. The commoners are vital for the sustainability of the forest as without the grazing animals, much of the forest would be swamped by gorse and scrub. As a result, a trust was set up in 1992 to ensure that commoners could continue to afford to live in the area at a time when much of the forest property was being snapped up by outsiders.

The **trees** of the forest are now much more varied than they were in pre-Norman times, with birch, holly, yew, Scots pine and other conifers interspersed with the ancient oaks and beeches. One of the most venerable trees is the much-visited **Knightwood Oak**, just a few hundred yards north of the A35 nearly three miles southwest of Lyndhurst, which measures about 22ft in circumference at shoulder height. But perhaps surprisingly, the Forestry Commission harvests some 50,000 tonnes of timber a year, most of it grown in fenced areas known as inclosures. Harvesting takes place in five-year cycles and care should be taken in areas where tree-felling is being undertaken.

Getting around

The New Forest was rated the world's finest **green destination** of 2007 in the annual Responsible Tourism Awards. This may seem strange to anyone stuck in a traffic jam on a hot summer's day, but is an acknowledgement of the area's drive to encourage people to arrive and get around by **public transport**. Many of the B&Bs and hotels offer incentives or discounts for those not arriving by car, while the area is fully geared up for **cycling**, with various cycleways and even an open-top bus that takes bikes (Ⓦwww.thenewforesttour.info) so that you can cycle sections of the forest and bus the less interesting bits. And with 150 miles of car-free gravel tracks in the Forest, cycling and **walking** are appealing prospects – pick up a book of route **maps** from tourist offices or bike rental shops. The Ordnance Survey Leisure Map 22 of the New Forest is best for exploring, and in the main towns you'll find numerous specialist walking books and natural history guides.

The main London to Weymouth **rail route** passes through the New Forest, with stops at Brockenhurst, Ashurst, Sway, New Milton and Christchurch – though fast trains only stop at Brockenhurst, where a small line links branches off to Lymington. The southern forest stretches have a reasonably efficient **bus** network. Useful **bus routes** include #56 from Ashurst to Lymington via Lyndhurst and Brockenhurst; #35 from Lyndhurst to Holmsley and Burley; the coastal route #X12 from Christchurch to Lymington via Highcliffe, Barton and Milford; and in summer the NFT circular route from Lymington to Beaulieu, Exbury and Lyndhurst, returning via Brockenhurst. Services are run by Wilts and Dorset buses (☎01202 673555, Ⓦwww.wdbus.co.uk) and Blue Star (☎01280 618233, Ⓦwww.bluestarbus.co.uk).

The **speed limit** through most of the New Forest is 40mph, and drivers should take particular care as ponies frequently graze at the side of – or even on – the roads, often with their foals.

The northern New Forest

The forest is split into two parts by the busy A31, each with its own distinct geography and character. The **northern section** is sparsely populated and much less touristy, perhaps because it's less accessible, with no towns, no main roads and no train line. It is also less wooded than the southern stretches, with open heathlands and rolling countryside that are great for walks or a picnic. There's a scattering of villages, such as the picturesque **Fritham** and **North** and **South Gorley**, rural pubs and campsites, but its main appeal is simply exploring a landscape that's far less visited than the southern sections. You'll need a car to get around – public transport is virtually non-existent; or you could explore by bike from the two towns just outside the forest, Ringwood (see p.161) or Fordingbridge (see p.159).

North Gorley to Linwood

Most drivers approach the northern section of the forest along the A338 (take care, the road is a notorious accident blackspot). A prettier route, however, is along the narrow road that runs north, parallel to the A338, via the diminutive village of **South Gorley**, where Hockeys Farm (Mon–Sat 8am–4pm, Ⓦwww .hockeysfarm.co.uk) has a farm shop selling its own and other local produce, as well as a café and mini aviary – you can also wander round and look at the resident animals or take an escorted trip to see its deer park. Right next door, Avon Valley Nursery has pick-your-own fruit and a seasonal toy steam train (weather permitting, daily March–Nov; £1.20), which trundles round the farm's perimeter. South Gorley merges into the picturesque **North Gorley**, home to the quaint, thatched *Royal Oak* pub (☎01425 652244), which has its own beer garden and serves good, if pricey, food. A few miles southeast of the village, the road splits at **Rockford Common**, a popular spot for picnickers and families, who cluster round a small ford. Here you'll also find a huge sand quarry, where children run up and down the giant dune; there are plenty of rope swings strung up on the surrounding trees and in summer the whole place is like a huge playground. Around two miles east of here, there's little to the tiny village of

Linwood, other than the popular *Red Shoot Inn*, a rural pub that brews its own ales and hosts a biannual beer festival (usually April & Oct). Behind it, the well-equipped *Red Shoot Camping Park* (Ⓦwww.redshoot-campingpark.com) is set in relatively flat land and is surrounded by beautiful forest.

Fritham and the Rufus Stone

From Linwood, the pretty road continues east through the northern part of the forest past rolling moorland – take the right-hand fork and you'll head back under the A31 to the southern section of the forest at Bolderwood (see p.179), or head left towards the spread-out village of **Fritham**. The road to Fritham ends at the delightful ⚘ *Royal Oak* (Ⓣ02380 812606; no cards), one of the best – and smallest – pubs in the forest. Inside, the three little rooms cram in open fires, wooden floorboards and assorted dogs, while the garden overlooks rolling farmland. Best of all is the limited but top-notch menu featuring local produce such as honeyed gammon, nettle and chilli cheeses, pork pies and summer crabs; main courses (£4.50–6) are served with great local chutneys. Just past the pub there are two forest car parks, the starting point of some lovely local walks or cycle rides (see box below).

The forest's most visited site, the **Rufus Stone**, stands southeast of Fritham, just off the A31, though you have to approach it by going north of the village and back via Brook. Erected in 1745, the stone marks the putative spot where the Conqueror's son and heir, **William II** – aka William Rufus after his ruddy complexion – was killed by a crossbow bolt in 1100 during a hunting expedition. William was not at all popular in these parts, so the official story – that Sir Walter Tyrell's arrow bounced off a tree and hit the king by mistake – is hotly disputed. Tyrell allegedly escaped by having his horse shod with the horseshoes the wrong way round to confuse his trackers. The memorial you see today was erected in 1865 by the Victorians who encased the original stone in a protective layer of metal to deter vandals; it states "King William the Second, surnamed Rufus, being slain, as before related, was laid in a cart, belonging to one Purkis, and drawn from hence, to Winchester, and buried in the Cathedral Church, of

A round walk or cycle route from Fritham

This 4.5-mile (approx 2hr) **round walk** is mostly on wide forestry tracks, and passes through a mixture of deciduous and coniferous forest and open heathland. It's also a popular cycle route: it starts on the well-signed cycle route to Frogham by the forest car park at Fritham, just past the *Royal Oak* pub (see above). Take this path to Islands Thorn Inclosure – keep to the main path and ignore a branch off to the right. The route becomes more wooded, and after thirty minutes you'll reach a pretty stream with a bridge over it. Cross the bridge and bear left where the path divides. This climbs a low hill and after ten minutes you'll see a gate to the left, which leads into Amberwood Inclosure. Go through the gate, continuing on the path as it winds downhill slightly (ignore a track to the right). Some twenty minutes beyond the gate you can rest at an ornamental wooden bench dedicated to local conservationist Eric Ashby. The path then crosses a bridge and continues straight through double gates; around thirty minutes beyond the bench you exit the inclosure through a gate – bear left where the path divides just past the gate. This last section of around twenty minutes goes through the open Fritham Plain, dotted with ponies and gorse bushes, and was where parts of Kevin Costner's *Robin Hood: Prince of Thieves* was filmed in 1991.

Forest campsites

In addition to several private sites, there are ten **campsites** in the forest run by the Forestry Commission (☎01313 146505, ⓦwww.forestholidays.co.uk). Some are very simple, with few or no facilities, so are suited to caravans and camper vans, others have full facilities for tents. The sites are particularly good for children, as they have open access to the forest, many have streams and fords running through them, and ponies and donkeys wander freely, often poking their noses in through open tent flaps. Most of the sites are also relatively low density to avoid the risk of fires, so there's plenty of space to run free. It's advisable to book beforehand to guarantee a pitch in high season, though some sites request a minimum stay of two nights if booked in advance. Unless stated, all the campsites are open from late March to late September.

Aldridge Hill Brockenhurst ☎01590 623152. Beautiful site beside the Blackwater stream, and just a mile from Brockenhurst. Suitable for caravans and motorhomes, but has no toilet or shower facilities. Open late May to early September.

Ashurst Lyndhurst Rd ☎02380 292097. Large site, a five-minute walk from Ashurst and the fine *New Forest* pub (see p.174). Full facilities for campers including a launderette, but no dogs allowed.

Denny and **Matley Wood** Beaulieu Rd, Lyndhurst ☎02380 293144. Simple woodland sites suitable for caravans and motorhomes, but with no toilet or shower facilities.

Hollands Wood, Lyndhurst Rd, Brockenhurst ☎01590 622967. Lovely wooded site, in easy cycling distance from Brockenhurst, with toilets, showers and a launderette.

Holmsley Forest Rd, Thorney Hill near Bransgore ☎01425 674502. Full facilities including children's play area and a shop. Open late March to late October.

Ocknell and **Longbeech** Fritham ☎02380 812740. Simple woodland and heathland sites with no toilets or hot water at Longbeech, and only toilets at Ocknell.

Roundhill Beaulieu Rd, near Brockenhurst ☎01590 624344. Wonderful, spacious site with showers, toilets and ponies galore.

Setthorns Wooton, New Milton ☎01590 681020. Wooded site with no toilet or shower facilities. Open all year.

---

that city". It's a tranquil spot despite its proximity to the main road. A short walk leads to the *Sir Walter Tyrell* **pub** (☎02380 813170), which serves good pub grub, has a children's play area and its own year-round **campsite**. There are two more good campsites in these parts, at Ocknell and Long Beech (see box above).

The central New Forest

South of the busy A31 lies the archetypal New Forest scenery of pony-flecked heaths and expanses of dense woodland, at its prettiest around the main tourist centres of **Ashurst**, **Lyndhurst** and **Brockenhurst**. These centres are packed in high season, but it doesn't take much effort to find solitude if you walk or cycle a little away from the roads. The eastern reaches of the forest are less wooded but contain the unmissable attractions of **Beaulieu** – a monastic estate with a superb motor museum – the ancient riverside **Buckler's Hard** and the sumptuous gardens at **Exbury**.

Ashurst and around

On the eastern edges of the New Forest, **Ashurst** can best be described as functional. However, it has a good range of shops, is right on the main rail line from Weymouth to London, and makes a handy base for local walks (see box, p.161) and alluring children's attractions.

The train **station** is on the edge of town; turn right out of the station and the centre is a couple of minutes' walk. Best of the budget **accommodation** options in Ashurst is *The Barn* (T02380 292531, Wwww.veggiebarn.net; ❷), 112 Lyndhurst Rd, which offers bed and breakfast in an Edwardian house. There are two tastefully furnished rooms and on offer is a fine organic, vegan breakfast: a ten percent discount is offered to those arriving by public transport. A mile and a half from the station, the upmarket *Hotel Terra Vina* in Netley Marsh (T02380 293784, Wwww.hotelterravina.co.uk; ❼) has comfortable boutique rooms, some with their own terraces, in lovely wooded surroundings. It has stylish decor, an outdoor pool and a highly regarded restaurant with an impressive wine list, overseen by the owner, a master sommelier. Just out of town on the Lyndhurst road is the well-appointed Ashurst **campsite**, though parts abut the railway line (see p.173 for details). For food, the best option is *The New Forest Hotel* (T02380 292721), Lyndhurst Road, a substantial pub right by the station, which has a large restaurant area and garden with a children's play area overlooking rolling New Forest countryside. There's live music some weekends and an excellent Sunday carvery; at other times, filling mains start at around £8 a head.

Longdown Activity Farm

Around a mile southeast of Ashurst off the Totton road, on Deerleap Lane, **Longdown Activity Farm** (daily: Feb–Oct & late Dec 10am–5pm, Nov & early Dec Sat & Sun 10am–5pm; £7, children £6; Wwww.longdownfarm co.uk) is great for younger children. There are various farm animals to admire and cuddle – so it's best to come in spring when there are plenty of cute babies

A round walk near Ashurst

This two-hour **round walk** starts at the **Ashurst campsite** (see above) and, despite its proximity to the A35 and main rail line, takes in some surprisingly unspoilt heath and woods. Turn right at the access road to the campsite and walk across the field, parallel to the A35. After ten minutes you'll reach a quiet side road (to Ashurst Lodge). Turn left and follow the road through ancient woodland. After fifteen minutes, you'll reach the entrance to the lodge. Turn right before the entrance and follow the track that skirts a high wooden fence and bears left across open heath, where you'll often see plenty of ponies. Follow this path, with the fence to the left, and it soon crosses a clear-flowing stream. The path then climbs a low hill. At the top of the hill, the path divides a couple of times – keep right both times and the path heads towards Mapley woods, full of ancient oaks. The path then veers right, following the edge of the treeline. Within ten minutes, a track crosses the one you are on. Turn right here and head back across open heathland, parallel to the way you came. You'll cross back over the stream over a different bridge, keeping straight on when smaller paths cross the main one. You may see deer on this open stretch, before the path enters another fantastic wood full of ancient trees, many of them hollow. Pick up a path through the woods shortly on the right. This follows the edge of the woods all the way back to the Ashurst Lodge road, which you cross to return the way you started, with the campsite ahead of you.

– and children can help feed the ducks, goats or calves and handle rabbits, chicks and guinea pigs, or collect eggs from the chickens. There are also tractor rides and go-karts and wet-weather activities including a ball park, a hay barn and trampolines.

Otter, Owl and Wildlife Park

Further south along Deerleap Lane is the **Otter, Owl and Wildlife Park** (daily: April–Oct 10am–5pm; Nov, Dec & Feb–March 10am–dusk; Jan Sat & Sun only 10am–dusk; £7.50, children £5.50; Ⓦwww.ottersandowls.co.uk). The park has a circular trail that takes you past and through various glass cages and enclosures, many containing animals that are (or were) native to the UK such as dormice, pine martens, badgers, wild boar and foxes. Most prevalent are several species of owls – kept in somewhat cramped conditions – and various species of playful otters: look for signs advertising the latest feeding times. You can also wander through enclosures containing wallabies and deer, and there's a butterfly house (summer only), a decent café and pleasant picnic area.

Eling Tide Mill

Further towards Totton on Eling Creek, at the head of Southampton Water, lies **Eling Tide Mill** (Wed–Sun & Bank Holiday Mon 10am–4pm; ☎02380 869575, Ⓦwww.elingtidemill.org.uk), one of the only functioning tide mills left in England. You can watch the flour being milled in the same way as it has been for thousands of years, though the times it works depend on the tide; there is also an attached Heritage Centre and café.

Lyndhurst and around

An attractive New Forest town, **LYNDHURST** is sadly blighted by a choking one-way system that funnels much of the New Forest's traffic right down the high street – in high summer it's often largely stationary. The town's main sight is the brick **parish church**, St Michael's, worth a glance for its William Morris glass, a fresco by Lord Leighton and the grave of Mrs Reginald Hargreaves, better known as Alice Liddell – Lewis Carroll's model for Alice, who spent her life in Lyndhurst. Most people visit Lyndhurst, however, for practical reasons: it has a good selection of accommodation and restaurants as well as the **New Forest Museum and Visitor Centre** in the central car park off the High Street (daily 10am–5pm; ☎02380 282269, Ⓦwww.thenewforest.co.uk), which also sells bus passes and maps. The **museum** (last entry 4pm; £3) is of mild interest, focusing on the history, wildlife and industries of the forest.

To escape the traffic, hire a bike (see box, p.176) and head out of town beyond the golf course and the marvellously named suburb of Custards. Alternatively, head a mile south to the neighbouring village of **Bank**, a typically pretty New Forest village with some great surrounding walks and one of the forest's best pubs, the *Oak Inn* (see p.177).

A couple of miles out of Lyndhurst on the Beaulieu Road, opposite Beaulieu Road station, you can see the **pony sales ground**, where several times a year there are New Forest pony auctions. Although most of the ponies live wild in the forest, they are actually owned by the forest commoners who have the right to train and ride them or sell them: for dates of the auctions, see Ⓦwww .newforestpony.com/diary_events.html.

Cycling in the Forest

The main **bike rental outlets** are in Burley (ⓦwww.forestleisurecycling.co.uk), Brockenhurst (ⓦwww.countrylanes.co.uk or ⓦwww.cyclex.co.uk) and Lyndhurst (ⓦwww.aabikehirenewforest.co.uk). There are over 100 miles of waymarked **cycle routes** in the forest – maps and routes are usually provided by the bike hire companies, or you can download cycle routes from ⓦwww.new-forest-national-park .com/bike-hire-in-the-new-forest.html. Cycle hire is typically £10–15 a day and most places also hire out tag-a-longs, trailers, childseats and helmets. Many of the New Forest's hotels and guest houses offer discounts for guests arriving by bike so it is easy to claw back the cycle hire fee if you are staying the night somewhere. It is worth noting, however, that though there are numerous off-road routes, you will find cycling on the New Forest roads themselves less pleasurable. Many roads are narrow with little room for cars to pass, so it is worth considering taking your bike on the **Open Top Bus** which links Brockenhurst with Lymington, Beaulieu, Exbury and Lyndhurst: you can get off at any point then get back on again at the end of your cycle route: details on ⓦwww.thenewforesttour.info.

Arrival, information and accommodation

Buses pull in on the High Street, which is well stocked with banks and shops. There's a decent choice of reasonably priced **accommodation**, most on the approach roads into town – with corresponding traffic noise. There are also two good campsites a short drive out of Lyndhurst at Denny and Mapley Wood; see box, p.173.

Beaulieu Hotel Beaulieu Rd ☏02380 293344, ⓦwww.newforesthotels.co.uk. Two to three miles out of Lyndhurst, by the disused Beaulieu Road rail station and opposite the pony sales ground, its isolated position makes this hotel a great place for kids to wander out into the forest and spot deer and ponies. It has well-equipped family rooms with foldaway bunk beds and a small indoor pool. ❼

Burwood Lodge 27 Romsey Rd ☏02380 282445, ⓦwww.burwoodlodge.co.uk; no credit cards. A good value B&B in a substantial Victorian house a short walk from the High Street. Back rooms are quieter and overlook the large lawned garden; there is also a family room and disabled access. ❸

Crown Hotel High St ☏02380 282922, ⓦwww .crownhotel-lyndhurst.co.uk. Traditional coaching inn dating from the 1600s, with a log fire and reasonably priced, comfortable rooms: make sure you ask for one at the back overlooking the gardens as the front rooms are right on the noisy high street. ❸

Forest Cottage High St ☏02380 283461, ⓦwww.forestcottage.co.uk; no credit cards; no smoking. On a busy road, but decent enough rooms in an eighteenth-century townhouse, with a well-stocked natural history library and attractive cottage garden. ❷

Forest Lodge Hotel Pikes Hill, Romsey Rd ☏02380 283677, ⓦwww.newforesthotels.co.uk. Attractive Georgian building in a good location a short walk from Lyndhurst high street but away from the main road, so there's less traffic noise. The rooms are comfortable and there's an indoor pool and sauna. The food is good at both restaurants (see the *Glasshouse* below). ❼

Rufus House Southampton Rd ☏02380 282930, ⓦwww.rufushouse.co.uk. A couple of minutes out of town on the Ashurst road, opposite some fine New Forest countryside, this characterful building has a four-poster bed in its tower room, though front rooms do face a busy road. The owner takes good care of the rooms and guests; good value. ❸

Eating and drinking

Crown Brasserie *Crown Hotel*, High St ☏02380 282922. Attractive, informal brasserie serving main courses such as seafood tagliatelle (£10) and rabbit casserole (£12.50): in summer you can eat outside in the garden.

Glasshouse *Forest Lodge Hotel* ☏02380 283677. Stylish restaurant serving British cuisine, much of it locally sourced and seasonal, in a contemporary setting. The £30 three-course menu features delights such as tea-marinated local venison, and

Dorset Blue Vinney and pistachio nut soufflé. Closed Sun afternoon & Mon.

La Pergola Southampton Rd ☎02380 284184. Lively Italian fare in an attractive building out on the Ashurst Rd, with its own garden. Sizzling meats from around £17, tasty pasta and pizza from £9 and superb home-made desserts, as well as daily specials. Closed Mon except bank hols.

Les Chocolats 23 High St. Step into this café-patisserie for a croissant and coffee, a light lunch or a hot chocolate and it's likely you'll leave with a slab of the handmade French chocolate under your arm.

Parisien 64 High St. French-inspired café with good coffee, pastries and lunches such as inexpensive *croques monsieurs* and baguettes, with a small terrace out back.

The Mill House Romsey Rd. Large pub with a spreading garden, children's play area and good-value pub nosh.

The Oak Inn Pinkney Lane, Bank ☎02380 282350. Fantastic little country pub around a mile out of Lyndhurst in Bank, with low wooden ceilings and a roaring fire in winter and a garden for the summer. Fine ales and great, if expensive food, featuring local ingredients such as river fish and venison – it's best to book in advance.

Waterloo Arms Pikes Hill ☎023 8028211. A pretty seventeenth-century thatched pub away from the busy high street. It's known for its food and real ales – as well as local fish and game, you're likely to find more exotic offerings such as wildebeest or tilapia on the menu: main courses start at £9.

Minstead and Furzey Gardens

A couple of miles north of Lyndhurst, the pretty, one-shop, one-pub hamlet of **Minstead** is an archetypal New Forest village with thatched cottages and a green. Its **church**, parts of which date from the thirteenth century, looks more like an extended cottage, and it is of interest for its unusual triple-decked pulpit as well as being the resting place of **Sir Arthur Conan Doyle**, creator of

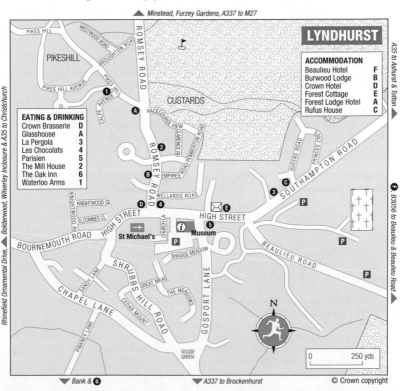

▲ Minstead, Furzey Gardens, A337 to M27

LYNDHURST

ACCOMMODATION
Beaulieu Hotel	F
Burwood Lodge	B
Crown Hotel	D
Forest Cottage	E
Forest Lodge Hotel	A
Rufus House	C

EATING & DRINKING
Crown Brasserie	D
Glasshouse	A
La Pergola	3
Les Chocolats	4
Parisien	5
The Mill House	2
The Oak Inn	6
Waterloo Arms	1

© Crown copyright

▲ Arthur Conan Doyle's grave

Sherlock Holmes. The church was initially reluctant to allow him to be buried here due to his fervent belief in spiritualism and his enthusiasm for mediums who claimed to be able to contact the dead – a séance was held at his funeral at his request. Eventually, however, it was agreed that he could be buried at the far edge of the graveyard, where his grave is often decorated by mementoes, such as pipes, left by fans of the fictional detective. Minstead is also home to **Furzey Gardens** (gardens: daily 10am–dusk; £5.50, children £2; gallery: March–Oct 10am–5pm; free; Ⓦ www.furzey-gardens.org), which are at their most colourful in spring when the azaleas and rhododendrons are out. Children will enjoy the climbing the tower and African-style tree houses and searching for the fairy doors that have been carved into trees around the gardens. There's also a café, art gallery and regular exhibitions of thatching, as well as a tiny thatched cottage, once home to a family of fourteen children, which has been restored to its original sixteenth-century condition.

A walk around Minstead

A lovely, bucolic **two-mile round walk** through native woods and over streams and fords starts from the **green in Minstead**. From here, head up the lane to the church, then take the path that runs alongside its graveyard down through a wood of oaks, beeches and silver birch. At the bottom, there's a lane with a ford across a babbling stream: cross the lane and follow the signs to Furzey Gardens. This takes you along a quiet path; take the first turning on the left and continue through a further ford until the lane bears sharply left and you see two footpaths. Take the right-hand track and carry on through the woods until you reach a stream; cross over the bridge and as the path climbs look for a yellow walk arrow on the right. Follow the arrowed path through further woodlands over a small stream, then bear left towards the Furzey Gardens car park. From the gardens it's a short walk back to the village: take the lane to the right, then turn right again round the bottom of the gardens. Continue along the lane until you see a style on your left and a footpath sign. Follow this path across two fields until you reach a road, where you turn right bringing you back to the village green.

Rhinefield Ornamental Drive

Signed off the main A35, **Rhinefield Ornamental Drive** was once part of the Rhinefield House estate. The house – now the *Rhinefield House Hotel* (see below) – was built in 1887, and exotic plants such as giant redwoods, azaleas and rhododendrons were planted on the surrounding land. Much of its former grounds are now part of the New Forest and have walking trails through them. You can see the giant redwoods – the two tallest trees in the forest – on the marked Tall Trees trail, a 1.5-mile walk from Brock Hill car park, signed half a mile along the Drive, or Blackwater car park, at the bottom of the Drive by Blackwater Arboretum a small enclosure packed with various trees from around the world. **Accommodation** here includes the upmarket *Rhinefield House Hotel* (☎01590 622922, ⓦwww.handpicked.co.uk/rhinefieldhouse; ❼), set in the stunning grounds with its own small lake, indoor and outdoor pool, and gastronomic restaurant. Not surprisingly, it is often overflowing with honeymooners, though the rooms are less characterful than the hotel as a whole.

Bolderwood and Wilverley Inclosure

Opposite the Rhinefield turning, a delightful narrow road winds through ancient woodland to Bolderwood; it's especially beautiful in the autumn, when the colours are dazzling – there are various car parks along the route if you want to stop off and explore. At the top of the slope, **Bolderwood** itself is a large open area of grassland with an information hut. Three marked trails depart from behind the hut, the longest just two miles, a pleasant and easy walk through a mix of deciduous and coniferous woodland, over a stream and back. All three trails pass a deer-feeding centre. The resident deer population thrives in these parts and they aren't worried about coming right up to the edges of the fenced paddock where they are fed weekly, except in winter during the rutting season.

A few miles south of Rhinefield, on the eastern side of the A31, lies **Wilverley Inclosure** – there are a few gravel laybys by the side of the road for parking. The New Forest has various inclosures – fenced areas for growing timber – and this is one of the densest, with impressively mature pines and deciduous trees. Various marked trails and cycle paths wend their way around the inclosure, though half the fun is getting lost in the thick, sloping interior, darkened by overhanging foliage even at midday. The surrounding area is also popular with local mushroomers, who often find rare edible species. For a more substantial **meal**, head a little south down the A31 and take the Burley turning for ⚹ *Station House*, Station Road, Holmsley (☎01425 402468, closed eves), set in the former Holmsley railway station – you can still see the signals and old tickets decorate the walls. The café serves sizeable breakfasts, sandwiches and daily specials (around £6–8), though it is best known for its superb home-made cakes and teas.

Burley

Set in a dip and surrounded by woodland, **BURLEY** is as attractively located as any village in the forest, pulling in day-trippers galore. There is not a lot to the village apart from a few pleasant pubs and a series of shops that seem to be permanently set up for Halloween. This plethora of bizarre stores all specialize in witchcraft, many opening in the wake of A Coven of Witches, the first shop created by local self-proclaimed white witch, Sybil Leek, in the 1950s – shortly after England's witchcraft laws were repealed in 1951. Black-cloaked Leek, who was usually seen with a jackdaw on her shoulder, became a local celebrity, billing herself as high priestess of the white witches – who believed in being guided by the sun, moon and the stars in their bid to spread goodwill. Another local, Gerald Gardner from nearby Christchurch, took on the mantle of "Britain's chief witch" in 1954, after writing a book on Wicca (or modern witchcraft), called *Witchcraft Today*. His book inspired an increased interest in witchcraft and his version of the "old religion" throughout the country. Burley shopkeepers claim there are still white witches who follow Gardnerian Wicca in the forest today, mostly "Hedgewitches" – those who work alone rather than part of a coven – and you'll find many of Burley's shops selling Hedgewitch spells.

Burley's secluded position helped it become the centre of the eighteenth-century New Forest smuggling trade, much of it conducted from *The Queen's Head* at The Cross in the centre of town, a good place for a drink. If you want to **stay**, the best option is a short walk out of town at Bisterne Close where the ☂ *White Buck* (☎01425 402264, ⓦwww.fullershotels.com; ❹) has decent doubles of various sizes, most of them recently refurbished. The pub below has superb food too, including local game, as well as a giant garden for kids to run around in; it also has occasional live music. Nearby, there's a YHA **hostel** in Cottesmore House, Cott Lane (☎0845 371 9309, ⒺBurley@yha.org.uk; £16), with simple hostel rooms and a lovely garden, where you can camp or stay in one of the ready-erected tents that sleep four (£40 per tent).

Brockenhurst

You'll frequently find New Forest ponies strolling down the high street of **Brockenhurst**, undoubtedly the most attractive and liveliest town in the forest. Surrounded by idyllic heath and woodland and with a ford at one end – which usually attracts crowds of children when cars splash through – it is a picturesque town with some fine shops and cafés. Spliced by the main London to Weymouth train line, this is also commuter territory, making it fairly upmarket. There are no specific sights – most people come just to wander through the charming lanes lined with thatched cottages, soak up the traditional village atmosphere and stock up on picnic supplies.

The New Forest Show

A mile or so north of Brockenhurst, the extensive New Park has been home to the annual **New Forest Show** since 1964. This three-day event gives a real insight into rural life in and around the forest, with demonstrations of skills little changed since medieval times, such as wood-turning, thatching and beekeeping. Part market and part fair, hundreds of stalls display the best of the local arts and crafts, food, antiques and countryside produce and you can buy everything from wet-weather gear to the latest rare breed of rabbit. There are also awards for the finest cattle, sheep, garden displays and vegetables. Throughout the day, several arenas host showjumping, horse and carriage competitions, tractor parades and spectacular motorbike stunts, along with the amusing pig-racing and dog handling.

Aim to spend a full day here and consider visiting on the last day when the prize fruit, veg and plants are sold off cheaply at around 5pm. The show usually takes place in the last week of July (check ⓦwww.newforestshow.co.uk for exact dates each year) and tickets cost around £15 a day for adults and £7 for children.

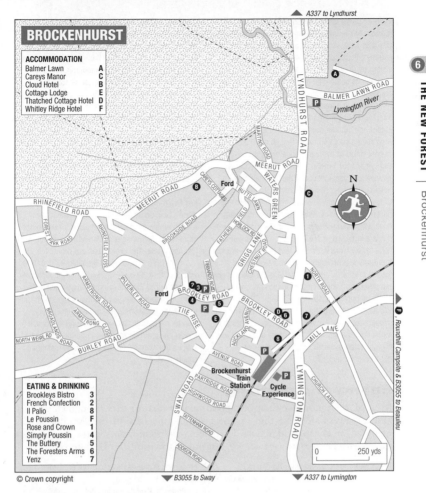

BROCKENHURST

ACCOMMODATION
Balmer Lawn	A
Careys Manor	C
Cloud Hotel	B
Cottage Lodge	E
Thatched Cottage Hotel	D
Whitley Ridge Hotel	F

EATING & DRINKING
Brookleys Bistro	3
French Confection	2
Il Palio	8
Le Poussin	F
Rose and Crown	1
Simply Poussin	4
The Buttery	5
The Foresters Arms	6
Yenz	7

A337 to Lyndhurst

Lymington River

N

0   250 yds

© Crown copyright   B3055 to Sway   A337 to Lymington

Arrival and information

Trains and **buses** pull in at the eastern edge of town – turn left and left again into the main Brookley Road which doubles as the High Street, where you'll find the bulk of shops, banks and places to eat and drink. Brockenhurst is also known for its cycling routes, and you can **hire bikes** from Cycle Experience right by the railway station (℡01590 623407, Ⓦwww.cyclex.co.uk; bikes from £11 a day), who also give out maps of the best local routes.

Accommodation

There's no shortage of **accommodation** in Brockenhurst, though much of it is on the pricey side and it is definitely a good idea to book well in advance for the top choices listed below. See box on p.173 for details of nearby campsites.

Balmer Lawn Lyndhurst Rd ☎01590 623116, ⓦwww.balmerlawnhotel.com. This giant Victorian pile was originally built as a hunting lodge and still exudes colonial splendour, if rather faded. Once visited by George V and used as a World War I army hospital, its communal areas still have a darkened, carpeted splendour. Some rooms have been refurbished in a more contemporary style, with interconnecting rooms for families, and there's an indoor and outdoor pool and restaurant. Forest-view rooms cost £45 extra, though room 37 sneaks in pool views at the lower price bracket.

Careys Manor Lyndhurst Rd ☎01590 623551, ⓦwww.careysmanor.com. This Victorian country house and former home of Charles II forester, John Carey, has a range of rooms, from traditional four-posters in the manor house to more contemporary ones with a terrace or balcony in the modern wing. It has a highly regarded Thai spa – though guests have to pay extra to use it – and three restaurants, the traditional *Manor* restaurant, a less formal French brasserie, and the *Thai Zen Garden*. You get ten percent off your accommodation bill if you arrive by public transport. ❽

Cloud Hotel Meerut Rd ☎01590 622165, ⓦwww.cloudhotel.co.uk. A lovely postion overlooking the forest with friendly staff. The rooms and decor are slightly dated, however, and it has a rather old-fashioned feel. ❼

Cottage Lodge Sway Rd ☎01590 622296, ⓦwww.cottagelodge.co.uk. A short walk from the High Street, rooms in the original forester's cottage here date back to the eighteenth century; some may prefer the more modern amenities in the modern extension. There are various rooms, with free tea and cakes for those arriving by public transport and environmentally friendly products used wherever possible; no smoking in any rooms. ❹

Thatched Cottage Hotel 16 Brookley Rd ☎01590 623090, ⓦwww.thatched-cottage.co.uk. Dating from 1627, this is indeed an ancient thatched cottage, with tiny, low-beamed rooms as crammed with character as they are with furniture. There are just five rooms, one with a small outdoor terrace; there's also an attached restaurant with its own garden which does great food using locally sourced ingredients, including New Forest mushrooms, wild fish and game. The cream teas are divine, too. ❷

🏃 **Whitley Ridge Hotel** Beaulieu Rd ☎01590 622354, ⓦwww.whitleyridge.com. A couple of miles out of Brockenhurst on the Beaulieu road, this sumptuous Georgian country house sits in rural splendour, with substantial grounds including its own tennis courts. Once a royal hunting lodge, it has lovely spacious rooms with period fittings, as well as the award-winning *Le Poussin* restaurant (see below). ❽

Eating and drinking

Most of the hotels have their own good-quality **restaurants**, though cheap–eats and takeaways are a bit thin on the ground, especially in the evenings when many of the cheaper cafés close. There are great picnic spots in the area around the *Bulmer Lawn Hotel* (see above), just out of town off the Beaulieu road.

Brookleys Bistro 58 Brookley Rd ☎01590 624625, ⓦwww.brookleysbistro.com. Small bistro and wine bar with a sunny terrace for breakfast, good-value lunches or drinks. Evening mains are around £16 for delicious steaks, grilled chicken or fish. Closed Sun & Mon.

French Confection 76 Brookley Rd ☎01590 624252. Great little *boulangerie* and patisserie on the high street, with a couple of outdoor tables catching the afternoon sun. The spinach pies are superb, as are the pizza slices, baguettes and strawberry tarts.

Il Palio Station Approach ☎01590 622730. Set in a former engine shed – you can watch the trains pass out of the window – *Il Palio* is an atmospheric traditional Italian restaurant. Prices for the pizza and pasta are slightly higher than the norm, but the portions are positively vast. Try the fried mixed fish or the seafood risotto, with a good

proportion of the day's catch well presented on your plate. Closed Mon.

Le Poussin *Whitley Ridge* hotel. Top-quality Michelin-rated cooking in a beautiful country house setting. Highly regarded chef Alex Aitken produces unusual combinations, such as cod cheeks with frogs legs, using local ingredients where possible. It's not cheap – the three-course Sunday lunch is £27.50 a head – but worth it for cooking and service of this quality.

Rose and Crown Lyndhurst Rd. A traditional forest inn dating from the thirteenth century with a pleasant garden and a skittle alley. It serves large portions of good-value pub grub, and a selection of real ales.

Simply Poussin The Courtyard, Brookley Rd ☎01590 623063. Also in the Alex Aitken stable (see above), but more affordable and less formal, this small restaurant is tucked away in a little

A round walk near Brockenhurst

A fine hour's **round walk** along a disused railway track begins just out of town on the **road to Sway**, taking in open heathland and some dense woodland. By car, follow the road out of Brockenhurst that crosses the main rail line, then turn right. The road shortly passes under a railway bridge – park on the right just afterwards, by a second raised railway line. The walk begins by passing under this line and goes along a wide track. When you reach a farm, turn left and follow the old dismantled railway line that once ran to Burley and Ringwood. After 20 minutes or so of passing through rolling heathland, you'll cross a bridge over a path by an electricity sub-station. Take the track down to this lower path and go past the substation. The path leads into shady woodland. After 200 metres or so, take the first main path off to the right. This heads out of the woods and back across the heath, rejoining the track you started on by the farm.

mews behind the high street. The menu is simple, featuring brasserie-style dishes, with mains, such as roast *poussin*, for £12–15, and an excellent value three-course menu for £17.50.
The Buttery 25 Brookley Rd. Bear-themed tearoom which attracts a steady stream of regulars for its inexpensive lunches, superior cream teas and delicious home-made cakes – the sugar-free, wheat-free fruit cake is much nicer than it sounds – with tea served in giant teapots.

The Foresters Arms 10 Brookley Rd. Friendly, traditional pub with a few outdoor tables, right by the station. It serves good portions of reasonably priced classic pub food and is popular with students from the nearby college.
Yenz Lyndhurst Rd. Delicious Chinese food in an attractive modern building – try the Szechuan chicken buried in chilli (£8.50) if you're feeling brave, or monkfish with shiitake mushrooms and vegetables (£9.50); also does takeaway.

Beaulieu and around

Situated in the southeast corner of the New Forest, the village of **BEAULIEU** (whose name originates from the French meaning "Beautiful Place", but is pronounced "Bewley") is embraced by the extensive land of the Beaulieu estate. The village feels rooted in some distant England of the past: its quaint high street is lined with traditional shops and a miniscule primary school, while donkeys and New Forest ponies amble at will. But most visitors bypass the village to head to the main attraction of Beaulieu House, or to the nearby village of **Buckler's Hard**, also owned by the Beaulieu estate.

Beaulieu originally was the site of one of England's most influential monasteries, a Cistercian house founded in 1204 by King John – in remorse, it is said, for ordering a group of supplicating Cistercian monks to be trampled to death. Built using stone ferried from Caen in northern France and Quarr on the Isle of Wight, the **abbey** managed a self-sufficient estate of ten thousand acres, but was dismantled soon after the Dissolution. Its refectory now forms the parish church, which, like everything else in Beaulieu, has been subsumed by the Montagu family who has owned a large chunk of the New Forest ever since one of Charles II's illegitimate progeny was created duke of the estate.

Beaulieu House

Owned by Montagus since 1538 and still the family home of Lord Montagu, **Beaulieu House** (daily: June–Sept 10am–6pm; Oct–May 10am–5pm; £15.75, children £9.50; Ⓦ www.beaulieu.co.uk) is a superbly arranged tourist complex, whose main draw, deservedly, is the **National Motor Museum**. Inside the museum, there's enough horse-power to make Jeremy Clarkson swoon – the collection of 250 cars and motorcycles includes spindly antiques and recent classics, Formula I cars rubbing shoulders with land-speed racers, vintage Rolls Royces, Ferraris and a Sinclair C5. Even if you're no petrolhead, you'll recognize many of the vehicles in the museum – Donald Campbell's record-breaking Bluebird, Chitty Chitty Bang Bang and even Mr Bean's Mini. You can clamber on the London double-decker bus and nose around the recreated 1930s garage, while the entertaining ride-through display, "Wheels", takes you on a trip through the history of motoring. The upper floor houses the motor-cycle gallery, home to the largest collection of Ducatti bikes outside Italy. Outside, a separate building houses the **James Bond exhibition**, where you can get up close to 007's amphibious Lotus and the world's first jet ski (from *The Spy Who Loved Me*), the Jag that Bond drove across the ice in *Die Another Day*, plus Jaws' giant shirt.

An undersized **monorail** runs round the estate and through the Motor Museum, which is worth riding for a bird's-eye view of the cars below, though it's an easy ten-minute walk from the museum through attractive gardens to **Palace House** and the other attractions. Formerly the abbey's gatehouse, the fourteenth-century Palace House is the well-kept if unexceptional family home of the Montagus: its history is brought to life by guides dressed in Victorian clothing, who relate anecdotes about the Montagu-related memorabilia. Other draws on the Beaulieu estate include a small museum, containing the Secret Army exhibition that traces how spies were trained here before being sent on missions in World War II, and the remains of a Cistercian **abbey** dating from 1204, whose undercroft houses an exhibition depicting medieval monastic life. Leave time, too, to explore the superb **gardens**, which spread alongside the river.

▲ Mr Bean's mini, The National Motor Museum

Practicalities

There's a small pay-and-display car park in Beaulieu village, or you can try and find a spot along the high street. The best place to **stay** in the village itself is the *Montagu Arms Hotel* (☎01590 612324, Ⓦwww.montaguarmshotel.co.uk; ❽) housed in an eighteenth-century building with open fires and a lovely garden, including four-poster beds; push the boat out for a meal at its **restaurant**, with sublime food created by Michelin-starred chef Shaun Hill. For more reasonably priced pub food, there's *Monty's Bar* next door. Alternatively, just off the high street, is the *Old Bakehouse Tearooms* (☎01590 612777), a good place for an inexpensive lunch of jacket potatoes or sandwiches, inside an eighteenth-century former bakery – you can still see the old oven doors. However, if the weather's good, you're best off getting a picnic from the *Beaulieu Delicatessen* (☎01590 611 266), on the high street, and taking it out to the green to eat in full sight of the donkeys, ponies and ducks: the deli has a good range of Spanish meats and superb local cheeses; there's a little seating area inside.

Buckler's Hard

If Beaulieu amply deserves its name, **Buckler's Hard** (daily: March–June, Sept & Oct 10am–5pm; July & Aug 10am–5.30pm; Nov–Feb 10am–4.30pm; £5.90, children £4.30), a couple of miles downstream on the River Beaulieu, has an even more wonderful setting. A lovely two-mile **track** links Beaulieu and **Buckler's Hard**, passing through meadows and woods. A slightly longer but more enjoyable path runs alongside the river itself, taking you past the mudflats and oak woods, most part of the North Solent nature reserve. If you park in Beaulieu and walk along the river, you can wander freely throughout the village of Buckler's Hard without paying the admission fee: you will need to buy a ticket, however, if you want to visit the museum.

Buckler's Hard doesn't look much like a shipyard now, but from Elizabethan times onwards dozens of men-of-war were assembled here from giant New Forest oaks. Several of Nelson's ships were launched here, to be towed carefully by rowing boats past the sandbanks and across the Solent to Portsmouth. The largest house in this hamlet belonged to Henry Adams, the master builder responsible for most of the Trafalgar fleet; it's now an upmarket hotel and restaurant (see below). This contrasts with the nearby simple Shipwrights Cottage, former home of Thomas Burlace, who worked on Nelson's favourite ship, the *Agamemnon*. At the top of the village, the **Maritime Museum** traces the history of the great ships and incorporates buildings preserved in their eighteenth-century form.

From Buckler's Hard, you can take a thirty-minute **boat trip** downriver (Easter to Oct: £4, children £2.50) past oyster beds, flashy yachts and rural scenery. It's hard to believe that this peaceful, attractive section of river was requisitioned during World War II by the armed forces, and Mulberry harbours were constructed here, with secret agents trained in the remote riverside houses before being sent abroad for daring missions.

The picturesque and peaceful *Master Builders Hotel* (Ⓦwww.themasterbuilders .co.uk; ❺) is a great place to **stay**. The hotel itself is in a wonderful old building with open fires and a superb location overlooking the river: the rooms are a mixed bunch, some newly refurbished with oriental flourishes and individually designed furniture, others more simple. The bar menu has sandwiches and snacks, as well as main courses, such as local mackerel, and linguine with New Forest mushrooms (£8–11), while the restaurant menu is slightly pricier and more formal.

East of the Beaulieu River

The eastern extremities of the New Forest are relatively unvisited – mainly because of the looming eyesore of the Fawley oil refinery, whose smoke stacks dominate what would otherwise be pleasant countryside. This section of the forest is a strange mixture of industrial blight and thatched rural idyll, but is worth exploring for its colourful gardens at **Exbury** and the interesting riverside communities of **Calshot** and **Hythe** that abut the Solent.

Exbury Gardens

Three miles southeast of Beaulieu, **Exbury Gardens** (daily March to early Nov 10am–5pm; £8, children under 15 £1.50; ⓦ www.exbury.co.uk) consist of 20 miles of pathways wending through superb cultivated and semi-wild gardens abutting the Beaulieu River; a small steam train (£3.50 extra) trundles round much of the grounds if you don't fancy the walk. The gardens were the brainchild of Lionel Nathan de Rothschild, who in the 1920s set out to create one of the best woodland gardens in the UK. His banking family was immensely wealthy, but Lionel saw himself more as a gardener than a banker and brought up the Exbury estate to indulge his passion. He dug ponds, laid irrigation pipes and planted the gardens with exotic species, only to die in 1942 before the gardens were completed. The Navy requisitioned the house, though after the war, Lionel's son continued work on the gardens and his family continue to develop it. Today you can wander round superb azalea and hydrangea walks, admire bog gardens and lawns, picnic by the river or visit the tearooms.

Lepe and Calshot

Beyond Exbury, the coast remains appealing, especially at **Lepe**, where there is a small country park complete with children's play area, café-restaurant and various marked trails along the coast. The beach here is a mix of fine shingle and sand – not the nicest for swimming, but great for a stroll, with good views over to the Isle of Wight. The sea turns into the river at the little village of **Calshot**, which has another pleasant shingle beach, though the scenery here is far more industrial. That doesn't prevent the beach huts here swapping hands for five-figure sums. The beach peters out at **Calshot Castle** (daily April–Sept 10.30am–4.30pm; £2.50, children £1.50; EH), a diminutive round fort with a little moat built by Henry VIII – there are great views from its upper rooms over the estuary, packed with ferries, boats and lumbering container ships. Next to the castle is the giant warehouse-like **Activities Centre** (☎02380 892077, ⓦ www.calshot.com), one of the largest outdoor activity centres in the country. As well as running a variety of watersports courses, there is also a dry-ski slope, velodrome and climbing walls: there is also a café-bar with good views.

Hythe

The small town of **Hythe** sits opposite Southampton on the busy Southampton Water and was where Sir Christopher Cockerell first developed the hovercraft. Its other claim to fame is that it was the home to the world's oldest **pier train**, a fantastic contraption that dates back to 1922 and carries passengers down an extremely long pier to a ferry terminal for connections to Southampton. You can walk, of course, in around ten minutes, but the ride (daily 6.10am–10.10pm; every 30min; £1 single) is much more amusing. The **ferry** trip itself to Town Quay in Southampton is also rather fun (departures connect with the pier train;

last return 10.30pm; £4.50 return or £5.50 during rush hour); from Town Quay, a free shuttle bus takes passengers to West Quay shopping centre (see p.225) and Southampton central station. There is not a lot else to Hythe, though a few Georgian buildings survive among the largely postwar high street and there is a lively Tuesday market. Also worth seeking out is the **marina** to the north of the pier, which has great views across the waters – especially impressive when the cruise liners sail into Southampton. Here, *Salt* at Shamrock Way (☎02380 845594) is a stylish **bar-restaurant** with outdoor seating and food ranging from inexpensive burgers and chicken ramen to more pricey monkfish in parma ham. Otherwise the best place to eat is the *Lord Nelson* pub, which has waterside tables opposite the pier.

The South Coast

The coast south of the New Forest is a continuous sprawl of fairly low-key development. The most attractive places to head are slightly off the beach, at historic **Christchurch** – with its enormous priory – and the harbour of **Lymington**. In between lie the fairly characterless seaside resorts of Highcliffe, Barton and the prettier village of Milford, most of them above shingly beaches. But though most of these places grew up postwar, there are a couple of older gems in the form of **Highcliffe Castle**, with its fine grounds, and **Hurst Castle**, dramatically sited on a shingle spit.

Christchurch and around

Formerly called Twynham, meaning "between two rivers", **CHRIST-CHURCH** is indeed shaped by its position, squeezed between the rivers Avon and the Stour. Separated from Bournemouth's sprawl by the River Stour, the town has a very different feel from its much larger western neighbour. Intimate and historic, it is at once likeable if generally sleepy – it has the highest percentage of retired people in the country. There is no beach here but its harbourside location is lovely, and you can easily take a boat out to the nearest sandspit beach in high season.

Arrival and information

Christchurch is on the main Weymouth to London line; the **train station** is about a mile north of the centre. Turn left out of the station then first right, and it is a ten-minute walk to the **tourist information centre**, 49 High St (☎01202 471780, ⓦ www.visitchristchurch.info), which can help with booking **accommodation**. Local **buses** from Bournemouth in the east, Lymington in the west and Ringwood in the north, pull up at the bus stop close to the tourist information centre right on the high street. Note that every Monday, the high street is closed to traffic for the weekly **market**, but there are plenty of pay-and-display car parks off the high street.

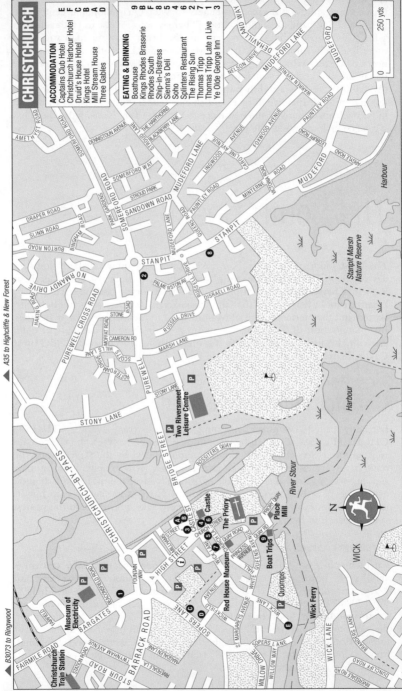

CHRISTCHURCH

ACCOMMODATION
Captains Club Hotel   E
Christchurch Harbour Hotel F
Druid's House Hotel   C
Kings Hotel   B
Mill Stream House   A
Three Gables   D

EATING & DRINKING
Boathouse   9
Kings Rhodes Brasserie B
Rhodes South   F
Ship-in-Distress   8
Sienna's Deli   5
Soho   4
Splinters Restaurant   6
The Rising Sun   2
Thomas Tripp   7
Thomas Tripp Late n Live 1
Ye Olde George Inn   3

Accommodation

As well as the **accommodation** listed below, there are several inexpensive bed and breakfasts on Stour Road, near the train station, though these can be noisy.

Captains Club Hotel Wick Lane ℡01202 475111, ⓦ www.thecaptainsclub.net. Right by the river, the modern glass exterior resembles a car showroom, but inside things improve and there is a fine riverside terrace, bar, restaurant and spa. The contemporary rooms come with great river views. ❼

Christchurch Harbour Hotel 95 Mudeford ℡01202 483434, ⓦ www.christchurch-harbour -hotel.co.uk. An upmarket option, in lovely harbour-side grounds with its own spa, pool, fantastic gardens and Gary Rhodes restaurant, *Rhodes South* (see p.191). The rooms vary: the new ones come with all mod cons, including flat-screen TV, free internet, iPod dock and power showers, though the real treat are the rooms that have their own terrace overlooking the harbour. ❻

Druid's House Hotel 26 Sopers Lane ℡01202 485615, ⓦ www.druid-house.co.uk. Well-regarded five-star guest house in a good location behind the high street, overlooking a park. ❷

Kings Hotel 18 Castle St ℡01202 483434, ⓦ www.thekings-chirstchurch.co.uk. A decent place to stay right opposite the castle ruins and above the *Kings Rhodes Brasserie* (see p.191). Each of the sixteen rooms has a boutique feel with flat-screen TVs and DVDs and includes breakfast in bed; note that parking is limited outside the hotel. ❸

Mill Stream House 6 Ducking Stool Walk ℡01202 480114, ⓦ www.christchurchbedand 0breakfast.co.uk. Just two en-suite rooms with all mod cons in this modern mews house overlooking the millstream. The location is quiet, but wonderfully central, a mere stone's throw from the *King's Hotel* and a short walk from the high street. ❸

Three Gables 11 Wickfield Ave ℡01202 481166, ⓦ www.3Gables-christchurch.co.uk. Just behind Druitts Gardens, a short walk from the high street, this simple B&B has clean and comfortable rooms and has friendly owners. One-week minimum let in August. ❶

The Town

Christchurch's historic centre looks up to the enormous **Priory** (Mon–Sat 9.30am–5pm, Sun 2.15–5.30pm subject to services; free), resembling a cathedral but actually England's longest parish church, parts of which date back to 1094. In the twelfth century, a legend developed about a miraculous beam which grew in length to fit the place it was intended for during the church's construction – a miracle only Christ could have performed – thus inspiring locals to change the town's name to Christchurch. The priory was added to over the centuries – look for the Lady Chapel, whose pendant vaulting is considered the earliest of its type in England. Henry VIII spared the priory during the Dissolution on condition that it was used as a parish church, which it has been ever since. There are free lunchtime recitals here most Thursdays and it often hosts concerts by the BSO amongst others: check the website (ⓦ www.christchurchpriory.org) for details. It's worth trying to take a **guided tour** that takes place throughout the year (check the website for dates and times); these visit parts of the church that are normally closed to the public, such as the crypt and the tower.

Behind the Priory in the riverside gardens, is the substantial ruin of a hilltop **Norman castle** – which offers great views over the old town – and a ruined house known the **Great Chamber**, built for the town bailiff. Dating from 1160, it's all that's left of stone buildings built to defend the town and contains a rare Norman chimney.

The riverside gardens spread down to an open area of grassland known as the **Quomps**, where you can visit the small water mill **Place Mill** (April–Oct Tues–Sun plus bank hols 11am–5.30pm; free), which is partly Saxon and was mentioned in the Domesday Book. Inside, you can clamber up the rickety ladders to see the workings of the mill, with the adjoining gallery hosting art exhibitions and a resident artist displaying local works. From just outside the mill, **boat trips** (and boat hire) head upriver to Tuckton and out to the beach at Hengistbury Head (see p.57). Boats run roughly every half an hour (☎01202 429119, Ⓦwww.bournemouthboating.co.uk/ferry); the full trip from Tuckton to Hengistbury Head takes around forty minutes.

Just back from the Quay, on Quay Road, **Red House Museum** (Tues–Sat 10am–5pm, Sun 2–5pm; free; Ⓦwww.hants.gov.uk/redhouse) is set in a Georgian former workhouse and now displays a fascinating mishmash of artefacts relating to local history, including some Arts and Crafts furniture. As well as detailing conditions in the original workhouse, there are archeological finds, traditional clothes from the eighteenth and nineteenth centuries, fossils and a lovely herb garden.

Some of the town's prettiest streets are tucked behind the *George Inn* on the High Street – look out for the **ducking stool**, used to punish miscreants until the nineteenth century, though what you see today is a modern replica.

The town's other main sight, tucked away off the busy Fairmile Road north of the high street, is the **Museum of Electricity** (Easter to late Sept Mon–Thurs noon–4.30pm, also Fri during school hols; free; Ⓦwww.scottish-southern.co.uk /museum) set in a former Edwardian power station. The gleaming fittings date back to 1903, and there are also electric vehicles including a Sinclair C5 and an old Bournemouth tram.

Christchurch Harbour, Mudeford and Steamer Point

East of the town centre, Christchurch's suburbs wrap round the substantial **Christchurch Harbour**, whose shallow waters make it ideal for novice sailors and windsurfers. The best approach to the harbour is via the suburb of Mudeford, a mile or so east of the town centre. Here, a small car park gives access to **Stanpit Marshes**, whose tidal inlets were once notorious for tobacco smugglers. Today there is a fine half-hour harbourside walk through the

▲ Christchurch from Hengistbury Head

marshes, which are usually full of resident ponies. Near the start of the walk, you'll pass a small information hut detailing local wildlife, which often includes rare wading birds. The road continues past here to **Mudeford Quay**, where ferries (every 10–15min, Easter–Oct daily 10am–dusk; Nov–Easter weekends only 10.30am–4pm, weather permitting; £1.20 single) depart to Mudeford sandspit and Hengistbury Head (see p.57). Once a fishing village, and still dotted with lobster cages, Mudeford is a great spot for crabbers and the starting point of a seaside promenade that heads for around a mile east, alongside a sand-and-shingle beach. You can also take the path up the cliff off the promenade to a nature area known as **Steamer Point**, where cliff-top woods offer superb views over the coast and lead on to Highcliffe Castle (see p.192).

Eating, drinking and nightlife

Christchurch has, in recent years, gained a reputation as a gastronomic town, with a good selection of top-class restaurants, regular **farmers' markets and an annual food festival each May** (Ⓦwww.christchurchfoodfest.co.uk). After dark the town is generally sleepy, though the pubs can be lively.

Kings Rhodes Brasserie 18 Castle St ☎01202 483434. A further outpost of the Gary Rhodes' empire, this stylish, buzzy brasserie serves interesting tapas-style dishes, such as bacon and egg soup (£5) or the more conventional tuna with green beans (£8), while the reasonably priced main courses include roast gurnard for £13. Also has a small but chic bar serving great cocktails.

Rhodes South *Christchurch Harbour Hotel*, 95 Mudeford ☎01202 483434. Celebrity-chef Gary Rhodes' second Christchurch project is a distinctive wooden restaurant with stunning views of Christchurch harbour. The waterside restaurant is in the grounds of the hotel, and its menu features interesting main courses, such as salmon, scallops and oysters in a ginger sauce for around £15–16.

ShipinDistress 62 Stanpit ☎01202 485123. Very atmospheric, friendly local pub full of maritime paraphernalia, with a highly regarded seafood restaurant at the back. The shellfish platters (£28) are fantastic, but there's also a wide range of less extravagant fish dishes on offer, such as tuna loin and sea bass (£17–18).

Sienna's Deli 20 Church St. The place to stock up for a picnic – delicious ciabatta sandwiches, soup, olives and nibbles, and home-made cakes to take out – or stop off for a cup of Christchurch's best coffee.

Soho 7 Church St. Comfortable bar-café-restaurant serving tasty pizzas cooked at the open kitchen: the more unusual toppings include Thai beef or crispy duck with hoi sin sauce. Also does sandwiches and snacks at lunchtime and has a lovely outdoor terrace overlooking the castle. Very different in the evenings, when it is more of a bar attracting large gangs of moneyed 30-somethings.

Splinters Restaurant 12 Church St ☎01202 483454. In a cobbled street down by the priory, this intimate restaurant has several dining rooms, one with wooden booths for added privacy. The top-quality cooking features unusual combinations such as seared scallops with pork belly, as well as more classic dishes, such as roast lamb.

🏃 **The Rising Sun** 123 Purewell ☎01202 486122. Excellent-quality Thai food, much of it organic and MSG-free, served at this pleasant pub. Prices are reasonable, and the Thai vegetable curries are particularly good.

🏃 **Thomas Tripp** 10 Wick Lane. Christchurch's liveliest pub defies the town's reputation for being full of retired people – a good-time, young crowd enjoy a great outdoor terrace, frequent live music and DJ sessions.

The Boathouse The Quay ☎01202 480033. In a lovely location overlooking the Quomps and the river with a huge outdoor terrace. By day, there's a decent range of breakfast dishes, followed by sandwiches and light lunches (around £6), or more substantial dishes such as moules frites, (£16) or mushroom risotto (£11), which are also available in the evening.

Thomas Tripp Late n Live 25–27 Bargates Ⓦwww.thomastripplive.com. The club venue for the *Tripp* (see above), with live gigs, tribute bands, comedy and local up-and-coming bands.

Ye Olde George Inn 2a Castle St. Christchurch's oldest pub, the *George* is an attractive former coaching inn with a great courtyard garden, and a warren of small rooms inside. Serves reasonably priced pub grub and a selection of real ales.

Highcliffe to Keyhaven

As its name suggests, **Highcliffe** sits on a high bluff above a fine stretch of shingle-and-sand beach. The town itself, three miles east of Christchurch, is unremarkable, and it's something of a surprise to find, amongst the sprawl of bungalows, the towering splendour of **Highcliffe Castle** (daily: grounds 7am–dusk, free; castle Feb–Dec 23 11am–5pm; £2.50, children free; guided tours Tues & Sun at 2pm; £3.50; Ⓦwww.highcliffecastle.co.uk). Actually an ornate early Victorian mansion rather than a castle, it was built by Lord Stuart de Rothesay in the 1830s and is lavishly embellished with gargoyles and stained-glass windows salvaged from medieval buildings in France. You can look round the partially restored state rooms and galleries, while guided tours also take in the old kitchens and upper floors. Much of the castle's appeal, however, lies in the small but ornate grounds (with its own café), whose lawns boast fantastic views towards the Isle of Wight. Head west and you can join the coastal footpath which leads into a wooded nature reserve off Steamer Point and on to Mudeford Quay (see p.191), or you can take numerous paths down the cliffs to the **beach**.

Motorbike fans should seek out the **Sammy Miller Museum**, a few miles inland from Highcliffe, on the road to Sway, at Bashley Cross Road (daily 10am–4.30pm, £5.90, children £3; Ⓦmuseum.sammymiller.co.uk). Named after the champion trials bike rider, who started the collection and is still very much involved with the museum, it houses a substantial collection of motorbikes including 400 rare and classic racers and prototypes. Outside, children may prefer the grounds, where they can pet alpacas and various rabbits and guinea pigs; there is also a shop and tearooms.

Three miles up the coast, **Barton-on-Sea** consists of a row of bungalows strung out facing the cliff-top above a shingle beach. There's a broad grassy strip above the cliffs, great for kite flying or a picnic. A **coastal path** wends all the way from here past the neighbouring golf course to **Milford-on-Sea**, a bracing hour's walk high above the sea. Set round a tranquil green, Milford is the most characterful of the villages on this stretch, though it only really comes alive during the August Bank Holiday Carnival, featuring the usual mix of floats, fancy dress and stalls. Just under a mile beyond the village, the picturesque harbour of **Keyhaven** is a popular spot for sailors; it has two sailing clubs and a fine pub, *The Gun* (see below). The **ferry** (Easter–Oct hourly 10am–5pm, return 10.30am–5.30pm; Nov to Easter weekends only; £4.20, children £2.50; Ⓦwww.hurst-castle.co.uk) to **Hurst Castle** leaves from here, and it's the starting point of a pleasant coastal walk across the salt marshes to Lymington (see p.194).

Hurst Castle

Best reached by ferry from Keyhaven (see above), or on foot along a 1.5-mile-long shingle spit from Milford, **Hurst Castle** (Easter–Sept daily 10.30am–5.30pm, Oct till 4pm, Nov–March weekends only 10.30am–4pm; £3.50, children £2.20) is spectacularly sited just under a mile from the Isle of Wight – there are great views from its various battlements and roofs. The castle was originally built by Henry VIII in 1544 as part of his coastal defences and was later used to imprison Charles I in 1648 before his execution. Much of the present structure was built during the Napoleonic Wars and in the 1870s, though its atmosphere derives from the fact that it has been largely untouched since soldiers were billeted here during World

War II, when it was manned with gun batteries and searchlights. You can still see the cramped dorms where the soldiers slept and the small theatre where they put on plays. Temporary exhibits are often held here and there's also a small tea room. Allow time, too, to explore the pretty shingle shoreline around the castle, and the tall lighthouse next door.

Accommodation

There's no shortage of places **to stay** along this stretch of the coastline, which has the advantage of relatively uncrowded beaches and easy access to the New Forest.

Chewton Glen New Milton ☏01425 275341, ⓦwww.chewtonglen.com. The most upmarket option in the area. Set in extensive manicured grounds leading down to the sea, it has a top-notch spa, its own golf course and tennis courts, indoor and outdoor pools and all the luxuries you would expect for the price. ❾

The Bay Trees 8 High St, Milford-on-Sea ☏01590 642186, ⓦwww.baytreebedandbreakfast.co.uk. Agreeable B&B in a seventeenth-century building that was formerly used as a shop, bank and poorhouse. It has lovely gardens – the downstairs room opens directly onto them – as well as a four-poster upstairs, and the breakfasts are great. ❹

The Rothesay 175 Lymington Rd, Highcliffe ☏01425 274172, ⓦtherothesayhotel.com. A short walk from Highcliffe Castle and its beaches, this great, family-run guest house is located off a fairly busy main road, and has an indoor pool, licensed lounge and separate coachhouse annexe. It has a wide range of rooms, some with four-poster beds and all with shower or bath, the best of which open onto an internal courtyard. ❹

Vinegar Hill B&B Mockbeggars, Vinegar Hill, Milford-on-Sea ☏01590 642979, ⓦwww.davidrogerspottery.co.uk. Has two smart, simply furnished rooms, and its own on-site pottery – the B&B is run by the local potter, and you can sign up for courses with him, if you fancy having a go. ❷

Westover Hall Hotel Park Lane, Milford-on-Sea ☏01590 643044, ⓦwww.westoverhallhotel.com. This is an opulent Grade II listed Victorian mansion designed for German industrialist Alexander Siemens in 1897. Its public rooms have lots of oak panelling, stained-glass windows and decorated ceilings, though the bedrooms are more contemporary, many with sea views. ❾

Eating and drinking

The Beachcomber Café, Marine Drive East, Barton-on-Sea. At the opposite end of the spectrum to *Pebble Beach* next door (see below), but sharing the same great views, this is a refreshingly old-fashioned café right on the cliff-top, with a lawned garden set with benches. It serves decent breakfasts until 11.30am, then a good-value lunch menu featuring fresh salads, sandwiches and tasty local kippers, or home-made fish pie.

Chewton Glen New Milton ☏01425 275341, ⓦwww.chewtonglen.com. A top restaurant with a daily-changing menu, designed to make use of local seasonal produce, such as wild mushrooms, vegetables and game from the New Forest: a three-course dinner costs £65, though for a more affordable taste of luxury, afternoon tea on the terrace includes cucumber and smoked salmon sandwiches and home-made cake for £22.50.

The Gun Keyhaven. A Grade II listed building, this friendly local pub, with a nautically themed interior is the hub of Keyhaven. It serves decently priced pub food, has a collection of 240 malt whiskies and a great beer garden at the back.

Pebble Beach Marine Drive, Barton-on-Sea ☏01425 627777, ⓦwww.pebblebeach-uk.co.uk. Highly rated restaurant which has great views over the Isle of Wight: it specializes in seafood and fish – the *plateau fruits de mer*, with crab, oysters, prawns and lobster, is £42 – though there are more affordable options, such as seafood pancakes (£11) or broad bean and mushroom risotto (£12); it also has a few comfortable rooms upstairs (❹).

Westover Hall Park Lane, Milford-on-Sea ☏01590 643044, ⓦwww.westoverhallhotel.com. Impressively grand restaurant using ingredients sourced locally and free range or organic where possible. You can sample the food here at a reasonable price, with the good-value £15 two-course lunch menu.

Lymington

The best point of access for the Isle of Wight (for ferry details, see p.196) is **LYMINGTON**, whose estuary harbour is jam-packed with yachts as luxurious as the houses that radiate outwards in its leafy suburbs. It's a lively harbour town that makes a good base for exploring the local marshy coastline facing the Solent, and the nearby forest inland.

Arrival and information

Lymington is on a branch **rail** line from Brockenhurst, where there are fast connections to London. Trains call first at Lymington Town, a short walk from the high street, and then run out to Lymington Pier for connections to the Isle

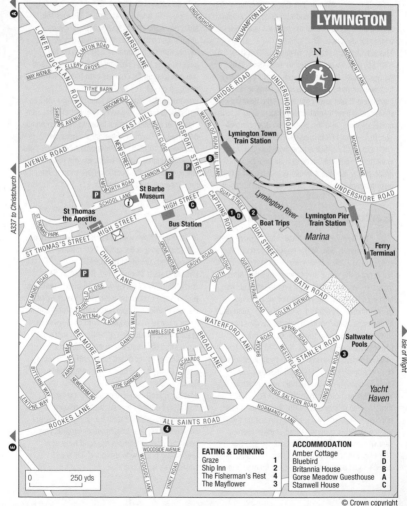

EATING & DRINKING	
Graze	1
Ship Inn	2
The Fisherman's Rest	4
The Mayflower	3

ACCOMMODATION	
Amber Cottage	E
Bluebird	D
Britannia House	B
Gorse Meadow Guesthouse	A
Stanwell House	C

© Crown copyright

of Wight ferry. The **bus station** is on the high street – there are regular services to Ashurst, Brockenhurst and Lyndhurst in the New Forest and along the coast to Christchurch. There are usually places to **park** along the high street, as well as signed pay-and-display car parks. **Information** is available by the museum in New Street, off the high street (Easter to Sept Mon–Sat 10am–5pm; Oct to Easter Mon–Sat 10am–4pm; ☎01590 689000).

Accommodation

There's usually plenty of places to **stay** in around the town– the tourist office can help with local B&Bs if the places below are full.

Amber Cottage 81 Wainsford Rd, Pennington ☎07793 059559, ⓦwww.ambercottagebedand breakfast.co.uk. Just two en-suite rooms in a handsome Edwardian house in the village of Pennington, a couple of miles north of Lymington. Guests get a welcome muffin on arrival and rooms come with flat-screen TVs. It is worth paying the extra £10 or so for the larger room overlooking the green. ❸

Bluebird Quay St ☎01590 676908, ⓦwww .bluebirdrestaurant.co.uk. Right in the thick of things in the old town, with decent en-suite rooms above a restaurant, though its position can be on the noisy side. ❸

Britannia House Mill Lane ☎01590 672091, ⓦwww.britannia-house.com. An upmarket, friendly and central B&B, right by the train station. Rooms are on the small side but there's a fine sitting room commanding views over the yachts. ❹

Gorse Meadow Guesthouse Sway Rd ☎01590 673354, ⓦwww.gorsemeadowguesthouse.co.uk.

A thirty-minute walk from Lymington, this lovely house is owned and run by mushroom authority, Mrs Tee, the only person with a licence to sell wild New Forest mushrooms commercially. Breakfasts feature the famous fungi, and you can opt for a three-course dinner with wine for £30, accompanied by tales from Mrs Tee and her husband, who has been band manager of Jimi Hendrix, The Who and The Animals in his time. The six rooms are comfortable and many have views over the grounds. ❹

Stanwell House High St ☎01590 677123, ⓦwww.stanwellhouse.com. The most upmarket choice in town is this handsome boutique-style hotel, whose array of individually designed rooms boasts rolltop baths and flat-screen TVs. Its seafood restaurant is also the top spot to eat, in a dining room with a distinctly colonial feel (mains from around £17); there is also a less formal bistro serving modern European cuisine. ❼

The Town

The old town around the quay is picture-postcard pretty, full of cobbled streets and handsome Georgian houses. Shipbuilding, using timber from the New Forest, helped the town flourish in the seventeenth and eighteenth centuries, boosted by smuggling – a warren of secret tunnels allegedly wends under the quay to the High Street. These days it's the yachting fraternity that drives the town's economy, with two marinas at Yacht Haven and Berthton. The only real sights of note are the partly thirteenth-century church of **St Thomas the Apostle**, with a cupola-topped tower built in 1670, and the small but informative **St Barbe Museum** on New Street (Mon–Sat 10am–4pm; £4; ⓦwww.stbarbe-museum.org.uk), which traces the town's history and has a gallery for temporary exhibitions, all inside a former school. Otherwise it's the boats' comings and goings and the town's fine array of shops that keep visitors busy. Summer **boat trips** run from the quay to the Needles on the Isle of Wight or to Hurst Castle (from around £7 per adult per hour; ⓦwww.puffincruiseslymingtonquay.co.uk). There are no beaches at Lymington, so locals make use of the giant **Salt Water pools** on Bath Road, near the yacht club (May–Sept daily 10am–5.30pm; £3, children £2.50). Beyond here you can pick up the lovely coastal footpath to Keyhaven (see p.192), a two-and-a-half-mile route through the salt marshes and mudflats that are a haven for wading birds.

The thirty-minute crossing from **Lymington** to **Yarmouth** on the **Isle of Wight** is the fastest vehicle access to the island and is also one of the prettiest routes there. Services are run by Wightlink (℡0871 3764342, ⓦwww.wightlink.co.uk) and depart every 60–90min; allow 30 minutes for check-in. Fares vary depending on the season and time of day, but expect to pay around £40–100 return for a car, or around £15 return for a foot passenger. Look out for special offers on the website when cheaper deals are usually on offer.

Eating and drinking

There are countless inexpensive places to eat and drink along the harbour and the old town, while the high street has many of the major chains. In addition to *Stanwell House* hotel (see p.195), the best options are listed below.

Graze 9 Gosport St ℡01590 675595. The liveliest spot for dining is the excellent *Graze*, whose good-value fusion food includes sumptuous courgette fritters, coconut shrimps and fried mixed fish for around £20 per person; it also has a trendy bar, serving great cocktails, and a small garden area. Closed Mon.

Ship Inn The Quay ℡01590 676903. With a terrace facing the boats, this classy pub has an interior of bleached woods and chrome which neatly embraces both style and a nautical theme. It also boasts a superior restaurant menu featuring modern British dishes such as Welsh lamb with sun-dried tomatoes and pork wrapped in Cumbrian ham, with mains from around £12.

The Fisherman's Rest All Saints' Rd. Slightly out of town, this cosy local is free of the tourist crowds and serves good-value daily fish specials such as local crabs and sea bass, from around £12.

The Mayflower King Saltern Rd. By the yacht club, this large pub does inexpensive but decent pub grub and also has a great garden facing the harbour.

Winchester and northern Hampshire

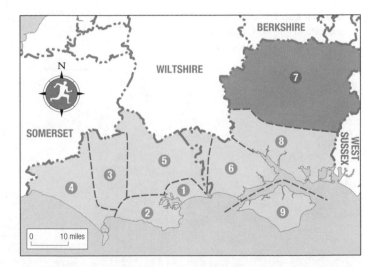

CHAPTER 7

Highlights

* **Winchester Cathedral** One of the most impressive and historic cathedrals in the country. See p.204

* **INTECH Planetarium** Feel the forces and wonders of space at this futuristic planetarium. See p.207

* **Wykeham Arms** Have a drink in this classic pub in the heart of Winchester. See p.208

* **Marwell Zoo** The extensive grounds of this zoo are as impressive as the beasts that you can see in them. See p.210

* **The Watercress Line** All aboard this great little steam train that chuffs through the heart of the region. See p.211

* **Chawton** Jane Austen's village is little changed from when the great author lived here. See p.211

* **Gilbert White's House** The former home of the original David Attenborough is surrounded by beautiful grounds. See p.213

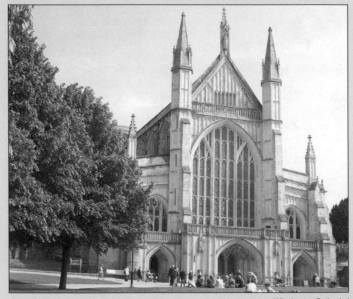

▲ Winchester Cathedral

7

Winchester and northern Hampshire

N ORTHERN HAMPSHIRE encompasses the quintessential English countryside of wooded valleys, clear flowing rivers and opulent farmland. In many ways this is the ancient heart of the kingdom, where Alfred the Great chose Winchester as his capital and where – allegedly – King Arthur set up his round table. To this day **Winchester** remains one of the country's most intriguing cities, its cathedral the resting place of ancient kings. The varied scenery of the South Downs National Park begins just to the east, embracing the **Itchen Valley**, with its pristine waters and attractive villages. The waters still feed the historic watercress beds that gave the name to the **Watercress Line**, a wonderful old steam train line that connects **Alton** with the pretty village of **Arlesford**. An England of bygone days is also in evidence at **Selborne**, where pioneering naturalist Gilbert White's house has been kept as a fascinating museum, though a more famous name from the past draws fans of **Jane Austen** to nearby **Chawton**, where the novelist spent much of her life. Further north there are more historical attractions round **Old Basing**, including the home of the Duke of Wellington at **Stratfield Saye**, **Highclere Castle** and the Roman remains at **Silchester**.

Winchester and around

Hampshire's county town now has a scholarly and slightly anachronistic air, embodied by the ancient almshouses that still provide shelter for senior citizens of "noble poverty" – the pensioners can be seen about town in medieval black or mulberry-coloured gowns with silver badges. A trip to this secluded old city is a must – not only for the magnificent **cathedral**, chief relic of Winchester's medieval glory, but for the all-round well-preserved ambience of England's one-time capital. Indeed, with its lovely riverside walks, medieval remains – including the ruins of the original Bishops of Winchester palace, **Wolvesey** and superb pubs and cafés, it warrants a day or two from anyone's itinerary. The surrounding countryside, too, is idyllic, with its pretty villages that follow the Itchen Valley to the east, which marks the boundary of the South Downs

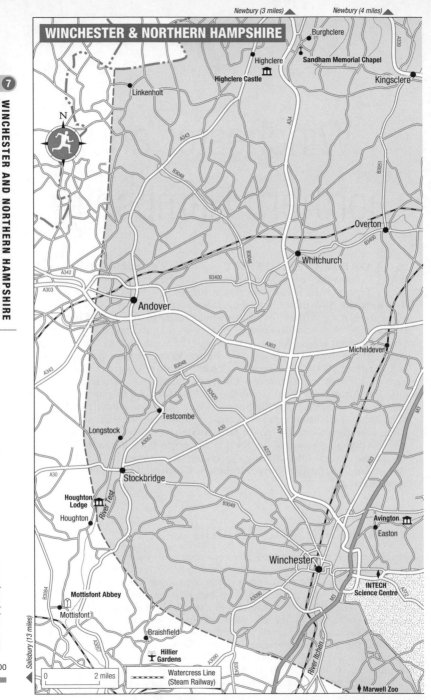

WINCHESTER & NORTHERN HAMPSHIRE

Newbury (3 miles) ▲   Newbury (4 miles) ▲

Burghclere

Highclere   Sandham Memorial Chapel

Highclere Castle   Kingsclere

N

Linkenholt

A343

A34

B3048

B3051

Overton
B3400

Whitchurch

A342
A303

B3400

Andover

A303

Micheldever

A343

B3048

B3420

Testcombe

Longstock
A3057

A30   A272

A30

Stockbridge

Houghton
Lodge   River Test   B3049

Houghton

Avington
Easton

Winchester

INTECH
Science Centre

Mottisfont Abbey

Mottisfont   River Itchen

B3084

B3090

B3043

A3057

Braishfield

Hillier
Gardens

0   2 miles   Watercress Line
(Steam Railway)

Marwell Zoo

Salisbury (13 miles) ▲

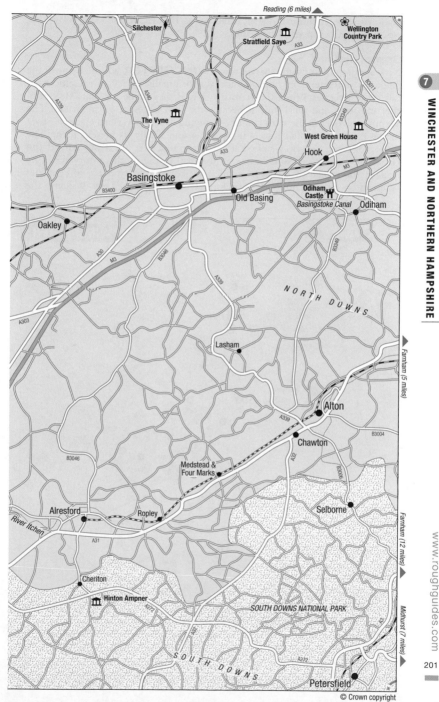

Reading (6 miles)

Silchester

Stratfield Saye

Wellington
Country Park

A33

The Vyne

B3011

West Green House

Hook

Basingstoke

Old Basing

Odiham
Castle

Basingstoke Canal

Odiham

Oakley

B3400

A340

A33

B3349

A30

M3

B3046

A339

M3

A303

NORTH DOWNS

Lasham

A339

Farnham (5 miles)

Alton

Chawton

B3004

B3006

Medstead &
Four Marks

A32

B3046

Alresford

Ropley

Selborne

River Itchen

A31

Farnham (12 miles)

Cheriton

Hinton Ampner

A272

SOUTH DOWNS NATIONAL PARK

Midhurst (7 miles)

A272

A32

A272

SOUTH DOWNS

Petersfield

© Crown copyright

National Park. A more modern attraction at **INTECH** also deserves a visit, especially for its superb planetarium.

Some history

Now a tranquil, handsome market town, **WINCHESTER** was once one of the mightiest settlements in England, and was originally capital of a Celtic tribe called the Belgares. When the Romans arrived they named it Venta Belgarum after the tribe, and for a time it became the fifth largest town in Britain. The Saxons took over in the sixth century, changing its name to Venta Caester – over the years this corrupted into Wintancaester and finally its present name. The Bishop of Wessex set up a cathedral here in around 676, but it was **Alfred the Great** who really put Winchester on the map in the ninth century when he made it the capital of his Wessex kingdom. For the next couple of centuries Winchester ranked alongside London, its status affirmed by William the

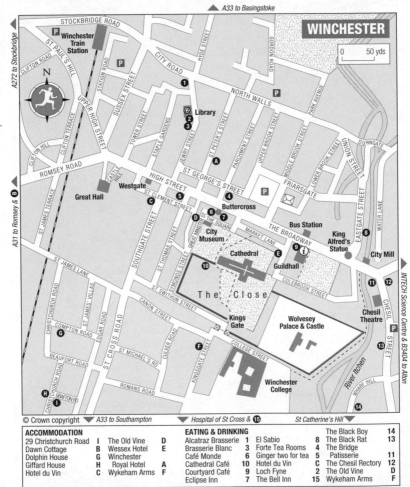

▲ A33 to Basingstoke

WINCHESTER

0   50 yds

© Crown copyright   ▼ A33 to Southampton   ▼ Hospital of St Cross & 15   St Catherine's Hill ▼

ACCOMMODATION				EATING & DRINKING					The Black Boy	14
29 Christchurch Road	I	The Old Vine	D	Alcatraz Brasserie	1	El Sabio	8	The Black Rat	13
Dawn Cottage	B	Wessex Hotel	E	Brasserie Blanc	3	Forte Tea Rooms	4	The Bridge	
Dolphin House	G	Winchester		Café Monde	6	Ginger two for tea	5	Patisserie	11
Giffard House	H	Royal Hotel	A	Cathedral Café	10	Hotel du Vin	C	The Chesil Rectory	12
Hotel du Vin	C	Wykeham Arms	F	Courtyard Café	9	Loch Fyne	2	The Old Vine	D
				Eclipse Inn	7	The Bell Inn	15	Wykeham Arms	F

Conqueror's coronation in both cities and by his commissioning of the local monks to prepare the **Domesday Book**. A palace was erected in the tenth century, though this was rebuilt in grander style by William the Conqueror – the Normans also built a new cathedral in 1079, the **Hospital of St Cross** in 1136 and also Wolvesey Castle as the bishop's residence. Winchester began to lose out to London in importance in the thirteenth century, though Bishop William of Wykeham founded Winchester College in 1382 and was also Chancellor of England.

It wasn't until the English Civil War, when Cromwell took and plundered the city in 1645, that Winchester began its decline into provinciality. Cromwell later destroyed Winchester's castle – only sparing the Great Hall – to prevent it falling into Royalist hands. Much of today's Winchester was built in the seventeenth and eighteenth centuries – Jane Austen died here in 1817 – and the resulting harmonious architecture has made it popular – if expensive – commuter territory, just an hour by train from London.

Arrival and information

Winchester is on the fast London to Southampton train line, with regular services to the capital (1hr). The **train station** is about a mile northwest of the cathedral on Stockbridge Road. If you arrive by **bus**, you'll find yourself on the Broadway, conveniently opposite the **tourist office** in the imposing Guildhall (May–Sept Mon–Sat 9.30am–5.30pm, Sun 11am–4pm; Oct–April Mon–Sat 10am–5pm; ☎01962 840500, ⒲www.visitwinchester.co.uk). **Drivers** should head for one of the well-signed central car parks, though note that the central area is mostly pedestrianized and that there is a somewhat confusing one-way system round the centre.

Accommodation

With a steady stream of year-round visitors to its sights, **accommodation** is never particularly cheap in Winchester – we list the best options below, or you may want to consider staying in one of the outlying villages (see p.209) where places are generally more affordable. The tourist board also has a list of various bed and breakfast options in the suburbs.

29 Christchurch Road 29 Christchurch Rd ☎01962 868 661, ⒲www.fetherstondilke.com. Reliable B&B accommodation in a charming Regency house located in a quiet residential part of town. No smoking. ❷

Dawn Cottage 99 Romsey Rd ☎01962 869956, Ⓔdawncottage@hotmail.com. About a mile out of town on the Romsey road (with frequent buses into town), this spacious ivy-covered cottage has three comfortable rooms, lovely grounds and its own sun deck, where breakfast is served in summer. ❷

Dolphin House 3 Compton Rd ☎01962 853284, ⒲www.dolphinhousestudios.co.uk. Good-value rooms in a lovely townhouse in a quiet part of town. Double or twin rooms share their own kitchenette and have access to the gardens; off-street parking. ❷

Giffard House 50 Christchurch Rd ☎01962 852628, ⒲www.giffardhotel.co.uk. Small hotel in an elegant Victorian building with high ceilings, its own William Morris stained-glass window and a range of rooms – most spacious and some overlooking the attractive gardens. En-suite rooms cost £10 more. There is also a great patio bar and off-street parking. ❺

Hotel du Vin Southgate St ☎01962 841414, ⒲www.hotelduvin.com. The first of the classy *Hotel du Vin* chain, this lovely Georgian townhouse has been given a stylish makeover and now comprises plush rooms – some cottage-style ones with their own private entrances and terraces – a lovely patio garden, chic bar and great restaurant (see p.207). First choice for accommodation in Winchester, especially if you can bag one of their periodic special offers, when luxury can be very good value. ❼

The Old Vine 8 Great Minster St ☎01962 854616, ⒲www.oldvinewinchester.com. Lovely, big rooms that combine period decor with modern touches such as widescreen televisions, above a fine bar-restaurant right opposite the cathedral. The street can be noisy at night. ❹

Wessex Hotel Paternoster Row ☎01962 861611, ⓦwww.mercure.uk.com. This ungainly hotel was built partly on concrete stilts in the 1960s and still has some fine retro fittings. Rooms are functional but it's just a stone's throw from the cathedral and there are good low-season rates. ❻

Winchester Royal Hotel St Peter's St ☎01962 840840, ⓦwww.forestdale.com. Very popular with wedding parties, rooms here are in a historic fifteenth-century building that has been a bishop's residence and a convent. The garden's lovely, though the carpets are as fusty as the atmosphere. Good low-season rates. ❻ or garden views for ❼

Wykeham Arms 75 Kingsgate St ☎01962 853834, ⓦwww.fullershotels.com. Small but charming rooms above this superb eighteenth-century hostelry with beamed, quirkily shaped rooms, or you can stay in larger, more contemporary rooms for the same price in the annexe opposite. Minimum two-night weekend stays at busy times. ❻

The Town

Winchester is fairly easy to find your way around. The largely pedestrianized High Street connects the Broadway in the east – where you'll find the bus station, tourist office and River Itchen – to the Great Hall in the northwest, from where it's a five-minute walk north to the train station. The **High Street** and the streets behind the city museum have the town's best shops, while the main attractions are just south of the High Street beyond the **Buttercross**, an impressive fifteenth-century monument dotted with figures representing, amongst others, the Blessed Virgin, St Swithun and Bishop William of Wykeham. Just off the High Street on the Square is the **City Museum** (April–Oct Mon–Sat 10am–5pm, Sun noon–5pm; Nov–March Tues–Sat 10am–4pm, Sun noon–4pm; free). Set on three floors, it is an imaginative medley of historical artefacts including recreated traditional shopfronts, some impressive Roman mosaics, medieval coins and skeletons.

Winchester Cathedral

The first minster to be built in Winchester was raised by Cenwalh, the Saxon king of Wessex, in the mid-seventh century, and traces of this building have been unearthed near the present **cathedral** (Mon–Sat 8.30am–6pm, Sun 8.30am–5.30pm; £5 donation requested, Tower tour £5), itself begun in 1079 and completed some three hundred years later, producing a monument whose features range from early Norman to Perpendicular styles. The exterior is not its best attribute – squat and massive, the cathedral crouches solemnly over the tidy lawns of the Cathedral Close. It is only once inside that Winchester Cathedral's glories become apparent. Its 1000-plus years of history are evident in every step – from the decorative tiled floors to the ornate ceilings, via the tombs of dignitaries and celebrities, fantastically carved altars and sumptuous stained-glass windows. Not only is this a revered church with the longest nave in England (170m), but it is a veritable treasure chest of memorabilia and specially commissioned art, spanning medieval times to the twenty-first century.

As you walk through the colossal cathedral entrance, light floods in from the giant **stained-glass window** in the east wall. During the English Civil War, horse-mounted soldiers rode thunderously into this giant space, plundering the church contents and smashing the stained glass. Under the reign of Charles II, the window was then pieced back together using whatever shards could be found. The result is an amazingly modern-looking mosaic – a head here, an angel there, but mostly a dazzling mishmash of colourful fragments.

The small upper floor **treasury** can be accessed from this corner of the cathedral. It contains displays of priceless silver from local parish churches –

though these constantly change, depending on what the churches can spare at the time.

The cathedral shelters various **tombs**, including Jane Austen – close to the north wall a short way in from the main entrance – and several of the earliest kings of England. Many of these were disinterred from the original Winchester Minster, which was demolished to make way for the new cathedral. As a result, the bones were placed in decorative chests on top of the choir screen – including Knut, William Rufus and King Cynegils (611–643).

Don't miss the superbly carved twelfth-century wooden christening **font**, or a peer into the Norman crypt – often flooded – where you can see **Anthony Gormley**'s contemplative figure *Sound II* literally and metaphorically reflect in the waters. The cathedral's original foundations were dug in marshy ground, and at the beginning of the last century a steadfast diver, William Walker, spent five years replacing the rotten timber foundations with concrete.

Other highlights include the **fisherman's chapel**, with ornate woodcarvings by contemporary artist Eugene Ball; and the **Lady Chapel**, in which every seat is imaginatively embellished with carved wooden animals. Look out, too, for the carved Norman font of black Tournai marble, the fourteenth-century misericords (the choir stalls are the oldest complete set in the country) and the memorial **shrine to St Swithun**. Originally buried outside in the churchyard, his remains were later interred inside the cathedral where the "rain of heaven" could no longer fall on him, whereupon he took revenge and the heavens opened for forty days – hence the legend that if it rains on St Swithun's Day (July 15) it will continue for another forty. His exact burial place is unknown.

The Great Hall and Westgate

Walk west along the High Street and it's a short walk to the **Great Hall** on Castle Avenue (daily except for occasional civic events 10am–5pm; free, donation requested; Ⓦ www.hants.gov.uk/greathall), the vestigial remains of a thirteenth-century castle. The current hall was built in 1235 as part of a replacement for the crumbling original castle built by William the Conqueror and would have served as the Royal's dining room as well as a court and assembly hall for dignataries. Most of this castle was destroyed by Cromwell during the English Civil War, though the hall was spared, being seen as useful to continue assemblies – indeed it was used as a court until 1974. It is now rated one of the best-preserved buildings of the genre in the country. Sir Walter Raleigh heard his death sentence here in 1603, though he wasn't finally dispatched until 1618, and Judge Jeffreys held one of his Bloody Assizes (see p.97) in the castle after Monmouth's rebellion in 1685. More recently, the wrought-steel gates, installed in 1983, commemorate the wedding of Prince Charles and Lady Diana. The main interest now, however, is a large, brightly painted disc slung on one wall like some curious antique dartboard. This is alleged to be **King Arthur's Round Table**, but the woodwork is probably fourteenth-century, later repainted as a PR exercise for the Tudor dynasty – the portrait of Arthur at the top of the table bears an uncanny resemblance to Henry VIII. At the back of the hall is the attractive **Queen Eleanor's Garden**, a recreation of a medieval herb garden named after the spouse of Henry III.

En route to the Great Hall from the High Street you'll pass **Westgate**, once one of the main gateways into the city. This was used as a debtor's prison and you can still see the prisoners' scribbles on the walls along with an assorted collection of relics including medieval weights, measures and costumes. There are fine views across town from its roof as well as activities for children, including the chance to try on some extremely heavy armour.

The City Mill

Head east along the High Street, past the Guildhall and the august bronze statue of King Alfred on the Broadway, to reach the River Itchen and the eighteenth-century **City Mill** (11am–5pm: Feb & late Oct to Dec Sun & Mon; March to late Oct Wed–Sun; school hols daily; £3.50; NT), where you can see restored mill machinery. The current building dates back to 1744, though there are records of a mill on this site in the Domesday Book. There's a video explaining the history of the building, attractive riverside gardens at the back and occasional demonstrations of flour milling. The highlight is the "Mill Race", where the water wheels are kept and you can watch the powerful water rushing through the building. Over the bridge you can head up St Giles' Hill, a ten-minute climb – there are great views over the town from the top.

Wolvesey Castle and Winchester College

Turning right before the bridge that leads up to St Giles' Hill, you pass what remains of the Saxon walls, which bracket the ruins of the twelfth-century **Wolvesey Castle** (April–Sept daily 10am–5pm; free; EH) – actually the palace for the Bishops of Winchester, who once wielded great clout over England's religious and political affairs. As a result, this was once one of the most important buildings in Winchester, encompassing its own stables, prison, chapel and gardens. The brainchild of Henry of Blois, who was Bishop from 1129 to 1171, the palace slowly declined with the influence of the bishops and was largely demolished in 1786, when it was considered too old-fashioned. Nevertheless, the ruins remain highly impressive and still dwarf the current dwelling place of the Bishop of Winchester alongside, a relatively modest house built in 1680.

Immediately to the west up College Street stand the buildings of **Winchester College**, the oldest public school in England – established in 1382 by William of Wykeham for "poor scholars", it now educates few but the wealthy and privileged. The cloisters and chantry are open for **guided visits** (Mon, Wed, Fri & Sat 4 daily; Tues, Thurs & Sun 2 daily; £4; Ⓦwww .winchestercollege.org), which includes a visit to the Gothic chapel and the red-brick school room, said to have been designed by Christopher Wren. Jane Austen moved to the house at nearby 8 College St (now privately owned) from Chawton in 1817, when she was already ill with Addison's Disease, dying there later the same year. The thirteenth-century **King's Gate**, at the top of College Street, is one of the city's original medieval gateways, housing the tiny St Swithun's Church.

Along the Itchen and St Cross Hospital

The eastern fringes of Wolvesey Castle and Winchester College back onto the River Itchen, with its cool, clear waters that pass idyllic water meadows – said to have inspired Keats' *Ode to Autumn*. It's around twenty minutes' walk south along the river to the foot of **St Catherine's Hill** and another twenty minutes to the top of this local wooded landmark that offers great views over the city. Alternatively, turn right over the river – or by road along St Cross Road – to **The Hospital of St Cross** (April–Oct Mon–Sat 9.30am–5pm, Sun 1–5pm; Nov–March Mon–Sat 10.30am–3.30pm; £3), the country's oldest continuing almshouse. Founded in 1132 as a hostel for the poor and extended in the fifteenth century, it even has its own surprisingly impressive twelfth-century church. You can still sample the Wayfarer's "dole" at the Porter's Lodge – a tiny portion of bread and beer – and stroll round the attractive Master's Garden.

INTECH Science Centre

Four miles east of Winchester at Morn Hill is the impressive-looking building for **INTECH Science Centre** (daily 10am–4pm; £6.95, children £4.65; Ⓦ www.intech-uk.com), a hands-on science and technology centre that's particularly interesting for children. The main hall has some well-used devices that explain scientific processes such as wind tunnels, cranes, sound waves, telescopes and locks amongst other things; downstairs is more suitable for older children, with a flight simulator, machines that create vortexes and information on recycling. Of more general interest for people of any age is the **planetarium** (£2 extra) with several daily shows about space projected onto a vast domed ceiling, in which you really feel as if you are floating in space or moving about in a rocket. The centre also has its own shop and café.

Restaurants

Alcatraz Brasserie 24 Jewry St ☎01962 860047. Spacious, modern Italian restaurant serving good-value pizza and pasta, with mains from around £8.
Brasserie Blanc 19–20 Jewry St ☎01962 8810870. Smart but laid-back French bistro bedecked with chandeliers and set in a former butcher's. Quality mains from around £12, including tasty *moules* and fine pancakes.
El Sabio 60 Eastgate St ☎01962 820233. Vibrant Spanish restaurant serving a fine range of tapas from £5, great fish platters and a tempting paella, as well as Spanish wines and beers. Closed Mon lunch.
Hotel du Vin Southgate St ☎01962 841414. Buzzy bistro-style restaurant in a series of attractive dining rooms, some with open fireplaces. The food is excellent, much of it locally sourced, and reasonably priced, with main courses such as roast pheasant around £14–17, and starters such as *moules marinières* around £7. The wine list, as you would expect, is impressive, with many wines available by the half bottle.
Loch Fyne 18 Jewry St ☎01962 872930. Classy fish and seafood restaurant with great cooking and a highly charismatic venue – in a converted jailhouse retaining its galleries and beams. Meals are not as expensive as you'd think (mains from around £12), and the oyster, mussel or shellfish platters are sublime.
The Black Rat 88 Chesil St ☎01962 844465. Quality modern British cuisine served in a cosy former pub. Ingredients are locally sourced (including veg from their own allotment) with dishes such as Weymouth crab, home-made black pudding, local pork loin and English cheeses, though expect to pay at least £30 a head. Reservations advised. Eves only except Sat & Sun.
The Chesil Rectory 1 Chesil St ☎01962 851555. This cosy, wood-beamed fifteenth-century building serves nouveau British cuisine from a former Fortnum and Mason chef – good-value lunches (two courses around £15), otherwise mains around £15. Closed Sun night and all day Mon.
The Old Vine 8 Great Minster St ☎01962 854616. Fashionable bar and bistro in a Grade II listed building – a great place for a drink or a full meal, with delicious starters and mains such as fish pie, Thai curry and pan-fried duck from around £10.

Pubs and cafés

Café Monde 22 The Square. The outdoor tables on this pedestrianized street get snapped up by those seeking a sunny spot for inexpensive lunches, breakfasts or tea and cakes.
Cathedral Café Inner Close. Part of the cathedral visitor's centre, this glass-fronted self-service café does a good range of inexpensive snacks, lunches and teas – the big appeal is the outdoor tables in a tranquil garden.
Courtyard Café Guildhall, The Broadway. At the back of the tourist office, this relaxed and spacious café with a small courtyard garden does good-value self-service lunches, as well as fresh croissants and pastries.
Eclipse Inn 25 The Square. Attractive sixteenth-century inn which has outside seating catching the last of the day's sun; also decent, mid-priced pub food.
Forte Tea Rooms 78 Parchment St ☎01962 856840. The best place in town for a healthy breakfast or meal. Great paninis, home-made soups, inexpensive salads, burgers or pastas in a homely upstairs dining room that attracts a lively, arty clientele. Closed Sun & Tues, Wed & Sat eve.

Ginger two for tea 29 St Thomas St ☎01962 877733. Small teashop in a warren of characterful backstreets, with inexpensive snacks, lunches, coffees and a huge array of teas.

The Bell Inn Saint Cross Rd. Right by St Cross Hospital, this historic pub serves a good selection of beer and decent food; also has a walled garden full of old pub signs.

The Black Boy Wharf Hill ☎01962 861754. Fantastic old pub with log fires in winter, walls lined with books and low ceilings hung with old coins and miniature bottles. Good cask ales and

reasonable pub grub from £8, as well as a small outdoor terrace.

The Bridge Patisserie 20 Bridge St ☎01962 890767. If you can make it past the counter groaning under the weight of delectable fruit tarts and pastries, you can grab a seat at the sit-down area for fresh coffees and various teas.

Wykeham Arms 75 Kingsgate St ☎01962 853834. This eighteenth-century pub is the best pub in town, with a warren of cosy rooms, great bar snacks and fine wines; it also has first-class bar food.

West to Stockbridge

Around eight miles west of Winchester, **Stockbridge**, literally meaning "bridge over the river", grew up at a crossing point over the River Test and a meeting place for two ancient roads – the east–west route between Winchester and Salisbury, and the north–south road along the Test Valley. Once a sizeable town used by Welsh sheep drovers as a stopping point on their way to markets further east – the thatched Drovers House still has a Welsh inscription on its walls – it's now little more than one street, laced with streams, and dotted with a few pubs, hotels, antique shops and restaurants. Its main *raison d'être* today, however, is fishing in the River Test – as the fishing equipment shops along the high street testify – in one of England's best chalk streams and the birthplace of fly-fishing. Salmon, trout and grayling can all be caught in the river and the chalk streams that feed it.

The best place **to stay** hereabouts is the *Peat Spade Inn* (☎01264 810612, ⓦwww.peadspadeinn.co.uk; ❺), a couple of miles north of Stockbridge in Longstock, which can organize fishing trips, guides and tuition as well as renting and selling equipment. It has comfortable rooms and an excellent restaurant serving classic English dishes, using seasonal produce, such as rabbit terrine (£8.50) and leek and potato pie with goat's cheese sauce (£11). For a drink or a decent pub meal, the riverside *Mayfly* **pub** (☎01264 860283), three miles north of Stockbridge in Testcombe, has a good range of real ales, a cosy interior and a lovely riverside garden.

The South Downs National Park

King Alfred's statue in Winchester marks the westernmost boundary of the **South Downs National Park**, created in 2010 to cover an area of 627 square miles. The park, which embraces woodland, chalk uplands and several areas of outstanding natural beauty, snakes across Hampshire and into Sussex, but has taken over 60 years to be implemented: years of public inquiries have held up a plan that was first mooted in 1956. It is now expected that up to 40 million people a year will visit the park, more than any of the other nine national parks in the country. The park should guarantee the safety of habitats for rare plants such as the musk orchid and wild thyme and birds like the nightjar and Dartford warbler, which were previously under threat from road and house building. Appropriately, the park includes the village of Selborne, where Gilbert White pioneered the study and protection of natural life around his village in 1789 (see p.213). Walkers can also enjoy the South Downs Way, a hundred-mile trail across the park from Winchester to Eastbourne. Full details are on ⓦwww.nationaltrail.co.uk/southdowns.

Cool counties

While you'll still find your fair share of cream teas, thatched cottages and blue rinses, in recent years the southern counties have upped their game in the cool stakes. You'll find Europe's first-ever artificial surf reef, some of the country's most cutting-edge chefs, striking architecture, and vibrant clubs and festivals that attract clubbers – both diehard and novice – from across the country. And if a night dancing till dawn is not for you, you can relax at one of the cool campsites or stylish, boutique hotels that dot the region.

Chic retreats

There are some extremely stylish hotels in the region, including two branches of Hotel du Vin, in both Poole and Winchester; the quirky 1930s Art Deco Portland Spa Hotel, high on a cliff-top in the Isle of Portland; and the chic Terravina in the New Forest. If you prefer camping, you can do that in style too, by renting a renovated 1950s Airstream caravan on the Isle of Wight with Vintage Vacations (Ⓦwww.vintagevacations.co.uk), or staying in a luxury tent on Featherdown Farm near Alton. For simple-but-chic camping, the wonderful solar-powered Eweleaze Farm, near Weymouth, has great cliff-top pitches and direct beach access, while Tom's Field, outside Swanage, is camping as it should be – in a field, with wonderful sea views and the added bonus of fresh croissants in the morning.

Camping at Featherdown Farm ▲

Terravina ▼

Rhodes South ▼

Hot cuisine

Once something of a foodie desert, the region is now firmly on the culinary radar thanks to several celebrity chefs. First of these was Hugh Fearnley-Whittingstall, whose *River Cottage* TV series and books not only highlighted the delights of rural West Dorset but also helped promote organic and seasonal "real" food. Gary Rhodes has also moved into the region with two restaurants in Christchurch, including the superbly positioned *Rhodes South*, lapped by the waters of Christchurch harbour, and its less-pricey brasserie neighbour, *King Rhodes*. Mark Hix is making similar waves in Lyme Regis, while Britain's youngest Michelin-starred chef, Robert Thompson, has set up shop in Ventor in the Isle of Wight.

A mile and a half south of Stockbridge, **Houghton Lodge** (Mon, Tues & Thurs–Sun March–Oct 10am–5pm, house visits by appointment only ☏01264 810502, ⓦ www.houghtonlodge.co.uk; £5) is a splendid and rare example of a late eighteenth-century *orné* (rural retreat) probably used originally as a fishing lodge for the local gentry. Built in the Natural Style its thatched roof and rounded form are designed to blend in with the surrounding landscape. The gardens, too, are a delight, full of wild woodlands and ornate topiary with some lovely walks along the River Test. There is also an orchid house and a hydroponic greenhouse showing how plants can be grown in enriched materials without the need for soil.

The Itchen Valley and around

East of Winchester, the **Itchen Valley** shows off rural Hampshire at its best. Well-marked footpaths follow the river valley through pretty villages full of thatched cottages, such as **Easton**, where you'll find the traditional, sixteenth-century *Chestnut Horse* **pub**, on the Ovington Road (☏01962 779257), which dishes up decent food and local beers. Around three miles beyond here, the road passes though Avington Park – you can pull up by a nature area with trails around a small lake, and an excellent view of **Avington House** (May–July & Sept Sun; Aug Sun & Mon 2.30–5.30pm; grounds free, guided tours of house approx every 45min £4.50), which may be all you get to see of the house, due to its limited opening hours. The park once belonged to Winchester Cathedral before passing into private hands at the time Henry VIII. In the mid-seventeenth century the house was owned by one of Charles II's staff, who had the property enlarged to accommodate his boss and his mistress Nell Gwynne. King George IV also stayed here before it was sold to John Shelley – brother to the poet – in 1847. It is still privately owned, but the inside has all the attributes of a royal palace to this day, complete with soaring painted ceilings, giant mirrors and chandeliers.

Four miles south of Avington, the lovely village of **Cheriton** is another idyllic medley of thatched cottages clustered round its own green. Here you'll find the wonderful 🍺 *Flowerpots Inn*, which brews its own beer and has its own beer festival in August. It also serves delectable home-made hotpots and steak baps from around £6. On a hilltop nearby lies a monument to the Battle of Cheriton that took place near here on March 29, 1644, during the English Civil War. Some 20,000 soldiers took part in a battle to halt the Royalist advance and the monument commemorates the many who died here.

A mile or so south of Cheriton is the estate of **Hinton Ampner** (mid-March to Oct Sat–Wed 11am–5pm, plus Sat & in Dec 11am–4pm; £7.10; NT) with its lovely landscaped gardens and vast grounds. Originally built in 1793 as a hunting lodge, the house itself has gone through many guises. Starting out as a traditional Georgian house, it was re-modelled and enlarged in 1867 in mock-Tudor style. However, the house that's seen today is largely a result of the work of Ralph Dutton, the last private owner of the estate. He demolished much of the old house in 1935, rebuilding it as a neo-Georgian house and landscaping the gardens in a similar style. Dutton also purchased all the land around the house, including a local village, in order to preserve the fine views. In 1960, a fire destroyed most of the house and its furnishings that Dutton had collected from all over Europe. Undaunted, Dutton rebuilt his empire, and collected more valuable antiques, including a fireplace from Marie Antoinette's palace in Saint-Cloud (now in the library), paintings by Pellegrini and an ornate Meissen clock.

The latest update allowed Dutton to include some mod cons in the house, such as his en-suite bathroom with a window specifically placed so that he could survey all he owned while sitting on his private lavatory. After Dutton's death in 1985 without heirs, the entire estate, including the local village was bequeathed to the National Trust.

South to Marwell

Deep in the countryside south of the Itchen valley, eight miles from Winchester, the wonderful **Marwell Zoo** (daily except Dec 25 & 26: Easter, May half-term, bank hols and summer hols 10am–6pm, £18, child £14; Nov & Dec closes at 4pm, £12, child £9; rest of year closes at 5pm, £16, child £12; Ⓦ www .marwell.org.uk) spreads over the grounds of the fourteenth-century Marwell Hall. It's home to tigers, leopards, rhino, lemurs, gibbons, penguins and red panda amongst others. The animals live in large enclosures over a 140-acre site, which is divided into various habitats, such as the Australian Bush Walk, where you can get up close to wallabies and kookaburra, and Tropical World with its rainforest flora and fauna – on a sunny day, watching the zebras and giraffes wander through the spacious African Valley, you could almost be on a real safari. A free road train runs around the park and there are plenty of picnic spots.

East of Winchester

To the east of Winchester, a series of attractive provincial towns and villages are worth a visit for their archetypal Englishness as well as for their literary connections. **Alton** and **Alresford** are linked by the **Watercress Line** along which a restored steam train chugs through pretty Hampshire countryside. The village of **Chawton** makes the most of its famous former resident, Jane Austen, as does **Selborne**, of its lesser-known but equally influential son, Gilbert White.

▲ The Watercress Line, Alresford Station

Cool clubs

Bournemouth and Southampton in particular support big club nights, a reasonable mix of touring bands and the odd little gem such as Boscombe's revamped O2 Academy, a great venue with big-name club nights and bands such as Florence and the Machine, Franz Ferdinand and Morrissey. In Bournemouth, the Old Fire Station hosts top commercial club nights and live music from the likes of the Fratellis and Gallows alongside student-orientated cheese. Down the coast in Southampton, Oceana is the UK's biggest club, hosting up to 4000 people and playing a mix of pop and house.

▲ Café Shore

▼ Urban Beach

▼ Kuti's

6 hip hangouts

▶▶ **Urban Beach** Boscombe, p.60. Friendly bar-bistro with a winning combination of great cocktails, live music, an outside deck and a laid-back vibe.

▶▶ **Café Shore** Sandbanks, p.67. Join the WAGs in this ambient café-bar with great views over Poole Harbour and admire the millionaires' yachts as they pass by.

▶▶ **Kuti's** Southampton, p.231. Renovated, Art Deco former ocean-liner terminal that now serves delicious Thai food and cocktails. Sit on the deck and watch the world's largest luxury cruise ships as they dock.

▶▶ **Graze** Lymington, p.196. A funky bar serving champagne and cocktails with delicious tapas-style dishes to nibble.

▶▶ **Lugleys** Cowes, p.259. Watch the yachting set at play, particularly during Cowes Week, from this waterside bar-restaurant.

▶▶ **Beach and Barnicott** Bridport, p.132. This former eighteenth-century pharmacy is just the tonic for a night out in Bridport, with live music and fine dining on three floors, each with their own distinct, fashionable decor.

Beach Polo Championships ▲

Wayne Hemingway's surf pods, Boscombe ▼

Spinnaker Tower ▼

The festival scene

Some of the country's best festivals take place in the region – indeed the Isle of Wight boasts more festivals per head of population than anywhere else in the UK. The Isle of Wight Festival in June is the grandee of them all; but don't miss the family-friendly Camp Bestival at Lulworth in July; its older sibling Bestival on the Isle of Wight and the End of the Road at the Larmer Tree Gardens, both in September. For the smarter set, other must-attend events include the Cowes Week sailing on the Isle of Wight, and the British Beach Polo Championships in Sandbanks. Film buffs should look out for the Purbeck Film Festival in October. For something totally off the wall, head to the World Stinging Nettle Eating Competition, held in a pub in Marshwood every June, and test your tastebuds with nettles and scrumpy.

Stunning structures

Who needs Newquay now that Bournemouth has its very own surf reef? The suburb of Boscombe has become the fashionable newcomer to the surfing scene with its designer "surf pods", aka chic, retro-style beach huts designed by Wayne Hemingway. Other great structures include the iconic Spinnaker Tower in Portsmouth. This fantastic viewing platform, shaped like a sail and complete with glass floor has been so successful that other towns are considering copying the concept. More low-key, but just as impressive architecturally, are the fantastic Art Deco buildings in the region that have been recently renovated, such as The Print Room in Bournemouth and The Shack, at Mottistone Manor Gardens on the Isle of Wight.

Alresford

The attractive Georgian town of **ALRESFORD** (pronounced Allsford) grew up on the cotton and tanning trade, but is now recognized principally as the final stop on the Watercress Line (see p.211). Watercress has long grown wild in the chalky streams around Alresford, but it was not until the advent of the railway that it became viable to grow it commercially, and Hampshire is still the main producer of watercress in England today.

The best way to explore the town is to walk the well-marked mile-long **Millennium Trail**, which takes you along the River Arle, a tributary of the Itchen. You may well see watercress growing wild here, though much of the marshy riverside is now a designated Site of Special Scientific Interest, home to otters and voles. The trail leads back via Broad Street, once the site of a major woollen market but today lined with the town's most handsome houses, shops and restaurants. May is a good time to visit Alresford to coincide with the annual Watercress Festival (Ⓦwww.watercress.co.uk), an extravaganza of food markets, live music and entertainment. If you want **to stay**, *Mulberry House* on Colden Lane (Ⓣ01962 735518, Ⓦwww.mulberryhousebnb.com; ❸, no cards) offers four rooms in a converted eighteenth-century stable block – meals are available on request or you can use the communal kitchen.

Alton and the Watercress Line

Once famed for its cloth manufacturing, today **ALTON** is pleasant enough, with a bustling shopping centre, though not much else to detain you apart from the fifteenth-century Church of St Lawrence with its Norman tower. The main interest to visitors here is as the starting point of the Mid Hants steam railway, better known as **The Watercress Line** (Ⓣ01962 733810, Ⓦwww.watercressline.co.uk). It takes its name from the fresh watercress that was transported along the line after it opened in 1865, initially all the way to Southampton. Nowadays the line, which also lays on special family days and events – including a "Real ale train" on alternate Saturdays that serves local ales – is maintained by volunteers on its ten-mile chug through rolling Hampshire countryside to Alresford. The tickets (roughly hourly, 10.50am to 3.55pm, last return 3.43pm; adults £12, £30 for family ticket) enables you to go up and down the line as often as you want – as many do, ensconced in the dining car (reservations for dining are essential) – or to hop off at one of the two intermediary stations: there's not a lot to the first, Medstead & Four Marks, though it does lay claim to being the highest station in southern England, a surprising fact considering the apparently flat landscape; the second stop, Ropley, has a pleasant picnic area alongside the tracks and steam buffs may wish to look round the workshed, where trains are repaired.

If you want to **stay** nearby, there's the splendid *Manor Farm*, a couple of miles east of Alton, in West Worldham (Ⓣ01420 80804, Ⓦwww.featherdownfarm .co.uk), where you sleep in well-equipped, ready-erected tents on a working farm; there's a wood-fired bread oven, hens to collect your eggs from and a shop selling local produce. The experience doesn't come cheap, however, with tents costing £100 or so a night in high season.

Chawton

"Everybody is acquainted with Chawton and speaks of it as a remarkably pretty village" wrote Jane Austen to her sister Cassandra. Indeed, **CHAWTON** is still a pretty village that's become a magnet for fans of the author, who lived here

▲ Chawton House

from 1809 to 1817, during the last and most prolific years of her life. Almost all her six books, including *Pride and Prejudice* and *Persuasion*, were written or revised here in **Jane Austen's House** (March–May & Sept–Dec daily: 10.30am–4.30pm; June–Aug daily: 10am–5pm; Jan–Feb Sat & Sun 10.30am–4.30pm; £5; ⓦwww.jane-austens-house-museum.org.uk), in the centre of the village. A plain red-brick building, it contains first editions of some of her greatest works, extracts from her original manuscripts, a lock of her hair, her jewellery and the desk at which she wrote her masterpieces – in reality, a small, simple table in the dining room. The house has been decorated and furnished as it would have been in Jane's time, with evocative details providing insights into her daily life, such as the tea chest in the dining room, whose key Jane kept because tea was so expensive that the servants kept stealing it. Upstairs is her sewing box and washing closet, as well as a beautiful patchwork bedspread made by Jane, her sister and her mother. You can also see two amber crosses given to the girls by their brother Charles – an event she used in *Mansfield Park*, when William Price gives his sister Fanny an amber cross.

A short walk from Jane Austen's house, past **St Nicholas Church**, which Jane regularly attended and where her mother and sister are now buried, is **Chawton House**, which belonged to Jane's brother, Edward Austen Knight. He inherited the house from the childless Knight family and, needing space for his eleven children, moved here, allowing Jane, her mother and sister to live in the smaller Chawton cottage – though in fact Edward spent little time in the Great House, as it was known. It passed on to his children who did live here and the house remained in the Austen family until 1987, when it was bought up in a sorry state of repair by American IT millionairess Sandy Lerner, who wanted a place to keep her historic manuscripts of women writers. It now contains the Chawton House Library, with an impressive collection of women's writing in English from 1600–1830. The house, which has now been fully restored, can be visited on a guided tour (book ahead on ☎01420 541010 as places are limited; Tues & Thurs 2.30pm; £6), or you can look round the gardens independently (Mon–Fri 10am–4pm; £3). The library is open to the public by appointment only (Mon–Fri 10am–5pm). For more on Jane Austen, see box opposite.

The Greyfriar's, opposite Jane Austen's cottage, is an excellent village **pub**, serving interesting dishes such as grey mullet and pistachios (from £11) as well as pub staples: many of the ingredients are locally sourced, including salad and vegetables from the gardens of Chawton House. Next door, *Cassandra's Cup* **tearooms** (closed Mon & Tues; also Wed Oct–April) has a lovely terrace that catches the last of the day's sunshine: it serves good home-made cakes, tea and scones, and has a few decent rooms (℡01420 83144; ❷).

Selborne

The attractive village of **SELBORNE** is best known as the home of the naturalist Gilbert White (1720–1793), whose book *Natural History and Antiquities of Selborne* documented the flora and fauna that he saw around him, becoming the first detailed record of natural history. His detailed observations and descriptions of the local wildlife lead to a pioneering understanding of the interdependence of animals and plants in nature. You can see the original manuscript of White's book in the **Gilbert White House and Oates Museum** (daily: 11am–5pm June–Aug; Sept–May Tues–Sun plus bank hols; closed last week in Dec; £6.95) on Selborne High Street, where White lived for much of his life and carried out his painstaking documentation: it has been restored according to his descriptions, with some of his original furnishings. Downstairs, the kitchen has been recreated with eighteenth-century utensils, while the parlour has some replica costumes from the era. Upstairs is White's study and desk, and his bedroom, with the original bed-hangings.

Also upstairs, the Oates Museum is dedicated to the Oates family: like Gilbert White, Frank Oates was a pioneering natural historian, who studied wildlife in Africa, bringing back artefacts and specimens from his intrepid expeditions over

Austen's powers

Jane Austen lived through the French Revolution and Napoleonic Wars – a time of great change. And perhaps this is one reason why her tales of small-town society and the minutiae of middle-class life in the early nineteenth century struck such a chord with readers. Her novels, dealing with local gossip, rumour and social conventions could be considered the reality TV of the day – a comfort in times of turmoil – and continue to fascinate readers today. Although she wrote only six novels, their influence has been far-reaching with her plots re-used, adapted and satirized over the years, culminating in *Bridget Jones' Diary* as a modern take on *Pride and Prejudice*, both parodying the novel whilst closely following its plotline.

The major draw for her fans, of course, is **Chawton**, where she spent the last seven years of her short life. Although she used fictional names for most of the towns in her novels, Chawton and its surrounding countryside fit many of her descriptions of places to this day. **Basingstoke**, then a small town, is probably the "Meryton" of *Pride and Prejudice*, while *Persuasion* is partly set in **Lyme Regis** (see p.134), where Austen liked to holiday. Jane and her sister Cassandra also attended regular dances and card evenings at **The Vyne** (see p.217), near Basingstoke, when her father was the vicar at nearby Steventon Church. Before Austen moved to Chawton, the family spent some time in **Southampton**, which also exploits its connections with the eighteenth-century writer. The city's Bargate (see p.230) marks the start of the Jane Austen Heritage Trail, commemorating the fact that the novelist was at school here in 1783, while **Netley Abbey** (see p.235), just outside Southampton, is thought to be the inspiration for Austen's *Northanger Abbey*. Austen died in **Winchester** – the house where she spent her last days can be seen from the outside (see p.206) – and now lies in Winchester Cathedral.

▲ Gilbert White's House and Oates Museum

there. However, it is his nephew, **Captain Lawrence Oates**, who is the family's most famous member – and most of the exhibition is devoted to him. Lawrence Oates sacrificed his life during Captain Scott's ill-fated Antarctic expedition of 1911, uttering the famous words "I'm just going outside. I may be some time" as he stepped into a blizzard, aware that his ill-health was slowing the progress of the expedition. Sadly, his death was in vain, as all the other team members also perished on their return journey from the South Pole. Despite the slightly tenuous connection with Gilbert White, the exhibition is fascinating. Viewing the original artefacts from the doomed polar expedition – including a sledge,

Selborne walks

A lovely hour's **round walk** starts in Selborne's churchyard, opposite the museum, which follows the valley of a small stream – for most of the way, keep the stream on your right on the way there, and on your left on the return, and you can't go wrong. It starts off along the signed Hanger's Way, which heads downhill across a stream (a lovely picnic spot) and into Short Lythe woods, past large, fallen trees. Ten minutes into the walk you'll pass through two sets of gates into Long Lythe woods. After a further ten minutes, you'll exit the woods into a meadow with a couple of small lakes – another fine picnic spot, though it can be muddy in wet weather. Pass between the two lakes over a stile into more woodland. Leaving the woods, you cross a field, bearing left towards Priory Farm. Turn right through the farm onto a track, picking up a footpath signed to the right again. You are now returning in the direction you came. The path goes up through a field into lovely woodland, which wends back to join a narrow road, Hucker's Lane, uphill back to Selborne.

If you still have the energy, you can continue the walk up Selborne Hill via the aptly named Zigzag path, which White and his brother cut into the hillside. From the village car park, it's a further twenty minutes or so up through beech woods to the top of the hill, where there are fantastic views back over the village and surrounding countryside.

wind suits and snowshoes – it's surprising that they managed to survive for so long with such poorly adapted equipment. There's also poignant footage from the actual expedition, with Scott, Oates and the other team members talking and joking on camera.

Gilbert White was a keen horticulturist too, and the stunning **gardens** are much larger and grander – 20 acres – than you would expect from the size of the house. Having been restored to their eighteenth-century condition, they are divided into different sections by topiary hedges, including a kitchen garden, a herb garden and a wild garden, with a series of marked walks ranging from fifteen to forty-five minutes. Partly cultivated but mostly lawned, the grounds are designed to make the most of various viewpoints, with an eighteenth-century "ha ha" – a wall set into the ground so as not to disturb the view. Back in the house, the small **café** has been furnished in eighteenth-century style and serves light lunches, teas and home-made cakes, as well as some traditional recipes including cinnamon or cheese and watercress scones.

Other good places **to eat** are on the one main through-road: the *Selborne Arms* has its own beer garden and serves a fine Winchester cheese ploughman's along with full meals such as Toulouse sausages and mash, steak and kidney pie and venison from around £10. Just up the road, the *Queen's* (☎01420 511454) does a fine Sunday roast and mains such as mushroom stroganoff from around £11. It also lets out somewhat basic rooms or a grander one with a four-poster bed (all ❷). Alternatively, the very pretty *Dorton's Cottage*, on Hucker's Lane offers bed and breakfast **accommodation** in a thatched building with its own large garden (☎01420 511276, ✉dortonscottage@btinternet.com; ❶).

Around Basingstoke

Even residents of **Basingstoke** would freely admit that it is rarely on anyone's tourist itinerary. For most of its past, it was little more than a small market town until the 1960s, when it was decided to make it an overspill town for London, with several major companies moving their headquarters this way. Today, it's a large, relatively affluent town with a population of around 90,000, good shopping facilities and transport links; being just off the M3 and only 45 minutes from London by train, it's also popular with commuters.

There are only really a couple of sights for visitors, Old Basing on the eastern edge of town (see below) and the impressive **Milestones museum**, Leisure Park, Churchill Way West (⊛www3.hants.gov.uk/milestones). Housed inside a huge, modern aircraft-hangar-like building, the museum contains life-size Victorian and 1930s street scenes that have been re-created, complete with shops, a village square and a pub. The staff are dressed in traditional costumes – children have the chance to dress up too – and you can wander along cobbled lanes, into the buildings and see artefacts from the past, such as prewar washing machines and hoovers, or buy sweets from a 1930s sweet shop. There's also a collection of steam engines and a reconstructed ironworks, with regular special events, street theatre and exhibitions.

The historic town of **Old Basing** on the River Lodden is home to **Basing House** on Redbridge Lane (April–Sept Wed–Sun 2–6pm; £2). Now little more than a ruin, it was once the impressive palace of the Marquess of Winchester, who built what was once the country's largest private house in 1535 with a room for almost every day of the year. It was built near the site of a Norman castle, the banks of which still remain. The Marquess' impressive estate was a popular spot for visiting Royals, including Henry VIII and Elizabeth I, but this imperial

The Basingstoke Canal Towpath

When it opened in 1794, the **Basingstoke Canal** was the longest canal in southern England, at thirty-seven miles. Built to link the market town of Basingstoke with the River Wey, and ultimately the Thames, it provided a 70-mile waterway to London, carrying timber and agricultural produce to the capital, and bringing coal back down to northern Hampshire. However, it was never really commercially viable, while the completion of the London to Basingstoke railway in 1839 hastened its demise. In sporadic use over the next hundred years or so, the canal was derelict by the 1950s and it wasn't until the 1970s that work began to restore it to its former glory. In 1991, 31 miles of the canal were finally re-opened for leisure boats and walkers. The Basingstoke Canal Towpath now runs the length of the canal, passing through woodland, heathland and rural villages, while the canal's clean spring waters are rich in wildlife and aquatic plants.

The pleasant Georgian town of Odiham is a good place to access the canal. Starting at the pleasant *Waterwitch* pub in Colt Hill, it's a thirty-minute walk along the towpath to the Greywell Tunnel. En route you'll pass the ruins of **Odiham Castle**, which was built by King John in the thirteenth century: it is thought that the location was chosen as it is halfway between Windsor and Winchester. The final five miles of the canal to Basingstoke have not been restored, and the **Greywell Tunnel** is its furthest navigable point, as well as being Britain's most important bat roost – some 12,500 bats of all native species live here.

Boat trips along the canal on the *John Pinkerton*, a restored traditional narrow boat, leave from Colt Hill Wharf, by the *Waterwitch* (mid-July to early Sept Wed, Fri & Sun; 2–2hr 30min; £6; advance booking recommended). Trips also run at other times of the year: phone or check website for details (℡01962 713564, ⓦwww.s-h-c-c.co.uk).

approval attracted the attention of Cromwell who laid siege to the estate during the English Civil War, leaving the palace largely destroyed. Nowadays you can still enjoy the riverside walks along the River Lodden and tour the grounds that include a re-created seventeenth-century garden and the Tudor Great Barn – the only original building still standing and which was used to store agricultural goods until the 1980s.

East to West Green House and Stratfield Saye

Around five miles east of Basingstoke in West Green, **West Green House** (gardens Easter to mid Sept Wed, Sat & Sun 11am–4pm; £8; NT) is an attractive eighteenth-century house (closed to the public) surrounded by stunning gardens. Here, you can wander around a walled kitchen garden, a "Nymphaeum" complete with a water staircase, topiary, aviary, water garden and lakes; it also lays on special events including summer opera; details on ⓦwww.westgreenhousegardens.co.uk. A couple of miles southeast in Winchfield, the *Barley Mow* **pub**, The Hurst (℡01252 617490) sits on the Basingstoke Canal (see box above) and so is popular with walkers and cyclists: it serves a good range of home-made pub dishes, such as steak and ale pie (£11) or leek and brie gratin (£7.50).

Four miles or so north of here, **Wellington Country Park** (daily: Feb–Nov 9.30am–5.30pm; £6.50, children £5.50) was established by the eighth Duke of Wellington in 1974 for local people to enjoy outdoor pursuits. Extensive woodland surrounds a large central lake and there are various playgrounds and marked nature trails, some leading to the resident Red deer. There is also a café, shop and a **campsite** set in woodland, which allows free access to the park (☎01189 326444, Ⓦwww.wellington-country-park.co.uk).

A couple of miles west, on the other side of the A33, lies the former home of the Dukes of Wellington at **Stratfield Saye**, though access is restricted to guided tours that take place a few weeks each year (usually April & July; £9) – check Ⓦwww.stratfield-saye.co.uk for the latest details. The house was bought as a country retreat for the first Duke Of Wellington, Arthur Wellesley, in 1817, shortly after he received his title after the abdication of Napoleon in 1814. By then Wellesley had successfully campaigned against the French Emperor in Spain and especially Portugal, where he helped drive the occupying forces out of the country. Wellesley later entered politics, becoming Prime Minister in 1827. The tour takes in an exhibition on his life – in which you can see his funeral carriage – and a look round the luxurious house, originally built in 1630 by Sir William Pitt. When it passed into Wellesley's hands, he had the property "modernized" by adding, among other things, central heating – the original radiators can be seen at the foot of the main staircase. Look out, too, for the entrance hall, which includes Roman mosaics pilfered from Silchester's Roman excavations (see below). The grounds, too, are suitably grand, though their most moving site is the ornate grave for Copenhagen – the Duke's favourite horse, which he rode during the Battle of Waterloo. The Duke later kept Copenhagen in his grounds for his children to ride. When the horse died in 1836 aged 28, it was buried with full military honours.

North to Silchester

Four miles north of Basingstoke, **The Vyne** at Sherborne St John (house March–Oct Sat & Sun 11am–5pm Mon–Wed 1–5pm; gardens Feb to mid-March Sat & Sun 11am–5pm; mid-March to Oct Mon–Wed, Sat & Sun 11am–5pm; ☎01256 883858; £9; NT) is a sumptuous, partly sixteenth-century house built by Lord Sandys, Lord Chamberlain to Henry VIII, who was a regular visitor to the property, as was Jane Austen who attended balls here. Later owned by the same family for over three centuries, the interior is a mishmash of aristocratic opulence including statuary, paintings and ornate carpets; highlights include a Tudor chapel with beautiful stained-glass windows and sixteenth-century Flemish tiles. The family substantially adapted the building over the years, adding what is believed to be the first classical portico on the front of the building (on the north side) in the mid-seventeenth century and constructing a walled garden in the eighteenth century. The rest of the surrounding gardens are also impressive, set round a lake and with various woodland walks, where you can also find one of England's oldest summer-houses, built around 1635. There's also a café and good-value restaurant as well as regular events laid on throughout the year, including performances at an open-air theatre.

Three miles further north, **Silchester** is the site of one of the oldest towns in England and home to one of the country's best-preserved Roman defensive walls, which can be visited at a small archeological site (free) just outside the village. This was once part of the Roman town of Calleva Atrebatum. Abandoned in the fifth century, the town was then largely forgotten, giving archeologists an exciting and rare example of ruins that have not been subsequently built on or altered in some way. The walls stretch for about 1.5 miles through open countryside, though little else remains – on the surface at least: digs at the site have revealed that there was a substantial town of around 10,000 people living here up to a century before the Romans arrived; the town minted

Village for sale

They say you can't buy tradition, but that is just what a wealthy businessman has done with the small village of **Linkenholt**, a few miles west of Highclere Castle. The village (permanent population around 40) was originally part of the estate belonging to the Abbey of St Peter of Gloucester before being purchased by Herbert Blagrave in 1964. When he died in 1981, he handed it to a charitable trust who in turn put the whole estate – consisting of 20 or so cottages, farmland, woodland, village shop, blacksmith and cricket pitch – up for sale in 2009. The billionaire purchaser spent around £23 million to bag one of Hampshire's most old-fashioned villages. Only the twelfth-century village church is not part of the package, with all the residents and shopkeepers having to pay rent to the new owner. Understandably, the inhabitants are worried that the sale will affect their long-standing traditional ways of life, which in theory the new owner could radically alter. But as the owner's big passion is said to be hunting, it is more likely that things will stay much the same.

its own coins and had its own running water. This would make it a clear rival to Colchester or St Albans as England's oldest town.

West to Highclere Castle

The towers and turrets of **Highclere Castle** (July to early Sept Sun–Thurs 11am–4.30pm: castle £8, exhibition £8 or joint ticket £14) rise majestically above grand trees and parkland just west of the A34. Built on land originally owned by the Bishops of Winchester, most of today's castle dates from 1838, when the Earl of Carnarvon used the latest Victorian know-how to build a mansion fit to impress his guests. He employed Sir Charles Barry, architect of the Houses of Parliament – the similarity of design is noticeable. But it's the interior that's really impressive, a series of ornate state rooms, richly carpeted with sweeping staircases and soaring ceilings, though the vaulted entrance hall is thoroughly Gothic, designed by George Gilbert Scott who also designed St Pancras Station in London. Look out for the leather wall coverings in the grand Saloon, brought from Cordoba in Spain in 1631, and the library, resembling a gentleman's club and now used for weddings. The house cellars also contain **The Egyptian Exhibition**, the private collection of the fifth Earl of Carnarvon, famed for his excavations of Tutankhamun in the 1920s. The collection includes his finds from other excavations in Thebes and Balamun including embalming shrouds, jewellery and coffins, along with photos of the discovery of Tutankhamun in 1922.

A couple of miles north of Highclere, just east of the A34 by Burghclere is **Sandham Memorial Chapel** (March & Oct Wed–Sun 11am–3pm; April–Sept Wed–Sun 11am–5pm; Nov–Dec Sat & Sun 11am–3pm; £4; NT), an unassuming 1920s building housing a superb display of wall paintings of World War I by Stanley Spencer. Spencer was already a promising artist when the war broke out, and then spent time as a medical orderly in Bristol and as a soldier in northern Greece. When he returned, he wanted to record the personal experience of soldiers and his idea was backed by a wealthy local family who had the chapel built for him to house his paintings. He spent several years on his work, attracting a steady stream of visitors to watch him painting, including Vanessa Bell and Virginia Woolf – the results are extraordinarily moving and powerful, though there is no artificial lighting in the chapel so it is best to visit on a bright day.

Southampton, Portsmouth and around

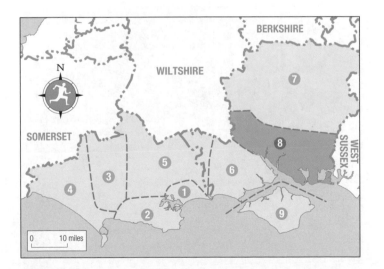

CHAPTER 8

Highlights

✳ **Kuti's, Southampton** Watch the cruise liners depart from the former gateway to America, now a sumptuous Thai restaurant. See p.231

✳ **Mottisfont Abbey** This superb house is filled with works by top artists and sits in lovely grounds by the River Test. See p.234

✳ **Hamble-le-Rice** Take a boat trip or riverside walk from this charming riverside town. See p.236

✳ **Spinnaker Tower, Portsmouth** Commanding terrific views over the town, this sleek tower is great to look at and even better inside. See p.241

✳ **The Historic Dockyard, Portsmouth** The heart of maritime Britain, with Nelson's HMS *Victory* as its jewel in the crown. See p.242

▲ The cannon deck on HMS *Victory*

Southampton, Portsmouth and around

Two of the UK's most important and historic ports, Southampton and Portsmouth, lie just a few miles apart facing the Solent. The *Titanic* departed from **Southampton**, once the main gateway to Britain's empire and the Americas. It is still the departure point for many cruise liners and Isle of Wight ferries, though these days it's the shops that pull in most visitors. These have gradually expanded in a centre that was largely destroyed in the last war; a series of interesting museums records the city's ancient past, however. Nearby, too, are some fine historical attractions, including **Netley Abbey**, one of the most complete Cistercian abbeys left in the country; **Mottisfont Abbey** and its stunning gardens; and **Romsey** with its handsome abbey and Broadlands estate where many of the Royals have honeymooned. Neighbouring **Portsmouth** shares Southampton's ferries and first-rate shops, but its harbour is usually filled with warships rather than cruise liners. This is the heart of the British navy – the best of the ships are shown off at the **Historic Dockyard**, home to HMS *Victory* and the *Mary Rose*. More naval museums – the **Submarine Museum** and **Museum of Naval Firepower** – are across the harbour in Gosport. Not surprisingly, the area's military role encouraged monarchs to heavily defend its environs, and there are several interesting castles in the vicinity including **Southsea Castle**, **Portchester Castle**, **Fort Nelson** and **Spitbank Fort** – the latter on an islet a mile offshore. But Portsmouth is not all military history. This is also home to **Charles Dickens' Birthplace**; the amazing **Spinnaker Tower** viewing platform; and the beaches of **Southsea**. Further beaches lie to the east at **Hayling Island**, while inland there's the child-friendly **Queen Elizabeth Country Park** and **Butser Hill**, with its recreation of an Iron Age fort.

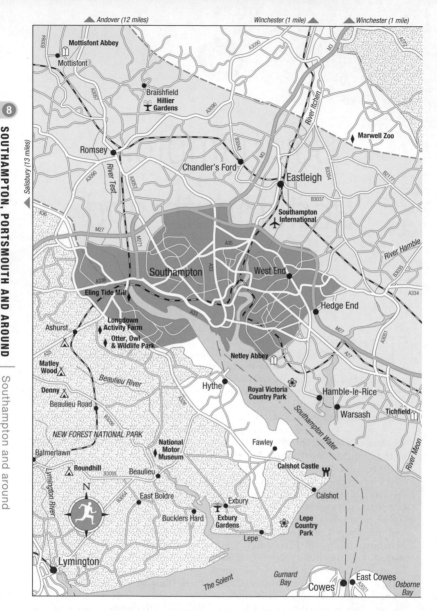

Southampton and around

One of England's most important ports thanks to its double tides, it was in **SOUTHAMPTON** that King Canute is alleged to have commanded the waves to retreat. And it was from its docks, too, that Henry V left to conquer

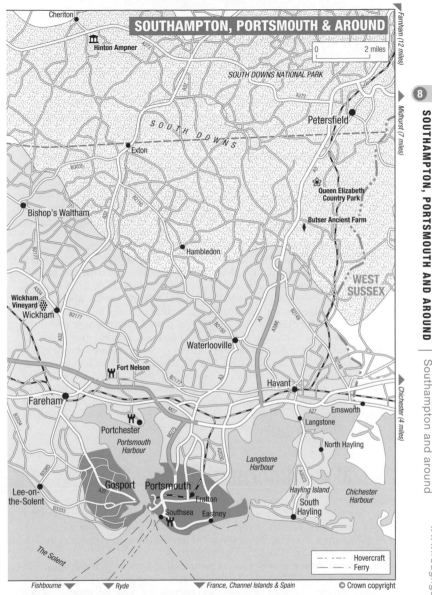

8

SOUTHAMPTON, PORTSMOUTH AND AROUND | Southampton and around

www.roughguides.com

223

Agincourt, the Pilgrim Fathers originally set sail for America in 1620, and the *Titanic* departed for its fateful voyage. The world's largest liners still berth here, but more than half a century after World War II, you feel the town is only just recovering from the dreadful pummelling it endured by the German Luftwaffe, which ripped out the heart of this ancient city. Though it sits on a peninsula where the Itchen and Test rivers meet Southampton Water – an eight-mile inlet from the Solent – the waterside is only gradually being opened up to visitors, largely round the Ocean Village development, though the city's numerous retail areas have turned it into something of a hub for serious shoppers. Indeed, many people see no more than its shops or ferry terminals and do scant justice to its leafy parks, fine museums, art galleries and superb, if incomplete, set of medieval walls, all of which merit further exploration.

Some history

The **Romans** built a small settlement on the Itchen called Clausentum, but it was the **Saxons** who gave the town its name, founding a port they called Hamtun in around 700 AD. The port thrived on exporting wool and even had its own mint by the ninth century, though the town was vulnerable to attack and was frequently raided by Danes. By the twelfth century, the **Normans** had built the church of St Michael and a castle, and the port flourished on trading wool and wine, as well as on shipbuilding. In the late thirteenth century, a stone wall was built to defend the town, however this did not stop French raids, so fortifications were improved throughout the fourteenth century. At this time most of the city walls, including Bargate, were built, along with several wealthy merchants' houses.

The first **docks** were built in the nineteenth century to handle the growing number of commercial ships and ferries. By the early twentieth century, Southampton had become the base for White Star transatlantic liners – including the ill-fated *Titanic*, which departed from the port in 1912 – and, in 1919, Cunard's services to New York. This helped Southampton thrive throughout the Depression, boosted by the manufacture of both flying boats and General Motors cars in the 1930s. The town's fortunes as a port have always fluctuated with changes in trade, but historically, until the mid-twentieth century, Southampton did best during wartime, as soldiers passed through. But this was not the case during World War II, when a series of bombing raids largely wiped out Southampton's prosperity. The 1950s saw much of the city rebuilt with a new road layout, but a combination of air travel and changes to shipping containerization saw its role as a port decline through the second half of the century. This century, the shift has been towards commercial activity, with numerous shopping centres opening alongside the former docks.

Arrival and information

Southampton's central **train station** is in Blechynden Terrace, a few minutes' walk west of the Civic Centre; the **bus station** is immediately southeast of the Civic Centre opposite Asda. A free City Link shuttle bus runs from the train to the coach station and on to Town Quay for ferry services to Hythe and the Isle of Wight. See p.232 for details of the airport.

The **tourist office** is at 9 Civic Centre Rd (Mon–Sat 9.30am–5pm, Sun 10am–3.30pm; ☎02380 833333, ⓦwww.visit-southampton.co.uk) and can provide transport timetables, maps and details of various themed walks, including a *Titanic* trail and Jane Austen trail. You can easily walk round central Southampton – from Town Quay to the station is around twenty minutes, or you can take the City Clipper **bus**, which runs in a loop from the stations to Town Quay and on to Ocean Village, the city centre and the university. Drivers should follow signs to one of the central car parks – the shops around West Quays are well served by several multistorey car parks, though note that you may have to queue to get into these at peak times.

Accommodation

The tourist office can help out with **accommodation** if the places below are full: there are also various inexpensive guest houses along The Polygon just north of the station.

De Vere Grand Harbour West Quay Rd ☎02380 633033, ⓦwww.devere-hotels.com. The impressive glass and steel exterior promises modern luxury, and though there is a pool, spa and restaurant, the rooms feel slightly worn. However, it's the plushest option in town and just a short walk from the harbour and main attractions. ❼

Eaton Court 32 Hill Lane ☎02380 80223081, ⓦwww.eatoncourtsouthampton.co.uk. Around half a mile west of the train station, this offers good-value if simple bed and breakfast accommodation with off-street parking. ❶

Elizabeth House Hotel 42–44 The Ave ☎02380 8022 4327, ⓦwww.elizabethhousehotel.com. A bit removed from the centre – around a mile north – this nevertheless offers large, well-furnished rooms in a couple of Victorian townhouses that now form a friendly two-star hotel. There is also a small bar, bistro and garden, plus parking and family rooms. ❸

Star Hotel 26 High St ☎02380 339939, ⓦwww.starhotel.co.uk. This seventeenth-century coaching inn now has well-furnished rooms above a decent Oriental restaurant (with Chinese and Malay cuisine); its great central position can entail a bit of street noise. ❹

White Star 28 Oxford St ☎02380 821990, ⓦwww.whitestartavern.co.uk. Stylish rooms, with comfortable beds and modern decor, above a trendy bar-restaurant (see p.232). ❹

The docks and the waterfront

Before transatlantic air travel became commonplace, Southampton was the main departure point for most liners across the Atlantic. These days its **waterfront** is rather tatty, though you do get the odd glimpse of what it must have been like in its heyday – have a look inside *Kuti's Thai* restaurant, for example, which is the former reception terminal for Atlantic passengers. The adjacent **Mayflower Park** is the best place to view some of the 250-odd cruise ships that call annually, and there are frequently fireworks and events held here to celebrate ships arriving or departing. Another way to see the cruise ships and other comings and goings on Southampton Water is to take the **Hythe Ferry** from Town Quay (daily every 30min; £4.50; ⓦwww.hytheferry.co.uk), which runs to the opposite side of the water to Hythe (see p.186).

Ocean Village and the Solent Sky

The waterfront area now known as **Ocean Village** is situated on what was originally Southampton's first dock, which opened in 1843. Then called the Outer Dock, it expanded in 1851 with the construction of the Inner Dock and after almost a century of handling freight and passenger ferries, was renamed Princess Alexandra Dock when she reopened it in 1967. Parts of the dock wall are listed, but the entire area has undergone much development in recent years and now houses an upmarket marina, the wonderful Harbour Lights art-house cinema (see p.232), and the trendy *Banana Reef* bar and restaurant overlooking the water.

A short walk back from the waterfront on Albert Road South, the **Solent Sky** aviation museum (Tues–Sat 10am–5pm, Sun noon–5pm; £6; ☎02380 635830, ⓦwww.spitfireonline.co.uk) takes an interesting look into the aviation industry in Southampton and along the Hampshire coast. In 1913, airplane production started in earnest in Southampton, kicked off by an aviation company called Supermarine, which produced flying boats – literally motor boats with detachable wings, that could be taken off when they landed. The company continued to develop new

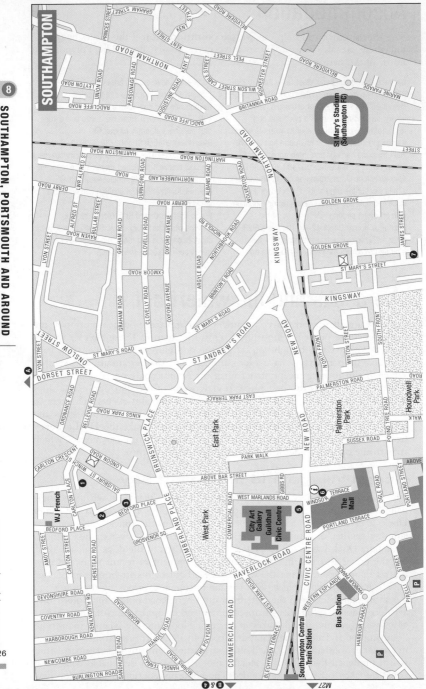

St Mary's Stadium (Southampton FC)

East Park

West Park

City Art Gallery
Guildhall
Civic Centre

Palmerston Park

Houndwell Park

The Mall

Southampton Central Train Station

Bus Station

WJ French

PRINCES STREET
GRAHAM STREET
KENT STREET
BELVIDERE ROAD
KENT ST
PEEL STREET
CABLE STREET
WILSON STREET
ROCHESTER STREET
NORTHAM ROAD
UNION ROAD
LEYTON ROAD
PARSONAGE ROAD
RADCLIFFE ROAD
AUGUSTINE ROAD
BRITANNIA ROAD
MARINE PARADE
BELVIDERE ROAD
STREET
HARTINGTON ROAD
HARTINGTON ROAD
NORTHUMBERLAND ROAD
ST ALBANS ROAD
WOLVERTON ROAD
NORTHAM ROAD
DERBY ROAD
DURNFORD ROAD
DERBY ROAD
LWR ALFRED ST
ALFRED ST
GRAHAM ROAD
CLOVELLY ROAD
OXFORD AVENUE
EXMOOR ROAD
ARGYLE ROAD
NORTHBROOK ROAD
ST JOHN'S RD
BRINTON'S ROAD
GOLDEN GROVE
GOLDEN GROVE
KINGSWAY
KINGSWAY
ST MARY'S STREET
JAMES STREET
LYON STREET
RAVEN ROAD
BULLAR STREET
GRAHAM ROAD
CLOVELLY ROAD
OXFORD AVENUE
ST MARY'S ROAD
ST ANDREW'S ROAD
ST MARY'S ROAD
NEW ROAD
LYON STREET
ONSLOW STREET
DORSET STREET
ORDNANCE ROAD
BELLEVUE ROAD
KINGS PARK ROAD
BRUNSWICK PLACE
EAST PARK TERRACE
PALMERSTON ROAD
NORTH FRONT
WINTON STREET
SOUTH FRONT
NEW ROAD
ROAD
CARLTON CRESCENT
WINDSOR ROAD
LONDON ROAD
SALISBURY ST
CARLTON PLACE
BEDFORD PLACE
PARK WALK
ABOVE BAR STREET
WEST MARLANDS ROAD
GIBBS RD
WINDSOR TERRACE
TERRACE
SUSSEX ROAD
POUND TREE ROAD
WALK
ABOVE
AMOY STREET
BEDFORD PLACE
CANTON STREET
HENSTEAD ROAD
GROSVENOR SQ
COMMERCIAL ROAD
HAVERLOCK ROAD
OGLE ROAD
PORTLAND STREET
PORTLAND TERRACE
PIRELLI STREET
CUMBERLAND PLACE
DEVONSHIRE ROAD
COVENTRY ROAD
KENILWORTH RD
MORRIS ROAD
THE POLYGON
WEST PARK ROAD
CIVIC CENTRE ROAD
WESTERN ESPLANADE
HARBOUR PARADE
PIRELLI STREET
HARBOROUGH ROAD
NEWCOMBE ROAD
SANDHURST ROAD
HANDEL ROAD
HANDEL TERRACE
MORRIS ROAD
COMMERCIAL ROAD
BLECHYNDEN TERRACE
HARBOUR PARADE
BURLINGTON ROAD

M27

M27

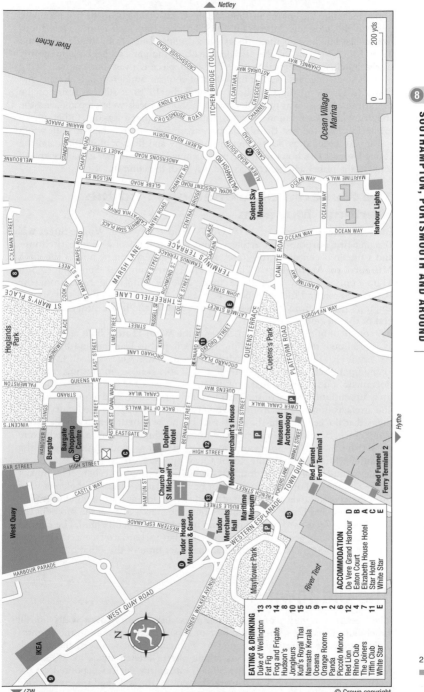

▲ Netley

River Itchen

West Quay

IKEA

ITCHEN BRIDGE (TOLL)

Ocean Village Marina

Harbour Lights

Solent Sky Museum

Queen's Park

Hoglands Park

Bargate Shopping Centre

Bargate

Dolphin Hotel

Church of St Michael's

Medieval Merchant's House

Maritime Museum

Tudor Merchants Hall

Tudor House Museum & Garden

Museum of Archeology

Red Funnel Ferry Terminal 1

Red Funnel Ferry Terminal 2

Mayflower Park

River Test

▼ Hythe

ACCOMMODATION
De Vere Grand Harbour	D
Eaton Court	B
Elizabeth House Hotel	A
Star Hotel	C
White Star	E

EATING & DRINKING
Duke of Wellington	13
Fat Fig	3
Frog and Frigate	14
Hudson's	8
Jongleurs	10
Kuti's Royal Thai	15
Namaste Kerala	9
Oceana	1
Orange Rooms	2
Panda	6
Piccolo Mondo	6
Red Lion	12
Rhino Club	4
The Joiners	7
Tiffin Club	11
White Star	E

▼ M27

N

© Crown copyright

0   200 yds

planes, including the Spitfire in 1936 and the C-class flying boat, the first passenger plane to fly across the Atlantic in 1938. The museum itself is in an enormous hangar-like building on three floors packed with planes, from the de Havilland Tiger Moth, via one of the last de Havilland Vampires to be built in nearby Christchurch, to an original Spitfire. The centrepiece is a vast four-engined flying boat, the only one preserved in the UK, that you can wander around, upstairs and down. In service in the Caribbean up until the 1970s, it still has some of the original interior, such as the galley, where elaborate meals were prepared, and the lavatory, which was far more spacious than today's cramped versions. Other quirky exhibits include the first British manpowered plane – more a bicycle with wings – that was invented by Southampton University and flew 55m in 1901; and the Flying Flea, a 1930s home-made flying machine. You can also sit in the cockpit of some of the planes and helicopters and play with the controls.

The Museum of Archeology and the Maritime Museum

Built into the town walls in 1417, **God's House Tower** in Winkle Street was Britain's first purpose-built artillery store. An amalgam of a simple gatehouse, and a fifteenth-century three-storey tower and gallery, it now houses the city's **Museum of Archeology** (Thurs & Fri 10am–6pm & 1–5pm, Sat & Sun 11am–6pm; £2.50). With three main galleries, displaying finds from the Roman, Saxon and medieval periods, it traces fifteen hundred years of South-ampton's history from its development as a port in the first century BC to the end of the medieval period.

A couple of minutes' walk further east is the **Wool House**, built around 1400 as a warehouse to store wool before it was shipped to Flanders and Italy. Today it's home to the **Maritime Museum** on Town Quay Road (Mon–Fri 10am–6pm, Sat & Sun 11am–6pm; £2.50), whose interesting exhibits document Southampton's marine history. Downstairs, the story of how the port grew up, and the history of the various different docks is told alongside models and artefacts from old steamships. Upstairs, the emphasis is on the luxury cruise liners that docked here in the early part of the twentieth century, with silver-ware, crockery and elaborate menus from the ships – many of which were crewed by men from Southampton. There is also a vivid exhibition on the **Titanic**, which left from the Town Quay opposite on 10 April 1912 on its maiden voyage, only to sink four days later after hitting an iceberg. The impact of the disaster on Southampton cannot be understated – most of the crew were from the city, and over five hundred families here lost at least one member. The owner White Star Line's policy of curtailing the crew's salary at the moment the ship went down caused further hardship to the families left behind. The exhibi-tion plays moving accounts of survivors and has various artefacts rescued from the ship, including a watch stopped at the exact time of the sinking.

The Old Town

The western extremities of Southampton's twelfth-century **town walls** are still largely intact, and are some of the best-preserved medieval walls in the country. Their sturdy structure was designed to withstand French raiders, and though much of the present structure was rebuilt after a French attack in 1338, large sections of the wall withstood the 30,000 incendiary devices deposited on the town during the last war. A well-marked circuit of the walls and towers is signed at strategic places, with the best stretch just west of Bugle Street. This street is also the most evocative of the old town, around which lie some of its most historic buildings, including the **Tudor Merchants Hall**, on Westgate Street, a distinctive, timbered building built in about 1492 by Sir John Dawtrey, but originally consisting of three dwellings dating back to around 1150. It was used as a hall for woollens and a fish market until the fifteenth century, when it became a warehouse. It is currently undergoing renovation and is due to re-open in 2011 along with the **Tudor House Museum and Garden**, on St Michael's Square.

Opposite, the **Church of St Michael's** is the city's oldest church and the only one to fully survive the war. It has beautiful stained-glass windows and a rare twelfth-century font made of black Tournai marble, one of six existing in England. The central Norman tower, built in around 1070 still exists, though later additions were made in the fourteenth and fifteenth centuries, with the current spire dating from 1878. Free classical concerts are frequently held here, currently on Tuesday lunchtimes.

From the church, a short walk down French Street brings you to the **Medieval Merchants House** at no. 58 (April–Sept Sun noon–5pm; £3.80; EH). Built in 1290 by John Fortin, a merchant who made his money trading with Bordeaux, it has been restored to its fourteenth-century condition, with replica furniture such as a canopied four-poster bed that a wealthy merchant would have enjoyed languishing in during medieval times.

The city centre

Along with parts of the Old Town, the modern centre fared far worse during World War II, where 45,000 buildings were damaged or destroyed. Hurriedly rebuilt after the war, most of what is left is a motley collection of tower blocks, cheap 1960s shops and offices. The one exception is **Bargate**, one of the last remaining of the city's seven town gates. Resembling a stone turret complete with carvings and defensive apertures, it is open to the public and you can climb up to the upper room that now serves as a gallery for temporary art exhibitions

▲ Bargate

Shopping

Southampton is something of a shopoholic's paradise, mainly thanks to its giant shopping mall **West Quay** (ⓦwww.west-quay.co.uk) – which includes large branches of the upmarket high street chains – and the other retail centres around it. Nearby on the long pedestrianized **Upper Bar Street**, you'll find further high street names. Alternative and surf-dude clothes can be found at **Bargate Shopping Centre** while **The Mall** on Above Bar has various designer outlets. For something more individual, seek out WJ French at 40 Bedford Place (☏02380 226542; closed Sun) a superb traditional **shoe shop** dating back over 200 years, though the designs are fully up to date. It also has a workshop for repairs.

(Wed–Fri 11am–6pm, Sat & Sun noon–5pm; free). This was used as the law courts until the 1930s – the downstairs served as a police lockup. Alongside Bargate a plaque marks the start of the **Jane Austen Heritage Trail**, highlighting the fact that the novelist was at school here in 1783, and visited frequently thereafter, attending dances and balls at the *Dolphin Hotel*, a few minutes' walk south on the High Street; pick up a leaflet from the tourist office (see p.224) if you want to follow the walk. Bargate is also the venue for regular markets (Fri–Sun).

North of here, the wide, pedestrianized Above Bar Street is one of the principal shopping streets, leading up past the West Quays shopping complex to the Civic Centre.

City Art Gallery

Inside the **Civic Centre**, with its distinctive clocktower, lies Southampton's excellent **City Art Gallery**, which is particularly strong on contemporary British art (Mon–Fri 10am–6pm, Sat & Sun 11am–6pm; free; ⓦwww .southampton.gov.uk/art); its entrance is round the back on Commercial Road. Although only a small proportion of its collection is on show at any time, you're likely to see works such as Chris Ofili's *Two Doo Voodoo*, displayed on two cushions of elephant dung; Antony Gormley's sculpture, *The Diver*, and some colourful abstracts by Bridget Riley. Earlier British works include Lucian Freud's *Bananas*, a couple of Lowry's – look out for his *Floating Bridge, Southampton* of the ferry that crossed the Itchen River until 1977 – and some fine pieces by the Camden Town Group, including works by Augustus John, Robert Bevan and Walter Sickert. The Impressionists are represented too, with works by Bonnard, Corot, Monet and Pissarro, while Sir Joshua Reynolds and Gainsborough – you can't miss his enormous portrait of *George Venables Vernon* – fly the flag for eighteenth-century British art. The remaining collection ranges from sixteenth-century Flemish and Italian paintings to Andy Goldsworthy's *Leaf Sculpture*: check out the website too, for details of the various temporary exhibitions held throughout the year. *The Fountains* café downstairs (Mon–Fri 8am–6pm, Sat 9am–5pm) serves reasonably priced food, while the adjoining gift shop is worth a browse for interesting, good-value jewellery by new designers.

Eating, drinking and entertainment

As you'd expect from a lively port town with two universities, there are lots of good places to eat and drink, whatever your budget. For bargain and ethnic cuisine, head to the popular student haunts along Bedford Place, north of the

Civic Centre, though the best restaurants are along Oxford Street or down towards the waterfront.

Cafés and restaurants

Fat Fig 5 Bedford Place ☎02380 212111. Greek café-restaurant, popular with students, serving superb *souvlaki*, falafels and Greek salads from around £5–8, along with a long list of starters, paninis and wraps. Closed Sun.

Hudson's 44 St Mary St ☎02380 232332. Simple café-restaurant in the student district of St Mary's with superb and authentic Carribbean food, including goat curry, jerk chicken and rice and peas. Mains around £7. Eves only except for Sun. Closed Mon.

Kuti's Royal Thai Gate House, Royal Pier ☎02380 339211. Excellent all-you-can-eat Thai buffets (£10 for lunch, £20 for dinner) are served at this superbly ornate waterside restaurant. There are great cocktails, an outside bar area and fine views across the water from the upstairs dining room, complete with chandeliers and a partly glass floor.

Namaste Kerala 4a Civic Centre Rd ☎02380 224422. Great-value lunchtime buffet for around £8 and a long list of fish, lamb and vegetarian dishes. Mains £6–8.

Panda 20 Bedford Place ☎02380 223153. Very good value Chinese restaurant using fresh ingredients, popular with students. Closed Sun lunch.

Piccolo Mondo 36 Windsor Terrace ☎02380 636890. Small but bustling and inexpensive Italian restaurant just round the corner from the tourist office. Filling pizzas and home-made pasta dishes along with daily specials. Closed Sun.

Tiffin Club 1 Oxford St ☎02380 233433. Upmarket Indian restaurant in a fine old building with modern art on the walls. The chef creates superb Indian cuisine using largely organic and local ingredients, though there is nothing local about its water buffalo *bhoona*. Innovative fish dishes include sumptuous Machli Biran, cooked with rainbow trout, and salmon *ka sula*, chargrilled with mushrooms. Mains from around £11.

Drinking and nightlife

Southampton's two universities ensure the town has an extremely energetic **nightlife**, at least during term time. Many of the best bars and clubs are around Carlton Place, five minutes' walk north of West Park. *Listed* magazine comes out once every two months and covers events such as theatre, films, gigs, festivals, clubs and restaurant reviews. It can be picked up free from bars, clubs and restaurants.

Duke of Wellington 36 Bugle St ☎02380 339222. Though the small interior is nothing special, take a seat outside this historic pub on a summer's evening and savour one of the oldest drinking holes in the town. Opened in the fifteenth century as the Bere House, it changed its name after the Battle of Waterloo and despite restoration from bomb damage, its exterior looks much as it would have when it first opened.

Frog and Frigate 33 Canute Rd ☎02380 335959. Earthy but usually extremely lively waterside pub with live music upstairs and regular DJs downstairs; open Thurs–Sat 7pm–4am, with a small entrance fee for entry after 11pm.

Jongleurs 2–4a High St ☎0844 4994074, ⓦwww.jongleurs.com. Lively venue for various events, though best known for its comedy nights featuring up-and-coming stand-up comedians.

Oceana West Quay Rd ☎0845 3132588, ⓦwww.oceanaclubs.com. One of the UK's biggest clubs, pulling in up to 4000 revellers into a giant place with various themed areas – a bar quarter, an al-fresco courtyard, a New York disco dancefloor, plus a live entertainment area and state-of-the-art sound and light systems: pretty much something for everyone.

Orange Rooms 1–2 Vernon Walk ☎02380 232333. Popular retro-themed lounge bar with great cocktails, decent food and various events from film screenings and live bands to regular DJs.

Red Lion 55 High St ☎02380 333595. One of the oldest and most atmospheric pubs in Southampton, dating from the twelfth century. The half-timbered apartment known as Henry V's "Court Room" was used for the famous trial of a group of hapless lords who had conspired to murder their king, Henry V, in 1415. They were subsequently condemned to death and executed outside the Bargate. Today the somewhat more peaceful pub serves fine real ales and traditional British food.

Rhino Club 5–6 Waterloo Terrace ☎02380 630171. Indie music club with regular DJs, retro music nights and a cool crowd.

The Joiners 141 St Mary St ☎02380 225621, ⓦwww.joinerslive.co.uk. This small, gritty pub is the place to catch live bands – it has hosted some of the biggest names since the 1980s including Oasis, Coldplay and Radiohead, all booked by the late owner, Mint, just before they made it big.

White Star 28 Oxford St ☏02380 821990, ⓦwww .whitestartavern.co.uk. Named after the White Star ocean line to the Americas, this chic bar-restaurant has comfy sofas and evocative photos on the wall from the heyday of ocean travel. The menu features generous and well-presented but largely meaty mains from £10–16, though you can also have less expensive bar food and sandwiches.

Listings

Airport Southampton's international airport (ⓦwww.southamptonairport.com) is a short drive north of the centre along the A335 near Eastleigh, which is ten minutes by train from Southampton Central at Southampton Airport Parkway, or take bus #U1 from Town Quay or the train station.

Bus information Information on local bus services is available on Traveline ☏0871 2002233. Buses to other local towns west are run by Wilts & Dorset bus company (☏01202 673555, ⓦwww.wdbus .co.uk). Long-distance buses are operated by National Express (☏08705 808080, ⓦwww .nationalexpress.com).

Car rental Easycar (☏08710 500444, ⓦwww .easycar.com); Hertz (☏0870 850 4881, ⓦwww.hertz.com); and Thrifty (☏02380 638437 ⓦwww.thrifty.co.uk).

Cinemas The Odeon, Leisure World, West Quay Rd (☏0871 2244007, ⓦwww.odeon.co.uk) and Cineworld, Ocean Village (☏0870 1555132) show the latest blockbusters. Harbour Lights, Ocean Village (☏02380 335533, ⓦwww .picturehouses.co.uk) shows art-house and independent films.

Disabled visitors Shopmobility schemes, offering battery-operated scooters or wheelchairs, are available for people with limited mobility at Above Bar Street (☏02380 631263) and West Quays (☏02306 36100).

Ferry services For details of Isle of Wight ferries, see p.253 or ⓦwww.redfunnel.co.uk.

Gay and lesbian For details of the best gay clubs, bars and contacts, see ⓦwww.gaysouthampton .com.

Police The central Police station is at Havelock Rd ☏0845 454545.

Taxi There are taxi ranks at the station and at many central points; fares from the station to the ferry terminals cost around £5. Try West Quay Cars (☏02380 999999).

Theatre The Mayflower on Commercial Rd (☏02380 711811, ⓦwww.mayflower.org.uk) is the south of England's largest theatre and frequently hosts shows from the West End.

Trains Southampton has regular departures to London (80–90min), Bournemouth, the New Forest and Portsmouth; train details on ☏08457 484950, ⓦwww.nationalrail.co.uk.

North along the River Test

The industrial hue of Southampton and Southampton Water quickly disappears as you head up the pristine waters of the **River Test**. Here you'll find the unspoilt townscape of **Romsey**, with its ancient abbey and neighbouring estate, Broadlands, where the Queen honeymooned. Continue up the Test and you reach the impressive **Mottisfont Abbey**, while nearby lie the attractive gardens at Hillier.

Romsey

Ten miles northwest of Southampton by the River Test, Romsey is a handsome and well-to-do market town that still boasts a great central market (Tues, Fri & Sat). The town grew wealthy in the fourteenth century thanks to its water wheels, which supported a thriving weaving industry, together with tanning and brewing; many of its products were exported from nearby Southampton. There are plenty of handsome buildings remaining from this time, most notably **King John's House and Heritage Centre** on Church Street (Mon–Sat 10am–4pm, £2.50, Oct–March £1.50), which embraces three historic buildings and the tourist information office. The Moody Museum here, named after the family who owned the properties, traces the history of Romsey and its links with

Florence Nightingale, who lived nearby, and includes a re-creation of a Victorian shop selling guns, which was on the site in the 1870s. Of more interest is King John's House, which dates back to 1256, and was probably built as a hunting lodge; you can still see the medieval roof timbers and Tudor fittings. There is also a small tearoom and fine gardens (free).

Romsey's best-known building is opposite, the Norman **Abbey** (daily 8.30am–5.30pm; free). It dates back to 1120, though the current structure is actually the third church on this site. During the Reformation, local townspeople purchased the abbey for £100 – a memorial to the Bill of Sale, signed by Henry III, can be viewed in the south choir aisle. The Abbey also houses the tomb of Lord Mountbatten, great-grandson of Queen Victoria and the last Viceroy of India, who was assassinated by the IRA in 1979. His former home was just south of the town centre in the Palladian mansion of **Broadlands**, superbly sited on the River Test in expansive parkland. Most of today's structure dates from 1767, when the second Viscount Palmerston commissioned "Capability" Brown to redesign the gardens and oversee rebuilding work. The mansion became the country residence of Lord Palmerston, Prime Minister during Victorian times (his statue is now in Romsey's main square) and still belongs to the Mountbatten family – the Queen honeymooned here in 1947, as did Prince Charles and Lady Diana in 1981. For now, the building and grounds are closed for substantial renovation until 2011, though concerts and events do still take place here; check the latest on ⓦwww.broadlands.net.

Finally, signed just beyond Broadlands, on Southampton Road, families shouldn't miss **Romsey Rapids** (Mon–Fri 7am–10pm, Sat–Sun 9am–7pm; £4.60, children £3.40; ⓣ01794 830333, ⓦwww.the-rapids.co.uk), a superb swimming pool complex with flumes and water jets, great for a rainy day.

Practicalities

Romsey is on the main Southampton to Salisbury **train** line (around 20min to both) and is also well served by **buses** from Southampton – the bus station is just a minute's walk from the main street. **Tourist information** is available from the Visitor and Heritage Centre opposite the Abbey at 13 Church St

▲ Romsey Abbey

(Mon–Sat 10am–4pm; ☎01794 512987, ⓦwww.visit-testvalley.org.uk), which can give out town maps and details of the five-mile/two-hour walk along the Test Way to Mottisfont (see below).

Accommodation is rarely a problem, though the town gets busy around the July Beggars Fair and Carnival and the Romsey Show in September. The best budget option is *The Courtyard* at 49 The Hundred (☎01794 516434, ⓔbabidge @btinternet.com; ❸), with spacious twins and doubles – some in an attic room – above a tearoom right on the main street. The top choice is the boutique *Silks* on the marketplace (☎01794 512431, ⓦwww.silkshotels.com; ❼), overlooking the marketplace in a former coaching inn – one of only three late-medieval purpose-built inns left in the county. There are characterful if small rooms at the front in former twelfth-century guest rooms for the nearby Abbey; others are in the wonky-floored Tudor part or you can take a spacious modern room in the 1960s extension at the back. Alternatively, around four miles west of town in West Wellow, *The Onion Store* (☎01794 323227, ⓦwww.theonionstore.co.uk; ❼, two-night minmum stay) is an extremely atmospheric B&B with its own pool. There are cosy rooms in a former onion storeroom, a former grain store complete with its own sun deck, or an apple store, with a silver birch tree as part of its bed.

Simply Silks brasserie in *Silks* is also the place **to eat**, with a courtyard bar and sumptuous mains such as monkfish wrapped in parma ham or New Forest venison from £14–20; look out for the good-value set menu. There are less expensive options along Bell Street, best of which is *La Parisienne* at no. 21 (☎01794 512067), an old pub given a French makeover and serving tasty salads, steak *haché*, quiches or scallops from around £7, as well as cheaper baguettes. *The Romsey Purbani* at 11 Bell St (☎01794 522107) serves reliable Indian and Bangladeshi food with mains from £8, and good vegetarian options. Slightly out of town towards Broadlands at 21 Palmerston St (☎01794 517353), *Prezzo* is also recommended, serving the usual chain-fare pizzas, salads and grills but in a great sixteenth-century manor house.

Mottisfont Abbey and Hillier Gardens

Around four miles north of Romsey up the Test Valley lies **Mottisfont Abbey** (house mid-March to Sept daily 11am–5pm except Fri in March, early May & July–Nov; gardens early Feb & Nov–Dec Sat & Sun 11am–4pm, late Feb to Oct daily 11am–5pm except Fri in March, early May & July–Nov; £8; ☎01794 340757; NT), which is less than a mile from Dunbridge train station (on the Romsey to Salisbury line). Note that on Sundays (May–Sept), a free bus service runs from Dunbridge and Romsey stations to Mottisfont and on to Hillier

---

Passing the Test

The Test, which runs for some 40 miles from near Basingstoke to Southampton Water, is one of the UK's cleanest rivers. Indeed, the pristine chalk stream river is rated one of the world's best for fly-fishing, with salmon, brown trout and grayling particularly prevalent thanks to the healthy population of shrimps and insects that breed in the waters – the area around Stockbridge (see p.208) is particularly favoured by fishermen. The river is also famous for its **watercress beds**, some of which have existed since the twelfth century. In the past, this peppery plant was known as Poorman's Bread and was a healthy staple for the working classes: it is still grown in beds alongside the river, especially around Arlesford and Whitchurch (see p.211). To see the best of the river, ask at local tourist offices for maps of the 44-mile long **Test Way**, which runs all the way from Southampton to Inkpen Hill.

Gardens (see below). Mottisfont is actually a mansion built on the remains of a twelfth-century priory, whose primary attraction is its superb position in lavish grounds by the River Test. In June, garden-lovers flock to its walled gardens when its National Collection of Old-Fashioned Roses is in full bloom. At this time, prices increase by about £1 and there are also extended opening times (usually to 8pm). The building was handed to William Lord Sandys after the Dissolution of the Monasteries. He converted the old abbey into a house, though most of the current structure dates from substantial rebuilding in the eighteenth century. By the early twentieth century, when owned by the Meinertzhagen family, the house was a popular London retreat for writers such as George Bernard Shaw. In 1934, the estate passed to the Russell family, who improved the gardens and employed artist Rex Whistler to decorate the drawing room, whose trompe l'oeil murals give the room a rather kitsch Gothic air.

Inside the house you can wander around the impressive Derek Hill collection of paintings, which is particularly strong on the twentieth-century Modern Movement, with works by artist such as Barbara Hepworth, Ben Nicholson, Vanessa Bell, Walter Sickert, Augustus John, Graham Sutherland and Lowry. There's also a good showing of Impressionism from Bonnard, Degas, Corot and Seurat. Outside the house, you'll have to search hard to see the beautiful mosaic Angel of Mottisfont, created by Russian artist Boris Anrep: it's hidden away in a niche in the outer wall of the chapter house, beneath the steps down from the Morning Room. The estate, which has its own café, also lays on various events during the year; check the National Trust website (Ⓦwww.nationaltrust.org.uk) for details.

Two miles northeast of Romsey and around three miles southeast of Mottisfont are the **Hillier Gardens** (late Oct to late March 10am–5pm, late March to late Oct 10am–6pm; until 7.30pm Thurs June–Aug; £8.25); note that on Sundays (May–Sept), a free bus service runs from Romsey station to Hillier Gardens and on to Mottisfont (see p.234). Named after its founder, Sir Harold Hillier, the gardens consist largely of over 40,000 trees and shrubs – including rare species from round the world – covering an area of 180 acres. Spring is particularly vibrant when the camellias, azaleas and magnolias are in bloom, but it also includes an impressive Winter Garden. Look out, too, for the Nepalese garden with plants native to the Himalayas. There is also a teahouse and smart restaurant, which has an outdoor terrace, while the website has details of various events, which include live music performances (Ⓦwww.hilliergardens.org.uk).

Along Southampton Water

The shipping motorway of Southampton Water heads south into the Solent, with the fringes of the New Forest on the west side (see p.186). Within easy commuting distance of Southampton, the east bank is fairly built up, but there are a couple of places that make an easy day-trip: **Netley Abbey** village, with its ruins of a Cistercian monastery and fine country park, and the quaint **Hamble-le-Rice**, a yachting town on the banks of the pretty River Hamble.

Netley Abbey

Around three miles east of Southampton over the Toll bridge (cars 50p) lies the village of **Netley Abbey**, which is also served by regular Southampton City buses #16A/#17A, or by train from Southampton Central. Overlooking the container ships and refineries of Southampton Water, it is not the most handsome of places, but it does boast some fine historic buildings. Foremost of these is the **Abbey**

(April–Sept daily 10am–6pm; Oct–March 10am–3pm; free), which gives the place its name. Though substantially ruined, this is nevertheless the most complete Cistercian monastery remaining in the south of England. The abbey was founded in 1238 by Bishop of Winchester Peter des Roches and housed monks from the nearby Beaulieu Abbey (see p.183). In 1556, Henry VIII granted the abbey to Sir William Paulet in 1536 after the Dissolution, and the new owner turned it into a Tudor mansion. This was abandoned in the eighteenth century, and the resulting ruins were later visited by various writers and artists – it was painted by Constable and thought to be the inspiration for Jane Austen's *Northanger Abbey*. Much of its appeal today is that it is open to the elements – in summer the walls of its ruined halls and rooms give shelter to families and picnickers. Paulet also built a castle in Netley as part of Henry VIII's coastal defences – this has now been turned into flats and is not open to the public.

Netley Abbey's other historic building is on the opposite side of the village in the expansive grounds of the **Royal Victoria Country Park** (daily: April–Sept 8am–9pm; Oct–March 8am–5pm; free), where the distinctive red-brick chapel and tower are all that remains of the once enormous Royal Victoria Hospital. You can look round what is left of the building, go up its distinctive tower, and learn about its fascinating history: it was opened in 1863 to treat casualties of the Crimean War, the injured arriving on hospital ships in nearby Southampton. The original hospital was a quarter of a mile long and had nearly 1000 beds, though Florence Nightingale – who was consulted about the design – felt that its layout was out of date before it even opened. During World War I, the hospital treated some 50,000 patients, including war poet Wilfred Owen. In World War II, the Americans used the hospital for the D-day landings, but it was closed in the 1950s and largely demolished in the 1960s. Elsewhere, the country park has numerous woodland trails, a shingle beach, playground, café and miniature train (£1.50) – enough to keep restless children amused for several hours.

Hamble-le-Rice

Some two and a half miles east of Netley Abbey (or slightly less if you walk the coastal path), and served by the regular bus #16 from Southampton via Netley Abbey, neighbouring **Hamble-le-Rice** ("rice" meaning a small hill) has a very different feel. This affluent yachties' village clusters round the attractive waters of the River Hamble with the focus of life being its sailing club and marina. It was also the location for the filming of the 1980s drama *Howard's Way*. There are no specific sights here, though you could easily while away half a day watching the comings and goings of the sailing boats or crabbing from the jetty, while in summer regular boat trips ply up and down the river (£6, children £4). You could also take one of the little bright-pink ferries across the river to Warsash: press the button if the ferryman is not there (daily 9am–6pm or dusk, weather permitting; £1.50 single). There are some great walks on this side of the river, especially heading north along the evocatively named Bunny Meadows.

Back in Hamble, half a dozen **pubs and cafés** cluster round the cobbled High Street that wends down to the waterside. Best of these is *The Bugle* on the High Street (☎02380 453000), with an interior of bare bricks and wood beams. As well as sandwiches and burgers, the pub serves excellent sharing platters for two such as paella (£18) and charcuterie (£14). An alternative is *Bonne Bouche*, further up the High Street (☎01703 455771), an inexpensive café-deli serving top-quality meats, cheeses, breads and some superb fresh salads, such as watermelon and haloumi, from around £3.50, with tables on outdoor decking. *The King and Queen*, on the High Street, is the place to go for real ales, while the *Driftwood*, on Rope Walk at the bottom of the High Street, does good Thai food.

The Solent Way

The seven-mile walk from Southampton to Hamble-le-Rice is the first of the eastern stretch of the **Solent Way**, a 60-mile coastal path stretching from Milford, south of the New Forest, to Emsworth, north of Hayling Island. Waymarked with a picture of a sea bird and also known as the **Solent Coast Path**, the best stretch of the path can be picked up from Netley Abbey from where it is an easy two-mile walk to Hamble. You can then take the ferry to Warsash for the next section, a pleasant seven-mile coastal walk to Lee-on-Solent along marshland and low cliffs. For details of the whole route, see ⓦ www.solentway.co.uk.

Portsmouth and around

PORTSMOUTH occupies the peninsula of Portsea Island, on the eastern flank of a huge harbour. This position has meant it has developed into Britain's foremost naval station, a flourishing port and a large industrialized city, its harbour swarming with naval frigates, dredgers, tugs and ferries bound for the continent or the Isle of Wight. Heavily bombed during the last war, much of the city is now made up of bland tower blocks, but it has a great array of attractions for visitors, which more than compensates. The still substantially walled **Old Portsmouth**, based around the original harbour, preserves some Georgian and Tudor character, while a little to the north, the revitalized **Gunwharf Quays** form an attractive waterfront hub of shops, cafés and restaurants, dominated by the impressive **Spinnaker Tower**. Head a little north and you'll find the historic ships and attractions of the **Historic Dockyard**, including HMS *Victory* and the *Mary Rose*, while half a mile beyond lies **Charles Dickens' Birthplace**. East of here is **Southsea**, a lively residential seaside suburb sitting alongside a shingle beach, where a long Georgian terrace overlooks a large green dotted with naval monuments as well as the engrossing **D-day Museum**, **Southsea Castle** and the **Royal Marines Museum**. Further military museums are over the water in **Gosport**, home to the Submarine Museum and Museum of Naval Firepower, while coastal defences can also be admired at nearby **Porchester Castle**, **Fort Nelson** and **Spitbank Fort**, the latter lying offshore.

Some history

The Romans raised a fortress on the northernmost edge of this inlet, but wealthy merchant Jean de Gisors is generally credited as the city founder when he built a settlement on the island of **Portsea** in 1180 at a sheltered spot for his fleet of ships. The town was given a royal charter in 1184 and by the following century it had become a major port exporting wool and grain. The 1300s saw the port employed as a base for the armies of Henry III and Edward I from which to attack France, but the following century, Portsmouth's wooden buildings were frequently torched by invading French soldiers. The town was pretty vulnerable until Henry VII improved its fortifications, established the world's first dry dock here and made Portsmouth a royal dockyard in 1495. Henry VIII invested further in Portsmouth, building **Southsea Castle** (1544), probably the spot from where he watched his flagship the *Mary Rose* sink in the harbour a year later. By the sixteenth century, Portsmouth's role as a port declined and it was hit heavily by the plague. During the English Civil War, the town governor's royalist leanings saw the city bombarded from

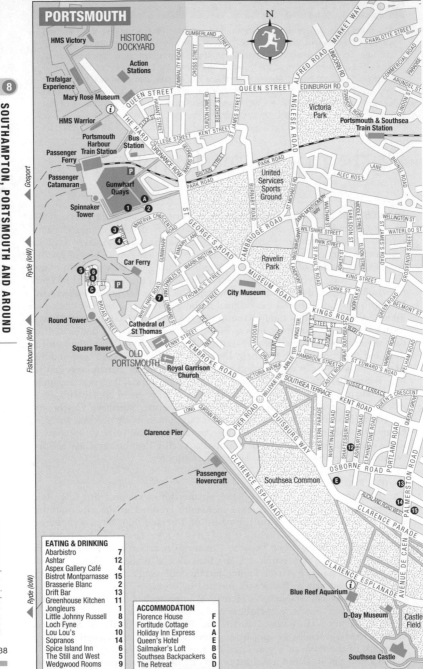

PORTSMOUTH

N

HMS Victory

HISTORIC DOCKYARD

Action Stations

Trafalgar Experience

Mary Rose Museum

HMS Warrior

Portsmouth Harbour Train Station

Bus Station

Passenger Ferry

Passenger Catamaran

Gunwharf Quays

Spinnaker Tower

Car Ferry

Round Tower

Cathedral of St Thomas

Square Tower

OLD PORTSMOUTH

Royal Garrison Church

Clarence Pier

Passenger Hovercraft

CUMBERLAND STREET

CROSS STREET

QUEEN STREET

Victoria Park

Portsmouth & Southsea Train Station

EDINBURGH RD

ALFRED ROAD

MARKET WAY

CHARLOTTE STREET

United Services Sports Ground

Ravelin Park

City Museum

Kings Road

Southsea Terrace

Pembroke Road

Victoria Avenue

Pier Road

Duisburg Way

Southsea Common

Clarence Esplanade

Clarence Parade

Blue Reef Aquarium

D-Day Museum

Castle Field

Southsea Castle

EATING & DRINKING

Abarbistro	7
Ashtar	12
Aspex Gallery Café	4
Bistrot Montparnasse	15
Brasserie Blanc	2
Drift Bar	13
Greenhouse Kitchen	11
Jongleurs	1
Little Johnny Russell	8
Loch Fyne	3
Lou Lou's	10
Sopranos	14
Spice Island Inn	6
The Still and West	5
Wedgwood Rooms	9

ACCOMMODATION

Florence House	F
Fortitude Cottage	C
Holiday Inn Express	A
Queen's Hotel	E
Sailmaker's Loft	B
Southsea Backpackers	G
The Retreat	D

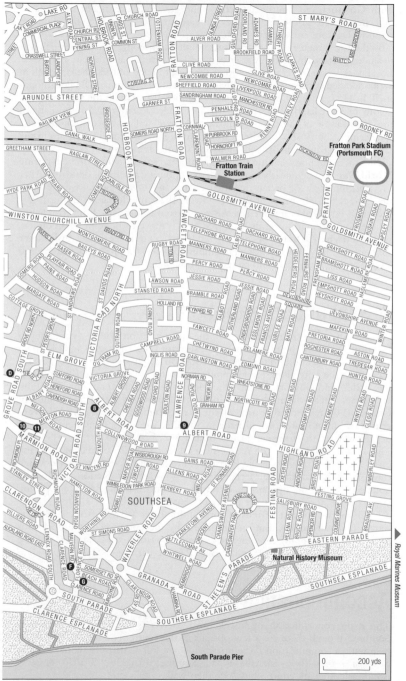

© Crown copyright

▶ Royal Marines Museum

both **Gosport** and Southsea Castle – the governor eventually surrendered and negotiated good terms after threatening to blow up the military gunpowder store and the city with it.

By the late seventeenth century, Portsmouth had become one of Europe's best defended ports, surrounded by a series of walls and castles, and the city flourished. Local dock workers were granted royal approval to build outside the city walls in a suburb called Portsea, which quickly expanded to be larger than Old Portsmouth itself. In 1787, a fleet of ships left from Portsmouth to establish the first European colony in Australia. By 1809, the city had expanded to embrace Southsea and in the 1860s, most of the now redundant old town walls were demolished. The nineteenth century also saw the birth of two highly influential Victorians in the city, Isambard Kingdom Brunel (1806) and Charles Dickens (1812).

Due to its military importance, Portsmouth was heavily bombed during **World War II**, when nearly ten percent of its housing stock was destroyed. After the war, hundreds of prefabs, council estates and tower blocks were put up throughout the city, many of them following the slum clearances of the 1950s. Industrial estates also appeared as the city looked to diversify from its reliance on the docks, though recently there has been a move to building retail outlets, with **Gunwharf Quays** opening in 2001. Its centrepiece is the **Spinnaker Tower**, originally conceived as a millennium project and finally opened in 2005 after years of controversy and budgetary wrangling.

Arrival and information

Portsmouth's main **train station** is in the city centre, but the line continues to **Harbour Station**, the most convenient stop for the main sights and old town and where you'll also find the main **bus station**. High-speed passenger **ferries** leave from the jetty alongside Harbour Station for Ryde, on the Isle of Wight (see p.253), and Gosport, on the other side of Portsmouth Harbour. Wightlink car ferries depart from the ferry port off Gunwharf Road, just south of Gunwharf Quays, for Fishbourne on the Isle of Wight (see p.267), while **hovercraft** leave from Clarence Esplanade in Southsea for Ryde. Continental ferries depart from north of the centre, just off the M275 (see p.247).

Most of central Portsmouth is accessible on foot, though you may need to use bus #16a, which runs from Old Portsmouth to Southsea's seafront or #5 which runs from the continental ferry terminal to Harbour Station and on to Southsea. As it is on a peninsula, **driving** into Portsmouth can be slow-going at peak times, though there are plenty of central car parks.

There are two **tourist offices** in Portsmouth (both ☎02392 826722, ⓦwww .visitportsmouth.co.uk), one on The Hard, by the entrance to the dockyards (daily 9.30am–5.15pm), the other at Clarence Esplanade on Southsea's seafront (daily 9.15am–5.30pm), next to the Blue Reef Aquarium.

Accommodation

The main concentration of **hotels and B&Bs** is south of the centre in Southsea, though there are a few options in the centre. The tourist offices can help with accommodation if the ones below are full. **Campers** should head to *Southsea Leisure Park*, Melville Road, Southsea (☎02392 735070, ⓦwww .southsealeisurepark.com) – bus #15, then walk.

Central Portsmouth

Fortitude Cottage 51 Broad St ☎02392 823748, ⓦwww.fortitudecottage.co.uk. Stylish B&B in Portsmouth Old Town overlooking the ferry terminal and Gunwharf Quays. The top-floor room has its own roof terrace (£105), two others have harbour views (£85), and the lower-floor rooms are least expensive (£65) but lack an outlook. ❷

Holiday Inn Express The Plaza, Gunwharf Quays ☎02392 894240, ⓦwww.hiexpress.co.uk. Rooms in this modern hotel are compact, and its position, right on Gunwharf Quays, can't be faulted. There's a large and airy breakfast room and bar too. ❺

Sailmaker's Loft 5 Bath Square ☎02392 823045, ⓦwww.sailmakersloft.org.uk. This modern B&B is just back from the waterfront, right opposite *The Still* pub, though top-floor rooms peer over the water. It's worth paying the extra £5 to have your own bathroom. ❷

Southsea

Florence House 2 Malvern Rd, Southsea ☎02392 751666, ⓦwww.florencehousehotel .co.uk. Very tastefully furnished, boutique B&B in a pleasant backstreet close to Southsea's waterfront. This Edwardian townhouse has a range of rooms over three floors, all spick and span with flat-screen TVs. There's a tiny downstairs bar, and communal lounge and parking permits can be provided. ❸

Queen's Hotel Clarence Parade, Southsea ☎02392 822466, ⓦwww.queenshotelportsmouth .com. This giant Edwardian pile sits in its own grounds overlooking Southsea's common and the sea beyond. Communal areas are extravagantly decorated – think chandeliers and soaring painted ceilings – though the rooms are contemporary (with wi-fi), with the best ones at the front having balconies. There's also a restaurant and champagne bar. ❺, breakfast £10 extra.

The Retreat 35 Grove Rd South, Southsea ☎02392 353701, ⓦwww.theretreatguesthus .co.uk. A clean, well-kept guest house in a Grade II listed building, an easy walk from the centre of Southsea. The rooms are bright with tasteful modern decor and flat-screen TVs. ❷

Southsea Backpackers 4 Florence Rd, Southsea ☎02392 832495, ⓦwww.portsmouthbackpackers .co.uk. Well-run hostel close to Southsea's front, with four-bed dorms (£15 per person) along with doubles and twin rooms (£34); there is also a communal kitchen, lounge, laundry, parking and use of garden.

Gunwharf Quays and Old Portsmouth

A short walk from Harbour train station lies the sleek **Gunwharf Quays** development, the shopping and social hub of the city and the place where you're most likely to have a night out or get an inexpensive meal. It shelters myriad stylish cafés, restaurants, nightclubs and retail outlets and is also the departure point for **boat tours** round the harbour (see p.246). It's also home to Portsmouth's iconic and hugely impressive **Spinnaker Tower** (daily 10am–6pm; £7). Opened in 2005, the elegant, sail-like structure rises 170m above the city, offering stunning vistas for up to twenty miles over land and sea. The three viewing decks can be reached by a high-speed lift, the highest one being open to the elements, though most people stick to View Deck 1, which has one of Europe's largest glass floors – despite its obvious strength, it is still nerve-wracking standing on it and peering vertically down. Also worth a visit is the **Aspex Gallery** in Vulan Building (Tues–Sat 10.30am–6pm, Sun 11am–5pm; ⓦwww.aspex.org.uk) in a former naval storehouse behind *Loch Fyne* (see p.246), which hosts temporary contemporary art exhibits and has a fine café.

It's a well-signposted fifteen-minute walk south of the tower to what remains of **Old Portsmouth**. Along the way, you pass the simple **Cathedral of St Thomas** on the High Street, whose original twelfth-century features have been obscured by rebuilding after the Civil War and again in the twentieth century. The nave was finally completed in 1991, leaving a pleasing light and airy building. The High Street ends at a maze of cobbled Georgian streets huddling behind an impressive fifteenth-century wall protecting the old port, where Walter Raleigh landed the first potatoes and tobacco from the New World. You can walk along the top of the walls past the Tudor **Round Tower** and neighbouring Square tower, both popular vantage points for observing nautical activities. The latter is open one Wednesday a month (May–July; free), and details its history as the home to the town Governor in Tudor times and later its use as a gunpowder store. Also in Old Portsmouth lie the atmospheric ruins of the Royal Garrison Church (free). Dating back to 1212, when it was built as a hospice for pilgrims on their way to Winchester, it was converted into a garrison church in 1560, before being partly destroyed by a fireball in 1941.

The Historic Dockyard

Portsmouth's biggest draw is the **Historic Dockyard** in the **Royal Naval Base** at the end of Queen Street (daily: April–Oct 10am–6pm; Nov–March 10am–5.30pm; last entry 1hr before closing; ⓦwww.historicdockyard.co.uk). It's made up of a series of warehouses and museums and ships that were the powerhouse of the Royal Navy for centuries. You can visit each ship separately (£12.50), though most people opt for an all-inclusive ticket (£18), which allows for one visit of the *Mary Rose*, HMS *Victory* and a harbour boat trip, plus unlimited visits to the remaining attractions – it is valid for a year. Part of the Dockyard's appeal is that it is unprettified, with plenty of guards on patrol and signs highlighting the latest security status adding an extra touch of authenticity.

Most first-time visitors head to the end of the long cobbled street to the historic highlight, the ornately wooden-fronted **HMS Victory**, famed for being the victorious ship against Napoleon in the Battle of Trafalgar. The ship was already forty years old when she set sail from Portsmouth for Trafalgar on September 14, 1805. Shortly afterwards, off the coast of Spain, Nelson was shot by a French musketeer after the ship had successfully broken through Napoleon's lines. A plaque on the deck marks the spot where he was mortally wounded, while the hold has a shrine marking the place where he finally expired. You can also see the wooden cask in which his dead body was preserved in brandy for its return to the UK. Arrows point you round various decks, which get progressively more claustrophobic as you head downwards. It is hard not to contrast Nelson and Hardy's lavish polished quarters at the rear – with private bedrooms and dining rooms – with the cramped hammocks strung up for the rest of the crew in the dingy lower decks. You can still see the leg irons and cat-o'-nine tails (see box, p.143) for those who disobeyed orders; the gallery's giant Brodie stove, the huge potential fire risk used to cook for the substantial crew; and the surprisingly airy sick bay. But above all else it is the ship's sheer size and power that are impressive – its cannons could fire shot almost a mile while a naval army of more than 140 marines could be stationed in the middle deck, ready for battle. Although badly damaged during the Battle of Trafalgar, the *Victory* continued in service for a further twenty years, before being retired to the dry dock where she rests today.

Opposite the ship is the **Trafalgar Experience** museum, which has a film show recreating the battle in vivid and noisy fashion. Here you can also learn about knots and shipbuilding techniques while upstairs you'll see an exhibition on the history of slavery and a fine selection of giant figureheads, rescued from various scrapped ships over the last couple of centuries. There is also Nelson's funeral barge, which was used to parade his body down the Thames in 1806.

Nearest the entrance to the complex is the youngest ship, **HMS Warrior**, dating from 1860. It was Britain's first armoured (iron-clad) battleship, complete with sails and steam engines, and was the pride of the fleet in its day. Longer and faster than any previous naval vessel, and the first to be fitted with

Naval vernacular

Many phrases still in use in English today owe their origins to the country's seafaring heritage. Below are some of the more familiar expressions believed to date from around Nelson's time.

"Three square meals a day" Sailors aboard the *Victory* were served a meagre trio of daily meals on square wooden plates.

"Let the cat out of the bag" and **"Not enough room to swing a cat"** Both refer to the cat–o'-nine-tails, a nine-thonged whip with knots at the end of each thong. Taking the "cat" out of its baize bag was obviously not a good sign, and floggings were carried out on the upper deck where there was enough room to get a good swing at the wrongdoer.

"Limeys" This nickname for Brits derives from the casks of lime juice ships carried to prevent scurvy.

"Grog" Slang for alcohol still current in Australia. In Nelson's time sailors were allocated a gallon of beer or a pint of rum a day: in the early 1700s, Admiral Vernon, noted for his coat made of grogram (a stiff silk and wool fabric) and so-nicknamed "Old Grog", became notorious for watering down the daily servings.

"Turn a blind eye" Part of Nelson's early reputation was made on his irreverent attitude to authority. At the Battle of Copenhagen, the arrogant second-in-command thought he knew best and "ignored" unnecessary signals from other ships by holding the telescope to his blind eye.

"Son of a gun" A scoundrel. Women unfortunate enough to give birth on ship did so between the cannons to keep the gangways clear.

---

washing machines, the *Warrior* was described by Napoleon III as a "black snake amongst the rabbits". The ship displays a wealth of weaponry, including rifles, pistols and sabres, though it was never challenged nor even fired a cannon in her 22 years at sea.

Close to the *Warrior*, the **Mary Rose Museum** (closes 5.30pm, Nov–March at 4.45pm) is dedicated to Henry VIII's flagship, which capsized off Spithead drowning almost all her seven-hundred-strong crew. The museum contains an absorbing collection of objects retrieved from the wreck, including guns, gold coins and implements from the Barber Surgeon's cabin. The ship itself is not on display as its remains are currently undergoing restoration (see box below), but it should be back on view by 2012 in a new high-tech boat-shaped museum currently being built behind HMS *Victory*. Lastly, nearby Action Stations has interactive games, videos and graphics to simulate life on board ship.

Mary Rose

Henry VIII's prize naval ship, built in 1511, the **Mary Rose** was sunk in Portsmouth harbour while fighting invading French forces in 1545 – the king watched it sink from Southsea Castle. It lay there preserved under silt in the Solent until 1982, when archeologists not only salvaged the boat but discovered extremely rare longbows and their arrows, some of them tipped with poison. They also found dice, backgammon sets and a shawm – a long-lost musical instrument. But it will take until around 2012 before the preservation programme will have safeguarded the finds and the boat itself, which is being sprayed with a special solution that will eventually replace the saline water that currently preserves the timbers with a long-lasting wax. In 2007, another section of the ship – the 13-metre-high castle-like bowcastle – was located under the seabed 1.5 miles from Portsmouth, and it is hoped that this can be added to the existing remains when a purpose-built museum opens in 2012.

Charles Dickens' Birthplace and the City Museum

In the north of the city, at 393 Old Commercial Rd is **Charles Dickens' Birthplace** (May–Sept daily 10am–5.30pm & Feb 7 for his birthday; £3.50), set up much as it would have looked when the famous novelist was born here in 1812. Charles' father, John, moved to Portsmouth in 1809 to work for the Navy Pay Office before he was recalled to London in 1815. So Charles was only here for three years, but nevertheless he is said to have returned often and set parts of *Nicholas Nickleby* in the city. The modest house not only contains period furniture but a wealth of information about the time Dickens lived here and the influences on his novels.

Another famous novelist also spent time in the city: Arthur Conan Doyle wrote his first Sherlock Holmes novels while working as a GP in Southsea having moved here in 1882. His house was destroyed in the war, but fortunately a stack of Conan Doyle memorabilia was left to the nation after the death of avid collector and Sherlock Holmes' expert Richard Green in 2004. Today, some of the 15,000 books and correspondence he amassed can be seen at **City Museum** at 3 Museum Rd (daily: April–Sept 10am–5.30pm; Oct–March 10am–5pm; free; Ⓦ www.portsmouthmuseums.co.uk), which also has re-creations of rooms throughout history together with various exhibits and paintings relating to the history of Portsmouth, as well as temporary exhibitions.

Gosport

With a couple of museums worth visiting, otherwise humdrum **Gosport** can be reached by taking the passenger ferry from Harbour train station jetty (every 10–15min daily 5.30am–midnight; £2.30 return; Ⓦ www.gosportferry.co.uk). The naval theme is continued here at the **Royal Submarine Museum** on Haslar Jetty (daily: April–Oct 10am–5.30pm; Nov–March 10am–4.30pm, last tour 1hr before closing; £9), with six submarines, some of which you can enter. Allow a couple of hours to explore these slightly creepy vessels – a guided tour inside HMS *Alliance* gives you an insight into how cramped life was on board, and the museum elaborates evocatively on the long history of submersible craft. Nearby, housed in the old armaments depot at Priddy's Hard, **Explosion! The Museum of Naval Firepower** (Sat & Sun 10am–4pm, last entry 1hr before

Spitbank Fort

A mile out in the harbour, **Spitbank Fort** is an offshore bastion of granite, iron and brick little altered since its construction. The circular sea fort was commissioned by Lord Palmerston in 1860 to defend Portsmouth from French attack, and was finished in 1878, actually never to be used in war. With over fifty rooms linked by passages and steps on two floors, the complex includes a 135-metre-deep well, which still draws fresh water from below the seafloor, and an inner courtyard with a café and sheltered terrace, where club nights, private parties and Sunday lunches are sometimes held. Every other Wednesday, Gosport Ferries runs a boat with guided tours of the fort (£14; Ⓦ www.gosportferry.co.uk), as well as Sunday lunches, club nights and events; contact ☎01329 242077, Ⓦ www.spitbankfort.com.

closing; £4) tells the story of naval warfare from the days of gunpowder to the present, with weapons of all descriptions, including mines, big guns and torpedoes, all backed up by vivid computer animations.

Southsea

Wrapped around a broad, grassy common, **Southsea** is an appealing suburb facing a shingle beach, with some fine nineteenth-century architecture, much of it designed by Victorian Thomas Ellis Owen. The main tourist sights are all lined along the seafront, though the inland streets are also worth exploring – Osborne Road for its ethnic restaurants; Marmion Road for quirky independent boutiques; and Albert Road for its trendy bars and cafés and antique and bric-a-brac shops.

Along the seafront, Southsea's most historic building, marked by a little lighthouse, is the squat **Southsea Castle** (April–Oct daily 10am–5pm; £3.50), built from the remains of Beaulieu Abbey (see p.183). You can go inside the keep and learn about Portsmouth's military history, as well as climbing up to the spot from where Henry VIII is said to have watched the *Mary Rose* sink in 1545 (see p.243), though in fact you can get just as good views by climbing along the adjacent seafront ramparts. Just back from the castle is the **D-day Museum** on Clarence Esplanade (daily: April–Sept 10am–5.30pm; Oct–March 10am–5pm; last entry 1hr before closing; £6), focusing on Portsmouth's role as the principal assembly point for the D-day invasion in World War II, code-named "Operation Overlord". The museum's most striking exhibit is the 90-metre-long *Overlord Embroidery*, which illustrates the Normandy landings. Just west of here, next to the tourist office, the **Blue Reef Aquarium**, on Clarence Esplanade (daily: 10am–6pm, last admission 5pm; £9, children £7) has the usual marine life, including tropical fish, sea horses, otters and giant octopus, with a walk-through tunnel and outdoor water play area for children.

Continue east along the seafront and it's ten minutes' walk to the **Natural History Museum** on Eastern Parade (April–Oct 10am–5.30pm; Nov–March 10am–5pm; free), a fairly modest museum detailing the wildlife that visits the area – mostly sea birds, though there is also a butterfly house you can walk through and changing exhibitions. Finally, half a mile or so further along the shoreside South Parade, just past South Parade pier, the **Royal Marines Museum** (daily: 10am–5pm; last entry 1hr before closing; £5.95) describes the greatest campaigns of the navy's elite fighting force from their origins in 1694 right up to recent campaigns in the Gulf. There are interactive exhibits, rifle simulators, displays of medals and military costumes and special events throughout the year. Of most interest are the details of what it takes to make a marine – which is not for the faint-hearted.

Eating and drinking

Places to **eat** are surprisingly scarce in Old Portsmouth, while Gunwharf Quays has all the usual chains, including *Pizza Express*, *Café Rouge* and *Strada*, all with outdoor tables overlooking the bustling harbour. For more independent places, head to Southsea, and Osborne Road, in particular, for its good variety of ethnic cafés and restaurants, including Ethiopian and Lebanese.

Central Portsmouth

Abarbistro 58 White Hart Rd ☎02392 811585. Vibrant bar-restaurant on the edge of Old Portsmouth, serving salads or simple dishes such as burgers and baguettes (£4–8) as well as bistro classics, including *moules* and fishcakes (£10), along with generous mains such as salmon with dill sauce, pasta or steaks from £13. Or just have a drink on the outside terrace.

Aspex Gallery Café Vulcan Building, Gunwharf Quays. Enjoy great coffee, cakes and snacks inside the arty bare brick interior of the Aspex art gallery. Closed eves.

Brasserie Blanc 1 Gunwharf Quays ☎02392 891320. Large modern brasserie with good-value early-evening deals (around £12 for two courses) along with tasty mains such as smoked haddock and leek fishcakes, scallops and fennel or Spanish omelettes (£11–16).

Loch Fyne Unit 2 Vulcan Buildings, Gunwharf Quays ☎02392 778060. Large and homely warehouse conversion serving top-quality fish and seafood including fresh mussels, trout and sea bass from around £12–16. Also has outdoor seating facing the Quays.

Southsea

Ashtar 31 Osborne Rd. Good-value, delicious meze dishes (£3–4), such as vine leaves, *baba ganoush* and falafel, as well as main courses such as chicken kebabs in pitta (£8), all served in an authentic Lebanese atmosphere.

Bistrot Montparnasse 103 Palmerston Rd, Southsea ☎02392 816754. Charming bistro serving two- or three-course set menus for £29–34. Modern British dishes include quail breasts with pomegranate, sea bass with Bombay potatoes and gorgonzola and pea risotto.

Greenhouse Kitchen 59 Marmion Rd ☎02392 815511. Small, friendly vegetarian and vegan café-restaurant with tasty breakfasts, soups, salads, pasta dishes (around £4–5) and some very tempting cakes (daytime only; closed Sun & Mon).

Lou Lou's 37 Marmion Rd ☎02392 825113. French-style brasserie with a lovely tiled interior, with *croques monsieurs, tartiflette*, and goat's cheese salads as well as good breakfasts from around £5. Closed eves & all day Mon.

Sopranos 108 Palmerston Rd. Good-value authentic Italian food, such as pizzas (£7–8), risottos and pasta (from £5), with an Italian moped on the wall for good measure.

Drinking and nightlife

Drift Bar 78 Palmerston Rd, Southsea. Hip lounge bar with a range of cocktails and snacks, including some very good-value lunchtime specials (mains under £4). Live music on Sundays and DJs on Friday and Saturdays.

Jongleurs Vernon Buildings, Gunwharf Quays ⊛www.jongleurs.co.uk. The usual mix of comedy, DJs and bands at this waterfront venue.

Little Johnny Russell Albert Rd ☎023 9282 6502, ⊛www.littlejohnnyrussels.com. Live bands, and club nights featuring DJs like Rob da Bank and Annie Mac, with a regular acoustic night on Tuesdays.

Spice Island Inn 1 Bath Square. Traditional pub in the old town with a lovely seafront terrace, wooden floors inside and good views from the upstairs rooms. It serves decent pub grub, such as steak and ale pie (£9), and has a takeaway fish and chips counter, so that you can sit outside along the harbour walls in true British fashion.

The Still and West 2 Bath Square. A waterfront terrace and cosy interior with views over the harbour make this pub worth stopping by: the food ranges from the traditional fish and chips (£9) to falafel and dips (£4.75) or smoked salmon risotto (£8.75).

Wedgwood Rooms 147b Albert Rd. Well-established Albert Rd venue hosting live music, comedy and club nights.

Listings

Boat trips Various boat trips go round the harbour and Historic Dockyard, and leave from the waterfront at Gunwharf Quays: Blue Boat trips (⊛www .blueboattrips.com) offers 45min tours from £4 a person.

Buses Information on local bus services is available on Traveline ☎0871 200 2233. Buses in the area are run by First Buses (☎02380 584321, ⊛www.firstgroup.com) and Stagecoach (⊛www .stagecoachbus.com). Long-distance buses are operated by National Express (☎08705 808080, ⊛www.nationalexpress.com).

Car rental Avis (☎0844 5446091, ⊛www.avis .co.uk; Europcar (☎02392 650880, ⊛www2 .europcar.co.uk); and Thrifty (☎02392 214888, ⊛www.thrifty.co.uk).

Cinemas The multi-screen Vue in Gunwharf Quays (ⓦ www.myvue.com) and the Odeon in Port Solent (ⓦ www.odeon.co.uk) both show the usual mainstream films.

Cycle tours The tourist office has leaflets of various cycle tours of the city, including the 4.5-mile Seafront Tour, which takes in all the major attractions, and the quirkier Famous Figures ride (7.5 miles), past Peter Sellars', Rudyard Kipling's and H.G. Wells' former homes, amongst others.

Disabled visitors The newer areas of the city, such as Gunwharf Quays are well set up for disabled visitors. There's a useful guide on disabled access in Portsmouth, which you can pick up from the tourist office or download at ⓦ www.visitportsmouth.co.uk/site /accessible-portsmouth.

Ferries Ferries to the Isle of Wight are run by Wightlink (ⓦ www.wightlink.co.uk) and Hovertravel ⓦ www.hovertravel.co.uk. The Gosport ferry is run by Gosport Ferries (ⓦ www.gosportferry.co.uk), and the Hayling Island ferry is run by The Hayling Ferry (ⓦ www.haylingferry.com). Ferries to France and Spain are run by Brittany Ferries (ⓦ www.brittany -ferries.co.uk) and Condor Ferries (ⓦ www .condorferries.co.uk).

Football The south's only Premiership team play at Fratton Park: for details of tickets, see p.34.

Trains Trains are run by Southwest Trains (ⓦ www .southwesttrains.co.uk) to London and South-ampton; First Great Western (ⓦ www.firstgreat western.co.uk) to Salisbury and Bristol; and Southern Railway (ⓦ www.southernrailway.com) along the south coast to Brighton.

Around Portsmouth

The countryside immediately around Portsmouth is not particularly inspiring, though there are a few **attractions** that are worth exploring, two just north of the city and one to the east. Northwest of the city, the countryside improves around Shedfield and Wickham.

Portchester Castle

Portchester Castle (daily: April–Sept 10am–6pm; Oct–March 10am–4pm; £3.70; EH), six miles out of the centre, is just past the marina development at Port Solent. Built by the Romans in the third century, this fortification boasts the finest surviving example of Roman walls in northern Europe – still over

▲ A view from Portchester Castle

seven metres high and incorporating some twenty bastions. The Normans felt no need to make any substantial alterations when they moved in, but a castle was later built within Portchester's precincts by Henry II, which Richard II extended and Henry V used as his garrison when assembling the army that was to fight the Battle of Agincourt. Today its grassy enclosure makes a sheltered spot for a congenial game of cricket or a kickabout with a football.

Fort Nelson and The Royal Armouries Museum

Just north of Portchester Castle, **Fort Nelson** (daily: April–Oct 10am–5pm, Wed from 11am; Nov–March 10.30am–4pm, Wed from 11.30am; free; ⓦ www .royalarmouries.org.uk) is another highly impressive castle, one of a chain of forts along a hill facing Portsmouth and the only one open to the public. Much more extensive than you would think from the outside, it sits in nineteen acres of land on top of Portsdown Hill, with fantastic views south over the Solent and north along the Meon Valley. It was built in the 1860s to protect Portsmouth from attack by the French and subsequently used in the last world wars. Inside you can visit a working blacksmith's forge, prison cells and several eerie underground tunnels. The fort is also home to the **Royal Armouries Museum**, displaying over 350 big guns and cannon from the national arms collection. The exhibits range from the trebuchet used in the film *Gladiator* to wonderfully ornate Portuguese cannons from the fifteenth century, along with guns used in the two world wars to the modern-day monsters, including the Iraqi "supergun" from the first Gulf War. There are also various demonstrations of the weapons during the day, and if you are feeling generous you can even buy your loved one a voucher entitling them to fire a deafening 25-pounder gun, or similar.

Titchfield Abbey

East of Portsmouth, around half a mile north of the village of Titchfield lies **Titchfield Abbey** (daily: April–Sept 10am–5pm; Oct–March 10am–4pm; free; EH), ruins of a thirteenth-century abbey, later rebuilt into a Tudor mansion. The abbey was founded by Peter des Roches, the bishop of Winchester, for the Premonstratensian order. Under the Dissolution, some of the structure was demolished and the rest was handed to one of Henry VIII's loyal civil servants, Thomas Wriothesley. He converted the abbey into Place House, a mansion suitably grand to entertain visitors who included, over the years, not only Henry VIII himself but also Edward VI, Elizabeth I, and possibly Shakespeare, who was a friend of the family and may have put on plays at the house. The house fell into ruins in the eighteenth century, leaving pretty much what you see today – you are free to wander round, with several panels detailing facts about the house and abbey's history.

Wickham Vineyard

In pretty Hampshire countryside northeast of Titchfield, **Wickham Vineyard** in Shedfield (Mon–Sat 10.30am–5.30pm, Sun 11.30am–5pm; £3.50), is a large estate planted with vines producing some decent English wines. You can look around the winery and the vineyard, followed by a tasting session, then meander freely around the surrounding nature reserve. The vineyard is also home to the award-winning *Vatika* restaurant (ⓣ01329 823405, ⓦ www.vatikarestaurant .com), run by Michelin-starred chef Atul Kochar. With a lovely terrace overlooking the vines, the restaurant's menu includes an innovative mix of

Indian-influenced dishes such as quail with strawberry chutney or water buffalo with aubergine: three courses cost £40, or the seven-course tasting menu is £65.

Hayling Island and Emsworth

An anvil-shaped islet jutting into the Solent, **HAYLING ISLAND** is four miles long and the same width at its southern point. Fringed by shingle beaches, its bland bungalows, run-down amusement arcades and bleak cafés won't tempt many beachgoers to linger. Apart from the beach, the main attraction is the somewhat shabby **Funlands** funfair (opening times and prices vary per day and per month, see ⓦ www.funland.info for details), with rides including a roller coaster and the Drop Ride that plunges 35 metres vertically. Of slightly more appeal, a narrow-gauge **railway** runs along the coast from outside Funlands (Wed, Sat & Sun every 20–45min 11am–dusk; daily during school hols; £2 single, £3.50 return) stopping at a couple of stations, Mengham's Road and Eastcoke Corner, a mile to the east.

In recent years, the island has become a popular venue for watersports – its southwest corner is particularly good for **windsurfing** and hosts the Fat Face Night Surf competition in September (ⓦ www.fatface.com/stry/nightwindsurf). Hayling Island even lays claim to founding the sport as local boy Peter Chilvers is credited (in some circles) with making the first windsurf board in 1958. Andy Biggs Watersports on Station Road (☎ 02392 467755, ⓦ www.andybiggs.co.uk) can provide windsurfing lessons, equipment and information on the latest conditions.

The island's only other claim to fame is as home to one of the UK's first holiday camps, used for the filming of the long-running TV series *Hi-De-Hi* and the film *Confessions of a Holiday Camp*. If you are tempted, *Mill Rhythe Holiday Camp*, 16 Havant Rd (☎ 02392 460044, ⓦ www.millrythe.com) still offers family holidays and adult-only breaks with discos and pool parties, spa and sauna and various activities.

Altogether more alluring is the pretty former fishing village of **EMSWORTH** two miles east of the bridge to Hayling Island, on the edge of Chichester Harbour. There are some attractive waterside walks along with a diminutive **museum** on North Street (Easter–Oct Sat 10.30am–4.30pm, Sun 2.30–4.30pm; also Fri in Aug 10.30am–4.30pm; 25p), which traces the town's history and includes information about author P.J. Wodehouse, who lived here for a time. Down at the waterfront, there are two-hour sailing trips on a nineteenth-century traditional sailing boat (☎ 01243 513201; £10), originally built to support the local oyster fleet.

Practicalities

Stagecoach **bus** #31 runs every 40min or so from Havant (for mainland train and coach services) for the 12min run to Hayling Island, or you can take a **ferry** from Eastney (Portsmouth) with departures every 20min (£2.40 single) to the southwest tip of the island. Hayling Island's **tourist office** on the seafront by Funlands (daily 9.30am–5.30pm) can give details of the various B&Bs on the island, though there is not much cause to stay here and you are better off heading for Emsworth, which is on the Portsmouth to London and Brighton train lines (hourly service). Here, comfortable, clean **rooms**, some overlooking the harbour, are at *36 on the Quay* (☎ 01243 375592 ⓦ www.36onthequay .co.uk; ❺) a seventeenth-century harbourside building, with a Michelin-starred **restaurant**: it's £47 for a three-course dinner, though the delicious, exquisitely presented food is more reasonably priced at lunch (£21 for two courses). Just up from here, in a former fisherman's cottage, superb food is also on offer at *Fat Olives*, 30 High St (☎01243 377914; closed Mon), which serves starters such as prawn *arancini* (£7) and mains such as braised lamb and samphire or sea bass with black olive oil; mains are around £15, or three-course lunch menu for £19. For a drink or simpler pub grub, head to the pretty hamlet of Langstone, at the entrance to Hayling Island, where there are a couple of good waterfront **pubs**. Overlooking the harbour is the fifteenth-century *Royal Oak* with stone floors, open fires and real ales, while the *Ship Inn* has a large waterfront patio and serves pub classics, as well as fresh local fish.

North of Portsmouth

Fifteen miles north of Portsmouth, **Hambledon** is an unexceptional village but one that has a special place in the heart of cricket fans, with one of the oldest cricket clubs in the world. Formed in 1750, Hambledon were England's top club for the second half of the eighteenth century and claim to have developed the modern game. The original cricket club in fact played in nearby Clanfield, where you'll find a memorial stone to the ground as well as the cosy *Bat and Ball Inn*. Once run by the club's captain, the pub was considered for a time the centre of the cricketing empire – especially after the village team soundly thrashed England in 1777. The President of Hambledon then helped form the MCC in 1787, establishing laws of the game already used by the village club and which now form the backbone of today's game.

Around five miles northwest, just off the A3(M), **Queen Elizabeth Country Park** spreads over the highest point of the South Downs and is Hampshire's largest park, passed through by a section of the South Downs Way. There's a visitor centre with café and shop (daily 10am–5.30pm, until 4.30pm Nov–Feb), which can give out maps detailing the various waymarked walking trails, cycle routes, children's play areas and barbecue areas. Once you've got your map, it's best to get clear of this part of the park, which is blighted by traffic noise – there are various car parks dotted round the park interior. The park also spreads northwest under the motorway onto the lower slopes of **Butser Hill** from where there are great views from alongside the radio mast (270m). This area is also a popular spot for hang-gliding and paragliding (check Ⓦwww.skysurfingclub.co.uk for details). Here, too, you'll find the **Butser Ancient Farm** (Easter–Sept Mon–Fri 10am–5pm; £6, children £3; Ⓦwww .butserancientfarm.co.uk), a reconstruction of an Iron Age village and a Roman villa. You can also reach this directly off the A3(M), a couple of miles west of Clanfield. Several Iron Age roundhouses have been built for visitors to explore and get an insight into family life in the Iron Age. There are also demonstrations of ancient techniques, such as spinning and thatching, as well as Roman cookery. Regular workshops (book in advance on ☎02392 598838) are also held, focusing on activities like bronze smelting and hedgerow basketry.

The Isle of Wight

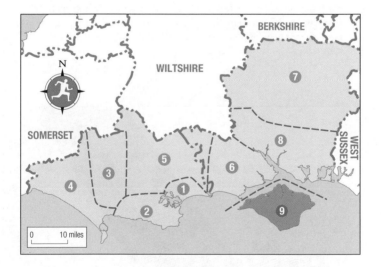

CHAPTER 9

Highlights

✳ **Cowes** At its liveliest during Cowes Week, this yachting town remains one of the island's most appealing, whatever the time of year. See p.256

✳ **Osborne House** It's easy to see why this house and gardens was Queen Victoria's favourite getaway. See p.258

✳ **Carisbrooke Castle** There are great views from a castle that has seen more than its fair share of historical events. See p.263

✳ **Bonchurch** There are some great walks around this pretty village, which has been an inspiration for several writers. See p.275

✳ **Compton Bay** One of the island's best beaches on the unspoilt southeast coast. See p.278

✳ **Tennyson Down** Walk out to the Needles along this exhilarating cliff-top path. See p.280

▲ Cowes week

The Isle of Wight

T here is nowhere in England quite like the **ISLE OF WIGHT**. Its beaches and scenery are as good as any on the south coast, yet it seems anchored in a past decade, before cars and multinationals ruled the roost. But though – or perhaps because – there are no motorways, few chain stores and a refreshingly laid-back pace of life, the island has started to attract a younger, livelier crowd. Parts of it, at least, can lay claim to being cool –

Sea routes to the Isle of Wight

There are three **departure points** from the mainland to the Isle of Wight – Portsmouth, Southampton and Lymington. **Fare structures** on all routes and with all carriers are labyrinthine, varying according to the time of day of travel, how long you are staying on the island and how far in advance you book: all companies, however, offer regular special offers, so check their websites for details. Note also that many hotels offer packages with the ferry included, which can work out cheaper than booking independently.

Lymington in the New Forest (see p.194) **to Yarmouth** is the most westerly and the fastest car ferry route, taking about 30 minutes. **Wightlink** car ferries (☎0871 376 1000, ⓦwww.wightlink.co.uk) run from 5.15am to midnight (also one ferry at 3.45am); frequencies vary from hourly to every 45 minutes at peak times, and every 90 minutes at quieter times. Trains from Brockenhurst, connecting with services from London Waterloo, run directly to the pier for the boat.

From **Southampton** (see p.222), there are two routes, both run by **Red Funnel** (☎0844 844 9988, ⓦwww.redfunnel.co.uk). The Red Jet Highspeed catamaran for foot passengers runs **to West Cowes** every 30 minutes throughout the day (hourly after 9pm) from 5.45am–11.43pm: the journey time is 25 minutes. A free shuttle bus from Southampton Central station to the ferry terminal connects with train services from London Waterloo. The car ferry runs from Southampton **to East Cowes** from 6am–10.15pm (April–Oct hourly; Nov–March every 90min), with an extra service at 4am; the journey time is 55 minutes.

From **Portsmouth** (see p.237) there are three routes. **Hovertravel** (☎023 9281 1000 or 01983 811000, ⓦwww.hovertravel.co.uk) runs hovercrafts from Clarence Esplanade in Southsea **to Ryde** every 30 minutes for foot passengers only (6.30am–8pm, 8.30pm in summer high season): the journey time is 10 minutes. **Wightlink** (see above for contact details) runs high-speed catamarans for foot passengers from Portsmouth Harbour to the end of Ryde Pier (4.15am–00.15am; every 30min at peak times; hourly at quieter times): the journey time is 20 minutes. Services at Portsmouth Harbour connect with trains from London Waterloo, while at Ryde, they connect with Island Line trains. Wightlink also runs a car ferry **to Fishbourne** from the Gunwharf Terminal in Portsmouth (every 30min: every 2hr from 9pm–5am); journey time is 40 minutes.

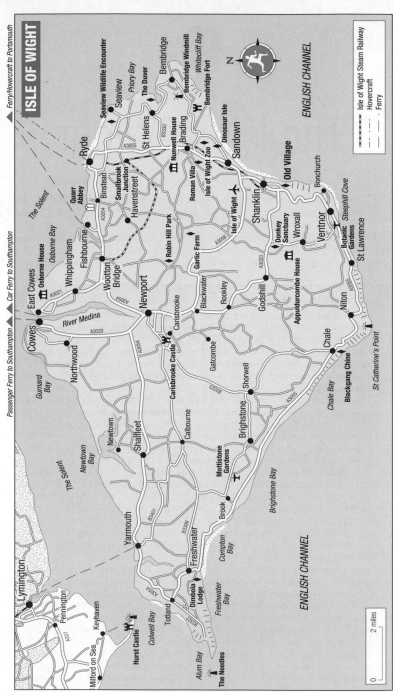

ISLE OF WIGHT

N

ENGLISH CHANNEL

— Isle of Wight Steam Railway
– · – Hovercraft
— Ferry

always popular with the yachting crowd, it now hosts two of the UK's best music festivals. It is England's smallest county – at least at high tide (at low tide, Rutland is smaller) – and measuring less than 23 miles at its widest point, the island packs in a surprising variety of landscapes. North of the chalk ridge that runs across its centre, the terrain is low-lying woodland and pasture, deeply cut by meandering rivers, while southwards lie open chalky downs fringed by high cliffs. All this makes it a terrific place for **walking** and **cycling**, and there are waymarked trails throughout the island.

The island has long attracted holiday-makers, and was favoured by such eminent Victorians as Tennyson, Dickens, Swinburne, Julia Margaret Cameron and Queen Victoria herself, who made **Osborne House** near **Cowes**, her permanent home after Albert died. This should be on anyone's itinerary, as should the sturdy remains of **Carisbrooke Castle**, near the island's capital, **Newport**, and the stunning landscape around **The Needles** at its westernmost tip. Most visitors, however, are drawn by its beaches, which range from the relatively remote **Whitecliff** and **Compton bays** to the popular sandy resort beaches at **Ryde**, **Sandown**, **Shanklin** and **Ventnor**. With its unreliable climate and the drawback of pricey ferry crossings, the island has also invested heavily in attractions that do not rely on the weather. These include a steam railway, a country park, funfairs, zoo, model village and dinosaur theme park, while the National Trust is also well represented in various country houses and historic buildings throughout the island. Though you can easily see much of the island on a day-trip, give yourself the best part of a week to do it justice and to tune in to the relaxed ambience.

For **information** on the Isle of Wight, call ☎01983 813818, consult ⓦwww .islandbreaks.co.uk, or call in at the tourist offices detailed in the text.

Getting around and information

Most places on the island are served by public transport, so it's possible to get around without a car, though the frequency of the buses is pretty patchy. You can pick up the free *Isle of Wight Public Transport Handbook* on your ferry crossing or from tourist offices on the island, which has detailed bus and train routes and timetables.

Buses are run by two companies: Southern Vectis (☎01983 827000, ⓦwww .islandbuses.info) and Wightbus (☎01983 823782, ⓦwww.iwight.com): both have timetable and route information on their websites. Southern Vectis also runs open-top tourist buses with commentaries along four different routes around the island. The price of an open-top bus tour is the same as a **day rover ticket** (£10, children £5), which gives you unlimited bus travel for 24 hours. Better value still is the **weekly freedom pass** (£20, children £10), which allows unlimited travel on all the island's buses, including the open-top buses. In addition, Ryde and Sandown have **road trains**, running along their seafronts, while Shanklin has a road train connecting its seafront to the old town and train station (all road trains every 40–50min).

There are two **rail lines** on the island: the eight-mile Island Line from Ryde Pier to Shanklin, via Brading and Sandown (ⓦwww.island-line.co.uk), which uses reconditioned London Underground tube trains; and the five-mile Isle of Wight Steam Railway from Wootton to Smallbrook Junction, where it connects with the Island Line (ⓦwww.iwsteamrailway.co.uk). **Cycling** is a popular way of getting around the island, but beware that in summer the narrow lanes can get very busy. For **bike rental** and guided rides contact Wight Cycle Hire (☎01983 761800, ⓦwww.wightcyclehire.co.uk), which has offices in Yarmouth and Brading, but also delivers and collects bikes anywhere on the island.

Cowes and around

COWES, at the island's most northerly point, sits opposite Southampton and is the first place many people see when visiting. And a good first point of call it makes too – it's an attractive town, bisected by the River Medina. **West Cowes** is the more interesting half, though **East Cowes** boasts the biggest tourist attraction in

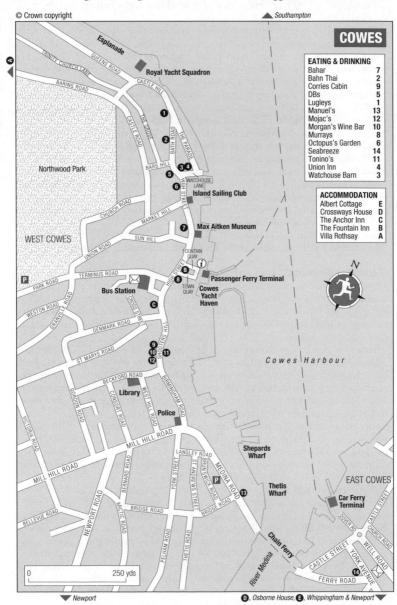

© Crown copyright ▲ *Southampton*

COWES

EATING & DRINKING
Bahar	7
Bahn Thai	2
Corries Cabin	9
DBs	5
Lugleys	1
Manuel's	13
Mojac's	12
Morgan's Wine Bar	10
Murrays	8
Octopus's Garden	6
Seabreeze	14
Tonino's	11
Union Inn	4
Watchouse Barn	3

ACCOMMODATION
Albert Cottage	E
Crossways House	D
The Anchor Inn	C
The Fountain Inn	B
Villa Rothsay	A

Royal Yacht Squadron

Northwood Park

Island Sailing Club

WEST COWES

Max Aitken Museum

Passenger Ferry Terminal

Bus Station

Cowes Yacht Haven

Cowes Harbour

Library

Police

Shepards Wharf

Thetis Wharf

EAST COWES

Car Ferry Terminal

Chain Ferry

River Medina

0 — 250 yds

▼ *Newport* ▼ *Osborne House, Whippingham & Newport* ▼

the form of Queen Victoria's holiday home, Osborne House. Just south of here, the village of **Whippingham** makes a good destination for a walk or boat trip.

Arrival and information

The **tourist office** is in **West Cowes** at the Arcade, Fountain Quay (April–Oct Mon–Sat 9am–5pm, Sun 10am–4pm, with extended hours during Cowes Week; Nov–March Tues–Sat 9.30am–4.30pm; ⓣ01983 813818), right by the terminal where the **passenger ferry** from Southampton docks. The **car ferry** from Southampton arrives at the terminal in East Cowes, just off Castle Street. The **bus station** is a short walk inland on Carvel Lane with connections to all the main towns on the island. **Parking** in West Cowes is very limited in the central area and drivers should head for one of the signed car parks or use the Park and Ride service. Alternatively you could park in East Cowes and go over the chain ferry to West Cowes.

Accommodation

Places to stay are somewhat limited in Cowes: there are a couple of decent options near Osborne House in East Cowes, though most of the bars and restaurants are in West Cowes so it's best to stay there. The tourist office can help with guest houses if the ones below are full, but note that rates almost double during Cowes Week when places need to be booked months ahead.

Albert Cottage York Ave, East Cowes ⓣ01983 299309, ⓦwww.albertcottagehotel.com. Adjacent to and once part of the Osborne estate, this lovely mansion has a country house feel to it. Set in its own grounds with a highly rated restaurant, rooms are very comfortable with flat-screen TVs. ❼

Crossways House Crossways Rd, East Cowes ⓣ01983 298282, ⓦwww.bedbreakfast-cowes.co.uk. This building was commissioned by Queen Victoria for the administrator of her Sea Cadets and sits right opposite Osborne House. Rooms are large, some with four-poster beds overlooking the gardens. Breakfast includes Belgian waffles, and evening meals are also available. ❹

The Anchor Inn 1–3 High St, West Cowes ⓣ01983 292823, ⓔtheanchorinn@gmail.com. There are seven simple en-suite rooms, including one family room, above the pub, which does reasonable food – front rooms can be noisy. ❷

The Fountain Inn High St, West Cowes ⓣ01983 292397, ⓦwww.fountaininn-cowes.com. The best budget option in town, with tastefully furnished rooms, the best ones overlooking the waterside, all above a fine old inn serving good-value pub food. ❺

Villa Rothsay Baring Rd, West Cowes ⓣ01983 295178, ⓦwww.hotels-cowes.co.uk. Upmarket boutique hotel that's maintained its Victorian roots with period decor throughout – think drapes, ornate stairways and stained-glass windows. Great views from the grounds and raised patio area. ❺, or ❼ with sea views and balconies.

West Cowes

One of the most attractive and upmarket areas on the island, the old centre of **West Cowes** consists of a warren of narrow streets lined with smart shops, historic pubs and restaurants. The town is inextricably associated with sailing craft and boat building: Henry VIII built two "cowforts" here (hence the name) to defend the Solent's expanding naval dockyards from the French and Spanish, one on either side of the River Medina, which splits the town in two. The castle in East Cowes was demolished in the 1960s, but the remains of West Cowes castle now form the Royal Yacht Squadron. In 1820, the Prince Regent's patronage of the yacht club gave the port its cachet, and it's now one of the world's most exclusive sailing clubs. In the 1950s, the world's first hovercraft made its test runs here, and hovercrafts continue to be made on the island today, though sailing eclipses it with a series of annual events, the most famous of which is Cowes Week (see box, p.258).

Cowes Week

The first week of August/last week of July sees the international yachting festival known as **Cowes Week** (ⓦ www.cowesweek.co.uk), the largest sailing regatta in the world. Up to 100,000 spectators watch around a thousand boats take part, commandeered by sailors of all abilities – from enthusiastic amateurs to Royalty and Olympic champions. The race first took place in 1826 (with just seven yachts) and has occurred every year since except during the world wars. Throughout the festival there's a great party atmosphere and dozens of organized events, including a spectacular fireworks display on the final Friday night. In addition to Cowes Week, most summer weekends see some form of nautical event taking place in or around town.

The best views of the comings and goings on the Solent are from the expanse of Northwood Park or the Parade and Esplanade to the northwest of the High Street. To learn something about the maritime history of the town, visit the small **Max Aitken Museum** at 83 The High St (May–Sept 10am–4pm; free), set in a renovated eighteenth-century sailmaker's loft and containing a motley collection of maritime memorabilia such as artefacts from royal yachts, model boats, figureheads and paintings, including some original Giles cartoons.

At the bottom of the meandering High Street, **boat trips** upriver and around the harbour leave from Thetis Wharf, near the chain ferry; for details contact Solent & Wight Line Cruises (ⓣ 01983 564602, ⓦ www.solentcruises.co.uk).

East Cowes and Osborne House

There is not a lot to recommend East Cowes, though it is fun to take the little **chain ferry** (or The Floating Bridge) that carries cars and passengers across the 70m width of the Medina (every 10min or so from 5am–midnight; cars £1.50, passengers & bikes free). This is just one of five remaining chain ferries in England, dating from 1975, though a ferry has run this route since 1720. Although East Cowes is a fairly run-down port, around a mile uphill is one of the island's top attractions in the form of Osborne House.

Queen Victoria's family home, **Osborne House** (daily: April–Sept 10am–6pm; Oct 10am–4pm; Nov–March Wed–Sun pre-booked tours only; call ⓣ 01983 200022; house and grounds £10.20, grounds only £8.40; EH) is signposted one mile southeast of town (bus #4 from Ryde or #5 from Newport; take either from East Cowes). The house was built in the late 1840s by Prince Albert and Thomas Cubitt as an Italianate villa, with balconies and large terraces overlooking the landscaped gardens towards the Solent. The state rooms, used for entertaining visiting dignitaries, exude an expected formality – the Durbar room is particularly impressive, clad almost entirely in ivory – while the private apartments feel more homely, like the affluent family holiday residence that Osborne was – far removed from the pomp and ceremony of state affairs in London. On the top floor, the nurseries and children's bedrooms still display their toys, cradles and tiny beds, while on the middle floor, you can peer into Prince Albert's bath, hidden away in a cupboard in true Victorian fashion. Following Albert's death, the desolate Victoria spent much of her time here, and it's where she eventually died in 1901. Since then, according to her wishes, the house has remained virtually unaltered, allowing an unexpectedly intimate glimpse into Victoria's family life.

The children were able to escape the confines and boredom of royal life by frolicking in the gardens and in their two-storey playhouse, the Swiss Cottage. Inside, you can view their miniature tea sets and toys: downstairs is now a lovely tearoom. Nearby, you can see the remains of a barracks with its own drawbridge, built by Prince Albert for the boys to play soldiers in, and Queen Victoria's original bathing machine. The grounds are large – it's a good fifteen-minute walk from the house down to the Swiss Cottage – so leave enough to time to explore. There is a shuttle bus that runs round the grounds, or you can take a horse-drawn carriage trip from the main entrance to the front door of the house (50p).

Eating and drinking

During Cowes Week, everywhere is pretty much packed to the gills, but at other times there are plenty of places serving good-quality food to suit all budgets. Unless stated, all the below are in West Cowes.

Restaurants

Bahar 44 High St ☎01983 200378. The best Indian in town – the owners gleefully remind visitors of the time Richard Branson visited, and he no doubt enjoyed the fine range of tandooris, baltis and specials such as garlic chicken masala. Mains from around £9.

Bahn Thai 10 Bath Rd ☎01983 291917. Cosy Thai restaurant with a long menu of sumptuous dishes from £8, including great king prawns, Thai fishcakes and good vegetarian options.

Corries Cabin 17 Shooters Hill ☎01983 293733. Something of an institution, with queues out of the door for the takeaway fish and chips. There's also a small sit-down area serving good-value, freshly caught fish.

🏃 **DBs** 3 Bath Rd ☎01983 291714. Small and intimate restaurant with a short but very alluring menu of tasty dishes such as sea bass with mango sauce, steaks and grilled chicken from £11–14. Evenings only, closed Sun out of season.

🏃 **Lugleys** The Parade ☎01983 299618. In a great position facing the sea, this fashionable bar-restaurant is a great place for a coffee, evening drink or quality meal, with a lunch menu featuring local pork and herb sausages or trout from around £9 and a more pricey evening menu of fresh fish, duck and the like from £14.

Manuel's Shepards Wharf, Medina Rd ☎01983 299566. It is worth heading out towards the chain ferry to eat at this friendly family-run Portuguese restaurant that serves excellent-value chicken piri-piri, grilled squid, sea bass and the likes from around £8, along with tasty tapas and Portuguese beers.

▲ Osborne House

Mojac's 10a Shooters Hill ☎01983 281118. Upmarket restaurant serving inexpensive lunches such as burgers and salmon omelettes, and good-value two course meals (around £16). Go à la carte and mains such as quality medallions of lamb or steaks start at around £15. Closed Sun.

Murrays 106 High St ☎01983 296233. Well known for its seafood, this does a reasonably priced set menu, with three courses at around £18.50. Great fish such as swordfish steaks, smoked halibut with leek and bacon, or salmon with spinach. Closed Sun night & all day Mon Oct–March.

Tonino's 8–9 Shooters Hill ☎01983 298464. Traditional Italian with a good range of well-prepared dishes such as pastas and pizzas from £9 and good fish and meat dishes at a more pricey £18.

Pubs, cafés and bars

Morgan's Wine Bar 15 Shooters Hill ☎01983 290730. With comfy sofas and bare brick walls, this is a fashionable spot for a coffee, drink or reasonably priced meal such as *moules*, risotto or pasta from around £8.

Octopus's Garden 63 High St. Fun high-street café stuffed with Beatles memorabilia – lots of framed photos and piped music to accompany unspectacular but inexpensive drinks and snacks.

Seabreeze Ferry Rd, East Cowes. If you find yourself in East Cowes, this is a decent café-restaurant serving good-value breakfasts, sandwiches and full meals, as well as fresh coffee.

Union Inn Watch House Lane. Historic pub with a cosy interior, decent pub food and delicious Sunday roasts.

Watchouse Barn 31 Bath Rd. Small tea and coffee shop that is a big hit with children thanks to the toy train that trundles overhead. Also serves inexpensive lunches such as jacket potatoes, omelettes and the like from £6.

Whippingham

The small village of **WHIPPINGHAM**, a mile south of Osborne, was once part of the Osborne House estate and the area would be largely recognizable to Victoria today. The highlight is another of Albert's architectural extrava-ganzas, the Gothic Revival **Royal Church of St Mildred** (Easter–Oct Mon–Fri 10am–5pm), where Victoria frequently worshipped. The German Battenberg family, who later adopted the anglicized name Mountbatten, have a chapel here. There is a lovely trail from here down to the Medina, a ten-minute stroll to the ☆ *Folly Inn* (☎01983 297171). This fine waterside pub has the river lapping its decking and serves fine wines, cask ales and very good pub food, including generous open sandwiches and sharing platters of smoked fish as well as wild mushroom lasagne, curries and the like from £8–10. The Folly Waterbus runs a taxi service from Cowes to the jetty next to the pub (call for details ☎07974 864627).

Newport and around

Inland, up the Medina, it is a short hop to the island's capital, **Newport**, and the nearby **Carisbrooke**, one of England's greatest castles, alongside the remains of a fine Roman villa. Close by is **Robin Hill Country Park**, a great expanse with its own toboggan run; it's also the venue for the annual Bestival music festival. Families will appreciate the steam railway, which begins its cross-island run from Wootton, via **Havenstreet**, to Smallbrook Junction, near Ryde.

Newport

NEWPORT, the capital of the Isle of Wight, sits at the centre of the island at a point where the River Medina's commercial navigability ends. The town isn't particularly engaging, though it is refreshingly free of the tourist trappings of the coastal resorts and has three small museums as well as some good shops and restaurants. It is also the administrative centre, where you'll find most of the

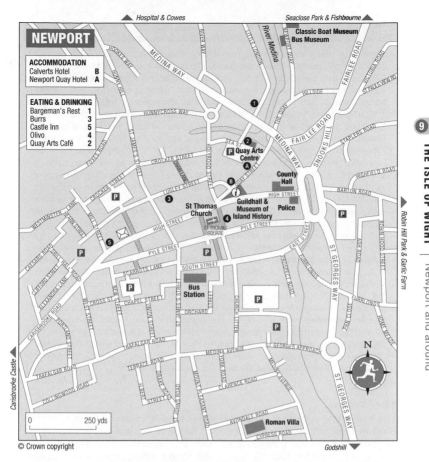

NEWPORT

ACCOMMODATION
Calverts Hotel   **B**
Newport Quay Hotel **A**

EATING & DRINKING
Bargeman's Rest **1**
Burrs **3**
Castle Inn **5**
Olivo **4**
Quay Arts Café **2**

Classic Boat Museum
Bus Museum

Quay Arts Centre

County Hall

Guildhall & Museum of Island History

St Thomas Church

Police

ST THOMAS SQUARE

Bus Station

Roman Villa

© Crown copyright

Godshill

9

THE ISLE OF WIGHT | Newport and around

Carisbrooke Castle

Robin Hill Park & Garlic Farm

0   250 yds

N

major supermarkets and the island's public facilities, such as the hospital, on Parkhurst Road, and the police headquarters and the county hall, both on the High Street. Newport is also the rather unlikely venue for one of England's best-known festivals, the **Isle of Wight Festival** (see p.262), held at Seaclose Park on the northern outskirts of town.

Arrival, information and accommodation

The **bus station** is a short walk south of the High Street, while drivers should follow signs to the central car parks. The **tourist office** is centrally located in the High Street in the Guildhall building (Mon–Sat 9.30am–5pm, Sun 10am–3.30pm; ☎01983 813813). There is not much reason to **stay** in Newport; if you do, the best option is the *Newport Quay Hotel* just down from the tourist office on Quay Street (☎01983 528544, ⓦwww.newportquayhotel .co.uk; ❹), a small B&B in a seventeenth-century townhouse with slightly flouncy rooms and a communal lounge. The best budget option is *Calverts Hotel* on Quay Street (☎01983 525281, ⓦwww.calvertshotel.com; ❷) in a charming seventeenth-century building opposite the tourist office: once the mayor's home, it now offers simple rooms above a lively bar.

The Isle of Wight Festival

The original **Isle of Wight Festival**, held in 1968, was a one-day hippy gathering near the village of Godshill – chosen because ley lines meet there – with Marc Bolan and T-Rex and Jefferson Airplane playing to a crowd of around 10,000 people. Due to its success, the following year, the festival moved to Wootton near Ryde, and hosted artists such as Bob Dylan, The Who and Free attracting an audience of around 1,150,000 people. However, the 1970 concert broke all records with an estimated 5,600,000 people swaying to performers such as Joni Mitchell, Miles Davis, Leonard Cohen, Joan Baez, The Doors and Jimi Hendrix at East Afton Farm on Afton Down – it remains today the largest festival ever held in the UK. The 1970 festival, however, had faced problems from the outset: local residents objected to the initial choice of sites and East Afton Farm was the last option offered – its location overlooked by a large hill meant that people could easily watch the concert for free from outside the site, leading to far greater numbers arriving than predicted. Added to this, poor organization by the promoters and a general feeling from the residents that naked hippies taking drugs were bad for the reputation of the island meant that controversy was assured. As a result, the following year the "Isle of Wight Act" was passed by parliament preventing gatherings of more than five thousand people on the island without a special licence. This put paid to the festival for 22 years, until it was revived in 2002 in its current venue of *Seaclose Park*, near Newport. Although this, too, has increased in size each year, critics argue that it has only become an accepted part of the Isle of Wight calendar because of its "safe" establishment reputation, with granddads of rock such as David Bowie, the Rolling Stones, Iggy Pop and Neil Young headlining in recent years. In 2009 the appearance of the Sex Pistols was a tad more adventurous, but to catch the rebellious spirit of the original Isle of Wight Festival, try the smaller, "boutique" Bestival in Robin Hill Park, which now pulls in 30,000 wackily dressed music fans for a much more contemporary programme of indie, dance and the odd nostalgia act. See also the *Cool Counties* colour insert.

The Town

The main draw in town is the **Guildhall** on the High Street. Designed by John Nash in 1816, the building has been used variously as a market, fire station and shop, not to mention a banqueting hall that once entertained the likes of Prince Albert and Garibaldi. Today it houses the tourist office, along with the small **Museum of Island History** (Mon–Sat 10am–5pm, Sun 11am–3.30pm; £2), a somewhat limited museum displaying fossils and dinosaur bones collected from round the island, together with old photographs, touch-screen displays detailing the island's history and some Anglo-Saxon jewellery, swords and axes. Newport's most interesting streets are in the pedestrianized stretch around the handsome **St Thomas's church**, on St Thomas Square, off the High Street, which contains the tomb of Princess Elizabeth Stuart, daughter of Charles I who died aged fifteen.

Newport also has an excellent arts centre, **Quay Arts** (☎01983 822490, ⓦwww.quayarts.org; closed Sun), set in converted riverside warehouses at Newport Harbour, which puts on exhibitions, concerts, films and comedy and has its own theatre and a fine café (see p.263). Over the river, under the flyover and just past the yacht-lined harbour, are two fun museums: first of these is the **Bus Museum** (10.30am–4pm: April, May & Oct Sun & Tues; June & July Sun, Tues & Thurs; Aug daily; check the website for other sporadic opening days, closed Nov–March; £4; ⓦwww.iowbusmuseum.org.uk) with a colourful collection of historic buses that once plied the island, including a Victorian tram, and pictures and paintings of various transport over the years. Check the website for details of the Island Buses Running Day, usually in May, when some of the buses that can still work leave their warehouse for a day out. Just beyond the Bus Museum in another warehouse is the **Classic Boat Museum** (10am–4pm: April–Sept daily; Oct–March Tues & Sat; £3; @www.classicboatmuseum.org), which houses a collection of vintage sailing and power boats, including Victorian rowing boats and gear from the *Gipsy Moth IV*, the yacht in which Sir Francis Chichester broke the round-the-world small vessel record in 1966.

Eating and drinking

Bargeman's Rest Little London, Newport Harbour. Spacious waterside pub with a big outdoor terrace. It serves good cask ales and a range of fresh pub grub, plus occasional live music.
Burrs 27–28 Lugely St ☎01983 825470. Upmarket dining with a short but quality menu featuring the likes of local pheasant, gnocchi with pesto and pine nuts and sublime steaks. Mains from £13.
Castle Inn 91 High St ☎01983 552258. Dating from 1684, this is the town's oldest pub. Housed in a fine old brick building, it offers decent beer and

pub food from £9, along with less pricey salads and sandwiches.
Olivo 15 St Thomas Square ☎01983 530001. Fashionable Italian café-restaurant opposite the church, with appealing outdoor seats and a modern interior. Reliably tasty pasta, pizza and salads from £8–9, and they do very good coffees.
Quay Arts Café Sea St, Newport Harbour. A good range of inexpensive meals such as chickpea curry and sweet and sour pork, along with coffees or cakes inside the arts complex, with a few tables outside a terrace facing the river (and flyover). Closed Sun.

Carisbrooke Castle and the Roman Villa

In the southwest suburbs of Newport, on the edges of Carisbrooke, lies one of the Isle of Wight's greatest attractions, the hilltop fortress of **Carisbrooke Castle** (daily: April–Sept 10am–5pm; Oct–March 10am–4pm; £6.50; EH; bus #7 or #11). This austere Norman keep's most famous visitor was Charles I, detained here (and caught one night ignominiously jammed between his room's bars in an attempt to escape) prior to his execution in London. The **museum** in the centre of the castle shows off many relics from his incarceration, as well as those of the last royal resident, Princess Beatrice, Queen Victoria's youngest

▲ Carisbrooke Castle

daughter. The castle's other notable curiosity is the sixteenth-century well-house, where donkeys still trudge inside a huge treadmill in order to raise a barrel 160ft up the well shaft. Children love watching the donkey demonstration and visiting the donkeys in their stables. Visitors can also walk round the well-preserved battlements, basking in the spectacular views over the island and the mainland.

The remains of a **Roman villa** stand a well-signposted ten-minute walk southeast of the town centre in Cypress Road (Easter–Oct Mon–Sat 10am–4.30pm, Sun noon–4pm; £2.50). Discovered in 1926 and dating from around 280 AD, it is thought to be the farmhouse of a wealthy estate. The remains of a well-preserved bathing suite with hypocaust underground heating are visible, and sections of the villa, such as the kitchen, have been reconstructed, though its sister villa in Brading (see p.270) is more impressive and gives a better idea of life in Roman times.

Robin Hill Park, Steam Railway and the Garlic Farm

Two and a half miles east of Newport and served by buses #10 and #8, **Robin Hill Park** (April to early Sept daily 10am–5 or 6pm; end Sept to end Oct Tues–Thurs, Sat & Sun 10.30am–4.30pm; last week in Oct daily 10am–4pm; £8.50) sits in 88 acres of woods and downs, and has a tree-top trail, a red squirrel tower, falconry and bird of prey displays, slides, a maze and zip wires. There are many different themed play areas designed for varying age groups – the African Adventure is very imaginative, with swings that look like giraffes and safari animals dotted around – as well as some low-key rides, such as the swinging galleon. All the attractions are included in the entrance fee – even the falconry displays, which are well worth catching – except for the fun toboggan ride (£1.50), which wiggles down a steep hill. The park is closed for two weeks each September, when it hosts the annual Bestival (see p.31).

The **Isle of Wight Steam Railway** (Ⓦwww.iwsteamrailway.co.uk; £9, children £4.50 tickets valid for unlimited journeys that day) runs from Wootton, a couple of miles east of Newport, through pretty countryside for five miles to Smallbrook Junction, where it connects with the Ryde to Shanklin electric rail line. The trains are all renovated steam engines, many of which were used for scheduled services on the island in the past, and some dating from as far back as 1876. A mile and a half from Wootton, the main station is at **Havenstreet**, where there's a children's play area and a **museum** containing artefacts relating to the island's steam trains, as well as a viewing gallery where you can watch the trains being worked on in the railway workshops.

The quirky **Garlic Farm** (Ⓦwww.thegarlicfarm.co.uk) lies about four miles east of Newport. Here, you can learn about growing and plaiting garlic, follow the 30min Garlic Farm Walk, or buy just about anything garlic related, from garlic pesto to garlic ice cream. There's also a very good café, with a large selection of vegetarian dishes, such as a meze of hummus and marinated garlic cloves. There's even an annual garlic festival nearby each August (Ⓦwww.garlic-festival.co.uk), and some self-catering cottages and converted barns on the farm (Ⓦwww.mersleyfarm.co.uk; £250 a week in low season, up to £790 in high season for a cottage sleeping four).

East Wight

East Wight contains some of the island's most historic sites, including the medieval remains of **Quarr Abbey** and the superbly presented Roman villa at **Brading**. It's also home to the island's other main entry point, **Ryde**, which has a very different feel from Cowes: it's a large, pleasantly old-fashioned Victorian resort facing a broad, sandy beach. Away from Ryde, the east of the island is pretty undeveloped, with relatively discreet beaches approached via small appealing villages, such as **Seaview**, **St Helens** and **Bembridge**, and the fine sandy beach at **Whitecliff Bay**.

Ryde and around

RYDE spills down a steep slope facing the mainland, enjoying great views over the Solent and the iconic Spinnaker Tower in Portsmouth opposite. Today, it's by no means the quaintest of places on the island, but its accessibility made it one of the principal Victorian resorts and as a result it has some fine old Victorian mansions and its own small Victorian shopping arcade. It's the main arrival point for foot passengers from Portsmouth, though the car ferry from Portsmouth docks a couple of miles west at the tiny village of **Fishbourne**.

Arrival and information

The **bus station**, **hovercraft terminal** and **Esplanade train station** (the northern terminus of the Island Line train line) are all at the bottom of the

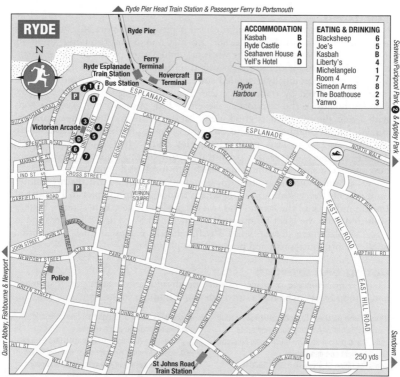

Ryde Pier Head Train Station & Passenger Ferry to Portsmouth

RYDE

Ryde Pier

Ferry Terminal

Ryde Esplanade Train Station

Hovercraft Terminal

Bus Station

ESPLANADE

Ryde Harbour

Victorian Arcade

ESPLANADE

ACCOMMODATION	
Kasbah	**B**
Ryde Castle	**C**
Seahaven House	**A**
Yelf's Hotel	**D**

EATING & DRINKING	
Blacksheep	6
Joe's	5
Kasbah	**B**
Liberty's	4
Michelangelo	1
Room 4	7
Simeon Arms	8
The Boathouse	2
Yanwo	3

Police

St Johns Road Train Station

0   250 yds

© Crown copyright

pier. **Ferries** dock at the end of it, from where connecting trains (roughly every 30min; £1.40 return) take you down to the Esplanade station. The **tourist office** (daily: March–Oct 9.30am–5.30pm, Sun 9am–5pm; Nov–Feb 9am–4.30pm; ☎01983 813818) is at the bottom of Union Street, the main drag lined with cafés, bars and restaurants. There are usually plenty of **parking** spots along the seafront esplanade, or follow signs to the pay-and-display car parks in town.

Accommodation

Surprisingly for such a big resort, **accommodation** is relatively scarce in Ryde and you may want to base yourself in neighbouring Seaview (see p.268). The best options are below, or ask about local guest houses in the tourist office.

Kasbah 76 Union St, Ryde ☎01983 810088, ⓦwww.kas-bah.co.uk. Stylish Moroccan-themed rooms above a funky café-bar (see below) which means they can be noisy at weekends, but great value. ❷

Ryde Castle The Esplanade, Ryde ☎01983 563755, ⓦwww.rydecastle.com. Recently renovated, this historic castellated building is said to date back to the time of Henry VIII and was used by the army during the last world war. Now it serves as a hotel with a spacious bar and brasserie with a range of comfortable en-suite rooms upstairs. ❸

Seahaven House 35–36 St Thomas St, Ryde ☎01983 563069, ⓦwww.seahavenhouse.co.uk. Homely seafront hotel with its own tastefully furnished lounge. Rooms are on the simple side, the best ones with sea views. ❶

Yelf's Hotel Union St, Ryde ☎01983 564062, ⓦwww.yelfshotel.com. Pleasantly old-fashioned hotel bang in the centre of town with its own café, restaurant and beer garden. Rooms are plain but spotless. ❺

The Town

Ryde's proximity to the mainland means it is a major transport hub, with ferries and hovercrafts regularly to-ing and fro-ing, and trains rumbling along its extensive **pier** that dominates the seafront. Unlike most piers, this one is essentially a giant jetty for the ferries to call at in deep enough water. First built in 1814 though substantially extended since, the structure is a quarter of a mile long and is served by trains (see p.255), or you can drive or walk along its wooden boards to the terminal at the end – little more than a giant car park with a café, though it offers good views back over town. But Ryde's principal attraction is its **beaches**, either to the west, or more alluring to the east, where the sands back onto leafy parkland, **Appley Park**. Here you'll find **Appley Tower** (summer daily, weather permitting, 10am–dusk; £1), a stone watchtower now open as a shop-cum-museum filled with fossils and gemstones.

The seafront promenade along this stretch is served by a **land train** (summer only, roughly every 40min; £2.50), which trundles from the pier to **Puckpool Park**, a mile east of the centre. This was originally a nineteenth-century battery built to defend the coast from possible French invasion. The walls were used as a gun emplacement during World War II, but now enclose a small park with a public tennis court, pitch and putt golf and play areas.

Eating and drinking

There is no shortage of places to **eat** and **drink**, largely along the Esplanade and Union Street, which is also where you'll find the nightlife.

Blacksheep 53 Union St, Ryde ☎01983 811006. Fashionable bar with comfy sofas and seats outside in a patio area. Live music most Fri nights and late night opening Sat.

Joe's 24 Union St, Ryde ☎01983 567047.

Inexpensive café-bar serving £5 brunches and good-value rice and pasta dishes.

Kasbah 76 Union St, Ryde ☎01983 810088. Lively Moroccan-themed bar and restaurant where you can chill out to world music and play a game of chess. The reasonably priced menu features home-made Moroccan dishes, with good veggie options, such as stuffed peppers and mushrooms for £6, as well as a variety of tapas (£3–4).

Liberty's 12 Union St, Ryde ☎01983 811007. A big and stylish continental-style café-bar with great salads, sandwiches and main meals (pasta from around £8 and fish and meat dishes around £13) in the upstairs dining room.

Michelangelo 30 St Thomas St, Ryde ☎01983 811966. This attractive seafront Italian restaurant has bright walls lined with bottles. Good-quality pizzas, pasta and salads from around £8 (closed Wed).

Room 4 30 Union St, Ryde ☎01983 611973. Bustling all-purpose Italian café-restaurant serving inexpensive breakfasts, snacks and a range of decent pizzas from £7.

Simeon Arms 21 Simeon St, Ryde ☎01983 614954. Tucked in a residential street, this is a pleasant local with decent pub grub, an outside terrace, darts and frequent live music.

The Boathouse Springvale Rd, Springvale ☎01983 810 616. On the front between Ryde and Seaview, this is a lovely gastropub decked out in bleached wood, with a fine beer garden. Classic English dishes such as sausage and mash, steak and kidney pie along with fresh fish dishes from around £9.

Yanwo 59 Union St, Ryde ☎01983 568818. Small, friendly restaurant specializing in Malaysian and Chinese food – including a spicy Thai tom yum seafood soup, wok-fried chilli chicken and Malaysian curries. Mains £6.

Quarr Abbey and Fishbourne

Two miles west of Ryde, outside the village of Binstead, is one of the island's earliest Christian relics, **Quarr Abbey**. The Abbey was founded in 1132 by Richard de Redvers, for the use of Savigny monks; the name was derived from the quarries nearby, where stone was mined for use in the construction of Winchester and Chichester cathedrals. Only stunted ruins survive the Dissolution and ensuing plunder of ready-cut stone, although an ivy-clad archway still hangs picturesquely over a farm track. In 1914 a new abbey was founded just west of the ruins, a striking rose-brick building with Byzantine overtones and still home to Benedictine monks (daily 9am–9pm; Vespers 5pm). There is a guest house for people wishing to stay, though guests will be expected to join in prayers (no set fee but donations accepted; details on Ⓦwww.quarrabbey.co.uk).

The Abbey is just outside the village of **Fishbourne**, where car ferries from Portsmouth make an incongruous arrival in such a small hamlet. There's nothing much there apart from a few houses, and the *Fishbourne Inn*, 111 Fishbourne Lane

---

Minghellas: ice cream and films

All over the Isle of Wight, you'll find **Minghellas ice creams**, certainly worth sampling. Made on the island by the Minghella family since 1950, using natural ingredients, including milk and cream from island cows, the ice creams come in a huge variety of flavours, such as gin and pink grapefruit sorbet, apple crumble ice cream, and frosted strawberry with balsamic vinegar. Italian immigrants, Edward and Gloria Minghella started out making and selling the ice cream from a small café on Ryde High Street, but by 1985 it was so popular that they moved to a larger factory in Wootton, where the ice creams are still concocted today. However, it is Edward and Gloria's son, **Anthony Minghella**, acclaimed director of *The English Patient* (winner of nine Oscars), *Truly, Madly, Deeply, Cold Mountain* and *The Talented Mr Ripley*, who has made Minghella a household name. Born and brought up on the Isle of Wight, he acknowledged its enormous influence on his film-making, calling his nine-Oscar win for *The English Patient* "a great day for the Isle of Wight". He was awarded a CBE in 2001, but died suddenly in March 2008 at the age of 54. A festival was held in his honour in Newport in March 2009, with stars such as Jude Law and Alan Rickman introducing his films, and there are plans to make it an annual event (Ⓦwww.minghellafilmfestival .com). Perhaps a more fitting memorial, however, is Minghellas delicious Cold Mountain ice cream, made from white chocolate and berries.

(☎01983 882823, ⓦwww.fishbourneinn.com; ❷), an attractive 1930s pub situated next to Wootton Creek and the ferry terminal. It has a few comfortable rooms, a pretty garden and serves decent pub food, such as a mixed grill for £12.

Seaview, Priory Bay and St Helens

The road southeast of Ryde follows the coast, but slightly set back in a delightful rural corner of the island. From Ryde the seafront promenade continues for two miles east along the old rampart walls to the neighbouring resort of **Seaview** (bus #16 from Ryde), which is very different in feel from its larger neighbour. There is no beach as such here, but a cluster of winding streets, pretty fishermen's cottages and fine Victorian mansions abut a rocky foreshore – most with great views over the giant tankers and container ships plying the Solent. It is now a fairly upmarket resort with a collection of hotels, cafés and restaurants. It is also home to **Seaview Wildlife Encounter**, formerly called Flamingo Park (daily: April–Sept 10am–5pm; Oct 10am–4pm; £7.85, children £5.85; ⓦwww.flamingoparkiw.com), a bird and animal sanctuary in a lovely position on a hillside overlooking the sea. Here you can feed penguins and flamingoes, stroll about with wallabies, watch meerkats and otters playing, and see baby chicks peeping out from their nests. An attractive series of pools and waterfalls running down the hillside is home to a huge variety of birdlife, and there's also a large indoor aviary where tropical birds fly amidst tropical foliage. The park is on Oakhill Road, just off the coast road, and is served by bus #16 from Ryde.

Beyond Seaview is one of the best beaches along this stretch, **Priory Bay**, a long sandy strip backed by tree-lined slopes: there's direct access to the beach from the *Priory Bay Hotel* (see below), though you won't escape the crowds here as plenty of yachties descend in summer. Alternatively, you can park in The Duver car park (see below) and walk round along the coast path.

The next bay south is Bembridge Harbour, flanked in the north by the village of **St Helens** (bus #14 from Ryde) – clustered round a pretty green, one of the largest in England – and by Bembridge itself to the south. From the southern side of St Helens, you can pick up a great section of the coastal path, which crosses a causeway across tidal mudflats and along the coast to **The Duver**, where you can see the stumpy remains of the Saxon St Helens Church. The tower is the only part left after a storm in 1703 washed the rest of the church away.

Accommodation

There's a good selection of accommodation along this coast, with *Nodes Point Holiday Park*, Nodes Road, St Helens (☎01983 872401, ⓦwww.park-resorts touring.com), being a superbly positioned **campsite**, with great views over Bembridge Bay. It's well equipped with an indoor pool and has caravans and ready-erected tents to rent, or you can bring your own tent or camper van.

Northbank Hotel Circular Rd, Seaview ☎01983 612227, ⓦwww.northbankhotel.co.uk. A traditional, family-run Victorian hotel dating from 1840, in a great location with direct beach access. Although the rooms are not en suite, many have sea views and it's a relaxed, child-friendly place. ❺

The Priory Bay Hotel Priory Drive, Seaview ☎01983 613146, ⓦwww.priorybay.com. This classy country house hotel in seventy acres of grounds pulls off the trick of being smart and luxurious without being too formal and stuffy. You enter through an impressive fourteenth-century stone doorway imported from France, and the rooms in the main house are plush with high ceilings; there are also self-catering cottages in the superb lawned grounds, which lead down through woods to the sands of Priory Bay. There's also an outdoor pool and a highly rated restaurant (see p.269). ❽

The Seaview The High St, Seaview ☎01983 612711, ⓦwww.seaviewhotel.co.uk. Contemporary

rooms with all mod cons in a Victorian townhouse in the middle of Seaview. It's child-friendly and has a highly recommended restaurant (see below). **⑧**
The Spring Vale Springvale, Seaview ☎01983 612533, ⓦwww.springvalehotel.co.uk. Attractive, seafront Victorian building opposite a shingle beach on the outskirts of Seaview. It's worth paying the £10 extra for a front room with superb sea views, though all are spacious with deep-pile carpets and comfy beds. There's also a reasonably priced restaurant and attractive gardens. **⑦**

Eating and drinking

Baywatch The Duver ☎01983 873259. Great sea-facing shack serving inexpensive breakfasts and lunches, as well as classy evening meals such as *moules*, fresh fish and gourmet burgers from £15. You can also pop in for a drink and there's a breezy outdoor terrace.
Ganders Upper Green Rd, St Helens ☎01983 872014. A cosy restaurant on the north side of The Green with contemporary decor. Two courses for £15.50, with local seasonal daily specials; there are good veggie options, such as mushroom strudel for £10.50. Open Tues–Sun 7–9.30pm, also Sun noon–2pm; closed Sun pm in winter.
The Old Fort The Esplanade, Seaview ☎01983 612363. Right on the seafront with superb views over the Solent, this lively café-bar serves a range of fresh food including curries, fish dishes, bangers and mash and baguettes, along with good coffee. Slightly pricey but the view is worth paying for.

The Priory Hotel Priory Drive, Seaview. The hotel has two restaurants, both with fantastic views over the grounds: the smart Island Room has two courses for £28, featuring local specialities such as veal, Bembridge lobster, and an Island cheese plate, while the less formal dining room next door serves main courses such as risotto or mussels from £10–15.
The Seaview The High St, Seaview. A top-quality restaurant specializing in local produce, some from the hotel's own farm in nearby Carisbrooke. There are two restaurants (three courses for £21), or you can have tasty bar meals in the bar, with a log fire, or on the terrace at the front in summer. The Sunday brunch is very child-friendly (adults £15, children £8), with a buffet plus hot dishes and entertainers laid on.
The Vine Inn Upper Green Rd, St Helens ☎01983 872337. Friendly local pub with views over The Green and a good range of local real ales. The food is good-quality home-made pub staples, local and seasonal where possible, with Bembridge crab featuring in summer.

Bembridge and around

Heading south, the coast path and road skirts Bembridge Harbour, a pretty bay lined with yachts and little moored houseboats. It is easy to pass through **Bembridge** without realizing it, but it pays to stop and linger to appreciate its charms. It's a well-to-do village of handsome houses and bungalows with its own deli, fishmonger's and assorted cafés and restaurants. The atmospheric **beach** of narrow shingle studded with weather-worn wooden groynes is a bit tucked away – follow signs to the coastal path or the *Crab and Lobster* pub (see p.270). Its main sight, however, is **Bembridge Windmill** (mid-March to Oct daily 11am–5pm; £2.90; NT), a Grade I listed windmill at the top of the High Street, just north of the village. The island's only surviving windmill, it dates from around 1700: flour ground here was sold to the navy who sent boats ashore at Bembridge to collect it, and Bembridge flour was probably used to feed the troops during the Battle of Trafalgar. The windmill is in a lovely position and you can climb up the steep stepladders inside to the second floor for great views over the nearby Culver Down.

Practicalities

The *Windmill Inn* (☎01983 872875, ⓦwww.windmill-inn.com; **⑥**), on Steyne Road in the middle of the village, has en-suite **rooms**, plus self-catering cottages to rent, though much more fun is the ⚓ *Xoron* houseboat, on Embankment Road (☎01983 874596, ⓦwww.xoronfloatel.co.uk; **①**), which offers B&B in a converted World War II gunboat on Bembridge Harbour: the en-suite cabins are cosy and centrally heated and the upper deck has a lounge and breakfast area with a lovely terrace at the back to watch the comings and goings in the harbour. Bembridge has a couple of good **pubs**: the lively *Pilot Boat Inn*, down by the harbour on Station Road (℡01983 872077), is decked out like a boat inside with portholes for windows, and a small waterfront terrace out front. It serves generous portions of pub food, steak for £12 and home-made veggie lasagne (£8), as well as local Isle of Wight beers. The *Crab and Lobster* (℡01983 872244, ⓦwww.crabandlobsterinn.co.uk) is harder to find, tucked away at 32 Forelands, Field Road – it is well signed, though. With views over the sea, the pub is always popular thanks to its friendly service and decent food: the seafood platters, grilled lobsters and fresh fish, such as trout with almonds, are good value. If you're self-catering, Captain Stan on the High Street sells locally caught fish, including lobsters and crabs, while Bembridge Deli, opposite, sells home-made cakes and tasty local picnic provisions.

Whitecliff Bay and Bembridge Fort

Southwest of Bembridge the coast becomes far more ragged, with the coast path skirting the top of the impressive **Whitecliff Bay**, a fine sandy swathe backed by cliffs. It's worth the steep walk down though the only facility on the beach is *Wonky Café* (℡01983 873077), a laid-back spot that serves everything from breakfasts and sandwiches to evening pizzas on Fridays and barbecues on Saturdays. Campers can head for the nearby *Whitecliff Bay Holiday Park* (℡01983 872671, ⓦwww.whitecliff-bay.com), a giant site complete with pool, spa and evening entertainment.

Southwest of Whitecliff Bay, on Bembridge Down, lies the remains of **Bembridge Fort**, an impressive hexagonal hilltop ruin built in the 1860s as part of the island's coastal defences, when it would have been manned by a hundred soldiers. Later used as a barracks and as a gun emplacement in World War II, it was subsequently abandoned. It is now owned by English Heritage who open it up for occasional tours (£3; details on ℡01983 741020).

Brading Roman Villa and Nunwell House

Just south of the ancient village of **Brading**, on the Ryde to Sandown A3055 (bus #2 or #3 from Ryde, Sandown and Newport or #10 from Newport and Sandown) lie the impressive remains of **Brading Roman Villa** (daily 9.30am–5pm; closed over Christmas; £4.50). It's the more impressive of two such villas on the island (the other is in Newport; see p.263), both of which were probably sites of bacchanalian worship. The Brading site is housed in an attractive modern museum and is renowned for its superbly preserved mosaics, including intact images of Medusa and depictions of Orpheus. It has Roman clothes for children to dress up in and a great café (10am–4pm) with a terrace and views over the coast.

Nunwell House (July to early Sept Mon–Wed 1–5pm; £4.25), signposted off the A3055 less than a mile northwest of Brading, was where, in 1647, Charles I spent his last night of freedom before being taken to Carisbrooke Castle (see p.263) and thence to his eventual execution in Whitehall. The house has been in the Oglander family for nearly nine hundred years; the present building blends Jacobean, Georgian and Victorian styles. There are guided tours of the house (2pm & 3.30pm), and five acres of lovely gardens, including a walled garden with views over the sea.

The south coast

The south coast of the Isle of Wight from Sandown to Blackgang Chine represents the island at its most varied best. Here you'll find the bucket-and-spade resorts of **Sandown**, **Ventnor** and **Shanklin**, the latter with its idyllic thatched old town, every bit as appealing as the inland village of **Godshill** that's proclaimed the prettiest on the island. Interspersed with these tourist magnets are the leafy, well-to-do villages of **Bonchurch**, **St Lawrence** and **Niton**, as well as the fine lighthouse at **St Catherine's Point**. Families are well catered for, with the cliff-top funfair at **Blackgang**, the **Isle of Wight Zoo** and **Dinosaur Isle** at Sandown, and the falconry centre at the splendid ruins of **Appuldurcombe House**. This corner is also ideal for walkers, with steep rolling downs, secluded coves and some superb coastal paths.

Sandown

The traditional seaside resort of **SANDOWN** merges with its neighbour Shanklin across Sandown Bay, and makes up the island's holiday-making epicentre. Usually lively but now rather worn at the edges, Sandown became a resort in Victorian times, thanks to its position on a five-mile stretch of soft golden sands, overlooked by the island's only surviving pleasure **pier**, which opened in 1879. There are also splendid coastal walks, especially heading east towards the headland of Whitecliff Point.

Arrival and information

The Island Line **train station**, served by trains from Ryde and Shanklin, is on Station Avenue, about a ten-minute walk inland from the pier. **Buses** #2 and #3 from Newport and Ryde and buses #8 and #10 from Newport pull in along the High Street, where you'll also find Sandown's **tourist office** at no. 8 (April–Oct Mon–Sat 9.30am–5pm, Sun 10am–4pm; Nov to Easter irregular hours; ☎01983 813818). There's usually car **parking** on the seafront esplanade.

Accommodation

There's plenty of **accommodation** in Sandown, in particular the inexpensive guest houses spreading from the High Street to Beachfield Road. A good first point of call is *The Reef*, The Esplanade (☎01983 403219, ⓦwww.thereef sandown.co.uk; ❶), above the excellent restaurant-bar (see p.272) with the best rooms facing the beach at a bargain £30 per person. It also has family rooms. Simple comforts are at *Mount Brocas*, 15 Beachfield Rd (☎01983 406276, ⒺLbrocas@netguides.co.uk; no smoking; no credit cards; ❷), at the west end of the High Street, very close to the beach. More comfortable is *Carisbrooke House*, 11 Beachfield Rd (☎01983 402257, ⓦwww.carisbrookehousehotel.co.uk; ❷), a decent family-run hotel a short walk from the beach with spacious rooms, its own bar and patio garden, or try *The Lawns*, 72 Broadway (☎01983 402549, ⓦwww.lawnshotelisleofwight.co.uk; ❹), a no-smoking guest house with its own gardens, bar and car park; plush rooms come with digital TV.

The Town

Away from the beach there are also a couple of year-round attractions. At the northern end of the Esplanade is the **Isle of Wight Zoo** (daily: mid-Feb to March & Oct 10am–4pm; April–Sept 10am–6pm; Nov open weekends weather permitting; £5.95; ☎01983 403883, ⓦwww.isleofwightzoo.com), built into the walls of a Victorian fort and housing Britain's largest collection of tigers including some endangered species that are virtually extinct in the wild. It's also home to panthers and other big cats, as well as some frisky lemurs and monkeys. Also on the Esplanade, just before the zoo, **Dinosaur Isle** (April–Sept daily 10am–6pm; Oct 10am–5pm; Nov–March 10am–4pm; Jan call for opening hours; £5, children £3; ℡01983 404344, Ⓦwww.dinosaurisle.com) is housed in a purpose-built museum shaped like a giant pterosaur. Its collection includes robotic dinosaurs and life-size replicas of the different species once found on the island, which is Europe's premier site for dinosaur remains as well as being one of the world's richest fossil localities.

Eating and drinking

Sandown's stylish *King's House Café*, 43 High St (℡01983 406445), offers sound **meals and drinks**, with great views over the sea, as does *The Reef*, The Esplanade (℡01983 403219), a bright bar-restaurant with a range of mid-priced dishes including pizzas, pasta, steaks and fresh fish, with mains from around £8–12. *Swad*, 18 High St (℡01983 400800) bills itself as a North Indian tapas restaurant and serves interesting traditional dishes such as tandoori prawns and *malai kofka* (potato balls) from around £7. You can eat for under £10 a head at *Barnaby's*, 4 Pier St (℡01983 403368) which serves bargain grills, breakfasts, sandwiches and pasta dishes, with sea views on the decking if you object to the naff interior decor.

Shanklin

Merging with Sandown to the southwest, **SHANKLIN** is split into three parts – a scenic old town at the southern end of the functional new town and, below steep cliffs, a lower beach resort. With its leafy cliff-top gardens and scenic Chine (a steep gulley running down to the beach) it certainly has a more sophisticated aura than its northern neighbour.

Arrival and information

The final stop on the Island Line from Ryde, Shanklin **train station** is about half a mile inland at the top of Regent Street, with the **bus station** (buses #2 & #3 from Ryde and Newport) a little south. Shanklin's **tourist office** is located at 67 High St (April–Oct Tues–Sat 9.30am–5.30pm, Sun 10am–4pm; Nov to Easter irregular hours; ℡01983 813818). There's a large **car park** in the Old Village and along the seafront, or try the side roads around Rylstone Gardens.

Accommodation

Aqua Hotel 17 The Esplanade ℡01983 863024, Ⓦwww.aquahotel.co.uk. Newish hotel in a great seafront location with its own garden and decent if unspectacular rooms. It's worth paying extra (£120) for a sea-facing room with a balcony; other rooms ⑤

Foxhills 30 Victoria Ave ℡01983 862329, Ⓦwww.foxhillsofshanklin.co.uk. Comfortable rooms in a well-run, Victorian guest house. The gardens are lovely, backing onto a stream and woodlands, and guests can use the free jacuzzi. ⑥

Luccombe Hall Luccombe Rd ℡01983 869000, Ⓦwww.luccombehall.co.uk (⑥) and **Luccombe Manor** Popham Rd ℡01983 869000, Ⓦwww.luccombemanor.co.uk (④). Owned by the same company, these two grand country houses sit side

by side on the cliff-top, with four acres of lovely gardens between them and splendid views over the sea. *Luccombe Hall* is slightly smarter, but both hotels share the same superb facilities, including indoor and outdoor pools, jacuzzis, children's play area and trampoline. Both hotels have a good range of family rooms.

Pink Beach Hotel 20 The Esplanade ℡01983 862501, Ⓦwww.pink-beach-hotel.co.uk. In a great location right on the beach, this Victorian building has its own garden and simple rooms. It is worth paying a little extra for sea views. ③

Rylstone Manor Rylstone Gardens ℡01983 862806, Ⓦwww.rylstone-manor.co.uk. This superb Victorian pile sits right in the middle of leafy public gardens on the top of the cliff. There's period decor

▲ Sandown

SHANKLIN

N

Shanklin
Train Station

Bus Station

OLD VILLAGE

Shanklin Chine

Entrance to
Shanklin Chine

Rylstone
Gardens

Cliff
Lift

Esplanade

◀ Godshill

0   250 yds

© Crown copyright

▼ Ventnor

EATING & DRINKING

Black Cat	2
Famous Pasty Shop	6
Fisherman's Cottage	5
Grand View Tea Gardens	8
Old Thatched Teashop	7
Pavarotti's	3
Steamer Inn	1
The Crab Inn	4

ACCOMMODATION

Aqua Hotel	B
Foxhills	D
Luccombe Hall	G
Luccombe Manor	F
Pink Beach Hotel	A
Rylstone Manor	E
The Havelock	C

and its own bar and dining room, though note children under 16 are not allowed and in high season there is a 2- to 3-night minimum weekend let. ❼ **The Havelock** 2 Queen's Rd ☎01983 8627847, Ⓦwww.havelockhotel.co.uk. Lovely cliff-top hotel with its own heated outdoor pool and fine gardens. The best rooms have sea views and balconies and there are also family rooms, while breakfast comes with superb fresh breads. Closed late Nov to early March.❸

The village and Chine

Shanklin's thatched **Old Village** is archetypically pretty – and correspondingly mobbed with visitors for much of the year. Escape the crowds in the lovely **Rylstone Gardens** that spread along the top of the cliff. This also marks the top of **Shanklin Chine** (daily: late March to May & mid-Sept to Oct 10am–5pm; June to mid-Sept 10am–10pm; £3.80), a twisting pathway with steps down a mossy gorge. There's a waterfall at the top and a series of minor attractions at the bottom of the narrow ravine including caged birds and chipmunks and a Victorian brine bath. Also here is a section of PLUTO, a metal pipe that once led from here under the Channel to supply troops with petrol during the Normandy Landings in World War II. Lights liven the Chine up on a summer evening, but it is all somewhat overpriced and once out of the bottom gate, there is no return without paying again.

Fortunately there are also steps down and a lift, along with an approach road to the broad **beach** at the foot of the cliffs, where you can hire kayaks and the like (Ⓦwww.wightwaters.com) in front of a row of guest houses and cafés.

Eating and drinking

Black Cat 83 High St ☎01983 863761. Tasty Thai menu with dishes such as duck and seafood specials from £8, along with good vegetarian options. Closed Sun.

Famous Pasty Shop 11 Shanklin High St. You can watch the delicious pasties being made here, then buy them cooked for a picnic, or uncooked to take home. Try the steak and stilton or pork and apple – prices from £2.50–3.

Fisherman's Cottage At the southern end of the Esplanade, and at the bottom of Shanklin Chine ☎01983 863882. An atmospheric thatched pub right on the seafront, with outside tables: it serves wholesome pub food, such as seafood pancake (£9) and leek and mushroom pie (£8).

Grand View Tea Gardens Popham Rd. In the grounds of *Luccombe Manor*, this small kiosk serves teas, coffees, light lunches and delicious home-made cream teas in a lovely cliff-top garden with great sea views.

Old Thatched Teashop 4 Church Rd. A warren of rooms in this friendly and efficient teahouse, with pretty gardens at the back. It serves lunches – soup and sandwiches – and is highly regarded for its delicious home-made scones and cakes.

Pavarotti's 105 High St ☎01983 863528. In the Old Village, this Italian has a good range of reasonably priced pasta and pizzas (around £8) and slightly more pricey meat and fish dishes (£14), as well as some fine antipasti.

Steamer Inn 18 The Esplanade ☎01983 862641. Prime seafront boozer with expensive pub food but great views.

The Crab Inn 94 High St ☎01983 862363. Quaint thatched pub in the old town with a range of good-value pub food including sharing platters such as a great deli board with cheeses, hams and chutneys or smoked fish and meats, as well as usual favourites such as steaks, burgers and curries. Mains from £7.

Ventnor and around

The seaside resort of **VENTNOR** and its two village suburbs of **Bonchurch** and **St Lawrence** sit at the foot of St Boniface Down, the island's highest point at 787ft. The Down periodically disintegrates into landslides, creating the jumbled terraces known locally as the **Undercliff**, whose sheltered, south-facing aspect, mild winter temperatures and thick carpet of undergrowth have contributed to the former fishing village becoming a fashionable health spa. Thanks to these factors, the town possesses rather more character than the island's other resorts, its Gothic Revival buildings clinging dizzily to zigzagging bends above a small but pleasant crescent of sands.

Arrival, information and accommodation

Ventnor is served by **buses** #3 from Newport and Ryde and #6 from Newport and Blackgang: they pull in along the High Street. The **tourist office** is on Salisbury Gardens, Dudley Road (☎01983 8138180). As well as the places listed below there's plenty of **self-catering accommodation** in the area: particularly worth a mention are the wonderful properties right on the shore at Steephill Cove (from £500–1500 in high season) including the stunning lighthouse; see ⓦwww.theboathouse-steephillcove.co.uk and ⓦwww.steephillcove.com for details.

Bonchurch Manor Bonchurch Shute ☎01938 852868, ⓦwww.bonchurhcmanor.com. Grand stone mansion with substantial gardens and sea views from the lounge and some bedrooms. Breakfasts are all free-range and use local products, and it is also home to the *Tiffin Room* restaurant, which serves delicious South Indian meals; booking essential. ❺

Hambrough Hotel Hambrough Rd, Ventnor ☎01938/856333, ⓦwww.thehambrough.com. Small but stylish, modern hotel above a restaurant

(see p.276). The minimalist rooms come with all the luxuries, including flat-screen TV and Molton Brown toiletries; most have sea views, and some have balconies. ❼

Horseshoebay House Shore Rd, Bonchurch ☎01983 856800, ⓦwww.horseshoebayhouse .co.uk. A lovely B&B right on the beach below Bonchurch at Horseshoe Bay. All the comfortable rooms have sea views and there's a great café with a sun terrace overlooking the beach. ❶

St Augustine Villa The Esplanade, Ventnor ☎01983 852289, Ⓦwww.harbourviewhotel.co.uk. Large Victorian mansion in a great location facing the beach with period fittings in the lounge. Rooms come in various sizes, but it's worth paying an extra £10 for sea views. ❹

The Lake Hotel Shore Rd, Lower Bonchurch ☎01983 852613, Ⓦwww.lakehotel.co.uk. Family-run hotel in a nineteenth-century country manor with lovely grounds, a short walk from Bonchurch village and the beach. It has an attractive sun lounge and terrace and twenty large, comfortable rooms, all en suite. ❹

The Troubadour Hotel 25 High St, Ventnor ☎01983 856537, Ⓦwww.troubadourhotel.co.uk. Simple but good-value en-suite rooms in a Victorian house, above *Merlins* restaurant. ❶

The Town

Ventnor's frayed-at-the-edges High Street has an interesting mixture of smart gift shops and delis sitting next to run-down antique and bric-a-brac shops. The main entertainment venue is the **Winter Gardens** on Pier Street (☎01983 855215, Ⓦwww.ventnorwintergardens.co.uk), which hosts comedy nights, bands, film nights and flea markets and has great views over the sea from its terrace bar-café. From here, the floral terraces of the Cascade curve down to the slender Esplanade and narrow fine shingle beach, which is lined with shops, cafés and restaurants. Ventnor Haven Fishery sells freshly caught fish from its stall on the jetty, while Ocean Blue Adventures runs catamaran tours along the Undercliff (45min; £10; ☎01983 852398, Ⓦwww.oceanblueseacharters.co.uk), as well as lobster and fishing trips.

From Ventnor's Esplanade, it's a pleasant mile-long stroll along the seafront (with some steep uphill sections) to the **Botanical Gardens** (free), 22 landscaped acres of flourishing subtropical vegetation. The plants grow naturally because of the mild microclimate of the south-facing Undercliff. There used to be a sanatorium here for patients suffering from consumption and diseases of the chest, as the climate was very conducive to their recovery. It's a lovely sheltered spot for a picnic, and there's a decent café too, with a children's play area and plenty of space for running around.

Just before you reach the gardens you'll pass the attractive **Steephill Cove**, a former fishing hamlet whose whitewashed cottages tumble down the cliff to a pretty beach. Right on the water's edge, the expensive *Boathouse* restaurant serves whatever fish or seafood the boats have caught each day, and there's also a beach café and the wonderful *Wheelers Crab Shed* (see p.276). There's no car access to the cove, but if you don't fancy the walk from Ventnor, you can park in a small car park on the main Ventnor–Blackgang road, and walk five minutes down a footpath to the bay.

Bonchurch

Back on Ventnor Esplanade, it's a lovely twenty-minute walk in the opposite direction along the seafront to Horseshoe Bay, just below the village of **Bonchurch**. An attractive village of thatched cottages and Victorian villas, many clustered round a picturesque pond, it was described by Charles Dickens as "the prettiest place I ever saw in my life, at home or abroad" and was where he wrote much of *David Copperfield*. Other notable literary fans of the village include John Keats and Algernon Swinburne, who is buried in the village graveyard. From the attractive if stony beach, there's a fine hour-long roundwalk: take the uphill path just east of the beach pottery and join the coastal path east (a short detour takes you to Bonchurch's Old Church, which dates from 1070). The coastal path crosses a field. You then follow the sign to Bonchurch Chute – the path climbs ancient woodland, home to red squirrels and the rare Glanville Fritillary butterfly. Soon you'll join a road, Bonchurch Chute. Turn left and head downhill and you return to Bonchurch's main street next to the ponds. Turn left here to go back down to the beach.

Alternatively, you can do the steep half-hour walk from the beach up the **Devil's Chimney**, a dramatic series of steps that wind up through the woods through a narrow crevice in the cliffs to the *Smuggler's Haven Tea Rooms* (see below) on St Boniface Downs, where you can reward your exertions with a cream tea.

Eating and drinking

Bonchurch Inn The Shute, Bonchurch ☎01983 852611. Old-fashioned, unspoilt inn, with an attractive courtyard. Serves delicious Italian food, such as home-made pizzas (£8–9) and risotto and steaks. It's very popular and with only one small bar and a small family room, booking is recommended.

El Toro Contento 2 Pier St ☎01983 857600. A cosy restaurant dishing up home-made tapas, such as chorizo in cider, and spicy squid, most for under a fiver. Also serves Spanish hams and cheeses and will cook paella for £10 a head (min 4 people) with 24hr notice. Closed Sun.

Goodman's Deli 14 High St. Great Italian coffee, and reasonably priced cakes and sandwiches to eat in – try the aubergine and gruyére panini – or assemble your own picnic from their great range of hams, cheese and olives. Closed Sun.

Smuggler's Haven Tea Rooms on the main Bonchurch to Shanklin road. Cosy tearooms in a great position overlooking the sea with its own lawn and small veranda. Serves cream teas, sandwiches and inexpensive lunches 10am–4.30pm; Easter to Oct daily; end Feb to Easter Sat & Sun only; closed Nov–Feb.

Spyglass Inn Ventnor Esplanade ☎01983 855338. Lively pub in a great location on the seafront with outdoor tables on the terrace. The meals are mostly pub staples in giant portions, such as fish pie for £9, while the home-made daily specials often include locally caught fish.

The Ale and Oyster Ventor Esplanande ☎01983 855674. Pricey but delicious seafood platters, including prawns, lobster and oysters, in a great seafront location.

The Café Steephill Cove. Simple café right on the beach with a lovely terrace overlooking the sea. Serves local crab sandwiches, home-made cakes and pints of prawns. Easter to Sept daily except Tues 11am–4pm; only opens if weather is fine; call ☎01983 855390 to check.

The Hambrough Hambrough Rd, Ventnor ☎01983 856333. Owned by Britain's youngest Michelin-starred chef, Robert Thompson, this award-winning restaurant uses local produce where possible and has great views over the sea. A two-course lunch, featuring dishes such as haddock chowder with quails' eggs, costs £18, with a three-course dinner including local partridge with chestnut pasta for £45. Closed Sun & Mon.

🏃 **The Pond Café** Bonchurch Village Rd, Bonchurch. Small and smart, this well-regarded restaurant overlooking the village pond is also run by Robert Thompson, but is cheaper and less formal than *The Hambrough* (see above). It has a short menu of good-value dishes, such as poached sea bream and Isle of Wight rib-eye beef; mains are £12–15 and starters around £5.

🏃 **Wheelers Crab Shed** Steephill Cove ☎01983 852177. Delicious home-made crab pasties, sandwiches and ciabattas served from a pretty shack on the seashore. Weekends and holidays 11.30am–3.30pm.

Wroxall and Godshill

A couple of miles inland along the B3327 and over St Boniface Down takes you to the unassuming village of Wroxall, where you'll find the small **Donkey Sanctuary** (daily 10.30am–4.30pm, free), home to some hundred or so rescued donkeys; go in spring and there are plenty of very cute foals.

Of more interest is **Appuldurcombe House** (daily: May–Sept 10am–5pm; mid-Feb to April & Oct 10am–3pm; £3.50; EH) half a mile from Wroxall – the island's grandest pre-Victorian house sitting in picturesque, rolling countryside. From the front of the house, the building looks intact, but it is in fact largely ruined. The present mansion was built in the late eighteenth century in the Palladian style, with gardens landscaped by "Capability" Brown. Soldiers were stationed here in both world wars – in World War II live ammunition was used for military training, exacerbating damage already caused in 1943 when a landmine was accidently dropped here. Semi-abandoned ever since, Appuldurcombe has been preserved in a scenic state of decay, the highlight being the partly renovated Great Hall, built 1701–1713, and once used for banquets.

The grounds are also home to the **Owl and Falconry Centre** (daily April–Sept; £7.25, children £5.25), which puts on regular talks and flying displays (usually 11am, 1pm & 3pm) from an array of falcons including kestrels, eagles and kites – though you can't help feeling the birds don't appreciate being tethered, and you may find the similar displays at Robin Hill Park more cost-effective (see p.264). Adjacent, too, is the beautifully sited *Appuldurcombe Gardens Holiday Park* (☎01983 852597, ⊛www.appuldurcombegardens.co.uk; closed Dec–Jan), a large campsite with its own heated pool.

You can pick up a great footpath by the Appuldurcombe House car park for a leafy two-mile walk to **GODSHILL**, which bills itself as the prettiest village on the island. With its medley of thatched cottages, gardens and medieval church it is undeniably lovely, but sadly it is now all but swamped by teahouses and souvenir stalls – indeed its historic Old Smithy is little more than a row of tacky shops set in historic buildings. Children should enjoy the **Model Village** (March & Nov–Dec 10am–3.30pm; April–June & Sept–Oct 10am–5pm; July & Aug 10am–6pm; £3.30, children £1.95); there are miniature versions of Shanklin and Godshill and a model railway neatly laid out among shrubs and plants.

Godshill is well catered for in terms of **pubs** and **restaurants**. Best of these is the *Taverners* (☎01983 840707), a fine old pub with its own garden famed for its fresh local produce. Dishes include local hams, Isle of Wight cheeses and traditional dishes such as shepherd's pie or faggots; mains from £8–10. Over the road in a thatched building, the *Loaves and Fishes* (☎01983 840232; closed Sun eve & Mon) specializes in excellent seafood dishes such as scallops in garlic butter, *moules* and sea bass; mains are £12–15.

Niton and St Catherine's Point

The western Undercliff at Ventnor begins to recede at the village of **Niton**, where a footpath continues to the most southerly tip of the island, **St Catherine's Point**, marked by a modern lighthouse. A great half-hour round walk leaves from in front of the old smugglers' haunt, the excellent *Buddle Inn* St Catherine's Road, in Niton (☎01983 730243), which serves real ales and good food in a beamed bar with an open fire, or outside in the garden with great views over the sea. From the pub, take the signposted path opposite and follow it down the hill. Turn right and join the footpath signed off to the right, which snakes through fields to join the coast path. Here, turn right to the lighthouse, then cross a stile onto the lane that leads (right) back up into Niton. The village is also home to the unusual *Enchanted Manor*, Sandrock Road (☎01983 730215, ⊛www.enchantedmanor.co.uk; 3- or 4-night stays from around £285 per person which includes ferry crossings, except at last minute), a fairy-themed guest house with luxurious rooms featuring fairy-tale artworks by Josephine Wall.

From Niton, there's a lovely 1- to 2-hour cliff-top walk to a prominent landmark on the downs **St Catherine's Oratory**, known locally as the "Pepper Pot", and originally a lighthouse, reputedly built in 1325. Take the road uphill past the *Enchanted Manor* and pick up the coast path on the left. This climbs to a walk along the lip of dramatic cliffs all the way to Blackgang (see p.278). Cross the road and pick up the footpath opposite the viewpoint car park and you'll see the Oratory on the hill above you. Return the same way, or you can head back to Niton over the hill.

▲ St Catherine's Lighthouse

Blackgang Chine

A short distance west, the theme park at **Blackgang Chine** (daily: April to mid-Sept 10am–5 or 6pm; mid-Sept to Oct 10am–4.30pm; Oct 10am–5pm; mid-Sept to mid-Oct closed Mon & Fri; £9.50) has a great location perched on the cliff-top. Opened as a landscaped garden in 1843, it now has a series of fairly low-key attractions on themes such as the Wild West, dinosaurs, nursery rhymes and goblins, along with a series of museum rooms tracing the history of local crafts. Most of the rides, which are ranged down the cliff, are suited to under-12s, though older children will enjoy the roller coaster and water chutes. Sadly parts of the park have had to be closed after much of the area slipped down the cliff – some say because of a monk's curse made after Henry VIII's Dissolution Act of 1539 closed the local monastery.

West Wight

The northwest tip of the island is fairly built up, from the bustling harbour of **Yarmouth** to the sprawl of **Freshwater** and **Totland**. However, the rest of the west of the island is largely undeveloped, especially along the south coast where rolling countryside backs onto fine bays at **Compton** and Freshwater itself. **Brighstone**, complete with its own bay, is a short walk from the superb gardens at **Mottistone**. But the big draw in this part of the island is the dramatic coastal formation on the westernmost tip, where the multicoloured sands of **Alum Bay** face the spectacular chalk stacks of the **Needles**. These also form the target for one of the island's greatest walks, along the cliff-top **Tennyson Down** where the great poet gained much inspiration.

Brighstone to Compton Bay

Brighstone is far less visited than the much-vaunted Godshill (see p.277) but just as pretty, with an idyllic cluster of low thatched cottages. One of the cottages on North Street has been converted into a **museum** (approximate hours Mon–Sat 10am–4pm, late May to late Sept also Sun noon–5pm; for exact opening hours see ⓦwww.nationaltrust.org; free; NT) of village life, with a re-creation of a Victorian cottage kitchen, complete with bread oven and hearth. The recordings of old villagers, reminiscing about their childhoods here give a fascinating insight into life in a rural community. If you fancy a stroll, there's a pleasant forty-minute walk round the village, which is detailed in a free leaflet that you can pick up at the village shop. *The Three Bishops* pub on the main road through the village, serves decent pub grub, such as haddock and spinach pie (£9), and has a large garden behind.

A couple of miles west of Brighstone, you can look round the beautiful **Mottistone Manor Gardens** (mid-March to Oct Sun–Thurs 11am–5pm; £3.50), though the manor house itself is still lived in and only open one day a year. The six acres of formal, terraced gardens, which are laid out up a hillside, form only a small part of the 650-acre estate given to the National Trust in 1963 by prominent architect John Seely, 2nd Lord Mottistone. The gardens at the bottom of the hill are more formal, with beautiful displays of camellias, roses and the like, then they give way to wilder areas the higher you go, such as bluebell woods and wild flower banks. There's a lovely walled tea-garden, which is also home to **The Shack**, designed in the 1930s by architects Seely and Paget as a country retreat, and a wonderful example of Art Deco style. Designed like a ship's galley, it was constructed to be as compact as possible, yet still incorporating all the mod cons of the time: ladders leading up to the bunks double as heated towel rails; the kitchen and gas boiler hide away behind walnut cupboards; and the dining table fits beneath the architect's desk.

If you want **to stay**, look no further than *Mottistone Farmhouse* opposite the gardens (☎01983 740207, ⓦwww.bolthols.co.uk; ❸), with its four rooms inside a lovely old farm building. It's a short walk or drive to the *Sun Inn* (☎01983 741124) in neighbouring Hulverstone, which serves good pub **food** (from around £8) and has a great beer garden. Alternatively there's *Grange Farm* campsite (☎01983 740296, ⓦwww.brighstonebay.fsnet.co.uk; closed Nov–Feb), which sits on the cliff-top at Brighstone bay and doubles as a rare breeds farm, complete with llamas and the odd water buffalo.

South of Brighstone, the coast path and road follow one of the least developed parts of the island to the superb expanse of sands at **Compton Bay**. Accessible only by foot from the car park at the top, the Bay is popular with surfers and kitesurfers. The gently sloping beach backed by crumbling red rocks is also good for bathing off, though at high tide it's a pretty packed patch of sand. The nearest campsite is the well-equipped *Compton Farm* in Brook (☎01983 740215, ⓦwww.comptonfarm.co.uk; closed Oct–April), around a ten-minute walk from the sands.

Freshwater and Totland

Joining both coasts of this end of the Isle of Wight, **Freshwater** is a sprawling community that merges with Totland in the north and Freshwater Bay in the south. **Totland** and neighbouring Colwell Bay have a pleasant seafront promenade, though the waters on the north coast are less alluring than those on the south at **Freshwater Bay**.

Just inland from Freshwater Bay, on the corner with Terrace Lane, **Dimbola Lodge** (Tues–Sun: March–Oct 10am–5pm; Nov–Feb 10am–4pm; bank holidays and daily during school hols; £4; ⓦwww.dimbola.co.uk) was the home of pioneering Victorian photographer Julia Margaret Cameron, who settled here after visiting Tennyson in 1860. The building now houses an eclectic collection of exhibits, including a museum of Cameron's work, with pictures of her contemporaries, such as Tennyson, Darwin, Robert Browning, the actress Ellen Terry, and Alice Liddell, the model for Lewis Carroll's *Alice in Wonderland*. There are also sections on the history of photography, a reconstruction of Cameron's bedroom, and a room where you can dress up as a Victorian and have your picture taken. In addition, there's an exhibition on the history of the Isle of Wight Festival (see p.262), with memorabilia from festivals past, such as posters, T-shirts, souvenirs and programmes. The rest of the space is given over to temporary exhibitions of photography (check the website to see what's currently on), and a fine **tearoom** on the ground floor with outdoor tables overlooking the sea: it serves light lunches such as kedgeree (£7), home-made cakes and cream teas and a good range of veggie options.

You can pick up the coast path alongside the museum or from Freshwater Bay itself, which leads onto **Tennyson Down**, a beautiful stretch of rolling downs stretching all the way to the Needles. It takes its name from Lord Alfred Tennyson who lived in Freshwater from 1852 to be "far from noise and smoke of town" (and where, it is said, he had an affair with Julia Margaret Cameron – see p.279). He frequently walked these downs to gain inspiration for his works, and it is fitting that the top of the down is marked by a monument to the poet, a half-hour walk from Freshwater Bay. Continuing west along the well-marked path, it is another hour to the Needles – a superb walk with great views over to the New Forest on the mainland. The energetic can then return along the northern coast path back to Totland (around 45min).

Practicalities

Totland and Freshwater are served by **buses** #7 and #11 from Newport. There are two small but well-equipped **campsites** in the area: *Stoats Farm* at Weston Lane, Totland (☎01983 755258, ⓦwww.stoats-farm.co.uk; closed Nov–Feb) and *Heathfield Farm*, Heathfield Road, Freshwater (☎01983 407822, ⓦwww .heathfieldcamping.co.uk; closed Oct–April). There's also a **youth hostel** in a Victorian house on Hurst Hill at Totland Bay (☎0825 371 9348, ⓦwww.yha .org.uk; £16). In Freshwater Bay itself, the *Sandpipers Hotel* (☎01938 758500, ⓦwww.sandpipershotel.com; ❷) is just a stone's throw from the beach, next to a large car park. It's a quirky warren of a **hotel** with a wide variety of rooms – some in the main Victorian house, others in the modern annexe – and a restaurant. About a mile inland is a more upmarket option, *Farringford House*, Bedbury Lane, Freshwater Bay (☎01938 752500, ⓦwww.farringford.co.uk; ❸), formerly Tennyson's home, surrounded by lovely grounds that look out to sea, with an outdoor solar-heated pool, tennis court, croquet lawn and adjoining golf course. You can stay in the luxurious bedroom of Tennyson himself in the main house, or in self-catering cottages in the grounds. There's a formal dining room that serves local produce, or alternatively there's the *Red Lion* **pub**, Church Place, Freshwater (☎01983 754925): it's a traditional place with log fires, real ales, a lovely big garden, and good selection of homely pub meals. Otherwise, try the *Fat Cat Bar* at the *Sandpipers Hotel* for its selection of amusing pub games and wide variety of local real ales and German beers.

Alum Bay and the Needles

The top attractions hereabouts, Alum Bay and the Needles, lie four miles west of Yarmouth. At the island's western tip, you'll find the multi-chrome cliffs at **Alum Bay** tumbling down to ochre-hued sands, which were used as pigments for painting local landscapes in the Victorian era. Alum Bay was also the scene of Marconi's early experiments, when he made the first telephone communications between here and Bournemouth (see box, p.52). You can still buy the multicoloured sands in a bottle that have long been popular souvenirs at the **Needles Park** (Ⓦwww.theneedles.co.uk) amusement park, at the top of the cliff: it's an assorted collection of rather tacky children's attractions, though the **chairlift** (£4 return) down the cliff to the bay is worth a ride for the stunning views. At the bottom of the lift, **boat trips** run by Needles Pleasure Cruises (Easter–Oct; Ⓣ01983 754477, Ⓦwww.needlespleasurecruises.co.uk) leave from a jetty to view the three tall chalk stacks known as **The Needles**: the standard trip lasts about twenty minutes and costs £5, and they also run high-speed RIB tours (£9; 15min).

From the car park by the amusement park, it's a lovely twenty-minute walk to the lookout on top of **the Needles**, and the **Old Battery** (mid-March to Oct daily 10.30am–5pm; £4.40), a Victorian fort that sits dizzily on the top of the cliff. It was built to defend Britain from the threat of invasion by the French and was active during both world wars. You can go inside the old guardroom, from where soldiers would have watched the D-day invasion force heading out to France, and clamber down a low tunnel to a nineteenth-century searchlight emplacement – once used to look out for night-time invasion – for some of the best views of the Needles. The fort include the remains of the original lighthouse, built in 1786 but partly obscured by the top of the cliff – the reason the current one was built at the end of the Needles in 1859. There's a small tearoom in the Old Lookout Tower, which has some of the best views over the headland (also open Sat & Sun 11am–3pm in winter).

Just above the Old Battery lies **The New Batteries** (mid-March to Oct Sat & Sun plus hols where possible 11am–4pm; free), built in 1895 as a gun emplacement. In 1956, the military started testing rockets here during the Cold War; the site became known as the High Down Test Site and once employed 200 people. Twenty seven rockets were tested here before being launched in Australia and the research undertaken pioneered much of the early space technology for the moon landings. Today you can explore the underground rooms where the secret testing took place; various exhibits explain what went on here.

▲ The Needles

Practicalities

Bus #7 runs from Yarmouth to the Needles Park car park every thirty minutes or so, but the only bus running from there up to the Needles themselves is the open-top Needles tour bus, a hop-on, hop-off tour of the west of the island (£10 for a day ticket). A ten-minute walk from the car park, along a path signed off the road towards the Needles, is the wonderful ⚘ *Warren Farm* **tearooms** (☎01938 753200, ⓦwww.farmhousecreamteas.co.uk), a working farm where children can play with pigs, goats and chickens and adults can refuel with delicious home-made scones, jams, cream and cakes served in a pretty garden, surrounded by verdant fields.

Yarmouth

Linked to Lymington in the New Forest by car ferry, the pleasant town of **YARMOUTH**, on the northern coast of the Isle of Wight, is one of the prettiest arrival points on the island. With its good array of places to eat and drink, it also makes the best base for exploring the western tip of the island, and for doing some local walks.

Arrival and information

The **ferry** from Lymington arrives pretty much in the centre of the town, with the **tourist office** next door, on The Quay (☎01983 813818). **Watertaxis** to Lymington and along the coast leave from The Quay too (☎01983 760776). You can **rent bikes**, a great way to explore the island, from Wight Cycle Hire, Station Road (☎01983 761800, ⓦwww.wightcyclehire.co.uk; £14 a day).

Accommodation

Jireh House St James's Square ☎01983 760513, ⓦwww.jireh-house.com. Right in the centre of town, this pretty seventeenth-century stone guest house once formed part of the old town hall. The six rooms are cosy, some with oak beams, and the lounge has a lovely stone fireplace. ❸

Medlars Hallets Shute ☎01983 761541. Just outside Yarmouth – a 15min walk from the town centre – this converted stone barn in a rural location has two comfortable rooms and a pretty garden. ❶

The Bugle Coaching Inn The Square ☎01983 760272, ⓦwww.buglecoachinginn.co.uk. Standard en-suite rooms, plus some smarter suites with four-poster beds, above a pub in a great location, right on the main square. ❹

The George Hotel Quay St ☎01983 760331, ⓦwww.thegeorge.co.uk. In a great position right by the ferry dock, with a lovely garden overlooking the Solent, this seventeenth-century hotel has comfortable, elegantly furnished rooms, some with balconies overlooking the water, that have hosted the likes of Charles II. It has two highly regarded restaurants (see p.283). ❽

The Town

Sitting at the mouth of the River Yar, Yarmouth is England's smallest borough. It's an appealing little town that has remained compact due to its position bordered by the river on one side, the sea to the north and marshland to the east. One of the earliest settlements of the island, the first recorded mention of the town was in 991, when it was known as Eremue, or "muddy estuary". It was the Normans, however, who laid out the town on a grid system, which is still in evidence today.

Yarmouth used to be the main port on the island, and suffered regular incursions from the French, being burnt down by them on two separate occasions. In order to protect the town, **Yarmouth Castle** (April–Sept Mon–Thurs & Sun 11am–4pm; £3.60; EH), tucked between the quay and the pier, was commissioned by Henry VIII. Completed in 1574, after Henry's death, the

The Yar Estuary and the Freshwater Way walk

There's a lovely **four-mile round walk** from Yarmouth that runs along one side of the River Yar, returning along the other bank. Head south from Bridge Road along the bridleway that runs behind the town car park, and follow the path for a couple of miles, through marshland and woods, looking out for red squirrels en route. Once you hit the road, turn right over the Freshwater Causeway to join the Freshwater Way with All Saints' Church on your right, and the *Red Lion* pub (see p.280) on your left. From here, you follow the Freshwater Way back up the western side of the River Yar through woods and fields to join the coast road that leads back into Yarmouth. If want to extend the walk, you can continue south along the Freshwater Way: to do this, instead of turning right at All Saints' Church, take the signed footpath on your left before you reach the church, just after crossing the stone bridge over the River Yar, which leads a mile or so down to Freshwater Bay.

castle was the last and most sophisticated of Henry's coastal defence network to be built, and the first to use the innovative arrowhead artillery bastion. Inside, some rooms have re-created life in a sixteenth-century castle, and there's also a display on the many wrecks that floundered in the Solent here. Outside, there are superb views over the estuary from the battlements. Yarmouth's only other real sight is the Grade II listed **pier**, England's longest wooden pier still in use.

Eating and drinking

Gossips Café on the pier, just off the main square. A great place for lunch or a snack – it does a huge selection of sandwiches (most around £3) and tortilla wraps, as well as hot dishes, and has a great view of the comings and goings of the boats.

Jirah Tearooms St James's Square. A seventeenth-century tearoom that serves dishes such as home-made hummus, soups and seafood in the evening, plus light lunches and cream teas during the day.

Salty's bar and restaurant Quay St ☏01938 761550. In a prime location in an old warehouse, next to the ferry terminal, with a nice balcony overlooking the street: it produces local seafood and meat dishes, with main courses around £17–18.

The Blue Crab High St ☏01938 760014. A simply decorated restaurant with cosy booths that offers fish and shellfish dishes such as plaice with parsley butter (£16). Also does top-quality fresh fish and chips to take away for £5.

The Boathouse Fort Victoria. About a mile east of Yarmouth in Fort Victoria Country Park, this daytime café has a great location right on the waterfront, with outdoor tables on the beach. It serves simple hot meals, such as ham, egg and chips (£7), as well as home-made soup and sandwiches. Wed–Sun 9am–4pm.

The Brasserie *The George Hotel*, Quay St ☏01983 760331. The place to go for an upmarket meal, specializing in top-quality seafood, such as monkfish in parma ham (£19). The two-course lunch menu is good value at £16.50, featuring dishes such as wild garlic and rocket risotto.

The Bugle Coaching Inn The Square. A seventeenth-century former coaching inn with several large bar areas with log fires and flagstone floors, and a small terrace out back. Serves large portions of traditional pub grub, as well as more fishy meals, such as bowls of mussels and chips.

Newtown and Shalfleet

Belying its history as capital of the Isle of Wight for 150 years, **NEWTOWN** is now little more than a peaceful village on the edge of an estuary on the north coast of the island. Founded in the thirteenth century by the Bishop of Winchester, the town grew in importance due to its location on a busy harbour that is now a peaceful nature reserve, and home to curlews, geese and other waterfowl. The only remains of the town's prestigious past are a trace of its gridded street pattern and an incongruous Jacobean **town hall** (2–5pm:

mid-March to June, Sept & Oct Mon, Wed & Sun; July & Aug Mon–Thurs & Sun; £2.10), stranded in the countryside with no town. There are pleasant walks in the vicinity, with footpaths leading out along a jetty and over the salt marshes around the nature reserve.

Just south of Newtown, the village of **Shalfleet** is of interest mainly due to *The New Inn*, Mill Road (℡01983 531314, Ⓦwww.thenew-inn.co.uk), a cosy **pub** with an inglenook fireplace, low beams and flagstone floors. It's also known for its food, which features locally caught fish and seafood, as well as good-quality pub dishes, such as home-made steak and ale pie (£10). If you want to stay in the area, there's a good rural **campsite**, about a mile inland at Newbridge, *The Orchards Holiday Park* (℡01983 531331, Ⓦwww .orchards-holiday-park.co.uk; closed Jan), with heated indoor and outdoor pools, café and shop.

Contexts

Contexts

History

Until Oliver Cromwell's rule in 1649, Winchester was one of England's most important cities, and the focal point for significant historical figures such as King Arthur, Alfred the Great and William the Conqueror. At one time it shared equal status with London and many of the country's major events took place in its hinterland, namely today's **Dorset**, **Hampshire and the Isle of Wight**. Below we pick the local places that were influenced by key moments in history.

Early settlers

Much of Dorset and Hampshire was inhabited in **Neolithic times** (around 3500 BC) when people first began to farm land and create defensive walls round their settlements. Their distinctive graves – long barrows – consisting of stone-chambered, turf-covered mounds can be found throughout the area, such as at Hambledon Hill (see p.152), off the Blandford to Shaftesbury road.

Bronze Age settlers from northern Europe (around 2000 BC) also left countless barrows, along with the famous stone circles at Stonehenge in neighbouring Wiltshire, but their earthen forts were unable to withstand the invading **Celts** (around 700–600 BC). The Celts' superior iron weapons, coins and ornaments brought in the Iron Age and they are credited with giving Dorset its name, calling it Dwry Triges, which evolved into Durotriges in Roman times – meaning "tidal waters". Maiden Castle was a typical Celtic stronghold, a multiple system of ramparts enlarging a simpler and older hillfort, though it was one of the first of England's Celtic forts to fall to the next set of invaders, the **Romans**, in 43 AD, the year Claudius led his successful invasion of the country. England flourished under the Romans, who established commerce and a political structure. Then called Venta Belgarum, Winchester became the fifth largest town in Britain.

From the fourth century, with the decline of the Roman Empire, the **Saxons** began to take over. The southwest of England became a stronghold of Celtic resistance, however, with semi-mythical figures such as **King Arthur** fighting to keep the invaders at bay. Some claim the wooden disc in Winchester's Great Hall to be Arthur's Round Table, and though it is unlikely to be authentic, it does suggest his activities were in this part of the country. But soon England was divided into Anglo-Saxon kingdoms – this area being the kingdom of **Wessex**. The Anglo-Saxons built stone churches, modelled on those in Rome, with round apses at their eastern end. By 664, England had adopted the **Christian faith** – though the last part of the country to be converted was the Isle of Wight, in around 686. By the eighth century, a Saxon port had grown up on the River Itchen known as Hamtun – later Southampton – which gave the county the name Hampshire. By 825, with the death of King Offa, Wessex became the dominant Anglo-Saxon kingdom and a fortress was built at Wareham to protect against marauding Vikings – its protective walls, later strengthened by the Normans, can still be seen today.

Vikings and the Norman Conquest

By 865, the **Viking** army had conquered much of England. They soon turned their attentions to **Alfred the Great**'s Wessex but, despite having inferior forces, Alfred stubbornly resisted the attacks, forcing the Vikings to sign a truce, agreeing to fix a border between Wessex and the Danelaw – the Viking territories to the north. Alfred made Winchester his capital, and for the next two centuries, the town was of equal importance to London.

After King Alfred died in 899, his successor, Edward the Elder, continued to build on Alfred's achievements and soon established himself as the de facto ruler of the country. His grandson Edgar then became the first ruler to be crowned King of England in 959. His son, Edward the Martyr, was crowned next, but in 978, aged 16, was murdered at Corfe Castle, it is thought by his stepmother – who was anxious to get her own son, Ethelred the Unready on the throne. Edward's tomb now lies in Lady St Mary's church in Wareham.

King Canute ruled from 1016–35, and it is in Southampton that he allegedly commanded the waves to retreat – some say not from a misguided sense of his powers, but as a rebuke to his obsequious courtiers. The king's bones now lie in Winchester Cathedral. By 1042, Edward the Confessor was king, but he allowed power to be wielded by Godwin, Earl of Wessex and his son Harold. When Edward died, Harold took over, only to be defeated at the Battle of Hastings in 1066, an event that quickly ushered in the **Normans**. They set about building various castles under **William the Conqueror**, who constructed abbeys and churches in the style of mainland Europe such as the cathedral in Winchester (begun in 1079), with its cruciform ground plans and huge cylindrical columns topped by semicircular arches. Appropriately, William the Conqueror's double coronation took place in both London and Winchester. William also used Winchester's monks to prepare the **Domesday Book** (1085–86) recording land ownership and the population of the country for the first time, providing the framework for taxation and feudal obligations. William also requisitioned the **New Forest** in 1079 as a game reserve. In 1066, the Normans gave the Isle of Wight its first ever lord, William Fitz Osbern, though actually he ruled very little – the Domesday Book records that at this time the island had just 126 properties, 24 water mills and 10 churches.

In 1087, William the Conqueror's son, **William Rufus**, became king, but was shot by an arrow while hunting in the New Forest at a spot now marked by the Rufus Stone (see p.172). There are plenty of theories surrounding his death – although officially it was a hunting accident, he was such an unpopular king that murder is a perfectly feasible explanation. His mortuary chest lies in Winchester Cathedral alongside the remains of England's early leaders. In 1100, William Rufus' successor, Henry I, gave the Isle of Wight to Richard de Redvers, who founded Newport in 1118. In 1292, the Isle of Wight became Crown property and the island's defences were improved.

The Hundred Years' War and the Tudors

In 1337, the **Hundred Years' War** with France began, with the French sacking Portsmouth and attempting to invade St Helens on the Isle of Wight. Six years later, King Edward III set sail from St Helens to invade Normandy, but the French returned later that century to attack Carisbrooke Castle and ransack Newport.

As frontline ports, Portsmouth and Southampton suffered numerous French attacks but were also the bases from which the English launched counter-offensives across the Channel. Henry V's famous victory against the French at **Agincourt** began when his troops departed from Southampton, largely securing the safety of the Isle of Wight.

One result of the war was the development of the Perpendicular architectural style, the first major style unique to England – before the Hundred Years War, the predominant Gothic style was copied from the French. The Perpendicular style was characterized by a rectilinear design, as typified by the chantry tombs in Winchester cathedral, where master mason William Wynford was one of the main driving forces of this style.

The start of the **Tudor period** in the fifteenth century saw England begin to develop as a major European power. With England's overseas expansion, Portsmouth was made the royal dockyard in 1495 and the world's first dry docks were built here.

Under Henry VIII, the English church was forced to secede from the Roman Catholic Church and instead recognize the king as its head (Supreme Head of the Church of England, to be exact), leading to the **Dissolution of the Monasteries**. This allowed the king and his nobles to take over monastic property, including the enormous estate of Beaulieu (see p.183), formerly one of England's most influential monasteries, and St Peter's monastery, now part of the Abbotsbury estate (see p.128).

By the time **Elizabeth I** became queen in 1558, England was divided on religious grounds, a consequence of the reign of her predecessor, Catholic half-sister, Mary. Though threatened by Spain under the powerful Philip II, Elizabeth governed wisely, reconciling Catholics and Protestants and allowing the merchant classes to flourish. Seafarers also were successful, with the likes of Walter Raleigh, who long lived in Dorset (see box, p.111), prospering from his raids on Spain's American colonies. Eventually, Philip II sent his Armada to attack in 1588, but after it was defeated, England became a major **maritime power**.

Early Stuarts and Cromwell

In the early 1600s, under the reign of Catholic James I, Catholics were tolerated once more. However, for those ardent believers who had suffered under the Protestant Queen Elizabeth I, the Stuart king didn't do enough for their cause, nor attempt to satisfy their demands. A small group, including a young and fervent **Guy Fawkes**, decided that enough was enough and conceived a plan to blow up Parliament in the **Gunpowder Plot** of 1605.

Life under James I was tricky for many Protestants, too: some turned to Puritanism and looked to move away from their turbulent island, keen to establish a "New Jerusalem" in North America. In 1620, the **Pilgrim Fathers** set sail from Southampton to establish a colony in New England, but their boat began to leak so they stopped at Plymouth before continuing in the *Mayflower* – a journey that would encourage thousands of Puritan emigrants to follow over the next few decades.

In 1645, **Oliver Cromwell**'s Roundhead troops effectively ended Winchester's position as a major player in English politics during the English Civil War, largely destroying its castle (now the Great Hall), breaking up the mortuary chests of previous kings and smashing the stained glass in the cathedral. Cromwell's troops were even more destructive in their siege of Corfe Castle, which lasted for six weeks before the Roundheads were victorious, blowing the castle into its current ruinous state. In 1647, Charles I fled to Carisbrooke Castle on the Isle of Wight, but he was soon captured and executed in London two years later.

The Restoration to Napoleon

In 1685, another Catholic, James II, became king. The Protestant Duke of Monmouth, an illegitimate son of James' brother, Charles II, raised a rebellion, landing at Lyme Regis in an attempt to overthrow James, but he failed and was beheaded. His followers were brutally dealt with by Judge George Jeffrey's **Bloody Assizes** in Dorchester, where the rebels were tried before a series of executions took place throughout the area – eighty were put to death in Dorchester, twelve in Lyme Regis and Weymouth and several others in Sherborne, Poole, Bridport and Wareham.

Under **Hanoverian** King George I, England's first de facto Prime Minister, Robert Walpole, governed a briefly stable period of growth. The wealthy spent huge sums of money on lavish buildings and their grounds – **"Capability" Brown** (1716–83), so-named because he assessed the "capabilities of landscapes", modified the estates of the gentry into ornate landscapes, complete with romantic ruins or pagodas. His work can be seen at Appuldurcombe House in the Isle of Wight and at Sherborne and Highcliffe castles, amongst others.

Under George III, England was engaged in the American Declaration of Independence and, busying itself with affairs across the pond, neglected France's woes over the Channel. In the bloody aftermath of the Revolution, **Napoleon Bonaparte** rose to fame but his military progress was interrupted by Nelson's victory at the **Battle of Trafalgar** in 1805 – you can see his victorious boat (and ultimate deathbed) the HMS *Victory* in Portsmouth (see p.242). Napoleon was finally defeated at Waterloo a decade later by the first **Duke of Wellington** – who lived in Hampshire's Stratfield Saye House, which has been home to the Dukes of Wellington since 1817, and still contains the original Duke's funeral carriage.

The Industrial Revolution and Victorian times

The late eighteenth century ushered in the **Industrial Revolution**, which accelerated after James Watt patented the steam engine in 1781. As industry flourished, so did the population, with towns and cities expanding rapidly. But rural England suffered, inspiring the pastoral yearnings of the Romantic writers such as Keats, who wrote many of his poems on the Isle of Wight, and Percy Bysshe Shelley – who was buried in Bournemouth (see p.56). Later, Thomas Hardy's novels traced the changing lifestyles of "Wessex" (see p.105), most notably in *The Mayor of Casterbridge*.

The great architect of the time was **John Nash** (1752–1835) who is associated with the Regency period of the Prince of Wales (later George IV). His stucco and decorous styles are evident today throughout Weymouth and at East Cowes Castle, Whippingham Church and Ryde Town Hall on the Isle of Wight. Under George IV, workers' associations were legalized, a civil police force was created and the Poor Laws alleviated the suffering of the destitute. This, however, did not stop the **Tolpuddle Martyrs** from being transported to Australia for joining an agricultural trade union in 1834 (see p.107). Poverty and injustice became the key political battlegrounds under **Queen Victoria**, a theme picked up in the novels of **Charles Dickens**, who grew up in Portsmouth (see p.244). This was also the age of the railway, with rail services opening up many of the south coast's resorts such as Bournemouth and the Isle of Wight to tourists – and royalty, with Victoria frequently holidaying at her family home at Osborne House (see p.258).

The twentieth century to today

In common with much of the country, World War I decimated much of the young male adult population throughout the region, but the area itself played a larger part in **World War II**. Several places were requisitioned in the war –

Blandford Camp, employed for training in World War I, was again put to use as a US hospital after the Normandy landings in 1944, while the whole village of Tynham and its surroundings were evacuated so it could be utilized for army training – the land around Tynham is army land to this day and the village stands eerily deserted (see p.88). US troops were based at Bridport and Poole while Studland was used for tank training exercises. **D-day landing** troops set off from several ports along the coast, including Portsmouth, Southampton, Poole and Weymouth to Omaha beach in France, while in 1943, the Fleet Lagoon near Portland was used to test Barnes Wallis' famous Bouncing Bomb, as depicted in *The Dam Busters*. The German Luftwaffe caused massive damage, damaging or destroying one in three properties in the three counties, with the ports of Portsmouth and particularly Southampton severely blitzed. Postwar, there was a massive rebuilding programme with an emphasis on office buildings and shopping centres to serve the hurriedly put up tower blocks and cheap housing – resulting in the bland cityscape of Southampton. Ironically, however, the land taken over by the army since the war has left much of the Isle of Purbeck wonderfully undeveloped – this area has escaped the explosion of bungalows and retirement homes that now blight much of the south coast.

Though **tourism** has increased vastly throughout the region, large areas of it have received future protection thanks to the awarding of World Heritage status to the Jurassic Coast in 2001, the creation of the New Forest National Park in 2005 and the South Downs National Park in 2010. Revitalization of Southampton and Portsmouth's docks and the creation of Bournemouth's artificial surf reef in 2009 (see p.56) have been further boosts to the region, which look set to continue with the focus turning to Weymouth for the 2012 Olympic watersports.

Wildlife

The counties of Dorset, Hampshire and the Isle of Wight cover a relatively small area but offer an extremely varied range of natural habitats, including deciduous woodland, tidal estuaries and jagged coastal cliffs. **Chalk ridges** make up the Dorset and South Downs, Cranbourne Chase, the Purbeck hills and Tennyson Down on the Isle of Wight, while **clay** is the dominant soil in the Frome and Stour valleys and the Hampshire basin. The New Forest and the area round Bournemouth consist largely of **heathlands** that survive on shallow sand, clay and gravel. Much of the coast is made up of hard **Portland** and **Purbeck stone**, revealed in sheer cliffs, while other sections of the coast – such as around Old Harry – are made of **soft chalk**. The Solent – once a river before sea levels rose, separating the Isle of Wight from the mainland some 7,000 years ago – itself creates a unique habitat thanks to its unusual double tides (caused by the irregular depth of the channel between Cherbourg and the Isle of Wight, giving additional tidal oscillation), while warm currents feed much of the Dorset coast, encouraging occasionally exotic foreign visitors to its waters.

Mammals

In common with much of England, mammals such as foxes, hedgehogs, badgers, roe deer, stoats and weasels are relatively common. The Isle of Purbeck has large colonies of various types of **deer**, many of which thrive on MOD land, which – the odd rocket aside – provides a safe haven for local wildlife. Sika deer in particular thrive on Purbeck, to the extent that they are creating a certain amount of damage to the protected wetlands at Arne. These deer – native to Japan – escaped from captivity in the nineteenth century and have been breeding here ever since. The New Forest, too, has a healthy deer population, though is best known for its **ponies**. These are not wild but belong to commoners, as do the pigs let loose to feed on acorns in autumn (see p.170). Grey squirrels, hailing from America, can be seen pretty much anywhere. These aggressive incomers have driven out the native **red squirrel** from most of England, however the Isle of Wight and Brownsea Island have resisted the grey invasion and on both islands red squirrels thrive.

The area's rivers – mostly extremely clean – support a good array of mammals including **otters** and water voles, though the latter are threatened by the introduced American mink.

The Isle of Wight and parts of southern Dorset and Hampshire are home to the very rare Bechstein's **bat**, which likes dense woodland and can live to up to twenty years of age. Even rarer is the Greater Horsehoe bat, which can live up to thirty years of age. There are around 200 breeding females in Dorset, where they are being encouraged to reproduce in some of the former stone quarries around Purbeck. The Greywell Tunnel on the Basingstoke Canal is Britain's largest bat roost with all the country's native species living here.

Insects and reptiles

Hampshire and Purbeck's chalky terrain provide a ready habitat for some beautiful and unusual **butterflies**, including the Lulworth Skipper – Purbeck is the only place where it flourishes – and the Chalkhill Blue, while the scarce Glanville Fritillary butterfly can be seen on the Isle of Wight. Durlston Head is also home for Dingy and Grizzled Skippers, Chalkhill and Small Blue butterfly. The heath **grasshopper** can only be found in Dorset and the New Forest, while Dorset's heathlands also support endangered reptiles such as the **smooth snake** and **sand lizard**. Rare **Natterjack toads** can be found in some coastal dune areas such as on Hengistbury Head. Prevalent throughout the regions are the harmless **grass snake** and the mildly venomous **adder**, often found basking on warm rocks in sunny weather. They are brown with a lozenge pattern down their back – they will flee if they sense you coming and only attack if they feel threatened. In the unlikely event that you are bitten, seek medical attention at once. Other summer nuisances are **mosquitoes** – anywhere near damp ground will see them flourish, while care should also be taken with **ticks**, which lurk in bracken.

Birds

The south of England is a rich habitat for a diverse range of **birds** including giant buzzards – usually seen swooping in pairs, often above the warm thermals created by hot tarmac roads in summer – kites, kestrels, nightjars and kingfishers. Dorset's heathlands support rare birds such as the Dartford warbler, while the increasingly uncommon skylark is thankfully still present on coastal grasslands such as on Hengistbury Head and Tennyson Down on the Isle of Wight.

The cliff ledges west of Portland Bill are home to some of the largest **sea-bird colonies** on the south coast and you can usually see guillemots, razorbills and kittiwakes. Similar bird colonies can be seen on the cliffs around Durlston in Purbeck, which also support the Manx Shearwater, European Storm-petrel, Pomarine Skua, Little Tern, puffins, Common Guillemot and Ring-necked Parakeet.

There are also some great **wetland areas** for very different birds. Particularly good for bird spotting is the wetland area around Lymington, Stanpit (Christchurch) and Arne (near Wareham), where you can see species such as marsh and hen harriers, peregrine falcons, lesser spotted woodpeckers and waders such as the avocet, little egret, whimbrel, sandwich tern, spoonbills and heron. The Fleet Lagoon by Chesil Beach is also *the* spot for birdwatchers, attracting thousands of summer and winter migrant birds as well as being home to England's largest population of mute swans (see p.128).

Marine life

The Swanage coast supports a diverse array of peripatetic sea life including **dolphins**, **porpoises**, the odd whale and occasionally giant leatherback turtles, which can be over two metres in length and drift along a migration route from their tropical breeding grounds usually in late summer, often on the trail of **jellyfish**. The latter can provide an occasional hazard, especially when the thankfully rare but poisonous Portuguese man-of-war drift into UK waters. Stings are extremely painful for up to three days. Also to be avoided is the weever fish, which lurks in the sands of shallow tidal waters. If you tread on the spines of their poisonous dorsal fins, it can be excruciating – the best treatment is to immerse the affected part in as hot water as you can bear for around 20 minutes. Another exotic but harmless marine life form native to the shores is the spiny **sea horse**, which is relatively common around Shell Bay – Britain's largest colony of the beautiful creatures lives off South Beach, though they are increasingly threatened by boats anchoring on their breeding grounds.

The clear waters of the rivers Test, Itchen and Avon are world famous for their **fish**, especially for trout and salmon, while tidal areas are rich in shellfish including crayfish, oysters, lobster and crab – a fact enjoyed by many of the pubs and restaurants around the Fleet Lagoon and the Isle of Wight, which regularly serve fresh seafood.

Books

We have highlighted a selection of books below that will give you a flavour of the area, or which were influenced by the area itself. Books marked 🏃 are particularly recommended.

Fiction

Richard Adams *Watership Down*. This classic children's story tells the tale of rabbits forced to move from Sandleford Warren in Berkshire to Watership Down in Hampshire – the locations are all based on the area where Adams grew up, south of Newbury.

🏃 **Jane Austen** *Pride and Prejudice*. The classic tale of love, intrigue and misunderstanding, partly set in "Meryton", based on Basingstoke. The book has been made into several films and adaptations, most famously with Colin Firth starring as the brooding Darcy who stirs the passions of feisty Elizabeth Bennett. Austen's *Persuasion*, set partly in Lyme Regis, is the tale of Anne Elliot's growing self-awareness of love and self-interest. Will she be persuaded to marry for money, or opt for the first love of her life, the once socially inferior Captain Wentworth?

Julian Barnes *England, England*. Barnes uses the Isle of Wight as the location for a witty novel about duplicating tourist sights at a theme park containing copies of, amongst others, Big Ben, Stonehenge and Princess Diana's grave.

Enid Blyton *Five on Kirrin Island Again, Five Have a Mystery to Solve, Five go to Mystery Moor*. Enid Blyton set many of her classic *Famous Five* children's stories in and around Purbeck (see p.78); Kirrin Island is based on Corfe Castle, while Mystery Moor is based on the area around Stoborough. Wonderfully dated, the books about the adventures of four children and their dog nevertheless are still hugely popular with children today, their plots regularly recycled in cartoons such as Scooby-Doo.

Arthur Conan Doyle *The White Company*. Best known for his Sherlock Holmes stories, Doyle also wrote this well-received historical novel about the Hundred Years War. It relates the tale of monks – the headstrong Hordle John and the brave Alleyne Edricson – who leave the sanctuary of the monastery in Beaulieu to join The White Company, a team or archers who set off to war in France.

🏃 **John Meade Falkner** *Moonfleet*. The late Victorian novelist and poet lived for a time in Weymouth. His most famous work is a gripping tale of an orphan who unwittingly becomes involved in smuggling, with the action taking place around Chesil Beach, Portland Bill (which he calls The Snout) and Purbeck.

🏃 **John Fowles** *The French Lieutenant's Woman*. Fowles, a keen fan of Thomas Hardy, wrote this classic tale in 1969 and it was later made into a successful film starring Meryl Streep. Set in Lyme Regis, it relates the tale of the mysterious Sarah Woodruff, a manipulated or manipulating woman – the book is given three alternative endings to help you decide.

Thomas Hardy *Under the Greenwood Tree, The Mayor of Casterbridge, Tess of the D'Urbervilles, The Return of the Native*. All of Hardy's novels depict the harsh conditions of rural life in nineteenth-century Dorset. *Under the*

Greenwood Tree, based on his childhood experiences near Dorchester, is perhaps the most cheerful, relating the tale of church musician Dick Dewy's awkward wooing of a new, beautiful school-teacher, Fancy Day. His other novels all describe places recognizable today (see box, p.102 & p.105). ⚔ *The Mayor of Casterbridge* traces the rise and fall of Mayor Michael Henchard, who seems forever cursed by his decision to auction his wife in a fast-changing society. *Tess of the D'Urbervilles* is perhaps his most famous novel: a bleak tragedy, it relates the tale of Tess, a poor girl who tries to better her lot by seeking out the wealthy D'Urbervilles who she believes are distantly related. Alec D'Urberville takes a shine to Tess, a one-sided relationship that eventually brings about Tess's tragic end in Wintoncester prison – based on Winchester.

P.D. James *The Black Tower*. Scotland Yard's Adam Dalgliesh, recuperating in Dorset, finds himself caught up in a murder mystery in which the tower – influenced by Clavell Tower in Kimmeridge Bay – plays a key part.

Ian McEwan *On Chesil Beach*. Virtually a short story and not perhaps his greatest book, but highly evocative account of a newly married couple's disastrous sexual experience while honeymooning on Dorset's famous pebble beach.

Edward Rutherford *The Forest*. A detailed and comprehensive, if rather lengthy, history of the New Forest, from the death of William Rufus to the twentieth century, told through the adventures of fictional and real characters.

Alfred Lord Tennyson *The Complete Works*. The works of the great Victorian Poet Laureate – who coined expressions such as "*Tis better to have loved and lost, Than never to have loved at all*" – include many of the poems composed while strolling on the eastern extremities of the Isle of Wight – now named Tennyson Down. His best-known works are *The Lady of Shalott* and *The Charge of the Light Brigade*.

Virgina Woolf *Freshwater*. This was Virginia Woolf's only play, a comedy of manners set in Freshwater on the Isle of Wight and centring on the excesses of Alfred Lord Tennyson and Woolf's great aunt, the pioneering photographer Julia Margaret Cameron. It was recently resurrected on Broadway in New York.

History and background

Bill Bryson *Notes From a Small Island*. American writer and anglophile Bryson's tour of Britain, mostly using public transport, includes his wry account of Bournemouth and much of the south coast: witty and enlightening to Americans and Britons alike.

John Burgess *A History of the Isle of Wight*. The most up-to-date book on the long and fascinating history of the island, published in 2008.

Mike Clement and Ted Gosling *Dorset Railways*. A photograph-based look at the steam trains and stations that once dotted the country, many of them now defunct.

John Leete *In Time of War: Hampshire*. A vivid account of the extraordinary activity that took place in the country during World War II, including photographs and first-hand accounts.

Richard Ollard *Dorset*. A fascinating roundup of the county's history, culture, folklore and buildings by a local author.

Nikolaus Pevsner and John Newman/David Lloyd *The Buildings of England: Dorset/Hampshire and the Isle of Wight*. Part of a series covering facts about virtually every building of note in the country, and though not updated for many years, its background information is still relevant today.

Nicola Sly *Dorset Murders/Hampshire Murders*. A look back in time at various evil deeds committed in the two counties, including unsolved mysteries and the real-life murder that inspired Thomas Hardy's *Tess of the D'Urbervilles*.

Peta Whaley *West Country History: Dorset*. A comprehensible account of key moments and figures in the history of the country, by a Shaftesbury-based author.

Nature guides

Martin Cade and George Green *Where to Watch Birds in Dorset, Hampshire and the Isle of Wight*. A comprehensive guide to the best sites for birdwatching throughout the year, including places with disabled access.

Dorset Wildlife Trust *The Natural History of Dorset*. A detailed round-up of the county's natural history, including detailed illustrations and photographs.

Barry Goater *The Butterflies and Moths of Hampshire and the Isle of Wight*. A scholarly look at the rich diversity of these insects, which flourish in this part of the country.

Gilbert White *The Natural History of Selborne*. This eighteenth-century account of the area's flora and fauna was written by a man who preceded Darwin by a century but who made many of the same observations. It also includes letters to explorers and fellow naturalists. See also p.213.

Walks and outdoor pursuits

AA *50 Walks in Dorset/50 Walks in Hampshire and the Isle of Wight*. A good range of walks with interesting introductions to each, though the maps are somewhat sketchy and not all routes are easy to follow.

Wayne Alderson *Surfing – A Beginner's Guide/Surf UK: The Definitive Guide to Surfing in Britain*. All you need to know before you hit the artificial surf reef in Bournemouth, whether you are a novice or an expert wave rider.

Nick Cotton *Cycle Tours: 24 one-day routes in Dorset, Hampshire and the Isle of Wight*. The title pretty much says it all, with routes on and off road and useful background information.

ed Juliet Gregor *25 Cycle Tours in and around Dorset and Hampshire*. Manageable cycle rides suitable for families along with more challenging rides of up to 62 miles.

David Foster and Jenny Plucknett *Hampshire and New Forest Walks*. Detailed descriptions of twenty-eight walks around the county, of different lengths, with excellent accompanying maps.

Philips *Cycle Tours Dorset and Somerset*. Very comprehensive guide to twenty cycle routes in both counties, with excellent OS detail maps.

Mike Power *Pub Walks in Dorset*. Details of forty manageable walks for those who like a pint or two at the end of a ramble. Maps are a bit sketchy so you'll need an OS map to help with some of them.

Martin Simons *Walk the Isle of Wight*. Excellent, detailed descriptions of forty walks, most with public transport access, throughout the island.

Roland Tarr *South West Coast Path: Exmouth to Poole*. The most comprehensive guide to the section of the South West Coast path that passes through the Jurassic Coast and Dorset.

John Wilks *Walks into History: Dorset*. Sixteen walks from 3 to 7.5 miles around key historical sites, including Cerne Abbas, Maiden Castle, Corfe Castle and Lyme Regis.

Robert Wood *Walks into History: Hampshire*. Sixteen circular walks in and around historical sites such as Winchester, Southsea Castle and the New Forest.

Books change lives

Book Aid International
www.bookaid.org

Poverty and illiteracy go hand in hand. But in sub-Saharan Africa, books are a luxury few can afford. Many children leave school functionally illiterate, and adults often fall back into illiteracy in adulthood due to a lack of available reading material.

Book Aid International knows that books change lives.

Every year we send over half a million books to partners in 12 countries in sub-Saharan Africa, to stock libraries in schools, refugee camps, prisons, universities and communities. Literally millions of readers have access to books and information that could teach them new skills – from keeping chickens to getting a degree in Business Studies or learning how to protect against HIV/AIDS.

What can you do?

Join our Reverse Book Club and with your donation of only £6 a month, we can send 36 books every year to some of the poorest countries in the world. For every two pounds extra you can give, we can send another book!

Support Book Aid International today!

 Online. Go to our website at **www.bookaid.org**, and click on 'donate'

By telephone. Start a Direct Debit or give a donation on your card by calling us on 020 7733 3577

Book Aid International is a charity and a limited company registered in England and Wales.
Charity No. 313869 Company No. 880754   39-41 Coldharbour Lane, Camberwell, London SE5 9NR
T +44 (0)20 7733 3577   F +44 (0)20 7978 8006   E info@bookaid.org   www.bookaid.org

So now we've told you about the things not to miss, the best places to stay, the top restaurants, the liveliest bars and the most spectacular sights, it only seems fair to tell you about the best travel insurance around

Small print and
Index

A Rough Guide to Rough Guides

Published in 1982, the first Rough Guide – to Greece – was a student scheme that became a publishing phenomenon. Mark Ellingham, a recent graduate in English from Bristol University, had been travelling in Greece the previous summer and couldn't find the right guidebook. With a small group of friends he wrote his own guide, combining a highly contemporary, journalistic style with a thoroughly practical approach to travellers' needs.

The immediate success of the book spawned a series that rapidly covered dozens of destinations. And, in addition to impecunious backpackers, Rough Guides soon acquired a much broader and older readership that relished the guides' wit and inquisitiveness as much as their enthusiastic, critical approach and value-for-money ethos.

These days, Rough Guides include recommendations from shoestring to luxury and cover more than 200 destinations around the globe, including almost every country in the Americas and Europe, more than half of Africa and most of Asia and Australasia. Our ever-growing team of authors and photographers is spread all over the world, particularly in Europe, the US and Australia.

In the early 1990s, Rough Guides branched out of travel, with the publication of Rough Guides to World Music, Classical Music and the Internet. All three have become benchmark titles in their fields, spearheading the publication of a wide range of books under the Rough Guide name.

Including the travel series, Rough Guides now number more than 350 titles, covering: phrasebooks, waterproof maps, music guides from Opera to Heavy Metal, reference works as diverse as Conspiracy Theories and Shakespeare, and popular culture books from iPods to Poker. Rough Guides also produce a series of more than 120 World Music CDs in partnership with World Music Network.

Visit www.roughguides.com to see our latest publications.

Rough Guide travel images are available for commercial licensing at www.roughguidespictures.com

Rough Guide credits

Text editor: Lucy White
Layout: Jessica Subramanian
Cartography: Katie Lloyd-Jones
Picture editor: Sarah Cummins
Production: Rebecca Short
Proofreader: Karen Parker
Photographer: Diana Jarvis
Editorial: Ruth Blackmore, Andy Turner,
Keith Drew, Edward Aves, Alice Park, Jo Kirby,
James Smart, Natasha Foges, Róisín Cameron,
Emma Traynor, Emma Gibbs, Kathryn Lane,
Monica Woods, Mani Ramaswamy, Harry Wilson,
Lucy Cowie, Amanda Howard, Lara Kavanagh,
Alison Roberts, Joe Staines, Peter Buckley,
Matthew Milton, Tracy Hopkins, Ruth Tidball;
Delhi Madhavi Singh, Karen D'Souza,
Lubna Shaheen
Design & Pictures: **London** Scott Stickland,
Dan May, Diana Jarvis, Mark Thomas, Nicole
Newman, Emily Taylor; **Delhi** Umesh Aggarwal,
Ajay Verma, Ankur Guha, Pradeep Thapliyal,
Sachin Tanwar, Anita Singh, Nikhil Agarwal,
Sachin Gupta
Production: Vicky Baldwin

Cartography: **London** Maxine Repath, Ed
Wright; **Delhi** Rajesh Chhibber, Ashutosh Bharti,
Rajesh Mishra, Animesh Pathak, Jasbir Sandhu,
Karobi Gogoi, Alakananda Roy, Swati Handoo,
Deshpal Dabas
Online: **London** George Atwell, Faye Hellon,
Jeanette Angell, Fergus Day, Justine Bright, Clare
Bryson, Aine Fearon, Adrian Low, Ezgi Celebi,
Amber Bloomfield; **Delhi** Amit Verma, Rahul Kumar,
Narender Kumar, Ravi Yadav, Debojit Borah,
Rakesh Kumar, Ganesh Sharma, Shisir Basumatari
Marketing & Publicity: **London** Liz Statham,
Niki Hanmer, Louise Maher, Jess Carter, Vanessa
Godden, Vivienne Watton, Anna Paynton, Rachel
Sprackett, Laura Vipond, Vanessa McDonald;
New York Katy Ball, Judi Powers, Nancy
Lambert; **Delhi** Ragini Govind
Manager India: Punita Singh
Reference Director: Andrew Lockett
Operations Manager: Helen Atkinson
PA to Publishing Director: Nicola Henderson
Publishing Director: Martin Dunford
Commercial Manager: Gino Magnotta
Managing Director: John Duhigg

Publishing information

This first edition published February 2010 by
Rough Guides Ltd,
80 Strand, London WC2R 0RL
14 Local Shopping Centre, Panchsheel Park,
New Delhi 110017, India
Distributed by the Penguin Group
Penguin Books Ltd,
80 Strand, London WC2R 0RL
Penguin Group (USA)
375 Hudson Street, NY 10014, USA
Penguin Group (Australia)
250 Camberwell Road, Camberwell,
Victoria 3124, Australia
Penguin Group (Canada)
195 Harry Walker Parkway N, Newmarket, ON,
L3Y 7B3 Canada
Penguin Group (NZ)
67 Apollo Drive, Mairangi Bay, Auckland 1310,
New Zealand
Cover concept by Peter Dyer.

Typeset in Bembo and Helvetica to an original
design by Henry Iles.

Printed in Singapore

© Rough Guides 2010

Maps © Rough Guides

No part of this book may be reproduced in any
form without permission from the publisher except
for the quotation of brief passages in reviews.

312pp includes index

A catalogue record for this book is available from
the British Library

ISBN: 978-1-84836-159-1

The publishers and authors have done their best
to ensure the accuracy and currency of all the
information in **The Rough Guide to Dorset,
Hampshire and the Isle of Wight**, however, they
can accept no responsibility for any loss, injury, or
inconvenience sustained by any traveller as a result
of information or advice contained in the guide.

1   3   5   7   9   8   6   4   2

Help us update

We've gone to a lot of effort to ensure that the
first edition of **The Rough Guide to Dorset,
Hampshire and the Isle of Wight** is accurate
and up-to-date. However, things change – places
get "discovered", opening hours are notoriously
fickle, restaurants and rooms raise prices or lower
standards. If you feel we've got it wrong or left
something out, we'd like to know, and if you can
remember the address, the price, the hours, the
phone number, so much the better.

Please send your comments with the subject
line "**Rough Guide Dorset, Hampshire and
the Isle of Wight Update**" to ©mail
@roughguides.com. We'll credit all contributions
and send a copy of the next edition (or any other
Rough Guide if you prefer) for the very best
emails.

Have your questions answered and tell others
about your trip at ®www.roughguides.com

SMALL PRINT

www.roughguides.com

Acknowledgements

Many thanks for all the people who helped us research the guide, especially Wightlink Ferries; Sian Brenchley at Visit Britain; Loraine Morris and Lara Nixey at the Dorset tourist board, Andrew Bateman at the Hampshire tourist board and Sue Emmerson, Antony Cook and Kellie Hodgson at the Isle of Wight tourist board; Ellie Hughes at English Heritage; the National Trust; Kim De Luce at *Priory Bay Hotel*; Charles Lotter at *Summer Lodge*; the Cycling Club of Southbourne; Viv McCrossen for Ventnor insights; Verity Chamley at *Hotel du Vin*; and all our friends and colleagues whose local advice has been invaluable, including Marion and Eva for their gastronomic expertise, Susie Long for retail tips, Amanda Heath for Shaftesbury insights, and Aley for museums. Thanks too to everyone at Rough Guides, especially Lucy White for her constructive editing, Sarah Cummins for photos and Katie Lloyd-Jones for maps. And special thanks to Alex and Olivia for their patience and enthusiasm.

Thanks also to the photographer, Diana Jarvis, for doing a sterling job.

Index

Map entries are in colour.

www.roughguides.com

Map symbols

maps are listed in the full index using coloured text

─── ··	County boundary	⛬	Lighthouse
─ ─ ─	Chapter boundary	❀	Country park
▬▬▬	Motorway	☗	Vineyard
═══	Main road	⁓‖‖	Cliffs
───	Minor road	⚠	Campsite
▬▬▬	Pedestrianized street	⬳	Swimming
-----	Footpath	ⓘ	Tourist office
─ ─	Ferry route	⊠	Post office
➤■➤	Railway	@	Internet access
⬝⬝⬝⬝⬝	Cliff railway	★	Bus stop
▬▬▬	Wall	✈	Airport
───	Waterway	🅿	Parking
♦	Point of interest	⊞	Hospital
∴	Ancient ruins	⊙	Statue
▲	Peak	⌂	Abbey
⊥	Gardens	⚑	Church (regional maps)
⚵	Viewpoint	✛	Church (town maps)
♙	Castle	▬	Building
🏛	Stately house	▭	Market
🏛	Monument	⬭	Stadium
♦	Museum	⊞	Cemetery
♣	Golf course	▓	Park
⟟	Windmill	░	Beach